Framing the Black Panthers

Also by Jane Rhodes

Mary Ann Shadd Cary:
The Black Press and Protest in the Nineteenth Century

Framing the Black Panthers

The Spectacular Rise of a Black Power Icon

JANE RHODES

THE NEW PRESS

NEW YORK
LONDON

"Revolutionary Generation" by Kenneth M. Boxley and Eric T. Sadler © 1990 Def American Songs, Inc., Your
Mother's Music. All rights administered by Songs of Universal, Inc./BMI.
Used by permission. All rights reserved.

Parts of chapter 3 first appeared in: "Fanning the Flames of Racial Discord: The National Press and the Black
Panther Party," *Harvard International Journal of Press/Politics* 4 (1999), 95–118; and in "Race, Ideology and
Journalism: Black Power and Television News," in Stuart Allan, ed.,
Journalism: Critical Issues (Maidenhead and New York: Open University Press, 2005), 30–41.

Gil Scott-Heron's "The Revolution Will Not Be Televised" is used with permission of
Bienstok Publishing Company.

Parts of chapter 4 first appeared in: "Black Radicalism in 1960s California: Women in the
Black Panther Party," in Quintard Taylor and Shirley Ann Moore, eds., *African American Women
Confront the West, 1600–2000* (Norman, OK: University of Oklahoma Press, 2003), 346–62;
and in "The *Black Panther* Newspaper: Standard-bearer for Modern Black Nationalism,"
Media History 7 (2), 2001, 151–58.

Requests for permission to reproduce selections from this book should be mailed to:
Permissions Department, The New Press, 38 Greene Street, New York, NY 10013.

Published in the United States by The New Press, New York, 2007
Distributed by W. W. Norton & Company, Inc., New York

LIBRARY OF CONGRESS CATALOGING-IN-PUBLICATION DATA

Rhodes, Jane, 1955–
     Framing the Black Panthers : the spectacular rise of a Black power icon / Jane Rhodes.
       p. cm.
     Includes bibliographical references and index.
     ISBN 978-1-56584-961-7 (hc.)
     1. Black Panther Party—History. 2. Black Panther Party—Public opinion. 3. Black Panther Party—Press
coverage. 4. Journalism—Political aspects—United States—History—20th century. 5. Mass media—
Political aspects—United States—History—20th century. 6. African Americans in mass media. 7. African
Americans—Race identity—History—20th century. 8. Black power—United States—History—20th century. 9. Public opinion—United States. 10. United States—Race relations—Political aspects—History—
20th century. I. Title.
E185.615.R48 2007
322.4'20973—dc22

                                                                        2007010436

The New Press was established in 1990 as a not-for-profit alternative to the large,
commercial publishing houses currently dominating the book publishing industry.
The New Press operates in the public interest rather than for private gain,
and is committed to publishing, in innovative ways, works of educational, cultural,
and community value that are often deemed insufficiently profitable.

www.thenewpress.com

Composition by Westchester Book

Printed in the United States of America

2   4   6   8   10   9   7   5   3   1

In memory of the women who taught me

Catherine L. Covert

and

Margaret A. Blanchard

And in memory of the editor lost to us all

Joe Wood Jr.

A Panther member stands vigil outside the Alameda County Courthouse during Huey Newton's trial. (Photograph by Jonathan Eubanks, courtesy of the African American Museum and Library at Oakland)

Contents

Acknowledgments

Over the last ten years I have labored in the quest to analyze the Black Panthers' enduring influence on American mass culture. This project would not have been possible without the assistance of many. As is often the case with scholarly projects, *Framing the Black Panthers* started as a graduate paper, at the University of North Carolina at Chapel Hill in a class taught by Professor Donald Shaw. Years later, that paper was vetted at a conference of journalism historians and I received valuable comments from the late distinguished scholar James Carey. From there this research took a circuitous rout through many venues. A former colleague at Indiana University, Carol Polsgrove, encouraged me to turn this research into a manuscript. At the final stages, I received invaluable feedback and advice from Robin D.G. Kelley, who gave the manuscript a close and insightful reading. Along the way, this research was made possible by financial support from the School of Journalism at Indiana University, the University of California, UC San Diego, and the Ford Foundation. A residency at the University of London enabled the start of my research on the Black Panthers in Britain. But most praise goes to the network of librarians who preside over a growing archive on the black power movement in the United States, including the Oakland Public Library, the San Francisco Public Library, the New York Public Library, San Francisco State University, the University of California at Berkeley, Stanford University, and the University of California, Los Angeles. I must single out three institutions that survive on public support, donations, and volunteers to bring alive the history of social movements and African American communities: the Southern California Library for Social Science and Research in Los Angeles, the African American Museum and Library at Oakland, and the San Francisco African American Historical and Cultural Society.

Thanks also go to those who generously gave of their time to grant interviews for this project. Last, but not least, I want to express my appreciation to the legion of undergraduate and graduate research assistants who helped me amass the enormous database for this study: Vanessa Hamilton, Albert Lowe, Ralina L. Joseph, Monika Gosin, Brian Chung, Jenee Darden, and Leslie Kuykendahl. Thanks to my colleagues at Macalester College, including Kathie Scott who keeps me organized, and Brian Longley for his technical assistance. This book was inspired, in part, by Ed Rhodes Jr., who ventured into the complicated terrain of black power activism and managed to survive the era intact and much wiser. Lynn M. Hudson, partner in daily and intellectual life, endured ten years living with this project while providing constant moral support and keen scholarly insight. For that, I am eternally grateful.

Framing the Black Panthers

INTRODUCTION

On July 18, 2002, ten months after terrorists attacked the World Trade Center and the Pentagon, a Moroccan named Zacarias Moussaoui was arraigned for the third time on charges that he was part of the conspiracy—"the twentieth hijacker." According to the grand jury indictment, Moussaoui trained in an al-Qaeda camp in Afghanistan, traveled from Pakistan to the United States with a large amount of money, enrolled in flight schools in Oklahoma and Minnesota, purchased small weapons including knives, and conspired to hijack the ill-fated airplanes. Moussaoui's activities aroused enough suspicion that he was arrested by federal authorities in August 2001; after September 11 he became the only living defendant in the government's quest to avenge the attacks and convict al-Qaeda and its leader, Osama bin Laden, in absentia. For a time, at least, Moussaoui was one of the nation's most notorious and reviled figures.[1]

During the arraignment, a group of African American men in paramilitary garb calling themselves the New Black Panther Party appeared as Moussaoui's self-appointed saviors. The group, which models itself after the 1960s black power icons, held a press conference outside the U.S. District Court in Alexandria, Virginia, to announce that they would offer Moussaoui legal assistance. Attorney Malik Shabazz first identified himself as a member of the Black Panthers and then told a group of reporters, "He [Moussaoui] is a black man, and it is our responsibility to see if he is being treated justly." The group thus presented themselves as the guardians of all black global subjects and the prosecution of Moussaoui as a racial matter in black-and-white terms. Their controversial statement was enhanced by their physical appearance—the black berets, the buttons with the insignia of a snarling black cat, and the men's determined, forceful glare. Like their predecessors thirty years earlier, the New Black Panthers marshaled the news media to capture public attention and to inject themselves into the vortex of this story. They also understood that the use of the Black Panthers' symbolism would spark immediate recognition.

To be sure, the New Black Panthers' presence was a marginal component of a news story that focused on the accused September 11 hijacker's initial plea of guilty. In May 2006 Moussaoui was sentenced to life in prison. Major news organizations, including CNN, the networks, and the *New York Times*, made no mention of the New Black Panthers' presence on that day. National Public Radio's *Weekend Edition* gave a brief report. But the conservative Fox Network News relished exploiting the suggested connection between black nationalist throwbacks from the 1960s and international terrorists. Following a thirty-second clip of the press conference, the news anchor raised her eyebrows, rolled her eyes, and shrugged as she uttered the words "Black Panther Party," signaling her disdain for the group. The producers and writers at Fox News knew that the image of the Black Panthers remains a potent symbol of black resistance and the nation's racial crisis gone amok. In the words of historian Nikhil Pal Singh, the Black Panther Party is "the privileged signifier of Black militancy writ large." Their claiming of Moussaoui as a "brother in need" only bolstered these implications. The New Black Panthers, who have been repudiated by the founders of the Black Panther Party and other black power activists, nevertheless sought to capitalize on their namesake's unique relationship with the mass media and enduring presence in the national consciousness.[2]

This was not the only connection made between the post-9/11 search for Islamic terrorists and the Black Panther Party. In November 2004, an investigative report by the *New York Times* revealed that an FBI agent in Germany posed as a former member of the Black Panthers who was "eager to give millions to terrorists." In this dubious intelligence scheme, a Yemeni sheik suspected of financing al-Qaeda and Hamas was lured into a meeting with the supposed Black Panther by a paid FBI informer. Transcripts of the encounter indicated that the FBI thought posing as a former Black Panther was an effective charade that a Muslim cleric would find credible. The agent's guise—as a Black Panther who sought to funnel millions of dollars to the Islamic jihad—linked the organization's legacy with the support of radical Islam and the notion that they have access to a vast financial network. The *Times* missed the irony that the FBI, who once pursued the Black

Panthers with vigor and deemed them the greatest threat to national security, had appropriated their identity to catch modern-day enemies. Equally intriguing was that the *New York Times* found no need to offer definitions or historical background regarding the Black Panthers. Like Fox News, the *Times* understood the symbolic resonance of the Black Panther Party—that readers would immediately recognize and understand its meaning.[3]

Nearly forty years after Huey Newton and Bobby Seale founded the Black Panther Party for Self-Defense in Oakland, California, this organization and its leaders are lasting fixtures in mass culture and popular memory. The passage of time has not eroded the strength of their symbols and rhetoric—the gun, the snarling panther, the raised fist, and slogans such as "All power to the people" and "Off the pig." Today representations of the Black Panthers linger in diverse arenas of commodity culture, from news stories to reality television to feature films and hip-hop, as they function as America's dominant icons of black nationalism. When Eldridge Cleaver, former Black Panther Minister of Information, died on May 1, 1998, he received more press attention than many heads of state, with his photo and obituary prominently displayed in the elite national media. He was eulogized as a relic of the sixties who left a timeless imprint on American history and culture. "Nicknamed 'El Rage' for his tendency to explode in outrage and anger, he quickly became the era's embodiment of black militancy," noted the *L.A. Times*. In the summer of 2000 the Black Panthers emerged again as signifiers of black rage and aggression in an entirely different context. At the start of the reality television craze a black male contestant on the CBS show *Big Brother* was exposed as a member of the New Black Panther Party. William Collins, one of two black contenders on the show, was the first resident evicted from the *Big Brother* group home because he delighted in confronting the white participants about racial issues. The ejection of Collins quickly sparked a nationwide debate on the Internet and in the press after it was revealed that he was a member of the New Black Panthers. The group received plenty of publicity in the aftermath; media such as the *San Francisco Examiner* reported that Williams was a follower of Khalid Abdul Muhmmad, who was ousted from the Nation of Islam for his anti-Semitic remarks. Following the eviction, Collins held a press conference and was interviewed by Bryant Gumbel on network television, all occasions for the media to juxtapose his involvement in the Panthers to his contentious behavior, which ultimately cost him a half million dollars in prize money. While his housemates and the program's viewers apparently disliked Collins, CBS was sorry to see him go—ratings dropped significantly after his departure.[4]

Indeed, ex-Panthers make good copy. In 1997 the national press closely followed the story of Elmer "Geronimo" Pratt, a former Black Panther leader from Los Angeles who had spent twenty-seven years in prison on a murder conviction. That summer a judge released Pratt after ruling that the prosecution had suppressed key evidence in his case. The decision and Pratt's subsequent exoneration were the result of a lengthy campaign by his supporters, who argued he was a political prisoner framed for murder by law enforcement because of his ties to the Panthers. The news of Pratt's release was featured on the front page of the *New York Times* under the kicker "Flashback," which made it plain that the newspaper was exploiting the Panthers' place in collective memory. The widespread attention to Pratt's case demonstrated the extent to which media producers and media audiences have maintained an intense fascination with the disciples of black power. Michael Kelly, writing in the *New Republic*, criticized the Pratt coverage and took the *Times* to task for perpetuating romantic notions of the Black Panthers while ignoring their underside. "[T]he myth of the Panthers has not been exposed by the *Times*," he wrote. "It has been institutionalized." Similarly, the intense media coverage of the arrest, trial, and conviction of former Student Nonviolent Coordinating Committee (SNCC) leader H. Rap Brown (Jamil Abdullah Al-Amin) for the murder of an Atlanta sheriff's deputy in 2000 was also predicated on memories of black militancy. Al-Amin, who spent a scant few months with the honorary title of Minister of Justice of the Black Panther Party, was nevertheless identified as an "ex-Panther" in most news accounts. Virtually every story of Al-Amin's case attributed to him the aphorism "Violence is as American as cherry pie," which he first uttered in 1967. H. Rap Brown's rhetoric of violence in the 1960s confirmed Al-Amin's violent acts thirty years later, making the reportage of his downfall—and his connections to the Black Panthers—irresistible.[5]

During the height of Brown's early activism, he argued that mass media framed him to conform to racial stereotypes. In his 1969 book

Die Nigger Die! he wrote, "I'm a crazy, dangerous nigger who hates white folks, according to the media. The news media is one of the greatest enemies to Black people. It is controlled by the ruling classes and is used to articulate their point of view." Yet, like many of his contemporaries, Brown relied on the media as an essential conduit through which to reach a mass audience. Brown, the Black Panther Party, and other black power proponents felt they were trapped by their dependence on the media and complained bitterly about the distortions it produced. Stokely Carmichael, who adeptly used the news media to convey his radical conception of black power, simultaneously decried its influence. "In this 'debate,' as in everything else that affects our lives, Negroes are dependent on and at the discretion of, forces and institutions within the white society which have little interest in representing us honestly," he said during a speech in 1967. In his influential study of Students for a Democratic Society, Todd Gitlin described this phenomenon when he wrote that "political movements feel called upon to rely on large-scale communications in order to *matter*, to say who they are and what they intend to publics they want to sway." In the case of the New Left, Gitlin found the media acted as agents of repression and containment as these young white radical activists suffered through the rise and fall of their movement. This study finds a similar process in the media coverage of the Black Panther Party, with one significant difference—the influence racial ideologies have on the processes of making meaning.[6]

Language, discourse, and images are the constitutive elements of representations, the cultural equipment that conveys ideas, beliefs, and knowledge. Blackness is not a fixed racial category, but part of a rather fluid and malleable set of representations that change meaning depending on time, place, and context. Blackness can be understood as a floating signifier that is under contestation by media producers, media subjects, and media audiences in what Stuart Hall calls a field of ideological struggle. Thus, race was a prime determinant of how the Black Panther Party would appear in mass culture and how the group would be understood. As icons of radical black resistance, its members were not mere victims of the media, but were participants in every aspect of their representations. This study uses the double entendre of "framing" as a way to understand this process at work. Subjects are placed within a formal frame that focuses attention on selected aspects of a visual or verbal text, or subjects are set up to appear to be something they are not. Conceptual frameworks help us make sense of the complexities of society, and journalists, photographers, and other cultural workers create frames to help simplify and organize the information they collect. Once the Black Panther Party became a recognizable media subject through the frames produced by mass media, the simple invocation of its name or image was sufficient to call up a host of ideas and assumptions about who its members were and what they stood for. *Framing the Black Panthers* seeks to identify and interrogate these powerful symbolic tools, and the dialogic relationship that developed between the Panthers and the media organizations that brought them into the public eye.[7]

This project is not intended to be a comprehensive history of the Black Panther Party; rather, it is a study of the group's rise to prominence at the hands of the mass media. Yet it necessarily takes into account many of the significant events, issues, and individuals central to their story. A major goal is to gain some understanding about what we see and how we see, about what media organizations told audiences about the Black Panthers and the range of possible interpretations of these messages. Studying the framing of a group such as the Black Panthers tells us about how blackness is represented in multiple facets of American society. Regardless of whether the Panthers are reviled or celebrated, seen as heroes or terrorists, they are subject to fundamental frameworks that are rooted in the history of race relations.

There have been numerous accounts of the Black Panthers' origins published in memoirs and histories and narrated in documentary films. Most begin with the 1965 meeting of two young African Americans, Huey P. Newton and Bobby Seale, at Merritt College in Oakland, California. Both were from families that migrated to California in the 1940s—the Newtons from Louisiana and the Seales from Texas. While Huey Newton knocked around in community college, law school, and music school, Seale, who was five years older, had served in the Air Force. They met when Seale was organizing black students at Merritt into a group that eventually became the Soul Students Advisory Council in his quest to bridge campus concerns with those in the local black community. Newton, who was increasingly disenchanted with what he considered the students' complacent and bourgeois interests, was an enthusiastic supporter of Seale's project. As a team, they found they shared a greater concern for the "brothers on the street," and each worked for a North Oakland anti-poverty program. In those militant times, the pair found solace in each other's commitment to a more confrontational politics focused on community needs. They left the Soul Students Advisory Council with the goal of creating their own organization; their emphasis was on the often violent tensions between Oakland's mostly white police force and the city's black citizens.

Newton and Seale were profoundly influenced by the powerful writing and rhetoric of Malcolm X, and they read the core revolutionary texts of the day, including the *Quotations from Chairman Mao Tse-Tung* and the works of Frantz Fanon and Che Guevara. In October 1966 Huey Newton laid out a program for this new group, and Seale wrote down his words, devising the now-famous ten-point program. In Seale's memoir, he recalled that they came up with the titles of "Minister of Defense" for Newton and "Chairman" for Seale and then blanketed black neighborhoods with ten thousand copies of their newly invented platform. They borrowed Marx's concept of the lumpen proletariat to describe the legions of working-class and underclass blacks whom they hoped to turn into revolutionaries. Indeed, much of the Black Panthers' early concepts were borrowed from other sources: the ten-point program was modeled on the Nation of Islam's platform, published weekly in its newspaper *Muhammad Speaks*, and their name and symbol were taken from the political party established by SNCC to facilitate black voter registration in the Deep South. By January 1967 Newton and Seale had opened a storefront office in Oakland and were recruiting members.[8]

In the first year of the Panthers' existence, their actions and rhetoric were based on a program of black community liberation through confrontations with state power. The group's agenda ranged from broad goals such as "the power to determine the destiny of our Black Community," full employment, housing, and education to highly controversial proposals including the exemption of black men from military service and the liberation of black men from prisons and jails. Point 7, "an immediate end to Police Brutality and Murder of black people," was the focal point for their early activities as they organized themselves to monitor the Oakland Police Department and openly carried weapons as a symbol of their self-defense agenda. Gradually, the emphasis on armed resistance waned as their defiant politics disintegrated into violent encounters with the police, resulting in casualties on both sides. Within a year, the group's leadership shifted their ideological perspective from one of explicit black nationalism to what they called revolutionary nationalism and intercommunalism as they increasingly identified with anti-colonial struggles in the Third World. The Panthers rejected any identification with the United States, which they deemed the source of black oppression, yet they embraced the nation's democratic principles in a hopeful quest for social change. They also began to court alliances with the white left, garnering support from the Peace and Freedom Party, the Communist Party, and others. The group's membership remained almost exclusively African American, and their social endeavors were always rooted in black communities, yet many scholars and black power activists have argued that the group falls outside the pantheon of black nationalism. But if we understand black nationalism as both political ideology and cultural practices that have shifted and changed over time, it is clear that the Black Panther Party is a part of this history. According to theorist Wahneema Lubiano, "Black Nationalism, in its broadest sense, is a sign, an analytic, describing a range of historically manifested ideas about black American possibilities that include any or all of the following: racial solidarity, cultural specificity, religious, economic, and political separatism." The most important aspect of black nationalism, perhaps, is that it is a movement that consistently critiques the racial order of the United States and the treatment and conditions of black America, and the Black Panther Party took on this role with relish.[9]

Framing the Black Panthers is based on an exhaustive study and comparative analysis of the media coverage of the organization from the moment they were picked up as a news story in 1967 through early 1970, when the organization underwent a dramatic transformation. By then, the Black Panthers were familiar fixtures in national and global culture. Daily newspapers provided a constant flow of stories about the Panthers and often set the agenda for other media. This study looks at virtually every article published on the Panthers and related subjects in the Panthers' hometown newspaper, the *Oakland Tribune*; one of the two dailies across the bay, the *San Francisco Examiner*; and the national newspaper of record, the *New York Times*. Articles in the *San Francisco Chronicle*, *Los Angeles Times*, *Wall Street Journal*, *Washington Post*, and others added to the compendium of daily journalism.

Television news had an equally powerful effect on how the Black

Panthers were seen and understood, but it took almost a year before the national networks gave them serious and sustained attention. Northern California television outlets, including the network affiliates and public broadcasting, provided the first visual and aural glimpses of the group to a mass audience. But while daily newspapers have been collected in digital and microfilm form and are easily obtainable in libraries, television footage is more difficult for researchers to study. Most of the footage at the local and national level is made available only to filmmakers and other broadcasters who pay a premium for broadcast rights. CBS, the dominant television news organization during this period, graciously provided footage and outtakes from its news archives at a fraction of the usual cost, but the other networks—NBC and ABC—refused to sell their materials for research purposes. Luckily, Vanderbilt University has maintained an archive of national television news programs since the summer of 1968, and these are available to the public. As is often the case, local histories are usually collected through the efforts of indefatigable librarians and archivists concerned with public access. Helene Whitson, former librarian at San Francisco State University, single-handedly established the Bay Area Television Archives, which provided some early footage of the Panthers on the CBS affiliate KPIX and public broadcaster KQED.

As the Black Panthers became national media subjects, the magazine world also took notice, providing additional material for consideration in these pages. The big three newsmagazines—*Time, Newsweek*, and *U.S. News and World Report*—as well as such venues as the *Saturday Evening Post, Life, Harper's*, and *Playboy* offer a contrasting array of media texts that employ styles and techniques different from the daily press but that generally conformed to the same frames. Once the group and its leaders achieved celebrity status, publishers followed the lead of other cultural producers and issued a flurry of books that created a more permanent record of the media's fascination with this subject.

Often ignored by scholars is the role of the black press and alternative media. The Bay Area's influential black weekly, the San Francisco *Sun-Reporter*, provides for this study a vital window into the attitudes and perspectives of area residents marginalized by the mainstream press. Other black-owned periodicals, including the *Los Angeles Sentinel* and *Ebony* and *Jet* magazines, illustrate the broad array of political perspectives among African Americans in this era. Many of the underground and alternative periodicals of the day, from the SNCC-influenced *The Movement* to the upstart student newspaper the *Berkeley Barb*, the socialist weekly the *Guardian*, and the independent magazine *Ramparts*, as well as Pacifica Radio's San Francisco–based station KPFA and the filmmaking collective Newsreel, all played a role in disseminating the Panthers' message and shaping their public image.

This book also benefits from efforts by scholars, librarians, and community activists to preserve the history of this organization. In the last decade, significant archival collections have emerged at Stanford University and the University of California at Berkeley. Smaller venues such as local public libraries and black history organizations have also devoted space and time to acquire and organize volumes of correspondence, records, publications, and ephemera that have been extraordinarily useful for this project. When I turned my attention to the Black Panthers overseas, I found a far less developed inventory of material but numerous organizations that were willing to provide assistance, including the Institute for Race Relations in London, the British Film Archive, the BBC, and the British Library newspaper collection at Collindale. The interviews gathered for this project are intended to provide personalized perspectives on the Black Panthers' relationship with the media from distinct positions—organization insiders, journalists, and activists. These accounts provide depth and what Clifford Geertz called "thick description" to the broader story but are not the definitive sources for this investigation.

Framing the Black Panthers strives to be a thorough, rigorous scholarly accounting of a complex political and social phenomenon that has a significant place in history. Undoubtedly, there will be those who argue that the group and its legacy do not deserve scholarly attention. This perspective was highlighted in June 2003, when an academic conference titled "The Black Panther Party in Historical Perspective" was held at Wheelock College in Boston. The gathering, which included more than forty scholars and this author, devoted two days to research papers and discussions on new methods of research and analysis, in the process attracting some media attention. In addition to several newspaper stories, the National Public Radio program *Talk of the Nation* devoted a segment to the conference. Although academic gatherings are rarely noticed beyond specialists in a field, this one was met with swift and fierce condemnation. The Sunday *Los Angeles Times* published a lengthy opinion piece by Panther critic Kate Coleman, who argued that "this bunch of thugs continues to capture the imagination of American intellectuals." Similarly, right-wing provocateur David Horowitz wrote on the Internet's History News Network, based at George Mason University, that the conference was "a celebration of the Panthers by acolytes, idolaters and the credulous." Such vituperative responses signify how the Black Panthers, a generation after their heyday, continue to elicit emotional and polarizing perspectives. This seems to be the case especially among former members of the New Left intent on repudiating the radicalism of the 1960s. Identifying a subject worthy of scholarly attention is not the same as reification, as these comments suggest. Ironically, these arguments are partly a reaction to the media's continued fascination with the Black Panthers, which is chronicled in these pages. *Framing the Black Panthers* is not likely to appease these critics, but it is hoped that this will be one of many serious intellectual incursions into a subject that remains an entrenched and resilient component of the national culture of the United States.[10]

1

FORTY YEARS IN HINDSIGHT: THE BLACK PANTHERS IN POPULAR MEMORY

It's just a matter of race
Cause a black male's in their face
Step back for the new jack swing
On the platter scatter huh
We got our own thing
Just jam to let the rhyth run
Day to day, America eats its young
                    —Public Enemy, "Revolutionary Generation" (1991)

In an early scene from the 1995 motion picture *Panther*, a small group of young, restless members of the Black Panther Party find themselves in an ugly confrontation with the Oakland, California, police as they attempt to monitor law enforcement activities in their neighborhood. They display all of the expected signifiers—afros, black berets, leather jackets, and scowling expressions. The rifle-bearing revolutionaries calmly line up as they resist the efforts of police officers to make them move and to disperse the growing, restive crowd of onlookers. In a particularly tense moment, Marcus Chong, the actor portraying Huey Newton, calls out to the crowd:

> This is your business. Stay right here. You don't have to leave. The man
> is trying to run his usual fascist bullying tactics on you. The law book
> says as long as you are a reasonable distance—and reasonable is defined
> as eight to ten feet to be exact—you've got a right to observe the police
> carrying out their duties.[1]

A voice from the throng answers, "Talk that good shit, brothers." Another yells, "Amen to that." As the standoff continues, the policeman in charge comes within inches of Newton and demands, "What do those guns mean?" The Black Panther leader responds: "They mean, *pig*, that the Black Panther Party declares that if you try to brutalize our community we are going to shoot you." The crowd goes berserk, cheering and clapping to Newton's bravado. The victory belongs to the Panthers. The police, stunned and intimidated, slink back into their patrol cars and drive away.

The film, written by Melvin Van Peebles and directed by his son Mario Van Peebles, captures the spirit and texture of many African Americans' collective memories about the revolutionary black nationalists of the 1960s and 1970s. Central to this memory are visions of direct, physical black resistance to white power; a resurgent black masculinity that protects family and community; a radical discourse that transforms the nation's democratic principles to serve the needs of the aggrieved; and a gleeful episode of triumph, no matter how fleeting nor at what cost. For a brief moment, these memories suggest, black folks were actually winning the war against white supremacy as embodied in the police. After watching the above scene, one black New York viewer repeated a line in the film and exclaimed, "Sweet Jesus, I thought I had died and gone to heaven." Black cultural critic Kristal Brent Zook took this sentiment even further when she declared, "Everyone I know loves *Panther*. . . . For a generation with no personal recollection of such a movement, *Panther* provides its viewers with the euphoria of possibility." Similarly, another black writer waxed poetic about the film's impact, calling it "a truly inspirational film that illumines a history that hasn't been taught to young people, while reminding older audiences what their generation accomplished with its protest." *Panther* was more than a film—it was an antidote to historical amnesia.[2]

This ecstatic response from a segment of the black audience suggests the powerful effect of recovering the memory of the Black Panther Party. To celebrate the image of the Panthers as heroes is an act of assertion and empowerment for many black Americans; to reclaim the Panthers is to return to a time when black rage openly identified and confronted the oppressor. Director Mario Van Peebles, like many African Americans of his generation, chose to create a nostalgic version of the Panthers and delivered this image to an audience eager to find hints of glory from the past. These memories draw on African Americans' history and their present, on African Americans' cultural productions as well as those from mainstream mass media.[3]

The act of remembering the Black Panthers is both individual and collective; people shape memories from their own subject position and from their exposure to images, words, and ideas. Collective memory is profoundly shaped by mass culture, which acts as the place where these memories emerge and make new meanings. Thus, collective memory is produced through the process of representation, and technologies including film, photography, and the printing press dominate how we remember. These technologies of memory, as Marita Sturken notes, can act as a screen by blocking out other memories that are difficult to represent. The prevailing memories of the Black Panther Party have been shaped by the images produced in the news media, art, and literature that circulated widely during the 1960s and 1970s and remain staples of contemporary culture.[4]

Cultural products in the last two decades, such as the film *Panther*, have been a force for producing countermemories—recollections that oppose or contradict the narratives produced by dominant culture. Often, dominant or official memories are those disseminated by historians, public officials, and journalists who establish themselves as authoritative chroniclers of the past. Groups on the margins of society—political, racial, and economic minorities—seek to refute mainstream interpretations and insert their own voices into how things are remembered. This is indeed the case for the Black Panther Party, whose legacy, according to two scholars, has been tarnished by inaccuracies and misconceptions that present the organization as anti-white, infantile leftist, controlled by a criminal underclass, and largely a creation of the mass media. Numerous writers, filmmakers, musicians, and other black cultural workers such as Mario Van Peebles rely on myth and history in the telling of the Panthers' story but "retain an enduring suspicion of both categories," in the words of George Lipsitz. These texts force a rewriting of history by calling on the audience's common experience with oppression and difference.[5]

Memory is manifest in many forms. It exists in oral histories and folklore, mass culture and government documents, built memorials and popular reenactments. Communities intentionally create archives, celebrations, monuments, and other sites of memory, or *lieux de mémoire*, to ensure that events and people are not forgotten. These popular texts and structures are open to endless uses and interpretations; they act at the intersection between history and memory and offer opportunities for catharsis and healing, or for inspiration and veneration.[6]

Since the 1990s, the Black Panther Party has been the subject of numerous memorializing projects—by those nostalgic for its brand of black nationalism, by those anxious to repudiate the excesses of the 1960s, and by those trying to find a middle ground between reification and condemnation. The prevailing sentiment of these memories is that the Black Panthers and their moment should not be forgotten. This is an impulse that resides deep within African American history. Frederick Douglass, the nineteenth-century freedom fighter and statesman, spent the last third of his life exhorting the nation not to forget the era of slavery and the trauma of the Civil War. In 1884 he said, "It is not well to forget the past. Memory was given to man for some wise purpose. The past is . . . the mirror in which we may discern the dim outlines of the future, and by which we may make them more symmetrical." In this sense, reclaiming memory is a radical act, a powerful political tool.[7]

The motion picture *Panther* begins as a historical narrative via black-and-white newsreel segments that juxtapose Martin Luther King Jr. against rabid white southerners, then move to the assassinations of Malcolm X and Robert F. Kennedy and on to images of random police brutality. The opening sequence establishes the Panthers as black America's logical response to the chaos of the era. The film tells the story of the rise and fall of the Black Panther Party through the eyes of a fictional character, Judge, a Vietnam veteran who joins the group in his search for meaning and political action. Within the dramatic story line, the film follows the key people and events in the Black Panthers' early days, from the founding of the organization by Huey Newton and Bobby Seale through the episodes of violent and sometimes fatal encounters with police and the protests to free Newton from prison that captured widespread media attention.

Panther's filmmakers also inject a sequence of events that emphasize government counterintelligence efforts to destabilize and eliminate the group. The local police and the FBI are portrayed as uniformly racist, corrupt, and inept. The film ends with the premise that a vast government conspiracy led to the introduction of crack cocaine in urban black America as part of a deliberate attempt to weaken the black power movement. Folklorist Patricia Turner, among others, has found that such conspiracy theories are part of the series of rumors that regularly circulate in African American communities. Turner notes that throughout history African Americans have embraced "the familiar notion that the dominant culture remains intent on destroying blacks—one body at a time," a perspective that resonates throughout *Panther*. The fact that scholars and journalists have uncovered ample evidence of the government's agenda against the Black Panther Party gives African Americans a reason to find such conspiracy theories plausible.[8]

Just as the Black Panthers are constructed as the embodiment of black radicalism in the 1960s, the film *Panther* itself is representative of a revived expression of black rage in the 1990s. Mario Van Peebles was one of many black filmmakers of the period who sought to capture the anger and restlessness brimming in urban communities through the experiences of heroic black male subjects. Directors such as Spike Lee, Bill Duke, and John Singleton all deployed some version of this government drug conspiracy motif as their films stimulated a boom in "ghetto-action cinema."[9]

These filmmakers were motivated by a desire for political expression and financial gain. In 1991 Mario Van Peebles spent $8 million and earned $47.6 million with his hit film *New Jack City*, an urban black gangster film that evoked the blaxploitation era with a hip-hop underpinning. This initial commercial success enabled him to land a major studio deal for *Panther*, which he made on a budget of $9 million. Hollywood hoped Van Peebles would produce another moneymaking venture that capitalized on the increasingly popular themes of black resistance and urban street life. His reputation for turning a profit also gave Van Peebles the power to negotiate the content of the film. "It took my previous movies to give me what they call, 'the juice' and the studio wanted a Mario Van Peebles' movie," he told one black newspaper. "[T]he most important element as a director was to have final cut because that is your film."[10]

Van Peebles, like his counterpart Oliver Stone, who directed the docudrama *JFK* (1991), presented his film as an authoritative version of the past that offered a counternarrative to prevailing assumptions about the Black Panthers. In keeping with the era, *JFK* also advanced a complex conspiracy theory, in the process contradicting the authority of journalists and historians who had previously established the "facts" of the Kennedy assassination. Van Peebles did precisely the same thing by appropriating the deeply politicized images and rhetoric fashioned by mass media during the 1960s to establish the realist texture of his film. *Panther* mixed original television news footage of key moments

in the black freedom struggle with invented scenes that mimicked realism down to the actions, words, and dress of actual Black Panthers.
This blurring of fact/fiction and history/memory is a common cinematic technique; it allowed Van Peebles to create a historical text that
established a kind of cultural authority in which he spoke for the generation of African Americans who came of age after the 1960s. This
self-authorization was the filmmaker's effort at shaping America's collective memory about the Black Panthers through the lens of black
masculinity. He counted on the power of popular culture to circulate
this perspective, in the process mobilizing and validating a form of
African American memory.[11]

In this text the Black Panthers are remembered as carrying out a
noble yet dangerous quest. They were valiant rebels who were unjustly
silenced or murdered. The film deliberately attempts to preserve a particular interpretation of black protest in the sixties, and in so doing to
shape the era's legacy. This underscored Van Peebles' political aspirations. As one reviewer commented, "*Panther* represents a call to consciousness much more than a call to arms—a message as applicable to
nineties youth as it was to sixties ones." Mario Van Peebles told one national publication that his goal was to valorize his subjects. "We take
the position that the heroes were common Black folks," he said.
"We've had plenty of time to see *their* heroes; when are we going to
canonize us?" In another interview, he added that he wanted to reach
contemporary urban youth who lacked the political ideology of activists in the sixties.[12]

But it was the involvement of Mario Van Peebles' father, Melvin, that
gave *Panther* its strongest and most strategic link with the black power
era. The elder Van Peebles wrote the screenplay, based on his novel of
the same name, and was deeply involved in marketing and promotion.
Melvin Van Peebles looked back to the sixties as a pivotal moment in
black history and identified the Panthers as "a living, breathing, all-
American Rorschach test" about the problem of race. His authority on
the subject can be traced to his 1971 independent hit film *Sweet Sweetback's Baadasssss Song*, which many view as the catalyst for the blaxploitation era. Melvin Van Peebles was the author, director, and star.
Sweetback, deemed a "maverick breakthrough," cost only $500,000 to
make but grossed $10 million, attracting huge black audiences across the
nation. The protagonist, Sweetback, was a defiant, hypersexualized black

hero who spends most of the film fleeing from the police in a series of daring and shocking escapades. Sweetback was an underclass icon, using his street smarts and sexual prowess to fight against white supremacy, characteristically represented by the police. That year, Van Peebles told *Life* magazine that *Sweetback* "tells you about black life like it is—not like the Man wants to hear it is. . . . For the black man, Sweetback is a new kind of hero. For the white man, my picture is a new kind of foreign film."[13]

Sweetback captured the imagination of young and working-class black audiences anxious for expressions of resistance. Black Panther Party founder Huey Newton hailed the film in a lengthy article in the *Black Panther* newspaper, saying it was "the first truly revolutionary Black film made and it is presented to us by a black man." Van Peebles was not a member of the Panthers and didn't know any of the Panther leadership, but his work was quickly embraced as representative of a burgeoning radical black aesthetic. In 1999, Van Peebles reminisced that because of the film, he was accorded serious black nationalist credentials. "*Sweetback* was just the nail to hang my political coat on," he said. *Sweetback* was successful in constructing a new category of black American cinema in part because of its ability to produce racially polarized audiences, thus setting the stage for a specifically black or white identification with the story and with the hero. One analysis found that white reviewers for both mainstream and leftist publications generally condemned the film for being exploitive and offensive, while black periodicals offered cautious support. The Van Peebleses, father and son, employed similar strategies in *Panther* by producing heroes that only some could love.[14]

Indeed, *Panther* contributed to, and was part of, a 1990s revival of popular interest in black power and radical protest. Prior to the film's release, the press heralded the resurgence of "Panthermania," a term first coined by journalist Gail Sheehy in 1971. "The black cat is back," announced a headline in *Essence* magazine, while the *San Francisco Chronicle* called new Black Panther organizations the "reincarnation of radicalism." Publishers released a flurry of books that highlighted the group from the perspectives of both insiders and outsiders—among them Elaine Brown's *A Taste of Power*, David Hilliard's *This Side of Glory*, and Hugh Pearson's *The Shadow of the Panther*. An accomplished black actor named Roger Guenveur Smith opened his one-man play about Huey Newton at a well-known independent theater in Los Angeles. Smith's *A Huey P. Newton Story* eventually made its way into the theatrical mainstream, with performances at the New York Shakespeare Festival and a film version on cable television directed by Spike Lee. The simultaneous appearance of these varied cultural products was mutually advantageous for all—readers of the Black Panther memoirs were a natural audience for *A Huey Newton Story*, while the play's program carried an advertisement for the film *Panther* with the provocative claim "There is a Black Panther born in the ghetto every 20 minutes." Implicit in this campaign to market the Black Panthers was a sense that the social and political conditions that were the catalyst for widespread black rebellion in the 1960s were producing another generation of the angry and disenfranchised.[15]

This resurgent interest in the Black Panther Party occurred during a period when urban communities of color across the United States boiled over with discontent, as starkly epitomized by the 1992 Los Angeles uprising. In the early 1990s, significant segments of the black population were gripped by economic disparity and decline. The black middle class increased significantly during the 1980s, with many moving to the suburbs, but the majority of African Americans were left out of this prosperity. The black-white income gap worsened after two decades of improvement, with college-educated black men earning about 80 percent of what their white colleagues made, and black unionized workers earning 85 percent of whites' wages. Meanwhile, one-quarter of young black males were caught up in the criminal justice system, and their life expectancy actually declined, leading scholars to conclude that life chances for African Americans were getting worse rather than better. By the mid-nineties, cities across the nation were displaying the disastrous effects of deindustrialization, with significant white flight, the loss of stable, well-paying jobs, declining public schools, and a political climate that allowed abuses by law enforcement agencies to go unchecked. This economic restructuring occurred against the backdrop of a lack of political leadership. The black political establishment of the 1990s was, according to Manning Marable, bankrupt in their theoretical outlook and failed to "take a qualitative step beyond the discourse and strategies of the Civil Rights Movement of a generation ago."[16]

Caught in this void, black youth looked backward to the black nationalism of the 1960s and 1970s for inspiration. As political scientist

Michael Dawson makes clear, "[b]lack nationalism grows in force when the nation is perceived to have turned its back on blacks." In the 1990s, ideologies influenced by black power tended toward a community-based framework with an emphasis on economic autonomy rather than outright separatism. As these sentiments emerged in African American consciousness, figures such as the Black Panthers and Malcolm X were appropriated as crucial symbols—reminders of an activist past to remedy an impotent and quiescent present. U.S. culture industries immediately capitalized on this climate. The release of the film *Panther* followed on the heels of Spike Lee's controversial biopic *Malcolm X* in 1993, the first feature-length motion picture to pay homage to radical black nationalism. Lee's influential movie, while criticized for its questionable historical interpretations, was enthusiastically embraced by young audiences—aided by an aggressive marketing campaign that made "X" baseball caps de rigueur garb. The so-called hip-hop generation looked to Malcolm X as a towering symbol of black male authority whose rhetoric defied white power every time he declared "by any means necessary." Spike Lee's *Malcolm X* also bolstered the 1990s resurgence of linking black liberation to idealized notions of masculinity and femininity. The film's emphasis on "all-male spaces and predominantly male relations" structured Malcolm X's story to "defend against threats to heteronormative black masculinity," notes theorist Maurice Stevens.[17]

Numerous rappers, DJs, artists, filmmakers, novelists, and other cultural workers emerged as spokesmen for this rediscovered black radicalism. This was epitomized in a 1994 feature story in the *New York Times Magazine* in which rapper Ice Cube argued that hip-hop was the most recent expression of black power: "We're our own people. And we gonna stand on our own, and we gonna try to get some of the fire that was given off in those times [the sixties] for today," he declared. So it is not surprising that hip-hop would be an important vehicle for the delivery of *Panther's* message. There were two spin-off recordings from the movie—the original motion picture sound track, and *Pump Ya Fist: Hip-Hop Inspired by the Black Panthers*. The sound track featured remakes of seventies funk anthems like Sly and the Family Stone's "Stand" and War's "The World Is a Ghetto." Meanwhile, a chorus belted out a hip-hop version of the civil rights anthem "We Shall Not Be Moved" to evoke the spirit of protest. The Last Poets, the poetry and rhythm ensemble that set the groundwork for modern–day rap, recited a verse that reinforced this nostalgic engagement with the past: "We are the children and the parents of an unfinished revolution." Perhaps most incongruous was the film's theme song, "Freedom," performed by a "We Are the World"–style chorus of seventy-five female soul and hip-hop singers, including Queen Latifah, Mary J. Blige, MC Lyte, and Me shell Ndege ocello. These performers' role was notable for the fact that women were visibly absent from the film's story line. The *Panther* sound track had its philanthropic objectives as well: proceeds from the recording were to be donated to the Huey P. Newton Foundation and the International Committee to Free Geronimo Pratt, a former party leader. *Pump Ya Fist*, unlike the music from *Panther*, was hailed as a hard-core assemblage of rap radicalism, with performances from KRS-One, Chuck D, and Tupac Shakur (whose parents were Black Panthers). This project placed the intersections between hip-hop and black activism squarely in the domain of gangster rap. This synergy between contemporary culture and historical memory created a powerful mix that reached a vast, youthful audience.[18]

Van Peebles' strategic use of hip-hop in a film about the sixties underscores the importance of the post-sixties generation in the memorializaton of the Black Panthers. The hip-hop generation has been in the forefront of appropriating, reformulating, and disseminating the images and ideas of black power activism through popular culture. Rap performers, dubbed "raptivists" by some, found a niche between musical expression, commercialism, and the articulation of a political consciousness. Political theorist Michael Dawson found that this was more than a mere entertainment fad; fans of rap music are more likely to see race as the defining social problem and believe that "the solutions to these problems are to be found within the ideology of black nationalism."[19]

In the late 1980s, the group Public Enemy burst on the music scene with an original, hard-hitting style of politically inflected, confrontational lyrics. Although their music invoked a range of black power icons, they intentionally adopted the persona of the "Black Panthers of Hip Hop." Historian Charise Cheney's study of masculinity and rap culture notes that Public Enemy's leader, Chuck D, sought this identification as a way to proclaim their role as "representatives of a revolutionary generation." On their album *Fear of a Black Planet*, the

song titled "Power to the People" evoked the spirit of black nationalism with lines like "Let's get it together make a nation." In Public
Enemy's 1991 video "By The Time I Get to Arizona" the scenario is
populated by black male figures wearing uniforms, red berets, and
dark sunglasses as gunfire and explosions suggest a racial apocalypse.
In this instance, the Panthers' wrath is summoned for a song that an-
grily complains about the refusal of Arizona officials to establish a
paid public holiday in honor of Martin Luther King Jr.'s birthday. At
one New York–area concert in 1988, they were introduced as "Long
Island's Black Panthers," sharing the stage with a paramilitary honor
guard called S1W (Security of the First World), in an overt nod to the
Panther militias and the Nation of Islam's security units. One of their
members, Professor Grif, had the title of Minister of Information, in
homage to Eldridge Cleaver. But the Black Panther connection with
Public Enemy was loose at best. It was largely a matter of style and
rhetoric—their defiant posturing harked back to the Panthers, as did
some of their lyrics. For example, in the title of the group's hit anthem "Party for Your Right to Fight," the Black Panthers are the
"party" in this double entendre. The song also makes reference to the
FBI's counterintelligence program:

J. Edgar Hoover, and he coulda proved to you,
He had King and X set up,
Also the party with Newton, Cleaver and Seale,
He ended, so get up,
Time to get 'em back.

What made Public Enemy influential, in part, was their call for black
resistance among young hip-hop audiences. They helped bring the
black power era of the sixties and seventies into the 1990s consciousness.[20]

Other rappers who took up the Black Panther banner included
KRS-One, Digital Underground, Digable Planets, and Tupac Shakur.
Rappers Common and Cee-Lo tell the story of Panther heroine Assata
Shakur's incarceration, during which "[s]he discovered freedom is a unspoken sound, / And a wall is a wall and can be broken down, / Found
peace in the Panthers she went on trial with, / One of the brothers she
had a child with." Tupac Shakur capitalized on his party lineage as the

son of Afeni Shakur, a member of the Panther 21 (a group tried on conspiracy charges in 1970), the stepson of Mutulu Shakur, and the godson of Geronimo Pratt. As a child of the original Black Panthers, Shakur had a legitimate claim of radical authenticity until his premature death in a drive-by shooting in 1996. He admitted that he felt like a Black Panther "[i]n a '90s way . . . I feel like every black person should own a gun." As the Black Panthers became increasingly visible in hip-hop circles in the early nineties, these ties worked well for Shakur's self-fashioning, as his music fell within the genres of both gangster rap and political nationalist rap, particularly when he repudiated his "thug life" after serving time in prison. "Building upon our cultural memory of the Black Panther Party, the image of Tupac Shakur, with his heavily tattooed body and his middle finger in the air, also stands in for black rebellion and dissatisfaction," notes Kara Keeling. Yet the point of Shakur's image was to sell records, not a political movement, she argued. Nevertheless, the ethos of protest, whether inherited or borrowed from his parents, permeated many of his lyrics. West Coast rappers such as Tupac "tended to weave their political consciousness into lyrical narrations on gang violence and police brutality," explains Charise Cheney, in the process addressing an issue raised twenty-five years earlier by the Panthers.[21]

Alternately, rapper Paris, who called himself the Black Panther of hip-hop, borrowed liberally from the group's writing and lore to underscore his political claims. On his 1989–90 album *The Devil Made Me Do It*, he quotes the ten-point program, calls for Panther power, and chants, "[R]evolution has come; time to pick up the gun," a quote from a Black Panther song. Paris rails against white supremacy and the police, and conflates his music with "the sound of the Panther movement." He often appeared with a quartet of dancers who held the Black Panther salute aloft as he rapped. On his 1992 album *Sleeping with the Enemy*, Paris devoted a song to Assata Shakur after meeting her on a trip to Cuba, where she lives in exile from the United States. Paris, who hailed from the Panthers' hometown of Oakland, was deeply conscious of the racialized nature of the memories surrounding the group. "You've got to understand, the Black Panthers were looked upon as terrorists by the white community, but much of the black community looked upon them as heroes," he told the *Los Angeles Times*. Thus, for much of the decade, black youth were dancing to songs exalting the spirit of the Black Panther Party; they were singing lyrics about Huey, Bobby, and Assata even if they knew little of the group's history, and they were being told that black revolutionary action needed to be revived. Indicative of this generational fascination was a two-part series in the magazine *Rap Pages* titled "The Black Panthers: Party of the People, Creating Commitment and *Real* Black Power." The article encouraged hip-hop fans to follow the ideals of the Panthers, rather than the contemporary emphasis on materialism and nihilism. This merging of rap and black nationalism produced a myth of radicalism rather than any significant political change, notes Errol Henderson. Nevertheless, films such as *Panther* and performers such as Paris and Public Enemy were powerful purveyors of the Panther memory.[22]

Politically inflected hip-hop has continued to invoke the Panthers as symbols of revolutionary nationalism. Dead Prez, who released their first album in 2000, railed against racism and government bureaucracy and promoted black self-determination on tracks such as "Assassination," "Behind Enemy Lines," and "We Want Freedom." They immediately won the label of the "millennial Black Panthers" because of their links to social movements and their desire to use rap as a political tool. Across the Atlantic, the politically conscious rap group Asian Dub Foundation has used the Panthers and other political icons as inspiration while promoting a transnational, transracial anti-racist movement. On their 2000 album *Community Music*, the voice of Assata Shakur is sampled on a song titled "Committed to Life," while a track on their 2005 album titled "Take Back the Power" pays homage to the spirit of the era's slogan "All power to the people."[23]

The responses to the movie *Panther* were deeply—and sometimes bitterly—contested as diverging contradictory memories of the sixties materialized. Perhaps the most vociferous critic was David Horowitz, a former leftist activist and editor of *Ramparts* magazine, who took out full-page ads in the trade publications *Daily Variety* and the *Hollywood Reporter* telling viewers to stay away and threatening demonstrations. Horowitz called the movie "a two-hour lie" in huge block letters, and distributed a seven-page statement to the news media with charges that the Panthers were "led by gangsters who committed hundreds of felonies, including arson, murder, extortion, and armed robbery." This was an instance in which fiction was accorded the status of history and the power to persuade. The simple act of going to the movie gave the Black Panthers credibility and heroic status, Horowitz feared. The campaign to discredit the film elicited a strident response from a group of well-known African Americans, including the Reverend Jesse Jackson, musician Quincy Jones, filmmaker Spike Lee, and basketball star Magic Johnson. Within three days these black luminaries purchased their own full-page ad in *Daily Variety* to defend the Van Peebleses' right to tell the story from their perspective. The signatories represented the collective outrage of segments of the black elite, who condemned Horowitz' ad as an "un-American persecution" of the film and an "attempt to quell the first amendment rights of any filmmaker." The statement emphasized the importance of injecting black voices into historical memory. "Rarely in the history of Hollywood have African Americans themselves had the opportunity to present our history, our hopes, our dreams, the story of our lives in our own way," they declared. This uproar turned a single motion picture into the site of a struggle over whose memory should be articulated, and how. As one article in the Hollywood press asked, "Whose '60s is it, anyway?"[24]

The reactions to *Panther* reflected distinct individual and collective memories and their investments in radically different narratives about race and radicalism in the 1960s. Film reviewers offered a wild mix of opinion. *Panther* was hailed as a celebration and hagiography, agitprop and mythology, shamelessly exploitive and "a rousing blend of drama, creative interpretation and likable performances." While *Time* magazine called the film a "whitewash," *New York Times* film critic Caryn James defended the Van Peebleses' use of dramatic license in the service of history and art. "*Panther* was created as a deliberate challenge to established power," she wrote. "If Mario Van Peebles rewrites history, he claims a power that seriously shakes up anyone who thought the Panthers were dead. . . . No historian can take that kind of license, but any artist can."[25]

Black cultural critic Michael Eric Dyson agreed with these sentiments. He argued that while the film was "willfully provocative" and biased in favor of the Panthers, it was also a "bold revisionist history" that captured "the intellectual ferment in the ghettos of Oakland as Newton, Mr. Seale and later Eldridge Cleaver . . . strategized against racism and capitalism." For Dyson, the Van Peebles team offered a distinctly black articulation of the past that superceded any question of veracity. Why should *Panther* be held to a higher standard than any other fictionalized version of history?, argued these critics. Michael Robinson, writing in the black history and culture periodical *American Visions*, went even further to suggest that regardless of its flaws, *Panther* was a vital tool for teaching the story of black radical protest: "[T]he Van Peebleses have created readily identifiable heroes for a young generation that is sorely in need of direction." But this debate cannot be reduced to racial essentialism, as many African Americans refused to embrace the film's premise. Criticizing *Panther* did not have to imply a lack of solidarity with the quest to tell the story of black American radicalism. Emblematic of this position was political scientist Clarence Lusane, who expressed outrage over the commodification of black power in films such as *Malcolm X* and *Panther*, which he called "a shameful amalgamation of conspiracy theories, action-movie antics, and political sophistry." Lusane was particularly dubious about "the unstable marriage of Black history and White Hollywood" and warned black audiences not to be duped by projects that ultimately support a conservative agenda.[26]

Another spirited discussion circulated around the film's gender politics. Dyson, among others, noted that *Panther* ignored the history of misogyny and sexual abuse that has dogged the group, particularly in recent memoirs. But perhaps more egregious was the total absence of any fully developed female characters in the film, effectively writing women out of the Panthers' history. Tracye Matthews, who has analyzed the status of women in the party, argued that *Panther* uncritically reinforced the idea that the struggle for black liberation is synonymous with the articulation of black manhood. At the core of *Panther*'s appeal was the way it inscribed the exaltation of a decidedly patriarchal black nationalism as it captured the gendered sensibilities of hard-core rap in a relatively safe space. This was epitomized by one black male reviewer, who unabashedly called the film "a stirring affirmation of black masculinity, an image of what the Panthers could have, and maybe should have, been." The responses to the film were shaped by gendered as well as political and racial identifications. One black female critic, who sat on the film's set during production, remembered being taken over by the cinematic spectacle of the Panthers, but later "left the screening room feeling strangely unaddressed" because of the absence of women in the narrative. Many viewers shared this dual experience of being both exhilarated by the mythology of the Panthers and equally disappointed with the obvious omissions.[27]

Ironically, it was Bobby Seale, Black Panther co-founder, who had some of the harshest words for the project. He called the film "bootleg fiction" and asserted that it distorted the entire history of the Panthers. "I know they [the Van Peebleses] say it's fiction but it's tantamount to a bunch of poetic lies," Seale told one black newspaper. "The average person is going to think these guys were street gang types. But we were part of a young black intelligentsia." Seale's comments demonstrate how surviving members of the Panthers remain intent on having the last word but may have little control in the process. Thus Seale told the news media that his own memoir, *Seize the Time*, was sold to Warner Brothers and that he was aggressively pursuing a movie deal. *Panther* clearly responded to the desire by some to celebrate the group as standard-bearers of black empowerment, but it simultaneously failed to conform to many African Americans' memories or to heal the wounds remaining from the sixties.[28]

Mario Van Peebles was keenly aware of the historical implications of *Panther*, and while the film played fast and loose with the facts, he found another venue through which to present a more straightforward version of the group's story. He collaborated with a historian and with a former Black Panther to publish a companion book, *Panther: The Pictorial History of the Black Panthers and the Story Behind the Film*, that offered a serious look at how the group fit into African American history. Ula Y. Taylor, a professor and author of a study of Amy Jacques Garvey, and J. Tarika Lewis, who identifies herself as the first woman to join the Panther, provided a thoughtful, detailed chronology of the group's activities. Taylor and Lewis assign a certain authority to Van Peebles' project, providing the seal of approval of a scholar and a Panther insider, particularly ironic that two women are given this influential voice, women are rendered invisible in the film. *Panther: The Pictorial History of the Black Panthers* is classified as juvenile literature, and like most accompanying a movie, it addresses a general audience with a and a stunning array of photographs. The book's first half presents tory of the civil rights struggle that situates the Panthers in context rather than as an isolated phenomenon. The second by Melvin and Mario Van Peebles, discusses their motives problems inherent in producing a controversial motion pi followed the path of Spike Lee, who has produced volumes about several of his films to discuss the political, economic, and artistic processes involved in filmmaking. Such books are also a clever marketing device, creating an intertextual dialogue between film and print and distributing images and scripts in venues beyond the local cinema. Indeed, the title of Lee's companion volume to the Malcolm X movie was *By Any Means Necessary: The Trials and Tribulations of the Making of* Malcolm X. Long after a film has retreated into video oblivion, books such as *Panther: The Pictorial History of the Black Panthers* keep the filmmaker and his or her story in circulation by relying on the permanence of print culture.[29]

The Van Peebleses' mythology of the Black Panthers stands in stark contrast to another film released just a year earlier. If *Panther* was the embodiment of a defiant African American memory of the sixties, *Forrest Gump* offered a white liberal alternative. The wildly popular 1994 film, directed by Robert Zemeckis, presented the tale of a feeble-minded southern white man whose mundane life intersects with crucial moments in postwar history. The film won numerous awards, including a best-actor Oscar for lead Tom Hanks. *Forrest Gump* strives to be a narrative of the social upheaval and transformations of the 1960s and early 1970s. Within this structure, the film functions as a parable about race relations in the United States as Gump, named after a Confederate hero and founder of the Ku Klux Klan, appears in pivotal events such as the desegregation of the University of Alabama. The foremost goal of the film, according to Robyn Wiegman, is "to demonstrate that difference and injury, even intellectual deficiency, are not impediments to the American way of life."[30]

When members of the Black Panther Party make their brief appearance in the film as stand-ins for all angry, destructive black males, they contradict every tenet of the American dream. In particular, they are placed in sharp contradistiction to Gump's best friend, Bubba, an equally slow, congenial southern black man who dies in the killing fields of Vietnam. Bubba, played by Mykelti Williamson, is warm and forgiving, while the nameless Black Panthers are cold and menacing. It isn't hard to discern the preferred form of black masculinity that is celebrated in the film.

On the day that Gump encounters the Panthers, he is decorated as a var hero by President Johnson, reunited with his true love, Jenny, and oerced into speaking to an anti-war demonstration by an Abbie

Hoffman look-alike. After the demonstration, Gump is confronted by a fierce-looking black man wearing a black leather jacket and beret who is clearly modeled on the image of Eldridge Cleaver—tall, dark, and handsome with similar gestures and facial expressions. The nameless character scowls at Gump and bellows, "Shut the blinds, man, and move your white ass away from that window." When the window shade is pulled down, it is adorned with photos and posters of Cleaver, Huey Newton, and other Black Panther leaders.

Gump is frisked by the same character, who taunts him with an endless tirade of black nationalist clichés: "Our purpose here is to protect our black leaders from the racist pigs who wish to brutalize our black leaders and rape our women" and "We the Black Panthers are against the war where black soldiers are sent to the front lines to die for a country that hates them." As the camera pans the room, a banner proclaims "No Vietnamese Ever Called Me Nigger" and posters celebrate "All Power to the People." The scene is little more than a contrivance to highlight Gump's innocence against the backdrop of such inflammatory rhetoric. In it he rescues Jenny from the blows of her violent, SDS-member boyfriend, beating him to the ground as a crowd of intimidating Black Panthers watch. When Jenny intervenes, Gump backs out of the room apologetically, saying, "Sorry I had a fight in the middle of your Black Panther party." The pun offers comic relief for a tense episode in which black and white radicals provide the specter of threat and danger. The portrayal of the Panthers as hate-filled, unstable, and politically bereft is a useful contrast to Gump's easygoing heroism, morality, and native intelligence, thus fueling a historical memory that lies somewhere between ridicule and condemnation. *Forrest Gump* is a successful counternarrative to African Americans' memories; it succeeds in constructing the Black Panthers as the era's anti-heroes rather than as idols of the black revolution.

2

BLACK AMERICA IN THE PUBLIC SPHERE

Planned Massacre of Whites Today; Negroes Seized in Arkansas
Riots Confess to Widespread Plot Among Them; Had Password
for Rising; and a "Paul Revere" Courier System—School House
an Ammunition Depot
                    —Headline, *New York Times*, October 6, 1919

Black Americans' intense desire to see themselves through heroic, self-
assured, and defiant figures—such as those in the film *Panther*—is a
product of the legacy of their place in mass culture. This was perhaps
best articulated by W.E.B. Du Bois, who used the metaphor of the veil
to describe black Americans' state of "double consciousness." Writing
at the dawn of the twentieth century, Du Bois explained that the nation's racial ideology forced black people to define themselves, in part,
through the ways they have been represented—"to see himself through
the revelation of the other world." Thus, the visibility of blackness is a
problem regarding not only how whites see them but also how they
see themselves. This phenomenon is all the more crucial because blacks
often lack the ability to shape their own image in mass culture. Rather,
they endure "this sense of always looking at one's self through the eyes
of others, of measuring one's soul by the tape of a world that looks on
in amused contempt and pity."[1]

From blackface minstrelsy to the penny press, dime novels, and motion pictures, blackness has been embraced and vilified, exalted and
ridiculed in American society. In his study of nineteenth-century minstrelsy in the urban North, Eric Lott explained that white males' crude
parody of black speech and culture on stage was a prime vehicle for
expressing their anxieties. "The black mask offered a way to play with
collective fears of a degraded and threatening—and male—Other while
at the same time maintaining some symbolic control over them."[2]
Throughout the 150 years since the abolition of slavery, African

Americans have had ample reason to view the mass media with suspicion and disdain. The media has been instrumental in circulating and
reifying racialized ideas and images and in maintaining a social and political climate that reinforced blacks' second-class status. Despite the
upheaval of the 1960s and the mediated politics of groups such as
the Black Panther Party, fundamental constructions of blackness have
proved to be resilient even as they are the object of criticism.

The image projected by the Black Panthers, and the frightened response from mainstream America, has its roots in the nation's history
of race relations. Since the arrival of Africans in seventeenth-century
Virginia, American society has been shaped, in part, by the ever-present
threat of black revolt. And mass culture relied on two contradictory
images of the black subject—the happy, contented slave and the black
as social danger. The fear of black people—especially armed and angry
black men—is as old as the United States itself. When Toussaint L'Ou-
verture led a successful insurrection in Haiti in 1792 that led to the
creation of a black republic, he confirmed slaveholders' worst fears—
that slaves could overthrow and take revenge on their captors. Historians have demonstrated that the Haitian revolution was the catalyst for
increasingly oppressive measures against blacks in the United States,
from the institution of slave codes that further circumscribed slaves' associations and movements, and attacks on the burgeoning abolitionist
movement, to the intense repression of the small population of free
blacks. "The hysteria unleashed by events on Saint-Dominque eroded
the freemen's legal rights like a torrent of rain on a grassless slope,"
noted Ira Berlin. With each successive rebellion, including Gabriel
Prosser's thwarted attempt to seize Richmond in 1800 and Nat Turner's
ill-fated uprising in 1831, the fear of black power became magnified
out of proportion. Thus, explained one historian, black people were
always suspect: "Southerners admitted their suspicion that duplicity,
opportunism, and potential rebelliousness lurked behind the mask of
Negro affability."[3]

The nation's statesmen were keenly aware that slavery made peaceful coexistence among the races impossible while sustaining the threat
of violent revolt. Thomas Jefferson, himself a slave owner, critiqued
the institution. Yet, Jefferson concluded, emancipation would only
bring greater chaos, and he instead supported the idea of repatriating
blacks to Africa or some other locale. Jefferson was fatalistic about the

damage done by slavery and by the enduring and fundamental differences between black and white. "Deep rooted prejudices entertained
by the whites; ten thousand recollections, by the blacks, of the injuries
they have sustained; new provocations; the real distinctions which nature has made; and many other circumstances, will divide us into parties and produce convulsions which will probably never end but in the
extermination of the one or the other race," he wrote in 1781. Senator Henry Clay, one of the architects of the Compromise of 1850, was
also a proponent of black colonization back to Africa, arguing "that
the slave system contained within itself the seeds of insurrection and
race war."[4]

In his landmark study *The Black Image in the White Mind*, George
Fredrickson mapped out a genealogy of the representations of blackness
as they changed over time. Slaveholders and abolitionists fundamentally
agreed that blacks could never be peacefully assimilated into society.
Free blacks were often characterized as degraded, vicious, and depraved,
supporting the rationale that blacks must be contained within the institution of slavery. Some argued that blacks were essentially inferior be-
ings, but many relied heavily on the belief that the hateful environment
in which blacks lived contributed to their wretched condition, particularly their propensity for crime and poverty. "The fact that the Negro
was, or had been, a slave and that the color of his skin was a permanent
sign of his origin was enough to prevent for all time his acceptance as a
social equal," Fredrickson wrote.[5]

The environmental rationale for black inferiority eventually gave
way to biological determinism and the idea that the races were separate
entities and that the black person was "a pathetically inept creature
who was a slave to his emotions, incapable of progressive development
and self-government because he lacked the white man's enterprise and
intellect." Simultaneously, a group Fredrickson defined as the romantic
racialists attempted to find redeeming qualities in racial differences,
culminating in the image of the African American as the natural Christian in Harriet Beecher Stowe's *Uncle Tom's Cabin*.[6]

After the Civil War, the aims of Radical Reconstruction, which
sought to give blacks the opportunity to develop some economic autonomy and political standing, were vehemently opposed by white
supremacists. Mass culture—the press, music, and theater—were essential

for maintaining and reinforcing this racial ideology. The rise of consumer culture in the United States coincided with post-Reconstruction
politics, and black stereotypes were a convenient, easily recognizable
source for selling products and creating brand loyalty. Kenneth Goings
suggests that the myth of the loyal and contented black servant became a
powerful advertising tool—ads for domestic products prominently featured grotesque images of the faithful Mammy and the happy Sambo.
"By producing and using in advertising everyday items that clearly depicted African-Americans as inferior . . . manufacturers were giving a
physical reality to the racist ideology," he argued.[7]

One popular racialist argument was fueled by social Darwinists of
the late nineteenth century, who used the "survival of the fittest" thesis to argue that there were only two possible outcomes for the Negro
race—extermination or mixture with whites. They employed the
principles of natural selection to argue that the Africans' naturally savage traits were an ongoing threat to white civilization. Social Darwin-
ism was an effective rationale for segregation, Jim Crow laws, and tacit
racial violence to keep restive negroes in check. It advocated "the need
to segregate or quarantine a race liable to be a source of contamination
and social danger to the white community as it sank ever deeper into
the slough of disease, vice, and criminality."[8]

Thus, by the arrival of the twentieth century, white supremacists
had created a discourse of "Negrophobia" that permeated racial ideologies in the North and South. Lynching reached its peak during this
period as the stereotype of the black brute was circulated with vigor.
Fredrickson noted that the debates on lynching could be boiled down
to the idea that it was "a 'necessary evil' in a segregated society, pending more effective methods to control the black population and curb
its 'criminal' tendencies." The black male figure as a beastly, lascivious
rapist was part of "the most extreme defamation of the Negro character that had yet been offered." The black brute, a particularly egregious
representation from this period, provided the major tension in D.W.
Griffith's 1915 silent epic *Birth of a Nation*, as the black male characters relentlessly pursued white females and generally wreaked havoc
on the Reconstruction South. The film's black brutes and bucks carried out a "rampage full of black rage," while Griffith "played hard
on the bestiality of his black villainous bucks and used it to arouse

hatred" in the name of white supremacy, according to film historian Donald Bogle.[9]

Twentieth-century mass media—newspapers, magazines, film, and later television—continued the transmission of these depictions of the black character. In Rayford Logan's study of northern newspapers during the post-Reconstruction period—what he called the nadir for African Americans—he found that the black image was consistently denigrated in print. He used the press as a gauge for the opinions of both the elite and the voting masses, and made a persuasive argument that print culture offered a vital window on the political and social ideologies of the day. "Then, as now, most Americans made up their minds about local affairs and their relations with their fellow man on the basis of news articles, many of them slanted, and the other less weighty ingredients of the paper, such as anecdotes, jokes and cartoons," Logan maintained. The northern press sought to condemn the South's disenfranchisement of blacks and the imposition of Jim Crow laws, while keeping the "Negro problem" at arm's length. By the turn of the century, only 10 percent of the black population lived in the North, and newspapers from Boston to St. Louis manifested little interest in blacks' well-being when discussing national political issues. Logan concluded that the North gradually accepted the concept of second-class status for blacks in an effort to eliminate the sectional crisis that had led to the Civil War: "the Northern press was not reluctant to sacrifice the Negro on the altar of reconciliation, peace and prosperity."[10]

But when Logan examined how these publications discussed the "color line" in their own cities, the picture changed significantly. Between 1877 and 1901, he found, the press exaggerated incidents in which blacks were involved, that the racial identification of "colored" or "Negro" distinguished blacks from white immigrants, and that these terms were frequently paired with pejorative adjectives such as "burly negro," "negro ruffian," "African Annie," and "colored cannibal." Newspapers often used inflammatory headlines—"Held Up By Masked Negroes"—followed by relatively tame articles, suggesting that editors recognized the marketability of the dangerous black figure. One of the more shameful practices of some newspapers was to play up lynching stories to capitalize on their lurid and violent content, and Logan found at least one publication that admitted doing so in its advertisements. Northern newspapers, Logan found, were also prone to believe the accusations of rape leveled against black men, in effect siding with white lynch mobs.[11]

The "comic Negro" was another staple figure in northern newspapers. Journalists took delight in mimicking so-called southern black dialect, and reproduced blackface minstrel characterizations in print. Blacks were ridiculed for being oversensitive about civil rights and were characterized as prone to instant violence; illustrations and cartoons reproduced the mammy, pickanniny, and Uncle Tom in exaggerated graphic terms. Simultaneously, they occasionally highlighted the activities and accomplishments of elite blacks, but there was little or no attention to the rampant segregation and discrimination they experienced. Logan found that the highbrow literary magazines, including *Harper's*, *Atlantic Monthly*, and *North American Review*, also took "evident delight in the lampooning of Negroes." Novelists, poets, essayists, and illustrators addressing a mostly northern audience "referred to Negroes as nigger, niggah, darkey, coon, pickanninny, Mammy, yallar hussy." Indeed, virtually every negative stereotype of blackness could be found in the pages of the five magazines he studied—rude descriptions of black phenotypes; ridicule of African American titles, names, and folk expressions; and depictions as thieves and liars or as sexually immoral—with, Logan complained, the overall goal of providing readers enjoyment "at the expense of the Negro." Perhaps most insidious was the way these newspapers and magazines fueled the anxiety about black sexuality and masculinity by highlighting the theme of black criminality, particularly in the attention paid to attacks on white women.[12]

Logan completed his analysis by looking at the black image in magazines and newspapers in the first eighteen years of the twentieth century. He despaired that little had changed, and that often the vicious representations of African Americans had worsened. Leading newspapers such as the *New York Times* and *Chicago Tribune* condemned lynching in their editorials, but others, including the *Cincinnati Enquirer*, "continued to present lynchings in a most sensational and lurid fashion that generally upheld the mob." He concluded that "on balance, the newspapers surveyed did not give strong support to Negroes in the struggle for equal rights. One can only conjecture as to the influence on the American mind of this continuing, though lessening, evidence of the violations of the basic principles of democracy."[13]

Logan is but one of numerous scholars who have studied the role of the press in circulating ideologies about race. One obscure study of six Philadelphia newspapers between 1908 and 1932 found that during this period, less than 1 percent of all news was about African Americans, and most of this coverage focused on crime. The researcher attributed this effect to the audience's prevailing assumptions about black criminality and the fact that the press constantly seeks the most sensational stories. Perhaps most telling was the commentary from the city's editors who were interviewed in 1936 for the study. An editor for the Philadelphia *Public Ledger* explained that blacks were not a significant part of the paper's readership "except a few of the more intelligent ones." He then critiqued a competing newspaper by noting, "The *Inquirer* is known as the paper with the largest nigger circulation."[14]

Even the muckrakers, who used print culture to rail against corporate greed and political corruption, perpetuated the prevailing mythologies of the black character. The major muckraking magazines of the early twentieth century—*Collier's, Cosmopolitan, McClure's, Everybody's,* and *Arena*—failed to critique Jim Crow segregation or the epidemic of lynching at the same time that they pushed for reform in other areas of American life. One historian noted that the magazines tended to apologize for southern racism, and the muckraking journalists often revealed their racist attitudes by deploying the argument that blacks were prone to rape and other acts of violence. Ray Stannard Baker, a leading investigative journalist of the era, took it upon himself to expose the problem of lynching in a series of articles for *McClure's,* but he also described blacks with phrases like " '[t]he animal-like ferocity' of the Negro criminal," revealing his own acceptance of racial stereotypes.[15]

These egregious constructions of African Americans occurred during the transition from the nineteenth to twentieth centuries, an era marked by momentous changes in the circumstances and politics of African Americans. In the post-Reconstruction era, African Americans faced an onslaught of legal decisions that opened the door to legally sanctioned segregation and discrimination, particularly in the

South, where 90 percent of the black population resided. Enforcement of the Fourteenth and Fifteenth Amendments to the Constitution waned as the federal protections were withdrawn after 1877. This was followed by the 1883 Supreme Court decision to invalidate the Civil Rights Act of 1875, and thirteen years later the infamous *Plessy v. Ferguson* (1896) decision, which rendered "separate but equal" facilities constitutional. Thus, by the 1890s, there were few if any barriers to the intensification of Jim Crow segregation and the racial violence that accompanied it.

This state of affairs prompted a range of oppositional strategies among African Americans. In 1890, for example, the brilliant journalist T. Thomas Fortune made it clear that many African Americans were prepared to engage in radical resistance to gain their civil rights. He told the founding convention of the Afro-American League that black Americans needed to follow the example of revolutionaries from ancient Greece to the American Revolution in the quest for justice. "The spirit of agitation which has brought us together here comprehends in its vast sweep the entire range of human history," he proclaimed. "Apathy leads to stagnation. The arsenal, the fort, the warrior are as necessary as the school, the church, the newspapers and the public forum of debate. . . . Ladies and gentlemen, it is time to call a halt. It is time to begin to fight fire with fire."[16]

Juxtaposed to this rhetoric of confrontation was the work of Booker T. Washington, who saw white supremacy as an irrefutable fact of life and argued instead that African Americans should engage in projects that would make them independent and self-sufficient. Washington argued on behalf of pragmatism—that blacks and whites were destined to live separately and that African Americans should remain in the South and concentrate their energies on bettering their economic condition. In his 1895 "Atlanta Compromise" speech, Washington reassured his largely white audience that the races should remain separate: "in all things that are purely social we can be as separate as the fingers, yet one as the hand in all things essential to our mutual progress." Washington also chastised activists such as Fortune, who demanded their civil rights: "The wisest among my race understand that the agitation of questions of social equality is the extremist folly," he argued.[17]

During this era, black activist intellectuals such as W.E.B. Du Bois, Ida Wells-Barnett, and William Monroe Trotter established organizations, schools, and publications that were the basis for the varied projects for black liberation. By 1900 the black literacy rate had risen from just under 10 percent to just under 50 percent, southern blacks slowly acquired property and businesses, and they increasingly engaged in acts of resistance such as protests against segregated public transportation. Meanwhile, African Americans escaping the land peonage and debilitating segregation of the South began a steady migration that accelerated during the years of World War I. Groups dedicated to the abolition of Jim Crow emerged to create a cohesive political opposition to white supremacy. By 1910, a biracial coalition calling itself the National Association for the Advancement of Colored People (NAACP) was founded with the goals of restoring the black vote in the South, ending the segregation of public facilities, and campaigning for anti-lynching legislation. Du Bois, one of the association's key organizers, emerged as a vocal opponent of Washington's accomodationist politics, calling him "a compromiser between the South, the North, and the Negro." In a stinging rebuke of Washington, Du Bois echoed Fortune's call to arms when he demanded, "By every civilized and peaceful method we must strive for the rights which the world accords to men"[18]

Black labor unions, historically black colleges and universities, black women's clubs, and black churches entered the new century with a commitment to protest and racial transformation. Within a few years, some African American activists also imagined a coalition with postcolonial Africa to build a unified front against white supremacy. In 1915 Du Bois called for a "negro brotherhood" across the globe that would fight Western imperialism on behalf of the darker races. Two years later, a charismatic Jamaican named Marcus Garvey opened an office of the Universal Negro Improvement Association (UNIA) in Harlem, attracting hundreds of thousands of supporters in the dream of black self-sufficiency and repatriation back to Africa. African American resistance was varied, alive, and well, but invisible to most of white America.[19]

The outbreak of World War I was a tempestuous period during which black Americans felt a sense of new economic strength and prosperity at the same time that they were deeply pessimistic about the potential for change. In the summer of 1917, the first of a series of violent race riots erupted, this time in East St. Louis, Illinois, where two hundred blacks were killed and thousands left homeless. The next year, as black men served overseas in a segregated military, seventy-eight African Americans were lynched, and the racial violence continued. Like the late 1960s, the period between 1918 and 1920 was marked by dissension, violence, and a national mood of unrest that reflected a crisis in American race relations. To aid this discussion, I picked up where Logan left off to study articles published in the *New York Times* for these two years.[20] The *Times* registered little, if any, of the spirit of protest and progress in black America expressed by figures such as Fortune or Du Bois. Instead, the fear of black insurrection prevailed in its pages. These long-standing anxieties were reflected in the *Times'* often hysterical coverage given to the race riots that culminated in the infamous Red Summer of 1919. The specter of an African American uprising was constant; black men emboldened by their contributions to the war effort had no qualms about avenging the legacy of racial hatred and discrimination at home, according to the city's prominent newspaper. The figure of the black beast—threatening and out of control— dominated the coverage. There were several elements routinely highlighted in these stories: blacks and whites engaged in hand-to-hand combat, black men wielded prodigious physical strength and weapons, and blacks lacked the internal restraints that would prevent violence. Numerous headlines provided a frightening image of uncontrolled black anger, such as "One Killed, 18 Hurt in Brooklyn Riot: Police Sailors, Whites, and Negroes Struggle Until Inciter of Fight Is Dead: 200-Pound Negro, Armed with a Shark Knife, Went to Defense of His Longshoreman Friend." In this bloody incident, the report noted that "excited negroes, armed with revolvers, knives, stones and bottles, swarmed out of the houses of the exclusively negro section and surrounded Prince Street, where six policemen were dodging about trying to close in on the crazed negro."[21]

Another article reported that the police were "powerless to subdue the infuriated whites and blacks" who fought each other with any weapon at hand. The headline read: "Race Riot in Philadelphia: Two Policemen Killed and Sixty Persons Injured—Many Negroes Held."[22] On the editorial page, the *Times* argued that the northward migration of African Americans undermined the southern economy and threatened northern stability because the South was where the Negro "is most at home, where he is best understood, and in reality best liked. . . ."[23]

In 1919 black soldiers returned from World War I and instilled a new sense of pride in their communities. When the renowned Harlem Hell Fighters, an all-black regiment of the New York National Guard who distinguished themselves on the front lines in France, marched down Fifth Avenue early that year, they were featured on the front page of the *New York Times* with the headline "Fifth Avenue Cheers Negro Veterans." The upbeat article noted that the multiracial crowd that lined the parade route was duly impressed by "the magnificent appearance of these fighting men."[24] But this was a rare moment in an otherwise sobering year during which the newspaper's attention to race riots continued unabated, nearly giving credence to the social Darwinists who predicted that emancipation would lead to all-out race war. In most of these accounts, blacks instigated the unrest, and it appeared that across the country race relations had deteriorated greatly. In one story, a white sailor was allegedly shot by a black man in a poolroom in Charleston, South Carolina, leading to a melee in which six were killed."[25] Meanwhile, in Harlem, a black man fired a gun at a fleeing white man after they argued about the war. "In a few minutes the negro became very much excited and when the white man disputed some statement he had made the negro pulled a pistol from a pocket," the *Times* reported.[26] Multiple articles described blacks spilling out of their homes at the hint of a disturbance, all ready to join in the fight.

The violent trend reached its apex in July, when the paper reported on what was characterized as an all-out race war in Chicago. "6,000 Troops Called Out in Chicago to Check New Riots; Negroes Fire at Soldiers, Attack Passing Trains," screamed the front-page banner headline.[27] The article offered numerous grisly details of the fighting, which killed thirty-one blacks and whites and left scores wounded. But there was little analysis of the cause of the discord. Two news briefs appended to the end of the article hinted at the larger political implications of the riots. A telegram from the Equal Rights League headed by William Monroe Trotter was reproduced, which condemned the rioting and called on the governor of Illinois and the city's mayor to punish white and black offenders equally. "It is unfair to disarm colored rioters and to allow white rioters to remain armed," the group maintained.[28] Below this item was a statement from the U.S. attorney general, A. Mitchell Palmer, suggesting that the "race troubles" in American cities were due to Bolshevik and other radical propaganda being circulated in black communities.

During the ensuing weeks, the *Times* gave voice to a new apprehension—that socialist agitators were the source of the nation's racial discord. This Red Scare, promulgated by Palmer and the Justice Department, swept the nation into a postwar frenzy in the wake of the Russian revolution. "Bomb-throwing anarchists, antiwar socialists, and plotting communists, harboring social visions as weird as their un-American names, were, many Americans truly feared, about to rip apart the fabric of a society already badly strained by economic unrest," noted historian David Levering Lewis. The *Times* joined in with stories such as "Reds Try to Stir Negroes to Revolt" and "Negroes of World Prey of Agitators." The articles gave credence to unnamed government sources who declared that the International Workers of the World (IWW), radical socialists, and Bolsheviks were seeking to "stir up discontent among the negroes, particularly the uneducated class in the Southern States." One brief article said the state attorney general claimed the IWW was the American counterpart to the Bolsheviks, and that "both movements called for the overturn of existing institutions by force, the murder of all who opposed the ideas embodied in them, and the setting up of a government of the proletariat."[29] A *New York Times* editorial denied there was any basis for racial discontent in the United States or that there was any organized form of black resistance. Instead, the newspaper inflamed the nation's fears by arguing that "outside influences" must be the source. "In other words, the situation presupposes intelligent direction and management," implying that such qualities were absent in black communities. One late-summer article reported that a southern congressman blamed the black press and figures such as Du Bois, Trotter, and A. Philip Randolph for inciting the racial violence when they condemned segregation and lynching. Yet, even in this limited recognition of a black critique, the article suggested that the IWW and figures such as Eugene Debs, not the black leaders themselves, were the inspiration for black Americans' dissent.[30]

Race riots continued to dominate the *New York Times'* coverage of African Americans in 1920, but a handful of articles also paid attention to the increasing demands of civil rights activism. The NAACP's ongoing denunciation of Jim Crow laws was published beside accounts of the prosecution of black rioters from the previous year. W.E.B. Du Bois, in particular, came to limited prominence in the press as his speeches pushed for the black vote in the South. Equally visible in the pages of the *Times* was UNIA leader Marcus Garvey, who invited the press to cover the group's enormous gatherings. In August, Garvey addressed a crowd in Madison Square Garden with a rousing speech demanding that blacks reclaim Africa for their own. "We shall ask, demand and expect of the world a free Africa," he declared. "The black man has been a serf, a tool, a slave and a peon for all the world and has been regarded as less than a man. That day has ceased."[31] Garvey, speaking to the first International Convention of the Negro Peoples of the World, captured the spirit of frustration and defiance that shaped the black politics of the era. He was at odds with Du Bois and other race leaders, whom he characterized as a light-skinned, bourgeois elite. Nevertheless, Garvey captured the attention and loyalty of the black masses, who found in his dream of an African homeland some relief from the exigencies of the day. Not surprisingly, the *New York Times* commented on Garvey's speech with condescension and sarcasm. An editorial published the following day, titled "Another Empire Builder," ridiculed Garvey's idea that African Americans "can evict all the white folk from Africa, and establish a negro empire." The paper lampooned the notion that Garvey's followers called him "your majesty" and that he wore military garb "of a solemn grandeur approaching that of mediaeval kings." In the *Times'* view, Garvey was ignorant of Africa's internal politics and "he does not know, either or has forgotten, that the whole of Africa never did belong to negroes."[32]

Such dismissive commentary was part of the overall discourse on African Americans in the national press during a time of great racial strife. The *New York Times*, an influential newspaper that was generally more sympathetic than other publications, uncritically mediated and disseminated prevailing ideologies of race. Black Americans existed only in narrow and closely definable frames—as a threat to the social order and political stability, as violent and impulsive, or as politically naive and immature. Articles about the efforts of established groups such as the NAACP were invariably brief and distanced—often generated by wire services and bureau stringers, suggesting that limited resources were allocated for this purpose. The *Times* also found it easy to believe that black protest did not emerge from strategic planning or from instantaneous expressions of rage, but rather was instigated by outside forces. The press, like much of white America, believed that most African Americans were invested in the national culture of individualism and upward mobility, and that while there were underlying social problems about race, it was only an unruly few who complained loudly. This theme would continue into the 1960s, as the nation reeled from the impact of widespread black resistance to the legacy of white supremacy. Novelist Toni Morrison reminds us that blackness is always a contested presence in the national imaginary; one that must be contained and manipulated. The black figure exists as "a fabricated brew of darkness, otherness, alarm, and desire that is uniquely American," even in contexts where race is not the dominant issue, she wrote.[33] It becomes the mass media's job to shape the disorderly fragments of human experience into a coherent, recognizable, and palatable product that audiences will consume. Thus, the media—particularly the fact-laden output of journalism—are central purveyors of the framing of black America.

In the second half of the twentieth century, the visibility of African Americans in the news media—particularly as agents of resistance—increased, but the categories remained remarkably similar. A marked transformation occurred as expressions of overt racism, which appears routinely in the journalism examined by Rayford Logan, slowly disappeared to be replaced by inferences of racial ideologies. Stuart Hall has explained that this process operates to produce a complex set of meanings—journalistic accounts appear on the surface to be dispassionate renderings of phenomena, but they rely on "unquestioned assumptions" that are inherently racist. In the news media "inferential racism is more widespread—and in many ways, more insidious, because it is largely invisible even to those who formulate the world in its terms," said Hall.[34]

In the period following World War II, the press in the United States sought to establish a set of practices that would bring it in line with other professions. Journalists, faced with complaints of sensationalism, bias, and corruption, appropriated many of the principles of science—objective observations, truth-telling, and careful scrutiny of information—to enhance their credibility. In 1947, the Committee on Freedom of the Press,

also known as the Hutchins Commission, obliquely addressed the problem of racial coverage when it announced that press responsibility included "projecting a representative picture of the constituent groups in
society." This guideline acknowledged that mediated images influence
public perceptions and that the press played an important role in building public understanding about racial and ethnic difference. This led to
efforts to eradicate offensive language, to accord courtesy titles to members of minority groups, and to highlight the "positive" accomplishments of these communities in print and, later, electronic media.[35]

The press was slow to heed this directive, however. Decades of
African American protest and resistance received scant coverage by the
news media until the strategies of mass marches, demonstrations, and
voter registration drives demanded their attention. A comprehensive
study of four newspapers over a thirty-year period found that in the
early 1950s black Americans were virtually ignored. "In the papers examined from this period, no stories or pictures about blacks were
found on any of the newspapers' society, financial, or obituary pages
except in the *Atlanta Constitution*," where such news was carried on a
segregated "colored" page, noted the study's author, Carolyn Martindale. "The papers did not seem to show blacks as part of the ordinary
life of the community."[36] When blacks were discussed, they were dis-
proportionately portrayed as criminals, or alternatively as entertainers
and athletes, not unlike the practices of a half century earlier. This
finding echoed the experience of African American journalist Simeon
Booker, who found that in the mid-1950s "Negroes cannot gain the
happy feeling of belonging, that dash of dignity or a degree of self-
respect" from white-oriented publications.[37]

In the South, a precise set of norms were employed by the press to
reinforce racial segregation. "The Southern newspaper constitutes the
greatest single force in perpetuating the popular stereotype of the Negro," noted a Southern Regional Council study done in the late
1940s. One small-town white Mississippi editor who considered
himself liberal on race issues outlined the five canons of southern
journalism that prevailed: the use of a Negro tag in any article concerning blacks, use of the descriptive term *colored*, segregation of people in columns by race, listings of local services such as hospitals under
white and colored categories, and the omission of courtesy titles

when referring to blacks. "Nigger stories," he explained, were items about black-on-black crimes that were either ignored or relegated to the back pages. On the other hand, stories of black crimes against whites were a front-page item while crimes by whites against blacks simply didn't exist.[38] Northern newspapers were not as explicit in their policies of segregation. Nevertheless, they too used racial identifications when referring to African Americans, and tended to lump "Negro" stories together.

This trend changed gradually beginning with the 1954 *Brown v. Board of Education* Supreme Court decision, which forced the press to attend to the problem of racial segregation across the country. Yet, as Taylor Branch noted, "the case remained muffled in white consciousness," as the national elite media relegated it to a legal affairs story with minimal sensationalism.[39] Newspapers in the South, on the other hand, responded to the *Brown* decision with expressions of defiance and outrage, mixed with calls for calm and acceptance. A study of Mississippi newspapers found that while their editorial responses ranged from "outright defiance to cautious acceptance, the latter usually followed by a quick reversal," many Mississippi editors also criticized state politicians who used the *Brown* decision to inflame segregationist sentiments.[40]

A pivotal episode in this process was the 1955 lynching of fourteen-year-old Emmett Till by two white men in Money, Mississippi. This event, which received heavy coverage from black periodicals such as the *Chicago Defender* and *Jet* magazine, pushed the mainstream press to move beyond the relatively safe terrain of a Supreme Court decision to consider the violent underbelly of racism. Indeed, there was a greater number of articles in newspapers and magazines concentrating on the Till case and its aftermath than on any single subject involving a black person in the previous five years. Given the scant coverage of blacks in the national press prior to 1950, the Till case represented a watershed.[41]

In particular, northern newspapers and the black press criticized Mississippi's corrupt judicial system and the state's obvious attempts to cover up or justify Till's murder. When a grand jury indicted two white men in the case, the *New York Times* maintained that "Mississippi stood at the head of the shameful list of the states in which lynching occurred."[42] The *Times* published more than fifty articles on the matter during the next twelve months. John N. Popham, the paper's only reporter based in the South, wrote, "The reactions to Till's murder reveals the wretched feelings of Mississippi. The picture is one of white supremacy that skates the thin ice separating it from white tyranny."[43] Others in the establishment northern press chimed in. An editorial in *Life* magazine expressed outrage when an all-white, all-male jury exonerated the pair accused of Till's murder, despite overwhelming evidence against them. "Sleep well, Emmett Till; you will be avenged. You will also be remembered, as long as men have tongues to cry against evil," proclaimed the magazine.[44] Yet even this expression of white sympathy had its limitations. In the accompanying *Life* article, members of Till's family or other African Americans were visibly absent, while the photos focused on the white defendants and their families. In her study of the magazine during this period, Wendy Kozol suggested that these editorial choices effectively denied African Americans "a presence in the narrative" while offering the illusion of a progressive agenda.[45]

Meanwhile, television news, still in its infancy, provided stark images of the Deep South to viewers who had never been there. This relatively new visual medium captured local whites sputtering racial epithets, blacks confined to the rear of the courtroom, and the intense climate of fear and suspicion that permeated the region.[46] Television networks rushed camera crews to this new media arena, and the images became part of the developing saga. When Till's mother, Mamie Till Bradley, talked to reporters outside the courthouse, what viewers saw was a poised, dignified, grief-stricken mother who contradicted all of the prevailing stereotypes of uneducated, backward blacks. This contributed to an emerging discourse in the media that posed justifiably aggrieved black Americans in opposition to bigoted southern rednecks. The added dimension of television was a catalyst for the press to perform responsibly—images did not lie, it was believed. Richard Valeriani, who covered the civil rights movement for NBC, remembered that despite its limitations, television "forced the print media to be more honest than it had been in covering these events. . . . Television forced [print journalists] to go there and see what was happening, and then they could not distort it," he said.[47] The media, especially television, also offered movement activists a measure of protection. Ruby Hurley remembered that the civil rights struggles were more difficult in the 1950s, when she opened the Deep South's first NAACP office, in Birmingham. "When I was out there by myself, for instance, there were no TV cameras with me to give me any protection. There were no reporters traveling with me to give me protection, because when the eye of the press or the eye of the cameras was on the situation, it was different," she said.[48]

In the case of Emmett Till, such attention to an event concerning an unknown African American was unprecedented; the northern establishment was taking a cautious stand against racial violence—and meddling in the affairs of southern racial relations. Segments of the southern press retaliated with fury, taking up the familiar position that un-American agitators were to blame. The "prejudiced communistic inspired N.A.A.C.P. organization will make little headway in their efforts to blacken the name of the great sovereign state of Mississippi, regardless of their claims of Negro haters, lynching or whatever," proclaimed the Picayune, Mississippi, *Item*. This comment was emblematic of the southern backlash, and of a disinformation campaign by the FBI that picked up steam in the 1950s and dogged black activists for decades afterward. Julian Bond, former Georgia legislator, NAACP Chairman, and a founder of the Student Nonviolent Coordinating Committee, explained that Bureau chief J. Edgar Hoover actively courted the press in his efforts to discredit the movement. In particular, says Bond, "a large number of American media outlets were fed a steady stream of 'secret' FBI-generated material on black activism, designed specifically to denigrate civil rights workers' motives and character, or to link them with international communism." Despite Hoover's best efforts, the press tended to eschew much of this bait, and Bond found journalists from the North were "eager to support the Struggle through their reporting." What those journalists could not predict was the effect their work would have on a younger generation of African Americans. Bond remembered that as a youngster, reading about the Till trial and the burgeoning movement shaped his political consciousness: "the media helped to raise my own appreciation of the sheer savagery of southern racism."[49]

The heightened attention to the lynching of Emmett Till and the trial of his attackers proved there was an appetite for news about the problem of race in America, and that the press had an important role to play in this evolving drama. When a coalition of civil rights activists in Montgomery, Alabama, the Montgomery Improvement Association, decided to protest segregation in public transportation by staging a widespread boycott, the news media was poised to respond. In December 1955, the story of Rosa Parks' refusal to relinquish her seat and the subsequent Montgomery bus boycott was primarily covered by the local paper, the Montgomery *Advertiser*. As the boycott dragged on through the winter, the national news media and the black press began to pick up the story.

The national press' attention was piqued when 115 members of the Montgomery Improvement Association, including Martin Luther King Jr. and other prominent ministers, were indicted by the local police to weaken the protest. After King was booked in the local jail and released, a mass meeting at the Reverend Ralph Abernathy's church attracted thirty-five reporters, including representatives of the elite newspapers and broadcast outlets. Within days, the *New York Times, New York Herald Tribune*, and the newsweeklies put the story on their front pages. "By the time the boycott case went to trial, the encampment of Negro reporters and domestic 'war correspondents' had been augmented by journalists from more than ten foreign nations," noted Taylor Branch. Montgomery and the southern struggle for social justice became a global issue.[50]

By the time the Till trial was over, a debate was under way in the journalism profession on how to handle sensitive racial issues. The editor of the Montgomery *Advertiser*, who had followed the issue for months, berated his northern counterparts for attacking southern racism while ignoring problems in their own communities. "[T]he race problem cannot be acted upon until the U.S. press at least locates the problem on the map," he argued.[51] Juxtaposed with the end of the Till case and the Montgomery indictments, the *New York Times* embarked on a five-week project using a team of ten reporters to produce a special "Report on the South" that appeared in March 1956. It sold seven hundred thousand copies, the largest sale of any single weekday issue in the paper's history. In 1958, the *Times*' publisher, A.H. Sulzberger, wrote a manifesto of sorts that argued the press must be used to help win civil rights and should "report, interpret and discuss the facts and attitudes involved in race relations." He also advocated providing black leaders with a wider audience through the press.[52] But it was far easier to make such recommendations than to actually incorporate them into the routine of news gathering.

Two years later, in September 1957, nine black children attempted to enroll in the all-white Central High School of Little Rock, Arkansas. Governor Orval Faubus responded by calling out the National Guard while angry white mobs gathered outside the school to prevent the students' passage. The resulting crisis, according to one historian, "made Little Rock the first on-site news extravaganza of the modern television era." Representatives of television networks, newsmagazines, and major newspapers—some estimate as many as 250 reporters—all descended on the Little Rock standoff, making it another episode in what would be a decade-long saga. But the results of this massive attention were mixed. Film historian Allison Graham argued persuasively that northern journalists, imposing a self-righteous support of civil rights and stereotypes about the South, focused attention on the problem of race while stigmatizing the entire region. According to one network television reporter covering the southern beat during the period, the attention on Little Rock "opened the eyes of the United States to the plight of the Negro" but also inspired the southern white opposition.[53]

Veteran reporters Gene Roberts and Hank Klibanoff contend that the Little Rock crisis also transformed news media coverage of race in the South. The legions of reporters who gathered for the story from organizations including the *New York Times*, the *Washington Post*, and the wire services, were poised to follow other events as they began to define their assignment as "the race beat." They describe an army of ambitious but ill-prepared reporters who spread into every state "picking off race stories as they emerged, seeking out stories that were hard to find, and seeing ordinary stories through a new racial prism." As these journalists pressed the story of racial discord and injustice, they encountered increasing opposition and violence. But it was the black press that suffered the most in this climate. Although black reporters understood the issues far better than their white counterparts, and had unprecedented access to black communities, they encountered opposition that made it difficult or impossible to do their jobs. Courts and police officials refused black reporters access to crucial sites, and white mobs beat and harassed them mercilessly. For example, L. Alex Wilson, editor of the Memphis *Tri-State Defender*, was among a group of black reporters who were brutally assaulted at Central High. Instead of covering the story, they became part of the story—emblems of southern white supremacy at its worst.[54]

These spectacles were also studied by civil rights activists, who realized that the media could be a crucial tool in disseminating their message. According to Julian Bond, the Montgomery bus boycott "showed
how the Movement, with the careful cultivation of sympathetic—or at
least acquiescent—forces within the media, managed to project the first
of its many faces to the American public." In the wake of the triumph
in Montgomery, Martin Luther King Jr. was catapulted into a new kind
of celebrity status. Six months after the boycott he was featured in *Time*
magazine, and he became the second African American to appear on
NBC's *Meet the Press*. Appearing on the front page of *Time* in February
1957 effectively made him the spokesman for the civil rights struggle. A
study of this coverage underscored that *Time* sought to construct King's
image, to make him nonthreatening and acceptable to white audiences
as a symbol of humility and nonviolence. Other media weren't so kind.
Newsweek refused to accord him much attention, and the conservative
U.S. News "had little sympathy for social change at any pace, and in
matters of race its sympathies were with segregationists," historian
Richard Lentz explained.[55]

Despite this visibility and his constant speaking engagements following the boycott, King found little changed in the basic fabric of southern segregation. What he craved was his own regular television spot.
The networks were not interested in providing King a platform, but he
did get a contract with a major publisher for a book to be named *Stride
Toward Freedom*. King, in his public relations quest, envisioned a movement that centered on mass meetings in select communities preceded
by intense publicity campaigns. The goal was to get civil rights workers
mobilized, to notify local politicians that blacks were organizing to
challenge segregation, and to attract the news media to garner national
attention. Just a few years earlier, no black resisters would have looked
to the press as a vital agent for their movement. Now that all had
changed. As the demonstrations and voter registration drives moved to
different battlefields, including Selma and Birmingham, Alabama, and
Albany, Georgia, and Greenwood, Mississippi, protest strategies hinged
upon what kinds of media attention could be attracted.[56]

The southern civil rights movement emerged as a definable and
marketable subject for the news media. The more visible, nonviolent
protests, led by ministers and other respectable black leaders, enabled
the northern press to fulfill its social obligation by endorsing the quest

for integration and black Americans' constitutional rights. But the processes of selection and framing were still at work. News organizations seized on the most palatable stories for their audiences, or built up periods of conflict that could be milked for their excitement and drama. In the Montgomery episode, for example, the news media aided in constructing a myth rather than generating a complete account. What they disseminated was the image of an innocent and solitary Rosa Parks engaging in a spontaneous act of protest rather than drawing on her years of civil rights activism. It was a better story to suggest that the black masses were led by the charismatic King rather than revealing the existence of a politically sophisticated organization led by the city's well-educated black middle class.

The image of the civil rights movement that was produced, and the one sustained in popular memory, was one-dimensional. More troubling instances of black aggression or radical initiatives were ignored through what one scholar has termed a "willful media myopia." While the press was busy covering King's press conferences and meetings of the Southern Christian Leadership Conference (SCLC), they ignored or marginalized moments when African Americans retaliated against white racism. "The press reports underrepresented the relatively high incidence of black violence—rhetorical and actual—that occurred around the edges, and occasionally in the midst, of the putatively nonviolent Movement," argues historian Jenny Walker.[57] Black leaders such as Robert Williams, who advocated armed self-defense when he was president of the Monroe, North Carolina, NAACP, were thrust back into the role of the black brute. In 1959, a black woman from Monroe was brutally attacked by a local white man, who was found innocent by a jury of his peers. The black community was outraged, and Williams articulated their frustration when he told reporters at the trial that "if it's necessary to stop lynching with lynching, then we must be willing to resort to that method." The national news media—including the *New York Times*—ran with the story that the NAACP leader advocated violence against whites. This prompted NAACP chairman Roy Wilkins to publicly denounce Williams' comments as antithetical to the organization's nonviolent principles. He was later suspended as president by the national NAACP board. According to historian Simon Wendt, newspapers in the North and South praised Wilkins for dissociating from William' seeming embrace of violence, in the process articulating what were acceptable and unacceptable modes of black protest. In this instance, as in so many others, the press was less an institution that passively chronicled events; rather, it served a disciplining function in keeping black activists in line. On occasions when real violence occurred between the Ku Klux Klan and Williams' followers, the press was silent. A black journalist covering the episode found that the elite media simply shut out the civil rights angle. When he proposed a series of stories on Williams to the *New York Post*, the editor "sent back the articles saying he'd read them and he liked them, but he wasn't going to print them . . . because he didn't approve of Williams."[58]

As the 1960s unfolded, news coverage of African Americans still comprised a tiny proportion of what filled most newspapers and other media, but what did appear had a new focus. Martindale noted that "if the press stereotype of blacks in the 1950s and earlier was of the criminal, entertainer, and athlete, in the 1960s the stereotype was the black demonstrator." In the *New York Times*, for example, three-quarters of its reportage about blacks during the 1960s was concerned with some aspect of the civil rights struggle. Most of what appeared in the daily press was focused on crisis and conflict—riots, interracial violence, protests and demonstrations, and white resistance to integration. Another study of Los Angeles newspapers between 1892 and 1968 concurred, showing that blacks were virtually ignored until the 1960s, when attention to civil rights and black power served to inflame long-simmering anxieties in white America.[59]

Despite the weaknesses and inconsistencies of the media's coverage of the early civil rights movement, the effects were undeniable. Through the marches, student lunch-counter sit-ins, and voter registration drives, the media recorded the events for a national audience. Movement organizers understood that they needed to provide dramatic events to fulfill the narrative of honorable black citizens facing a hostile and violent white South. Bond notes, for example, that King and the SCLC joined the local protests in Birmingham and Selma, in part, because they knew law enforcement officials would overreact, providing the kinds of action that would make the evening news. Thus, figures such as Birmingham's public safety commissioner, Bull Conner, became an instant and recognizable villain when he turned dogs and water cannons on black demonstrators. Back in Mississippi, the efforts of James Meredith to integrate the state university in 1962 attracted the press corps after Governor Ross Barnett himself blocked the effort and President John F. Kennedy had to intercede. The National Guard was called in to control rioters on the campus after two people were killed and dozens wounded. At the peak of the conflict, the *New York Times* published four stories about the Ole Miss integration on its front page with blaring headlines that literally palpated with excitement: "3,000 Troops Put Down Mississippi Rioting and Seize 200 as Negro Attends Classes; Ex-Gen. Walker is Held for Insurrection."[60] Headlines such as this borrowed the same techniques as those published fifty years earlier—they relied on the excitement of violent clashes and racial discord to tell the story. But now the perpetrators were reversed—whites were to blame for the insurrection, and blacks exhibited restraint and moral fortitude. In so doing, the same tried-and-true journalistic formulas could operate on behalf of the civil rights movement.

After the matriculation of James Meredith at the University of Mississippi, and the violent attacks on demonstrators in Birmingham, Alabama, movement leaders wanted to focus on the growing frustrations of African Americans in the pursuit of jobs and education. Veteran black activist and labor leader A. Philip Randolph joined with Bayard Rustin and others to plan a March on Washington for the summer of 1963 that would highlight black America's grievances on the doorstep of the U.S. government. The march's themes were unity, racial harmony, and passage of the Civil Rights Act. Because of their adept planning, the march on August 28 was a monumental media event that attracted over a quarter of a million marchers, and a television audience of more than a million. According to Taylor Branch, "It was the first—and essentially the last—mass meeting ever to reach the national airwaves." Rustin, SNCC leader John Lewis, influential religious figures, and assorted entertainers all made hard-hitting speeches about the need for social justice in America. But it was King who emerged as the most memorable figurehead of the event. The networks broadcast the speeches and performances for hours, blocking out regularly scheduled programs. Newspapers showed images of the humanity that stretched from the Lincoln Memorial to the Washington Monument, and excerpted parts of King's speech, highlighting the words "I have a dream." Black and white Hollywood celebrities—Charlton Heston, Marlon Brando, Harry Belafonte, and Diahann Carroll among them—appeared at the march en masse, a symbol of the importance of the entertainment industry in civil rights causes. The spectacle had a lasting impact on America and on how black American protest would be seen. As a restless seven-year-old, I remember being placed in a chair in front of the television by my parents on that day and told, "Watch this. You are witnessing history." I complied, and the televisual event made an indelible impression I never forgot.[61]

The news media found, in King's speech, a message of hope and triumph that quelled the fears of black insurrection. The news media reflected a national sigh of relief that the march had not devolved into riots and violence. Instead, participants quoted by the press called it an uplifting and transformative experience. *Time* and *Newsweek* discussed the March on Washington as "a rite of national idealism" and "a cause made sacred by the Constitution," and they juxtaposed the "moderate" King to the more "radical" John Lewis of SNCC. Martin Luther King Jr. was anointed the leader of his race. A *New York Times* editorial followed up the march by declaring, "What Negroes *do with the day* will be determined in the weeks and months ahead," putting the onus for social justice back on black Americans rather than the government. The newspaper's position suggested that it missed, or was resisting, the event's main point—that racism and discrimination were a national problem that blacks could never hope to eradicate alone. On the same day, *Times* correspondent Claude Sitton suggested that the most important outcome of the March on Washington was the communication of African Americans' grievances to a wider audience: "More are aware of the distance the nation yet must travel if all citizens are to enjoy those ideals." The march was surely a success, but Sitton was congratulating the news media for disseminating the story as much as the organizers for creating the event.[62]

This national illusion of calm and moderation was shattered two weeks later when three Ku Klux Klan members planted a bomb in a stairwell at Birmingham, Alabama's Sixteenth Street Baptist Church, killing four black girls and injuring twenty others. Days earlier, a federal court had ordered that black students be allowed to attend the city's public schools. This violent backlash, amid a Sunday morning service, plunged Birmingham into a chaotic state of grief and anger, reprisals and recrimination. Reporters rushed to the scene and struggled to illustrate how the incident shattered any illusions that racial harmony was on the horizon. It was not a time to be dispassionate. Atlanta *Constitution* editor Eugene Patterson wrote an editorial in which he denounced the crime and the traditions of southern white supremacy. *CBS Evening News* broadcast the entire column, and wire services distributed it across the country: "We know better. We created the day. We bear the judgment. May God have mercy on the poor South that has so been led," he wrote. Once again, the mainstream press provided a forum in which white America could discuss race; black people were visibly absent except as victims.[63]

In his study of grassroots civil rights activism in Mississippi, Charles Payne noted that one of the media's greatest failings was their inability to convey a sense of how the movement developed and changed over time. The narrative of actual people's lives was rarely told, nor was the difficult, routine labor of organizing communities and building the confidence of individuals gripped by fear. "In order to play, the story had to be packaged with violence or with white involvement or with the involvement of nationally known celebrities," Payne found. By relying exclusively on the frames of conflict or celebrity, "[t]here was never a time when the simple deprivation of constitutional guarantees or the murders of Black activists were enough to seize and hold national attention," he argued. Former activists bitterly recount that the deaths of James Chaney, Michael Schwerner, and Andrew Goodman in 1964 received significant attention because two of the civil rights workers were white. Yet the press ignored the numerous occasions when black southerners were murdered because of their connections to the movement.[64]

White journalists were limited by their own prejudices and their ignorance regarding racial matters, the arrogance of editors who made decisions from their offices in New York and Washington, and the constant worry that the wrong news about black America would alienate white audiences. The media represent the values of their owners and practitioners and generally portray any resistance to the state in a negative light. The civil rights movement was an aberration in this system; in this instance, the resisters argued for easily definable rights and they opposed governments that were deeply corrupt and antithetical to the national creed. Thus, coverage of the movement tended to be sympathetic and supportive, though narrow and lacking in complexity. Just a few years later, this fragile relationship between the media and black American activism would be sorely tested as urban riots and cries of "black power" overtook the public arena. Meanwhile, civil rights organizers had proven that media attention was essential for any political project to succeed.

3

BECOMING MEDIA SUBJECTS

In secret recesses of any ghetto in the U.S. there are dozens and
hundreds of black men working resolutely toward an Armaged-
don in which Whitey is to be either destroyed or forced to his
knees.

—Russell Sackett, "Plotting A War on Whitey,"
Life (June 1966)

In the 1960s, Oakland, California, was representative of the West's economic and racial woes. The San Francisco Bay area's industrial base—
particularly the growth of naval shipyards—was a magnet for African
American migrants seeking employment in the region. During World
War II, black southerners were actively recruited to work on the docks
and in the warehouses of Oakland and San Francisco. But postwar
deindustrialization shook the region's economy, displacing black workers and throwing many into poverty. Oakland's overall population declined between 1950 and 1970, with whites fleeing the city in large
numbers. During the same period, the number of blacks grew by 150
percent, making them a quarter of the total inhabitants. In the 1960s,
two-thirds of Oakland's nonwhite population lived in poverty, there
was an acute housing shortage, and urban renewal projects were deci-
mating black neighborhoods. By the era of the Black Panther Party the
city was in a full-fledged crisis. In 1960, two-thirds of the Bay Area's
black workers were in semiskilled, unskilled, or service positions, and a
quarter of black teenagers were unemployed. Apprenticeships were
closed to them and new industries refused to hire blacks. Thus, as
Quintard Taylor noted, Huey Newton and Bobby Seale were part of a
disadvantaged generation who, "unlike their shipbuilding parents,
could not secure places in the post-war Bay Area economy."[1]

Despite the increasing number of blacks in Oakland, it remained a
largely segregated city. Poor and minority residents were confined to

the flatlands, while affluent whites settled in the hills overlooking San Francisco Bay. Local retailers were notorious for refusing to hire blacks, there were only nineteen black officers out of six hundred on the Oakland police force, and the city's one daily newspaper, the *Oakland Tribune,* had a reputation for ignoring the concerns of black residents. In 1964, a group calling itself the Ad Hoc Committee to End Discrimination launched a campaign against the *Tribune,* charging that the paper refused to hire African Americans and other minorities. The Oakland Police Department harassed members of the group who picketed outside the *Tribune*'s offices, and several members of the committee were arrested. One of those arrested was a young activist named Mark Comfort, who would later become a core member of the Black Panther Party for Self-Defense.[2]

The Knowland family, one of the pillars of Oakland's economy, owned the *Tribune.* Former Republican senator William Knowland took over as publisher during the 1960s and used the newspaper as a platform to critique the social movements of the day. When UC Berkeley students demanded an end to the ban on campus political activities, Knowland referred to the university as "the Little Red School House" and actively opposed the student campaign. He steadfastly defended the Oakland police against charges of racism and harassment, and he resisted the establishment of anti-poverty programs during the Johnson administration. The *Tribune* would not welcome the arrival of a more radical black activism.[3]

In 1963, civil rights organizations such as the Congress of Racial Equality (CORE) and the NAACP targeted Oakland, San Francisco, and neighboring Berkeley for boycotts and demonstrations to protest discrimination in housing and employment. Oakland's small but vocal black political leadership forged a coalition that actively pushed an agenda to attain some political and economic clout in the city. It seemed as if their efforts paid off when Oakland received a major federal development program in 1966 that promised to provide new jobs and training. But the program failed, the city's black leaders were bitterly disappointed, and national observers predicted that Oakland would follow Watts as the next city to spill over in riots of anger and despair. The area's disaffected black youth looked for other, more radical outlets. During the summer of 1966 Bobby Seale was working at the North Oakland Neighborhood Anti-Poverty Center, and he and

Newton were active in the black student organization at Oakland's Merritt College. The Black Panthers would emerge from these circumstances and be catapulted into public consciousness through the mass media to become the best-known proponents of a new black movement.[4]

The emergence of black power politics was a logical extension of the southern-based civil rights struggle, which had its basis in the black church and civic organizations and its focus on demands for inclusion and citizenship. Although the news media tended to present this transition as a generational conflict, there was considerable continuity among black activists as the direction and tone of the movement shifted.

Former NAACP chapter president Robert Williams was one civil rights activist who exemplified this relationship. Although he was ousted as head of the Monroe, North Carolina branch, he remained committed to the project of desegregation and voting rights while arguing that nonviolence was not the only route to black liberation. In his 1962 manifesto *Negroes With Guns*, Williams complained that so-called "responsible Negroes" bowed to the wishes of white liberals and feared being replaced by a new militant black leadership. "When people say that they are opposed to Negroes 'resorting to violence' what they really mean is that they are opposed to Negroes defending themselves and challenging the exclusive monopoly of violence practiced by white racists," he declared. In Williams' view, assertive acts of resistance served to empower black Americans and to shift the balance of control between the races. Similarly, in Jonesboro, Louisiana, a civic group calling themselves the Deacons for Defense was founded in 1964 to resist Ku Klux Klan terrorism. The Deacons initially organized to provide protection for CORE members working on voter registration. Using guns and shortwave radios, the Deacons patrolled neighborhoods and met threats of violence head-on. They adopted a language of self-defense and exhorted black men to "stand up" for their community. In February 1965 the *New York Times* thrust the Deacons into the national spotlight with a generally sympathetic article that outlined their activities without demonizing their strategy. This media attention positioned the Deacons as "a political challenge to nonviolence" and the civil rights mainstream, noted historian Lance Hill.[5]

By the end of the decade many of the tangible successes of the earlier civil rights project, such as the Voting Rights Act, were overshadowed by persistent segregation, overt expressions of racial discrimination, and wide economic disparity between blacks and whites in places such as Oakland, California. Leaders of the civil rights movement were forced to confront the discontent among its members, particularly within SNCC and CORE. Economic depression and despair fueled urban rioting in cities across the North and South, beginning with the Watts uprising in August 1965. A growing, more radical cadre of black activists began to promote confrontational tactics and a black nationalist orientation in the light of what they considered to be an intolerable state of affairs. Black power was their call to action. As Clayborne Carson notes, many SNCC staffers "were losing faith in the New Left dream of an interracial movement of the poor." Black Panther Party co-founder Bobby Seale gave voice to young blacks' frustrations with traditional civil rights activism when he declared in 1967: "Black people have begged, prayed, petitioned, demonstrated and everything else to get the racist power structure of America to right all the wrongs which have historically been perpetrated against black people. All of these efforts have been answered by more repression, deceit, and hypocrisy." In their landmark book *Black Power: The Politics of Liberation* published in 1967, Stokely Carmichael and Charles Hamilton laid out a political framework in which they called for black Americans to redefine themselves, embrace their history, reject integration and assimilation, and question the basic values and institutions of society. "The concept of Black Power rests on a fundamental premise: *Before a group can enter the open society, it must first close ranks*," they argued. This call for group solidarity had a profound effect on the shifting tactics of black activism and how they would be understood in the public sphere.[6]

The news media played a crucial role in delivering this developing strain of black protest to a national audience. Black power surfaced as a regular news item in the spring of 1966, and early on this new political entity was associated with something called the Black Panther Party. While Huey Newton and Bobby Seale were still months away from launching their organization, the news media focused attention on a voter registration effort in Lowndes County, Alabama, led by SNCC. The political entity established to empower this Deep South community's black majority was called the Black Panthers. Perhaps the most visible and telegenic figure leading this crusade was the young SNCC staffer Stokely Carmichael, who announced that the Alabama Black Panthers intended to exercise black power in their quest for the franchise.[7]

In May the *New York Times* devoted page-one attention to the Alabama state primary, in which the wife of Governor George Wallace, Lurleen Wallace, was nominated to run for governor to succeed her husband. The Wallaces represented an intractable southern segregationist constituency that maintained a base in the Democratic Party. This was juxtaposed with the story of heavy black voter turnout spurred by the SNCC voter registration drive. "Today's primary was perhaps the most interesting in the state's history, as Negroes and whites swamped polling places," noted the report. SNCC "urged Negroes there to join the independent 'Black Panther Party,' which nominated its own all-Negro slate for November." Black voters failed to garner a victory for Wallace's rival, but several black candidates won the chance to run for seats on the state legislature and as sheriffs. This was a dramatic transformation for a state best known for blatant segregationism under the Wallace regime.[8]

A week later, the *New York Times* followed up with a report that SNCC had been taken over by "militants" advocating third-party politics for African Americans. Stokely Carmichael was elected the group's chairman, in the process displacing an earlier generation of civil rights activists, particularly John Lewis. The *Times* credited Carmichael's leadership in organizing the Lowndes County Black Panthers for his ascension to the chair's position. The story played up the idea that there was a fundamental conflict between more or less militant members of the organization, ignoring the fact that Carmichael actually opposed a black separatist agenda promoted by another SNCC faction. Other newspapers, including the *Los Angeles Times* and the *Atlanta Constitution*, heralded Carmichael's election as a victory for black nationalism. This early reporting situated black power and black nationalism in the national lexicon, and issued a warning to white Americans that a new threat was on the horizon.[9]

The national television networks brought a visual and narrative dimension to this complex story, offering viewers a glimpse of SNCC's influence on southern politics. ABC and CBS sent journalists to interview Black Panther workers in the town of Haynesville, Alabama, a place that had come to represent the intransigence of Jim Crow segregation. It was in this town where an all-white jury acquitted four Ku Klux Klan members for the murder of civil rights worker Viola Liuzzo in 1965. One reporter stood in front of the Lowndes County courthouse, using the edifice as a metaphor for southern racism. "The hue of its fresh white paint is more than symbolic," he intoned. "In it white officials collect taxes, regulate schools, choose jurymen, and handle the law in a county where they are outnumbered four to one by Negroes." This CBS account presented the Black Panthers as an instance of noble black resistance to white supremacy. The enemy was embodied in the town's white sheriff, who drawled on camera: "All the niggas as far as I'm concerned know I've been fair and straight with all of them." The most powerful visual image came as the cameras lingered on the emblem of the snarling black cat, created because Alabama law required that political parties have a symbol for illiterate voters to identify. In these media constructions, the black power movement operated within the legitimate realm of electoral politics and through the discourse of equal rights. This news report ended with correspondent John Hart concluding that this story demonstrated the triumph of right over wrong: "The potential power of Negroes here has changed the climate of county politics."[10]

The mass media were wholly unprepared to report on or interpret these developments. Newspapers were "largely ignorant of the growing black resentment in their own communities," noted one media historian. Despite the growth in civil rights reporting, the national press of the 1960s was exceedingly complacent, fostering an "editorial sloth" that was the result of declining competition in most newspaper markets and a decided lack of vision by many in the industry. The nation's newsrooms were virtually all white, and reporters relied almost exclusively on official government sources, paying little or no attention to the concerns of minority communities. In the aftermath of the nation's worst urban rioting in 1967, the National Advisory Commission on Civil Disorders, also known as the Kerner Commission, criticized the news media's poor performance in attending to the needs of black America: "the news media have failed to analyze and report adequately on racial problems in the United States and, as a related matter, to meet the Negro's legitimate expectations in journalism."[11]

Newspapers were also thrown into disarray by the new competition from television; for the first time in the nation's history the press could no longer assume that daily news coverage was their exclusive domain. By the mid-1960s, television had moved from its status as a novelty medium to becoming a permanent part of national culture, with 92.6 percent of all households having at least one TV set. But television news lagged far behind entertainment programs in audience and budget. News shows were not a regular fixture of prime-time programming until 1961, and in 1963 CBS and NBC lengthened their newscasts from fifteen to thirty minutes; ABC waited until 1967 to do so. Network news shows attracted limited advertising, and many local affiliates refused to carry them. Television news in the mid-sixties was still attempting to define its position in the media marketplace and generally lacked innovation and initiative. Most newscasts aired during this era consisted of light and inexpensive features, or anchors reading wire service leads. Public officials, who were able to reach the public through long, uninterrupted sound bites, dominated most news.[12]

The poor economic showing of television news during the sixties forced the industry to focus on building audience and advertising revenue. Throughout this period, the entertainment value of news was being discovered, which placed a premium on style and holding audience attention rather than content or social responsibility. Pacing, format, packaging similar stories together, the use of charismatic anchors, and the avoidance of complex ideas were pressed into service. The ideological bias projected by broadcast journalists, according to political scientist Edward J. Epstein, was whatever was in the interest or service of the network. The civil rights movement and the transition to black power politics satisfied the media's growing need for sensationalism, continuing stories, and compelling visual content. While television news strove to deliver action and indelible images to their audiences, their print counterparts—newspapers and newsmagazines—sought to maintain their dominance by setting the agenda about how these stories would be told.[13]

The collision between the black power movement and the news produced a potent means for transmitting ideas about race through public venues. Journalists wedded to the principles of truth and objectivity could play the role of neutral arbiters in this heated national battle over the future of race relations. Meanwhile, their news coverage was dependent on their presentations of events and situations, which "have racist premises and propositions inscribed in them as a set of unquestioned assumptions," explained Stuart Hall. Dominant values shape and enable the expression of racist discourses, and such discourses are circulated and exchanged via truth claims and representations.[14]

The press customarily framed stories about the civil rights movement within binary oppositions that reproduced the standard values of American journalism: good versus evil, justice versus lawlessness, and North versus South. Previous events are crucial in defining and altering media frames. The early news reports on the emergence of black power struggled to fit Stokeley Carmichael, SNCC, and other figures into the existing frames of black protest. The logics of news coverage for civil rights would not be extended to the burgeoning black liberation movement, however. As Julian Bond observed, "amid calls for black power and scenes of urban rioting, white media sympathy and public support for further action on behalf of African Americans steadily evaporated." The name and image of the Black Panthers would soon leave the battlefield of the black South to enter the sphere of northern, urban racial discord. Black power advocates would no longer be associated with the legitimate claims of the civil rights establishment. Instead, they would be constructed in the mass media as racialized "others" who, as Herman Gray described in another context, fulfilled the stereotypes of blackness "along a continuum ranging from menace on one end to immorality on the other, with irresponsibility located somewhere in the middle."[15]

As the spring and summer of 1966 passed, SNCC leaders gained considerable media attention as they rallied young, radical civil rights workers behind cries of black resistance. The term "black power," derived from "black power for black people," was a popular slogan among SNCC members. A June 1966 march and rally in Greenwood, Mississippi, was widely covered by the news media, which recorded Carmichael uttering his dissatisfaction with traditional civil rights tactics. "We been saying freedom for six years and we ain't got nothin'," exclaimed Carmichael. "What we gonna start saying now is Black Power!" As the crowd of SNCC workers shouted "Black power!" before the national press, the era of black nationalism was ushered into the public sphere. The slogan became the primary focus of news media coverage, obscuring the larger issues of black disenfranchisement and violent white resistance. Martin Luther King Jr. worried that this deployment of black power would alienate white supporters. But as SNCC leader James Forman recalled, "black power" also resonated in black communities beyond the South. "[T]he slogan had tremendous force. It struck a responsive chord, because by 1966 the problems of black people across the United States had become similar in all their fundamentals." The phrase also attracted new, if ambivalent, media attention. Early news accounts were confused and inconsistent in their framing as they searched for clearly definable leaders and symbols while they emphasized the inflammatory rhetoric.[16]

While SNCC deployed the "black power" slogan, *Life* magazine published a two-part series on what it called "the critical new phase of the Negro revolution." The series helped fuel national anxieties about black protest and established new frames for media discourse: responsible versus irresponsible approaches to acquiring racial justice. The first article signaled a crisis with the title "Growing Alarm of the Responsible Negro Leaders," while the second was structured around an obvious fear appeal. The cover photograph of film star Elizabeth Taylor was juxtaposed to a searing headline: "Plot to Get Whitey: Red-Hot Young Negroes Plan a Ghetto War." Writer Russell Sackett used provocative language to report that a growing legion of hate-mongering extremists, armed to the teeth, lay waiting to wreak havoc on white America. In particular, he focused on the clandestine Revolutionary Action Movement (RAM) founded in 1963 by adherents of Robert Williams. RAM, according to the article, was "the most influential and feared of the black revolutionary groups," and though small was plotting urban race riots and assassinations. The *Life* articles underscored the idea that angry northern black youth, many considered the brightest of their generation, were chafing for revenge and social transformation. Bayard Rustin told the reporter that as long as poverty and inequality structured the life chances for African Americans, such revolutionary groups would thrive. "While we're talking about a poverty program, the extremists are telling him [black youth] how he can be black and still feel like a *man*. I don't agree with their conclusions, but there are a lot of brothers—too many—who think it sounds pretty good," Rustin warned. *Life* set the tone for a media discourse that praised certain forms of black activism, and condemned others, while sounding the alarm that whites had much to fear.[17]

The *Oakland Tribune*, like most of the press, followed these developments and disseminated them to their Bay Area audience. A wire service article on the June demonstration in Mississippi headlined the idea
that "black power" was the new rallying cry for civil rights advocates.
The reporter warned that the mood among southern blacks had
changed; they were no longer focused on enactment of civil rights
laws. Rather, "[t]hey talk about bread on the table, money in their
pockets, and Negro officeholders in the towns and counties." As the
weeks passed, the *Tribune* reported on the deployment of black power
as a political and strategic tool. It carried multiple articles about debates over black power within the NAACP leadership, clearly anticipating its rejection by the civil rights mainstream. One front-page
headline was "NAACP Aide Raps 'Power' Declaration," with the article noting that executive director Roy Wilkins condemned black
power as "[t]he father of hatred and the mother of violence." This was
followed by articles interviewing Stokely Carmichael and reports on
the proclamations of SNCC, CORE's Floyd McKissick, and New
York congressman Adam Clayton Powell Jr. as the de facto leaders of
this new movement. In particular, the *Tribune* sought to routinely
frame these stories as one of internal conflict—that there was a split
among different factions of black activists—through headlines and articles. The basic question seemed to be whether black power posed a
threat to white America, and whether it would capture the imagination
of mainstream blacks.[18]

The *Tribune* clearly viewed these debates as newsworthy; more than
a dozen articles on the meaning of black power were published during
the summer and fall of 1966, just as Huey Newton and Bobby Seale
were setting up shop. The Black Panther Party appeared in a *Tribune*
headline in November 1966 when Stokely Carmichael, now a media
celebrity, called on blacks in Lowndes County, Alabama, to vote the
Black Panther ticket. Ironically, the Oakland Black Panthers had already organized, but the *Tribune* failed to make the connection or its
editors were unaware of the burgeoning black power movement in
their own backyard.[19]

The Black Panthers of SNCC origin gradually moved north and
spread their message of black power in numerous political venues. The
New York Times published a feature story on the group's political transformation in its Sunday magazine, further enshrining them as subjects

worthy of popular attention. The article also solidified the framing of
SNCC in its black power phase, expressing disdain for its professed
black nationalist politics along with empathy for the larger goals of the
black freedom struggle. The reporter, Gene Roberts, a North Carolin-
ian, was the *Times'* chief southern and civil rights correspondent.
Roberts' reporting expressed a familiarity with the southern racial crisis that was often missed by white northern journalists. In this feature
article, he claimed that SNCC members were comfortable calling
themselves "radical" and that they asserted that the quest for integration was "irrelevant"—making sure to put both terms in quotation
marks. Members of SNCC were disillusioned and alienated from society, and there was "an increasing tendency in Snick to wonder if white
civilization wasn't inherently evil," he wrote. The author perhaps accurately reflected the national anxiety about the emergence of black
power. On one hand, Roberts reduced the group's membership to
blacks who spouted Malcolm X, read Frantz Fanon, and dressed in
Afrocentric garb. Yet he wrote convincingly of Carmichael's sincerity
and the membership's tireless commitment to their cause. The article
both demystified SNCC for *Times* readers and simultaneously cast the
group's members as part of a larger social problem—disgruntled black
youth lured by the promise of black nationalism.[20]

The cult of celebrity that surrounded SNCC continued unabated.
When they held a press conference in Chicago in January 1967 to announce support for embattled New York City congressman Adam
Clayton Powell Jr., the Black Panther insignia was once again in the
foreground of a CBS news report, although nothing was actually said
about the organization. The Black Panthers were no longer an organization based in Alabama—it had become a signifier for black militance
and resistance nationwide. Television news coverage of these activists
was sporadic and brief—only one or two stories a month through
mid-1967. Nevertheless, the media were clearly fascinated with their
visual expressions of controlled rage and frustration. Journalists sought
to identify clear leaders around whom stories could be structured—
Carmichael, H. Rap Brown, and Floyd McKissick of the Congress on
Racial Equality (CORE). Thus, when Carmichael received a defer-
ment from his draft board (13 March 1967), was jailed in Atlanta (23
June 1967), or visited France (6 December 1967), he made the network
news. Predictably, television did little to explain the context of these

organizations or the reason for their visibility. In the spring of that year McKissick targeted the media's framing tactics when he told the annual meeting of the American Society of Newspaper Editors that the press consistently ignored all but the most negative aspects of black life. The story was broadcast on the *CBS Evening News*, but there is little to suggest that his comments had any influence on how the news media covered the black power movement. James Forman has argued that the mass media worked assiduously to discredit the rise of black power: "The press attacks on SNCC became ferocious in this period, as reporters and columnists tried to make our spokesmen—particularly Carmichael—into monsters thirsting for the blood of whites."[21]

Within a year, Carmichael, SNCC, and the Alabama Black Panthers were supplanted—both in the arena of black politics and in the media's field of vision—by Huey Newton and Bobby Seale's Black Panther Party for Self-Defense. In spring 1967 Carmichael relinquished the SNCC chairmanship to H. Rap Brown, another advocate of black power, and later he had a brief association with the new Black Panther Party. Carmichael's role in introducing black power into public discourse was undeniable; black youth across the United States were profoundly influenced by the media models of dissent provided by the evening news and in newspapers and magazines. Even the scanty television coverage of earlier black radicals had a powerful impact on those poised to become activists. Former Black Panther Party Minister of Culture Emory Douglas reminisced that his early days in the Black Panthers were "like being in a movement you'd seen on TV and now you could participate and share in that movement; when you'd seen Malcolm on TV, when you had heard talk about Stokely Carmichael, Rap Brown. . . . To become part of that brought a sense of pride." For him, being and watching had become almost indistinguishable. Douglas read these news accounts as evidence of political and social expressions that answered his desire for action. In that respect, the media was a powerful recruitment tool for groups such as the Black Panther Party.[22]

Huey Newton and Bobby Seale appropriated the Black Panther name and symbol after reading a SNCC pamphlet about the Alabama project. Undoubtedly, they also were influenced by the media visibility of Carmichael and SNCC. The name Black Panther was loaded with symbolic significance. Newton and Seale expected that taking on the

Black Panther mantle would accord their group immediate political relevance and be a vital tool in attracting would-be activists on the margins of black political culture. Newton told Hilliard, "We're gonna organize the brothers. All these other organizations deal with students or the churches. We're gonna get the brothers and sisters off the block like you and me."[23]

In early 1967, small groups of Black Panthers conducted armed patrols of black neighborhoods in Oakland and nearby Richmond to confront what they deemed to be racially motivated acts of police brutality. This activity garnered attention and support from the community but little from the press. The group rose from obscurity in February when Oakland's Black Panthers volunteered to provide security for a visit by Malcolm X's widow, Betty Shabazz. Newton and Seale were hoping to overshadow a rival group calling themselves the Black Panther Party of Northern California, and they sought a connection with the legacy of Malcolm X. Dressed in their uniform of black beret, leather jacket, and guns, they escorted Shabazz from San Francisco International Airport to the offices of *Ramparts* magazine, where she was going to be interviewed. Police descended on the magazine's San Francisco offices, followed by a group of local reporters. According to Bobby Seale, a reporter and cameraman from the ABC affiliate station pursued the action as the Panthers shouted down the police and got into a shoving match. The cameras captured Huey Newton staring down a policeman poised to pull his weapon, taunting him, "OK, you big fat racist pig, draw your gun." The Panthers, Shabazz, and the police emerged unscathed, but Bay Area residents had their first glimpse of the Panthers' bravado on local TV.[24]

The print media failed to report on the Panthers' early activities until April 1967, when the *San Francisco Sunday Chronicle and Examiner* put them on page one. The article "It's All Legal: Oakland's Black Panthers Wear Guns, Talk Revolution" sought to tell local readers about this new, threatening organization that was capturing the public imagination. In this news account, the Black Panthers were described as "stars of a movie melodrama of revolution," a theme that would follow the group throughout its tenure. The writer was captivated by Newton's physical attractiveness and the Panthers' dramatic uniform. He was also struck by the way guns were deployed as a central part of their image. "The melodrama is real, the guns are real. The two young men are real revolutionaries." The lengthy article also confirmed the suspicions that the Black Panthers were blatantly anti-white, and outlined parts of their ten-point platform, including their indictment of police occupation of black neighborhoods and opposition to black participation in the Vietnam War. Why and how the Panthers armed themselves was a crucial focus; the reporter noted that "not much can be done about the guns, under California law," which allowed their public display. The accompanying photograph, perhaps the first to appear in a major newspaper, showed Seale and Newton outside the group's Oakland headquarters, appearing both confident and defiant in their paramilitary attire, with Newton brandishing a shotgun. The caption read, "They make no bones about being anti-white or about being revolutionaries." Hence, the Panthers were framed as a threatening entity to be feared, particularly by whites. Although their platform was indistinct, what they represented was not. These visual and verbal images tapped into white Americans' primal fears of black male sexuality, black American violence, and the potential of an all-out race war. "The figure of the Black male out of control is a cultural nightmare for whites," noted media scholar John Fiske. Subsequent media coverage continued in this manner.[25]

But it was not until their arrival at the California capitol the next month that the national elite media took notice of the group. On May 2, 1967 a group of thirty young black men and women wearing black berets and dark glasses, some carrying weapons, assembled at the California state capitol in Sacramento to protest a pending gun-control bill. The legislation had been introduced by Assemblyman Don Mulford, in part, to stifle the Panthers' open use of guns. The Black Panthers seized on this issue to heighten their visibility. Newton knew that their carefully planned appearance at the capitol would turn into a "colossal" media event. He also anticipated the media framing of the incident, predicting, "Now the papers are going to call us thugs and hoodlums."[26]

On this particular spring day, the armed Panther delegation met a startled press corps, including wire service stringers who were assembled for the usual political stories. The protesters marched past Governor Ronald Reagan, who was busy greeting a group of schoolchildren. Amid the commotion, Bobby Seale stood on the capitol steps and read a statement asserting that the proposed gun bill was "aimed at keeping black people disarmed and powerless" and was part of a policy of "terror, brutality, murder and repression of Black people." Seale announced, "The Black Panther Party for Self-Defense believes that the time has come for Black people to arm themselves against this terror before it is too late." Still and television cameras recorded the Panthers being jostled by police, and later searched and arrested against a backdrop of shouting and disarray.[27]

Next the Panthers strode into the visitors' gallery of the legislative chambers in a scene described as a media circus: "news cameramen and photographers jumped back and forth in front of them, filming and clicking away." One chronicler of the event blamed the media for inflaming the situation: "The rally [of the small group of Panthers] became less placid as newsmen flocked around, shouting questions, and snapping pictures." Reporters asked Seale to read the manifesto twice more so they could get it right. Meanwhile, some in the Panther delegation scuffled with police and capitol security guards. Over the din, the broadcast microphones captured one man's voice shouting, "Am I arrested? Am I arrested? Get your hands off of me." As the Panthers left the Legislature building they were followed by the police, who searched them at a nearby gas station, confiscated their guns, and charged most of them with assorted violations, including intent to disrupt legislative proceedings.[28]

The story hit the Bay Area press by storm, and it was fitted in between accounts of the wedding of Elvis and Priscilla Presley and heavy American troop losses in Hanoi. The *Oakland Tribune* devoted considerable space to what was termed the "Panther Invasion," in the process establishing its role as the dogged pursuers of the group. The *Tribune* would simultaneously function as the Panthers' greatest critic and most reliable news outlet. The paper's initial story was furnished by the Associated Press with the headline "Armed Men Invade Assembly." The front-page account told readers, "A group of young men, armed with loaded pistols and rifles, entered the Capitol today." They were identified as Black Panthers, but there was no mention of race for two-thirds of the article until the decisive explanation, "All the men were Negroes." The skeletal report noted that the police "herded the men" out of the assembly chamber and took away their guns amid "protests and some struggling." Bobby Seale's statement was excerpted, offering a first glimpse at the Panthers' political ideology. He was quoted stating that the "racist California legislature" was considering a law "aimed at keeping the black people disarmed and powerless" while "racist police agencies throughout the country are intensifying the terror, brutality, murder and repression of black people." The article concluded with a response from Governor Reagan, who declared the Panther protest "a ridiculous way to solve problems," and in a foreshadowing of the framing strategies that were yet to emerge, the *Tribune* noted that the governor denounced "even the implied threat weapons might be directed against fellow Americans."[29]

The Panthers were still on the front page the next day as a reporter for the paper's state capitol bureau amplified the sense of intrusion and assault that framed the Sacramento incident. According to the *Tribune*, the State Assembly was "shocked by an invasion by armed members of the East Bay's 'Black Panther Party for Self Defense.'" A recapitulation of the event charged that the Panthers "knocked down a sergeant-at-arms and barged into the Assembly chamber." The reporter also noted that the media was very much a part of the story: "The Panthers were surrounded by cameramen as they entered the chamber." The protest was so unsettling in Sacramento that concerns for the governor's security were expressed. Reagan's press secretary, Lyn Nofziger, typified this anxiety when he said, "[T]hese guys could just as easily burst in the Governor's office as the Assembly. You don't like to feel the Governor is not safe in his own office." In a few paragraphs this article captured the official response to the Panthers' first large-scale mediated event. They were unwanted intruders and invaders, they "stirred the wrath" of the political establishment with their bold appearance, and their presence aroused great fears that this "armed band" might take vengeance on white America. Although photographers were present at the protest, the *Tribune* failed to provide a visual context. Instead, the story was juxtaposed against a photograph of a U.S. Marine and his "fallen comrade" following a particularly bloody battle just below the border that divided North and South Vietnam. The dialogue between the two news accounts was far from subtle—on one side were the heroic soldiers, on the other, the Black Panther anti-heroes.[30]

The *Oakland Tribune* also provided an explanatory sidebar titled "Background of Black Panthers" that gathered anecdotes and observations about this new group of radicals. The paper used quotation marks to highlight their cynicism toward the group. The salient information

was that they were the "Black Panthers," who were self-described "revolutionaries," known for their black uniforms "and lugging pistols, rifles and shotguns around in public." They had engaged in other public
forays, and they "appeared armed on Eastbay streets on a number of occasions, mostly at night, and are usually kept under close surveillance by
police." Clearly the *Tribune* felt compelled to reassure readers that the
police department had this group under control. No Black Panthers
were quoted for this piece, and the information undoubtedly came
from the Oakland Police Department, since the Panthers considered
themselves to be keeping the police under surveillance, not vice versa.[31]

If this attention wasn't enough to inflate the Sacramento protest far
out of proportion, the *Oakland Tribune* also published an article headlined "Conspiracy Charge Faces Gun-Toters" that listed the names and
addresses of all of the Panthers arrested in Sacramento. Among those
charged were Bobby Seale, Eldridge Cleaver, Emory Douglas, and
nearly two dozen other party members, most under the age of twenty.
Another defendant was Mark Comfort, who had participated in the
protests against the newspaper several years earlier. The *Tribune* milked
the story further the next day with a front-page photo of Assemblyman
Hugh Burns holding a toy cannon under the headline "Man the Barri-
cade." The caption stated that the cannon was a gift from the governor
following the visit by the Black Panthers. "The governor's note jok-
ingly said the cannon would help 'resist aggression,'" read the caption,
which clearly made the Panthers the object of ridicule. Yet another
front-page article reported that the Assembly Rules Committee began
hearings to investigate how to improve security at the capitol in the
wake of the Panthers' protest. Said one official at the hearing, "They
came more or less like a flying wedge of humanity," as he explained
how it was impossible to repel the group of black activists.[32]

All of these stories were fodder for the *Tribune*'s major attack on the
Black Panthers—a particularly vicious and condescending editorial
titled "Playtime in Sacramento." The editorial began with an allegory
about children acting out their fantasies in a world of make-believe.
But, according to the writer, "one day most of us had to grow up." In
this case, groups such as the Ku Klux Klan and the Black Panthers
acted out their fantasies by dressing up, posturing, and threatening people, the editorial asserted. "They get the whole gang together, think up
a secret name like 'The Black Panthers,' put on berets and carry guns,"

the editorial declared. "Then they go out and pretend they're just as grown up and honorable as the man who wears a badge and is paid to carry a gun to preserve law and order." While the *Oakland Tribune*'s contempt for the Panthers was evident in its news stories, this editorial laid bare their position. There would be no support for a critique of the local police, nor would the elite—as embodied in the newspaper— tolerate the theatricality of the Panthers' protest style. The paper failed to acknowledge, or perhaps understand, that the name Black Panther was far more than a childish invention: it had a history rooted in the civil rights movement that made the comparison to the Klan all the more egregious. The frame was established: the Black Panthers were to be condemned and repudiated.[33]

The *San Francisco Examiner* also went wild with the story, running a banner headline announcing, "'Panthers' Invade Capitol," with a front-page story and photo. The *Examiner* used many of the thematic devices that appeared in the *Oakland Tribune*. The group's name was also placed in quotes as if to suggest the questionable nature of their identity. The article reassured readers that no shots were fired at the capitol, that the police intervened and arrested the protesters, and that the Panthers insisted they had the right to demonstrate. There were repeated references to the Panthers' loaded guns, and one paragraph that outlined their armaments in detail: "They carried such weapons as rifles, semi-automatic rifles, double barreled shotguns, of which at least one was sawed off." The article also highlighted the Panthers' rhetoric, placing in quotes phrases such as "white power structure" and "cop dogs" to emphasize the outrageous and marginal nature of their language. Perhaps most inflammatory was the accompanying photograph, which showed Seale and two other Panthers being force-fully pushed out of the capitol building. The caption read: "State po-liceman, carrying rifles taken from Panthers, escorts extremists outside." The local press was simultaneously excited and repulsed by these black activists—the article framed them, once again, as threaten-ing and out of control, while the police were essential for bringing order to the incident. The Black Panthers were cast as the villains and the police as the conquerors.[34]

The press coverage of the day's events also marked the emergence of the Black Panther Party as national media subjects. Short accounts of the Sacramento incident appeared in the *New York Times* and *U.S.*

News and World Report. More substantial articles and critical commentary quickly followed. The *New York Times* published a wire-service story the next day, with a headline proclaiming, "Armed Negroes Enter California Assembly in Gun Bill Protest." The wire service story, which was picked up by newspapers across the country, filled the paper's news hole on page twenty-four and was illustrated with a photograph from the incident. There were two themes dominating the article: the Panthers' fear-inspiring militancy and the media spectacle. "It was one of the most unusual incidents in California legislative history, involving grimfaced, silent young men armed with guns roaming the Capitol surrounded by reporters, television cameramen and stunned policemen and watched by incredulous groups of visiting schoolchildren," said the report. The single-sentence lead captured the reporter's preoccupation: "young Negroes armed with loaded rifles, pistols and shotguns . . . barged into the Assembly chamber." The operational words referred to weapons, the race and demeanor of those who were carrying them, and the shock they registered among observers. Verbs used to describe their actions included *armed, roamed, barged,* and *shouted.* The Associated Press article acknowledged that "during the whole incident there was no real violence, and no shooting occurred." Indeed, an alternative lead for the story could have used the words *marched, assembled,* and *demanded*—all terms that described countless demonstrations of the 1960s. Yet the threat of what these protesters represented—belligerent black men with weapons, and hence the potential for violence—was the real story. One historian would later point out that the presence of a sizeable "gun lobby" at the Assembly hearing that day went virtually unnoticed by the press. Out of the five-paragraph manifesto read by Bobby Seale, the article offered a brief reference to the "racist California Legislature . . . and racist police agencies," giving readers little information about the Black Panthers other than their blunt indictments of institutional racism. What was disseminated instead were powerful, selective words and images about the Panthers as a menace. The Panthers had deliberately fashioned themselves as a paradox—on one hand claiming a constitutional right to bear arms, on the other hand abandoning the tactics of nonviolence and reconciliation. These subtleties were lost in the rush to produce a story in a recognizable frame.[35]

Bobby Seale remembered that as the Panthers left the state capitol ranting about repression and racism, some stunned whites in the crowd mumbled the words, "Niggers with guns, niggers with guns." This racialized anxiety was reflected in the AP photo selected by the *Times,* which showed several stern-faced Panthers wearing black berets and holding rifles at attention in a corridor of the capitol. This image was America's visual introduction to the Black Panther Party, and it was guaranteed to stir fear and concern in a populace already wracked by war and social unrest. This scant coverage was shaped, in part, by the reliance on the wire services to report this story. The *New York Times*, exerting its authority as leader of the East Coast media establishment, determined that this story had minimal national importance. Without a reporter based in Sacramento, the *New York Times* had little firsthand access to the event.[36]

The press beyond the San Francisco Bay area knew little or nothing about the Panthers, leading them to search for categories to construct a media frame. These new media subjects shared some of the character- istics of student anti-war protesters and black civil rights activists. But the Panthers' symbolic use of guns was the primary determinant for the fear frame. This new visual specter of black protesters brandishing weapons contradicted the image of a nonviolent, religiously inflected civil rights movement or a harmless, predominantly white counter- culture. By contrast, Gitlin noted that early national news accounts of Students for a Democratic Society offered a respectful analysis of the group's politics and approach "heralding the emergence of a 'new stu- dent left.'" No media heralded the arrival of the Black Panther Party.[37]

Nevertheless, the Black Panthers were invested in the fear frame that they helped to shape. They hoped that this visual representation of de- fiance would attract new members and generally impress the black masses. They fully intended "to use the mass media as a means of con- veying the message to the American people and to the black people in particular," wrote Bobby Seale. He added that their expectations for Sacramento to become a colossal event had been realized: "[M]any, many cameramen were there. Many, many people had covered this event of black people walking into the Capitol, and registering their grievance with a particular statement."[38]

The *Times* rapidly followed up on the Sacramento story, again leav- ing it to the wire services. A short UPI dispatch published the next day said that Governor Reagan ordered a review of security in his office at the capitol in the wake of the Panthers' protest. Reagan's fear response added authority and specificity to the day's events. The story recapped the events of the previous day, describing the Panthers as "an armed band of Negroes" who "intruded" or "stalked" or "burst" into the Assembly carrying loaded shotguns, rifles, and pistols. The Panthers were to appear in state superior court that day to face charges of felony conspiracy. The four-paragraph article noted, with some irony, that the standing law in California only prohibited carrying concealed weapons without a permit—not ones displayed in the open. Thus, despite the furor, it did not appear on the outset that the Panthers had broken any state laws. However, six out of the original twenty-four Panthers arrested in the incident, including Bobby Seale, would eventually serve jail time under a little-used section of state law that forbade disruption of legislative sessions.[39]

In the Sunday edition of that week's *New York Times*, the paper's editorial board had already decided what stance to take regarding the Black Panthers. The issue's leading editorial, titled "The Spirit of Lawlessness," condemned the group for their tactics and style of protest. Ironically, the *New York Times* followed the lead of the *Oakland Tribune* in conflating the Panthers and Stokely Carmichael with southern white supremacists. By framing the Panthers as extremists in the vein of the Ku Klux Klan, the news media demonstrated an inability to see beyond action, to distinguish between the donning of a white hood and the wearing of a black beret as symbolic practices. The *Times* editorial writer was unwilling to differentiate between the Panthers' assertive demands for civil rights and white Alabama segregationists' mission to deny the franchise to black citizens. This framing revealed the raw fear the Panthers inspired; these editorials assumed the Black Panthers sought to terrorize whites in the same way the Klan terrorized blacks.[40]

In the few days since the Sacramento protest, the *New York Times'* writers were now experts on the Panthers, and this position contributed to the paper's characterizations of the group. The editorial denounced the fact that "military training, racist conspiracy theories and a contempt for the law have spread among some Negroes," particularly the Black Panthers. A "spirit of lawlessness pervades the American scene," despite the fact that "laws protect liberty as long as certain unalienable

individual rights are secure," bemoaned the *Times*. Blacks might be justified in their anger about racial discrimination, stated the *Times*, but
they should rely on "lawful means of protest" in the tradition of groups
such as the NAACP. With this pronouncement, the pattern was set for
future treatment of the Black Panthers by the press. The editorial's tone
was both paternalistic and harsh, irritated with this new breed of black
activists and certain that the Panthers were wrong in their expression
of dissent. The *New York Times* assumed that the Panthers' strategy in
Sacramento was unlawful, although it was unclear what laws they had
broken. This was a group to be criticized, shunned, and even silenced.[41]

If the *New York Times* functioned as the agenda setter for the national
press, the weekly newsmagazines were America's interpretive guides.
Each of the three weeklies had a distinct personality and political ideology as they competed for an audience niche. *Time* magazine, the old-
est and most established, took a middle-of-the-road position on most
matters, as it catered to a middle-class, middlebrow audience. Richard
Lentz notes that during the civil rights era, *Time* founder Henry Luce
was deeply committed to defeating segregation but was equally critical
of black radical politics. "Social reform, implemented with delibe-
ration, was one thing, radicalism another; America was to be set right,
not torn asunder," said Lentz about the magazine's editorial policy.
Newsweek differentiated itself from *Time*, in part, by embracing a
slightly more progressive, left-leaning politic. "In the turbulent 1960s,
Time's polished prose put it at a disadvantage: It had the smell of a library; *Newsweek* reeked of the streets." The third national weekly, *U.S.
News and World Report*, was the voice of conservatism, expressing a
strident anti-Communism and consistent criticism of the era's social
movements. It took the weekly newsmagazines several weeks to pick
up on the story of the Black Panthers in Sacramento, and only *U.S.
News and World Report* gave the event significant coverage. The magazine used the story to lead its national news section. The headline announced: "An 'Invasion' by Armed 'Black Panthers.'" The use of
carefully placed quote marks seemed to challenge the validity of calling the protest an "invasion," in the process questioning the hysterical
tone of previous press reports. The account used verbs such as *swarmed*,
marched, and *pushed* to describe the day's events, claiming that the
demonstration "resembled an armed invasion." Yet later in the text the

article raised the following query: "No shots were fired. There was no violence beyond a few scuffles with police. What was it all about?" Equally suspect, according to *U.S. News*, were these new militants who dubbed themselves "Black Panthers" and protested racism while carrying guns. The same photograph of several stern-faced demonstrators that was published in the *New York Times* accompanied the article. The image of one Panther holding a rifle aloft in the foreground produced the center of visual impact. That both the *Times* and *U.S. News* chose this one photograph out of the many available from news agencies and wire services suggests the inclination of the national press to select, highlight, and reinforce the emphasis on guns and the threat of black masculinity. At the same time, these images aided the Panthers' public relations agenda.[42]

By mid-May, the Panthers were no longer a big story in the *New York Times*. One brief wire service dispatch, however, revealed the emerging law enforcement response to the Black Panther Party that would further influence their media frame. An article titled "Hoover Links Carmichael to Negro Leftist Group" announced that the FBI chief had identified the Panthers as a special subject of scrutiny. In testimony before the House Appropriations Subcommittee, J. Edgar Hoover alleged that Stokely Carmichael was tied to several Communist groups, and that they were both linked to a Black Panther chapter in New York City. Hoover was quoted as stating: "The action-movement is dedicated to the overthrow of the capitalist system in the United States, by violence if necessary." The article provided no evidence to back up this assertion, nor did it seek comments from Carmichael, the Panthers, or others mentioned. Nevertheless, the Black Panthers were now labeled enemies of the government, and the *New York Times* presented this uncritically. The use of such highly charged terms as *leftist, Communist, overthrow*, and *violence* marked the Panthers as traitors and a threat to the social order at the height of the Cold War. Unwittingly, perhaps, this story signaled the press' complicity with Hoover's public and covert pursuit of the Panthers, which Kenneth O'Reilly described as "unique only in its total disregard for human rights and life itself." The *Times*' condemnation of the Panthers was now supported and reinforced by a key government spokesman.[43]

U.S. News and World Report trumpeted similar themes in subsequent stories on the Panthers and their black power allies. Another lead story in the "March of the News" section was provocatively titled "We're Going to Shoot the Cops." This combined a report on a Stokely Carmichael speech with Hoover's assertions about Communists, the Black Panthers, and urban racial unrest. The magazine sought to juxtapose the outrageous rhetoric on both sides of this ideological divide. Carmichael reportedly declared, "We're going to shoot the cops who are shooting our black brothers in the back," while Hoover claimed there was "a highly secret all-Negro, Marxist-Leninist, Chinese-Communist-oriented organization which advocates guerrilla warfare to obtain its goals." The hyperbole of the news subjects did not overshadow the story structure, however, which posed Carmichael and the Panthers as a threat and Hoover and the FBI as the solution. A photograph of Carmichael showed him flashing a broad smile with two fists in a black power salute, while the caption ridiculed his message: "Mr. Carmichael—His summer job: building 'black resistance' to the war."[44]

The other national weekly newsmagazines, Time and Newsweek, published virtually nothing on the Panthers or the heightened alarm toward black power advocates through most of 1967. The Red-baiting theme linking black nationalists to a nebulous Communist threat was established as the frame of choice for representing the Black Panthers in U.S. News and World Report. In the ensuing months, the magazine published articles such as "Is Castro Behind Guerrilla War in U.S. Cities?" "How Red China Stirs U.S. Racial Strife," and " 'Black Power': Tool of the Communists?"[45]

The Bay Area press continued to be preoccupied with the aftermath of the Sacramento protest. The Oakland Tribune avidly followed the progress of a state Assembly proposal to review California's security. The paper published an editorial in support of this measure, reminding readers that "the recent Black Panther incident at Sacramento" as well as anti-war protests in the area made it essential that the state be prepared for "large-scale natural disasters or public disorders." A follow-up story dubbed the legislation the " 'Panther' Curb Bill." The newspaper clearly expected that the Black Panthers would be the catalyst for widespread urban rioting, and promoted this idea on multiple occasions. The Tribune also followed the cases of the Panthers arrested in Sacramento, publishing several articles on their court appearances and subsequent jail sentences.[46]

The *San Francisco Examiner* followed the legal travails of those Panthers arrested in Sacramento as well, but the newspaper was also investigating the threat closer to home. In late May, a front-page article headlined "S.F. Panthers Armed with Deadly AR-15" continued the alarmist discourse swirling around the group. The article reported that a secret, well-armed squad of Panthers was organizing in San Francisco and that they were preparing for a race war—"a last-stand guerrilla fight in what its members believe will be a white war of extermination against Negroes." The reporter who uncovered the group kept the names of his informants confidential while inflaming readers' fears with a detailed description of the armaments that "can be easily converted into fully automatic rifles with a shattering rate of fire." The "underground" Panthers were portrayed as deeply paranoid, fearing attacks from right-wing white extremists, and maniacal in their quest to defend African Americans to the death. This was likely a group of San Francisco black activists who also called themselves Black Panthers, although they were not affiliated with the Oakland party. The San Francisco Panthers eventually dropped the name and reorganized after pressure from Newton and Seale. This theme of threatening armed radicals was repeated in the *Examiner*, which used the phrase "gun-toting Panthers" in several headlines in the ensuing months.[47]

Although the *New York Times* ignored the local saga of the Panthers in the Bay Area, its editors recognized that there was an audience for a discussion of black radical activism. In late May, an article titled "A Gun Is Power, Black Panther Says," explored the group's politics and strategies. It was based on an interview with Huey Newton, one of the first big media coups for the attention-hungry activists. Every element of the article reinforced the framing of the Panthers as a threat to be feared. The article also revealed the press' growing fascination with this clandestine, exotic, and dangerous world. The lead was a description of Newton as he "toyed with a foot-long stiletto that he said he had taken from an American Nazi party officer in a scuffle." Newton's bravado and arrogance, which he displayed for the reporter's benefit, was translated into a portrait of someone frighteningly anti-social. The second paragraph described Newton's bodyguards; one "held a 12-gauge shotgun between his knees," another displayed a 45-caliber automatic, and the third, "a karate expert, flexed his muscles." After numerous descriptions of weapons, the article presented Newton's background and explained his commitment to protecting the black community. The Black Panthers had succeeded in gaining access to a national audience. They provided a sensational scenario of guns and aggression, and the press put these into operation. Newton used the *Times* venue to explain that the Panthers were interested in defensive strategies rather than initiating conflicts with authority. "Force, guns and arms are the real political arena," he told the reporter. This article foreshadowed new framing strategies that would emerge—particularly an emphasis on individual personalities among the Panthers, rather than the group as a whole. By profiling Newton, the *New York Times* offered the first detailed discussion of the Panther organization. Yet the coverage provided no context for the rise of militant black nationalism, no background on the communities where the Panthers were gaining popularity, nor any comparison to other protest movements. Instead, it emphasized Newton's personality and the Panthers' obsession with guns.[48]

As the Black Panther Party for Self-Defense continued to organize and recruit members, massive urban rebellions spread across the country. The summer of 1967 was marked by more than two dozen uprisings that rocked major American cities, including Detroit, Newark, Tampa, Cincinnati, and Atlanta. In Detroit, scene of the worst rioting, federal authorities called up fifteen thousand National Guardsmen and state police to stem the violence. The crisis devastated Detroit, killing forty-three, injuring thousands, and leaving behind destroyed homes and businesses. This red-hot summer followed a troubling pattern: since 1964, African Americans and other minorities expressed their grievances by pillaging and burning the communities where they lived, with the most notorious being the Watts riots of 1965. The catalyst for this backlash was often incidents of police harassment or brutality, and they were fueled by massive unemployment, substandard housing, and a general sense of hopelessness.[49]

During July and August the pages of the *New York Times* were filled with dramatic accounts of the rebellions; photographs portrayed tense standoffs between rioters and National Guardsmen, or the burning remains of urban communities. The newspaper published several feature stories during this period that sought to interrogate African Americans' deep anger and despair. Among these stories was a lengthy feature in the paper's Sunday magazine titled "The Call of the Black Panthers," which helped launch the group's cult of celebrity. It was written by Sol Stern, an editor at *Ramparts* magazine, rather than a *New York Times* staffer. *Ramparts*, a slick, widely circulated magazine of the New Left, had several ties to the Panthers: Eldridge Cleaver had been a regular correspondent, and Stern was a former Berkeley activist who knew the key players.[50]

Stern's article offered a generally sympathetic analysis of the Panthers' politics, while using personalities—particularly Newton and Seale—as recognizable symbols. The Panthers had become a commodity. The first page was illustrated with the Panthers' own iconography: a photograph of Huey Newton seated in a fan chair holding a rifle in one hand and a spear in another, and a photo of Bobby Seale resplendent in the Panther uniform of beret and black jacket. The *Times* helped to make the Newton photo an internationally recognized image, as it later adorned posters, book jackets, and the *Black Panther* newspaper. The six-page story discussed the Panthers' political inspiration, including photos of Marcus Garvey, Mao Tse-Tung, W.E.B. Du Bois, and Malcolm X, under the caption "Required Reading." Stern attempted to allay readers' fears, asserting that "[d]espite Huey Newton's fatalism, the Panthers are not simply nihilistic terrorists." And he argued that the Panthers were a manifestation of black Americans' unspoken frustrations. The article suggested that while many considered the Panthers a radical fringe group, they had a growing following. This was underscored with a photo captioned "Followers," showing the armed Panther delegation at Sacramento flanked by black male and female party members. Gone was the language of fear and condemnation; the Panthers were not characterized as violent intruders or a national threat. There were numerous quotes from Newton and Seale, and anecdotal material about their families and background, thus humanizing these previously fearsome individuals. The *Times* had commissioned an article that diverged dramatically from the tone of its earlier coverage. Five days later, a short wire service article in the *Times* reported that a California judge had sentenced some of the Sacramento protesters to up to three months in jail, officially ending the story of this event.[51]

In October, almost a year to the date of the Panthers' founding, a young Oakland police officer named John Frey was killed in an exchange of gunfire with Huey Newton. The *Oakland Tribune* announced the story with a front-page skyline head in bold letters announcing "Officer Slain, Panther Leader Wounded." For many, the prophecy had been realized. The gun-wielding Panthers acted out their violent drama with the worst possible outcome—the death of a police officer. The *Tribune* provided local readers with an intensive, detailed account of the incident based on police department information: Frey and his partner had stopped Newton's car and asked him and another occupant to get out, somehow shots began to fly, and when the smoke cleared Frey was dead, his partner and Newton were injured, and the Panthers were officially enemies of the state. An accompanying photo showed the police car, noting this was where Frey "was found dead in a pool of blood." Other grisly details were also outlined. For the next few weeks the *Tribune* kept the case on page one as a "mystery witness" to the shooting was pursued, Newton was transferred from the hospital to San Quentin prison, and he made his first court appearance. Local television outlets also gave the story considerable attention. CBS-affiliate KPIX broadcast a feature in which a reporter was filmed on a dismal Oakland street, replete with empty storefronts and ramshackle buildings, to recount the sketchy details of the shooting. "A pool of blood marks the spot where twenty-three-year-old police officer Fry was fatally wounded from multiple gunshots," said the reporter, who noted the victim left behind a three-year-old daughter. There was little new information offered in this piece, but it gave visual evidence to the bleak surroundings in which the shooting took place. The *New York Times* reported this development in a scant four paragraphs on page 86. But when Newton was arrested and charged with the murder, the national press began to cover the Panthers with vigor and Newton became a household name.[52]

Time magazine, in an issue dedicated to examining the nation's racial crisis, used Newton and the Panthers to exemplify the frightening potential of black nationalism. This was the magazine's first discussion of the Black Panther Party, and its disdain was readily apparent. " 'Thinking black' is Huey Newton and his rage—a rage so blinding he can look on white America comfortably only through the cross hairs of a gun." In this lead sentence, *Time* reverted to the frames of fear and condemnation. The Panthers were out to get white Americans, who should view them with alarm, argued the magazine. The logical outcome of this directive is that white Americans must respond defensively to this threat. *Time* also used ridicule and skepticism to discuss the organization. It placed quotation marks around Newton's title of Defense Minister, calling into question the Panthers' use of paramilitary terms. It referred to the Panthers as a "Negro splinter group," though never defining from whom or what they split. The five-page article sought to outline this new militancy with a degree of understanding: "The spread of 'black consciousness' ought to surprise no one; the Negro in America has never been permitted the luxury of forgetting that he was black." Nevertheless, this framing of the Black Panthers made a clear moral judgment: the Panthers' brand of "thinking black" inevitably led to a violent outcome.[53]

The Black Panther Party had succeeded in striking fear into the hearts of the white-owned mainstream press, but the Bay Area's largest African American newspaper, the *Sun-Reporter*, had little to fear from this latest incarnation of black power activism. The *Sun-Reporter*, a weekly, was founded in 1947 after the merger of two rival black newspapers, and it was—and continues to be—the major voice of African American culture and politics in the Bay Area. By the late 1960s, the paper's publisher was Carlton Goodlett, a black psychologist and entrepreneur, and its senior writer was Thomas C. Fleming, a former editor and well-known local resident. The *Sun-Reporter* claimed to have a readership of well over a hundred thousand across the region. It was firmly rooted in the tradition of the black press, which strove to articulate African Americans' political and cultural perspective while supporting black-owned businesses and community institutions. Such periodicals gave voice to the concerns of black Americans ignored by white-owned media.[54]

Such was the case for the *Sun-Reporter*'s coverage of the region's black power movements. The paper took the position that African Americans must debate the merits of the strategies promoted by Stokeley Carmichael or Huey Newton and should not leave that conversation to a hostile white press. In the fall of 1966, for example, the *Sun-Reporter* published an editorial on Carmichael that encouraged readers to listen to his ideas for themselves rather than relying on the "misrepresentation and misinterpretation" provided by the news media. "Even if you do not agree with all that he says, there is a clarity and simplicity in his utterances," the editorial maintained. The *Sun-Reporter* was not enthusiastic about the Panthers' Sacramento protest, calling it "a bit too audacious" in an editorial. The paper argued, "This truly astonishing caper probably did more harm than good for the Negro's cause." The next week, Thomas Fleming interviewed the Oakland activist–turned–Black Panther Mark Comfort, who had been arrested at Sacramento. Fleming wrote that activists such as Comfort became Panthers "because of the failure of all the picket lines in the last 13 years to bring about any meaningful changes in the social position of American-born Negroes." Comfort rejected both the nonviolent philosophy of the civil rights movement and black Americans' reliance on Christianity. Instead of writing about Newton or other celebrity Panthers, this article presented the voice of a person well known to local residents and echoed a shared sense of frustration. Fleming also reported that there were conflicts between the Panthers in Oakland and the San Francisco chapter, details missed by the mainstream press, which failed to make a distinction between the rival groups.[55]

When the *Sun-Reporter* covered the shoot-out between Newton and the Oakland police, the headline read "Black Panther Shot by police," a deliberate effort to subvert the dominant frames presented in the mainstream dailies. Because the *Sun-Reporter* is a weekly publication, the article was published much after the fact. This gave writer Thomas Fleming the opportunity to summarize the events, emphasizing Newton's treatment in the hands of police authorities. After a brief recitation of the case, Fleming reported on Newton's arraignment in a heavily guarded hospital room. After the judge formally charged Newton, his defense attorney requested round-the-clock aid for the defendant, charging that police were verbally and physically harassing him. A photograph showed Newton lying on a hospital gurney, surrounded by tubes, shortly after he was shot. The paper's sympathies clearly did not lie with the Oakland Police Department.[56]

The following week, the *Sun-Reporter* published an unusual letter from a physician who was outraged by Newton's treatment, titled "Doctor Apologizes to Huey." The doctor noted that she had read Newton's essays and heard him speak on several occasions, and that she was struck by his intellectual abilities. She apologized not only for the aggravation of his wounds but "for the subhuman conditions and horrors of the ghetto in which an immoral political and social system . . . makes it inevitable that men like you are gunned down in the streets of our town." Beneath this testimonial was the Black Panthers' official version of the incident, and a coupon to send money to Newton's defense fund. A brief note by the editors stated that the Panther point of view did not necessarily express the opinions of the newspaper. But in this deeply polarized climate, the *Sun-Reporter* sought to publish the perspectives of the Panthers and their supporters. Another article sought to vindicate Newton, suggesting that Newton was a victim of the police department's desire to avenge the death of a fellow officer. In this opinion piece, the writer made Newton the figurehead of a justifiable black radicalism: "Huey Newton is a symbol of the militancy of men who believe that a hundred years is long enough to wait for equality and democracy." The *Sun-Reporter* did not proclaim Newton's innocence, but it was in solidarity with the restless anger that he represented. The article ended with a call for activist journalism, noting that what was needed was "a press that recognizes that the Black Panther Party of [sic] Self-Defense was created because of the criminal flaunting of the plea for democracy by 22 millions of Americans." This was the *Sun-Reporter*'s assigned mission.[57]

Unlike what appeared in the *Sun-Reporter*, the record shows that the early mainstream press coverage of the Black Panther Party was not as widespread and sympathetic as some have contended.[58] It was another nine months following their first media event before the Panthers became routine figures in national news. For much of this time, the Black Panthers were considered a regional (West Coast) story—not one of national importance—and consequently were accorded limited space and attention. The *New York Times* set the media agenda in making the Black Panthers national news subjects. When the Panthers did move into the spotlight, they were fit into narrow, unidimensional frames that told the public little about why the organization existed, its appeal to black youth across the nation, or its relationship to the nation's racial crisis. As Robert Entman has suggested, these limited frames played several roles. They defined the problem as young black males who used radical, inflammatory rhetoric and targeted government and law enforcement for their enmity. Nowhere was the problem defined as racism, discrimination, poverty, unemployment, the decay of urban landscapes, or other social ills. Rather, the cause was identified as a "spirit of lawlessness" and a "hatred of whites" that was gripping black America. The press made clear moral judgments: the Panthers were wrongheaded, anti-social, and a national threat. The remedy was for black nationalists to adopt the more palatable model of protest exemplified by the southern civil rights movement or risk being eliminated. The ideologies about race and social protest disseminated by the national press were quite explicit: black power advocates were a problem population to be addressed by law enforcement practices of containment. Groups such as the Black Panther Party "who confronted the state from radical positions were met with intense repression," argued Michael Omi and Howard Winant, and the press was complicit in this process.[59]

For the most part, the elite national media failed in their explanatory role, so badly needed in this story of race relations and radical protest. Instead of enabling meaningful conversation about the nation's problems, they fanned the flames of racial discord. The national press was profoundly influenced by its own fears and repulsion, the rhetoric of conspiracy used by political figures such as J. Edgar Hoover, and the Panthers' considerable efforts at spin control. The press failed to differentiate between the theatrics and hyperbole of the Black Panther Party and any real threat they presented to individual whites or to national security. Rather, the coverage registered white Americans' shock and dismay over the Panthers' style of protest. During this early period, the press, like FBI director J. Edgar Hoover, seemed to dread the *potential* of the Black Panther Party—the possibility that this movement could spread to disaffected black youth nationwide.

At the same time, journalists were crucial for publicizing the group's activities and raising public awareness. Bobby Seale wrote that the Sacramento protest was designed with the press in mind: "those hungry newspaper reporters, who are shocked, who are going to be shook up, are going to be blasting that news faster than they could be stopped." At this formative moment in the group's history, the Panthers cared less about being demonized in the news and more about having a national platform. They expected a racialized discourse and hoped to exploit it. However, another former Panther remembered that although Sacramento "put the name of the Panthers on the lips of people across the country," the publicity ultimately damaged their efforts at self-representation. "The end result was that the white people at the mercy of the news media were led to believe that black men were beginning to march armed on their policy makers—a belief sure to spread a wave of panic in white suburbia," he recalled.[60]

These press accounts about the Black Panthers relied heavily on certain racially coded frames that communicated deeply held beliefs about black Americans—as a group, prone to violence and criminality, lacking in the ability to behave reasonably and responsibly, and driven by an irrational (and dangerous) hatred of whites. The racial discourses embedded in the early news coverage of the Black Panther Party sought to avoid overt, or traditional, racism with its egregious stereotypes and offensive language. Yet when the press reported on the Black Panthers, stereotypes about black people were barely hidden, and fear of and disdain for black power were subsumed under a rhetoric of law and order.

In these early days of the Black Panthers' visibility, the national weekly newsmagazines and the Bay Area press took a uniformly hostile stance, relying heavily on the kinds of racial discourses described above. By contrast, the *New York Times'* coverage vacillated between criticism of black radicalism and attempts to turn them into commodifiable celebrities. The *Times* found the Panthers irresistibly primitive and exotic, and the daring of Eldridge Cleaver and the charisma of Huey Newton gradually seduced writers for the paper. What we see are the nuances of racial ideology at work. As Stuart Hall has explained, the media provide a place where ideas about race are "articulated, worked on, transformed and elaborated."[61]

The national press coverage of the Black Panther Party functioned within a segregated news universe as well. Invariably, stories about the Panthers would appear on what could be called "Negro pages"—news sections of the *New York Times* and the weekly newsmagazines that packaged stories about black Americans together while they remained invisible elsewhere. The prevailing journalistic values of conflict and crisis dominated the news about black America, and the presence of white elite subjects in a story, be they police officers or Governor Ronald Reagan, increased their newsworthiness. In this world of separate black and white media, it was San Francisco's black newspaper, the *Sun-Reporter*, that offered some insight into how they were understood and received in black communities. The Panthers anticipated that the mainstream media's framing would demonize them, and they believed this would be their most effective recruitment device. Bobby Seale anticipated that many blacks would see beyond the news frames to find something appealing in their mediated image: "They've been calling us niggers, thugs and hoodlums for 400 years, that ain't gon' hurt me, I'm going to check out what these brothers is doing." Seale's prediction was right on the mark, as the Black Panther Party would experience a meteoric rise during the next two years.[62]

4

REVOLUTIONARY CULTURE AND THE
POLITICS OF SELF-REPRESENTATION

You will not be able to stay home, brother.
You will not be able to plug in, turn on and cop out.
You will not be able to lose yourself on skag and skip,
Skip out for beer during commercials,
Because the revolution will not be televised.
                    Gil Scott Heron, "The Revolution Will Not
                        Be Televised," *Pieces of a Man* (1971)

The Black Panthers played to the press, and the press responded with a flurry of prominent coverage. This was more than a strategy to attract attention; it was crucial to the way the group's leaders understood their mission. The Black Panthers wanted to reach the oppressed and the disenfranchised beyond the boundaries of Oakland, California. Global media were necessary to accomplish this goal. They exploited their visual appeal and usefulness as commodities through their determined display of guns, their garb and expressions of black pride (i.e., the Afro), paramilitary spectacles, and the deployment of inflammatory rhetoric, such as the use of *pig* to describe police and other authority figures. The images of the Panthers reinforced stereotypes such as blacks' propensity for violent confrontation, but they also helped make them objects of intense curiosity. In the early days of the organization, mass media represented the Panthers as agitators who moved outside of conventional forms of protest—picketing and demonstrations—to march in uniformed formation and conduct armed surveillance of the police. Reporters captured the tense confrontations between Black Panthers and white authority figures in which they used rhetoric such as "racist white power structure" and "racist pigs" to establish their volatility and potential threat. Huey Newton explained that the use of *pig* was a deliberate choice as the young Panthers fashioned themselves as new kinds of radicals. Their routine use of *pig* aided in their framing on the evening news as belligerents who displayed disrespect, if not outward hatred, toward symbols of authority. These were not protesters who were asking for their rights; these were armed and angry black figures who maintained they would take what was theirs "by any means necessary."

Part of the Black Panthers' legacy lies in how they invented themselves and the culture of their organization. This group of radical black activists created a collective subjectivity—a shared way of life and system of meaning. The creation of a "revolutionary culture" was crucial to the Panthers' efforts to influence black Americans' consciousness about race and self, to create autonomous and self-sufficient institutions, and to defy the sites of political and social power in the United States. Communication—the process of representing shared beliefs and rituals and disseminating them to an audience—took up a significant portion of the Black Panthers' labors. The newspapers and pamphlets they published, their speeches and carefully orchestrated rallies, their posters and buttons, and their political education classes all constituted a unique discursive universe. Their synthesis of rhetoric and images from the Nation of Islam, Malcolm X, SNCC, and Mao Tse-Tung melded with the urban street vernacular of the 1960s to produce a revolutionary culture that was often imitated, parodied, and vilified, but never entirely appropriated by others.[1]

Several scholars have viewed the culture generated by black nationalism in the 1960s and 1970s in more conventional terms. Relying on a high/low dichotomy, they have defined it as certain practices that depend on recognizable cultural institutions, and exist separately from the political sphere. William Van Deburg, for example, has declared that black culture was the seedbed of the black power movement—that it was the structural underpinning of "the movement's more widely trumpeted political and economic tendencies." Culture was, from this perspective, synonymous with artistic production. At the same time, culture was to be the instrument of a black revolution. Many writers located this imperative in the profound influence of Malcolm X and his proclamation that "[W]e must launch a cultural revolution to unbrainwash an entire people." This liberatory culture involved developing pride in black history and affirming a distinctive black culture rooted in an identification with Africa as a homeland. Stokely Carmichael maintained that black Americans must reclaim their identity "from what must be called cultural terrorism, from the depredation of self-justifying white guilt."[2]

Cultural nationalism, or the claiming of African identities by African Americans, was the most visible manifestation of this phenomenon. This involved the acquisition of significant lifestyle changes—the use of African names, the celebration of African-based holidays, and the wearing of African-inspired dress. The ethos of protest also evolved through popular culture in the rhythm and blues of artists ranging from the Last Poets to Marvin Gaye and Curtis Mayfield, from the avant-garde jazz of the Art Ensemble of Chicago, Pharoah Sanders, and Archie Shepp through the literary production of poets and playwrights such as Amiri Baraka, Don L. Lee, and Sonya Sanchez, and in the visual arts in work by Faith Ringgold, Betty Saar, and Robert Colescott, among others. The cultural workers of the black power movement argued that their efforts were central to the project of black liberation. "A people without their culture are a people without meaning," wrote poet Don L. Lee, later known as Haki R. Madhubuti. This position had particular appeal for those African Americans who were alienated from both national politics and high culture. The ideas of black nationalism and black power became inextricably connected to these cultural forms. But for the Black Panther Party, revolutionary culture was less dependent on traditional artistic expression. There were no overt boundaries between art and life.[3]

The Panthers theorized that the Afrocentric preoccupation with culture was counterrevolutionary, and some of their major ideological and physical conflicts were with adherents of this perspective, including the northern California chapter of the Black Panthers and Maulana Karenga and the US organization. Huey Newton derisively referred to cultural nationalism as "pork chop nationalism" and spent considerable energy differentiating the Panthers' perspective. "It seems to be a reaction instead of responding to political oppression," he wrote. "The cultural nationalists are concerned with returning to the old African culture and thereby regaining their identity and freedom. In other words, they feel that the African culture will automatically bring political freedom. Many times cultural nationalists fall into line as reactionary nationalists." Newton was profoundly influenced by Frantz Fanon's refusal to embrace a romantic African history. "In no way should I dedicate myself to the revival of an unjustly unrecognized Negro civilization," wrote Fanon in *Black Skin, White Masks*. "I will not make myself the man of any past. I do not want to exalt the past at the expense of my present and of my future."[4]

Huey Newton and Bobby Seale's critique of cultural nationalism was, in part, a class-based analysis. They associated Afrocentrism with a form of bourgeois blackness that was preoccupied with style rather than content. Only those with money and education had the luxury of wearing dashikis and taking Swahili classes, they believed. In one particularly stinging indictment, Panther member Linda Harrison wrote a lengthy essay arguing that "cultural nationalism has no political doctrine" and "offers no challenge or offense against the prevailing order." She critiqued black women who paid large sums for professionally styled Afros, hair accessories, and traditional African dresses: "On the way to and from this shopping and spending they are still observing the oppression and exploitation of their people—in different clothes." Of course, the party's founders had much in common with the cultural nationalists, but they chose to repudiate the outward trappings of this framework and construct their cultural milieu out of the vernacular of the underclass and working class—or more precisely the decaying urban ghettos such as Oakland. This was the case, in part, because the party's founders, Newton and Seale, were firmly ensconced in the rough-and-tumble street culture of their hometown. Although they met as college students, both had engaged in their share of extralegal activity, violence, and substance abuse, and each waged a constant struggle to find secure and rewarding labor. Their political ideology was focused on those black Americans inhabiting this space; they sought to reproduce the language of the street and use it as an organizing tool for the black lower classes. "Huey P. Newton knew that once you organize the brothers he ran with, he fought with, he fought against, who he fought harder than they fought him, once you organize those brothers, you get niggers, you get black men, you get revolutionaries who are too much," remembered Bobby Seale.[5]

Thus, the Black Panthers cultivated their revolutionary culture through the social practices of the inner city that straddled the boundaries of acceptable behaviors—a swaggering, sometimes violent, hypermasculine aggressiveness that masked the uncertainties and real dangers of everyday life. David Hilliard remembered that the party leaders hung out at Bos'uns Locker, a dank little bar in Oakland where fights and prostitution were regular fixtures. To raise money they held poker parties and sold fried chicken, chili, and gumbo out of friends' apartments. After the Panthers marched on the California state capitol in Sacramento in May 1967, Hilliard and Newton raised the money for their comrades' legal defense, in part, by selling nickel bags of reefer. They attracted the curious and hungry to huge rallies in Oakland and Berkeley by selling barbecue and potato salad for a dollar.[6]

The founding Panthers eschewed the religiously inflected, genteel discourse employed by their civil rights predecessors. Gilbert Moore, one of *Life* magazine's first black reporters and one of the few outsiders to get close to the Panthers, immediately recognized their class roots—characteristics that helped forge a unique but threatening radical culture:

[T]hese weren't tennis-playing niggers or button-down niggers with big shiny hard-kicking cordovans when those are the shoes to wear or skinny little soft toes from Switzerland when those are the shoes to wear. These were not slick cocktail niggers shooting down slick white chicks at parties. These weren't smooth-talking niggers that could fool you on the telephone . . . these were the cats off the block. These were the bad motherfuckers, who came up hustling and pimping and taking numbers and kickin' ass just to stay alive just because they didn't know how to do anything else.[7]

But the Panthers' cultivation of a streetwise culture did not mean being illiterate, inarticulate, or accidental. Over time, their self-fashioning became deliberate and strategic. Newton, in particular, was intent on translating the philosophies of Third World revolution into a language that was accessible to the young men and women he recruited from inner-city Oakland. He wanted to develop a discourse through which the "brothers" on the street could, for example, find a source of empowerment in Fanon's analysis of cultural dislocation and political oppression. The memoirs of former Panthers always situate this political education—this process of intellectual struggle—as the formative moment in their decision to commit to the group. David Hilliard recalled feeling utterly frustrated in his early attempts to read *The Wretched of the Earth*, a task Newton urged him to complete. "But if I read and study the book, apply myself, struggle to understand the concepts, rather than just become frustrated by them, I will begin to understand what Fanon is saying. The wretched of the earth—that's not only the peasants Fanon talks about, but us," wrote Hilliard. Similarly, William Lee Brent remembered standing around with other Panther recruits, drinking a mixture of white wine and lemon juice, and discussing the ten-point program. "You could find small groups of Panthers discussing politics in the office, on the way to a meeting, or just hanging out and getting high. Less than a week after I joined the Panthers, I had memorized the entire platform and program," he said.[8]

The Panthers' political education classes could be frustrating as well. After Assata Shakur joined the Harlem, New York branch, she surmised that the group lacked a "systematic approach" to political education. Many of the party's teachers failed to put the material into context and lacked a background in black history, she complained. While the sessions were enlightening, she doubted that they produced the kinds of subtle understanding and analysis among the rank and file that were envisioned by the Panther leadership. "To a lot of Panthers, however, struggle consisted of only two aspects: picking up the gun and serving the people," she wrote.[9]

The *Black Panther* newspaper, first called the *Black Panther Black Community News Service*, was the most important site for the party's efforts at self-representation. It was, particularly during the early years, the only medium completely under their control, and it set the stage for further spin-off publications. The Panthers considered themselves under siege, not only from law enforcement agencies but also in the world of public discourse. Huey Newton would later grumble that mainstream media exaggerated the Panthers' rhetorical use of guns as political instruments while the other projects of the party were obscured. "What never became clear to the public, largely because it was always de-emphasized in the media, was that the armed self-defense program of the Party was just one form of what Party leaders viewed as self-defense against oppression," he argued. Thus, it was up to the party itself to shape its image and promote its programs, and the newspaper was the most consistent site through which to accomplish this goal.[10]

The newspaper first appeared in the spring of 1967 amid a flurry of influences. It was part of a surge of "underground," politically influenced periodicals published during the sixties, including the Nation of Islam's *Muhammad Speaks* (founded by Malcolm X in 1960) and the student-run Los Angeles *Free Press* (1964) and *Berkeley Barb* (1965). Malcolm X was a pioneer in the use of mass media for black national-ity formation, and he single-handedly launched the *Muhammad Speaks* newspaper to spread the word of the Nation of Islam. Seale and New-ton had fashioned the party's ten-point program from the platform of the Black Muslims, and they sought to emulate their successful news-paper as well. These publications, made possible by the recent availabil-ity of inexpensive mimeograph machines and offset printing, captured the zeitgeist of the era. Noted one historian, "[U]nderground newspa-pers were written by the alienated for the alienated." These periodicals were colorful, partisan, and often outrageous, flouting the principles of conventional journalism and cultivating a mostly youthful audience.[11]

Newton and Seale avidly read these publications and understood the necessity of a mass medium to serve the organization. They conceived of the newspaper primarily as a propaganda tool—a means for political education and the recruitment of followers. It was also to play a cen-tral role in the construction of an imagined community of black revo-lutionaries across the United States and eventually across the globe. Theorist Benedict Anderson has aptly explained that throughout his-tory, print culture has been an essential component in linking widely dispersed populations together in the first step toward forging a na-tional identity. "These fellow-readers, to whom they were connected through print, formed, in their secular, particular, visible invisibility, the embryo of the nationally-imagined community," he noted. This was clearly the objective of Huey Newton, who wrote in an early issue of the *Black Panther Black Community News Service*, "It is of prime impor-tance that the vanguard party develop a political organ, such as a news-paper produced by the party."[12]

It was equally important for the newspaper to respond to the particu-lar needs of those considering themselves black nationalists—the desire for an independent presence within a larger and often hostile nation-state. Since the early nineteenth century African Americans have imag-ined a race-based collectivity in the United States that offered the possibility of independence, autonomy, and protection from discrimina-tion. The Black Panther Party could not offer a geographic refuge, but rather presented adherents with an ideology, sense of purpose, group identity, and plan of action that had nothing to do with locale. Media that enabled patterns of interaction and a sense of belonging were the glue for such a movement, in the absence of a "place." The "imagined community is, in fact, usually constructed in the language of some particular ethnos" that accords membership in a political formation, argued David Morley. The *Black Panther Black Community News Service* was the principal vehicle for this nationalist language and culture.[13]

The catalyst for the paper's first issue was the death of a twenty-two-year-old black man, Denzil Dowell, of nearby Richmond, California, who had been shot and killed by the police in April 1967. Despite evidence that suggested otherwise, the case was ruled a justifiable homicide, inspiring outrage among Bay Area blacks. The Dowell family asked the newly formed Black Panthers to investigate, and the controversy emerged as an ideal showcase for the group's ideology and image. The Panthers organized a demonstration in North Richmond to demand that the police in the incident be charged with murder. Two dozen uniformed Panthers with rifles prevailed over a large crowd of community residents, exhorting the onlookers to demand their civil rights and reciting the group's ten-point platform. The rally culminated in another tense standoff with the police, and the Panthers emerged victorious.[14]

Bolstered by their success, the Panthers set to work getting out a publication to further publicize the issue. In a recent account, Seale recalled that he and Elbert "Big Man" Howard, one of the party's earliest recruits, designed and wrote the inaugural issue at a North Oakland community center where Seale worked. On April 25 the *Black Panther Black Community News Service* appeared, emblazoned with the headline "Why Was Denzil Dowell Killed?" The four-page mimeographed sheet laid out the details of the case, critiquing both the Sheriff Department's findings and the local press. Dowell's death was cited as justification for the Panthers' quest for community protection. "We believe we can end police brutality in our black community by organizing black self-defense groups that are dedicated to defending our black community from racist police oppression and brutality," the paper proclaimed. The paper was clumsy—headlines were handwritten and columns hand-drawn with black lines. Nevertheless, it bore the markings of the Panthers' self-fashioning—the snarling black cat, the expressions of black rage, the combative tone that openly condemned the sites of power. It was also a useful organizing tool, announcing a public meeting to support the Dowell family and urging black men to join their armed community patrols. The Panthers distributed five or six thousand copies, getting children on bicycles to assist them. This first issue attracted the attention of the San Francisco press, which sent a reporter to interview the Panthers, culminating in the April 30 feature story in the Sunday *Examiner and Chronicle*. The Panther's mimeographed pages circulating free across the Bay Area were weapons far more powerful than any rifles.[15]

Newton and Seale followed up the inaugural newspaper with an array of planned media events. After the rally in Richmond, Newton proposed a demonstration in front of a city building where they would "talk to the people and hold a rally there, so we could get a message over to the mass of the people. And the mass media would come along and cover it," remembered Seale. "We all read the papers and realized that the news of the existence of the Black Panther Party was being widely distributed, especially in the Bay Area." Seale and Newton understood that publishing a newspaper was a key strategy in maintaining this momentum. The second issue of the Black Panthers' newspaper followed the media coup in Sacramento in May. While they fielded questions from reporters in the mainstream press, they stayed up nights to produce the next issue. This time, the focus was on the Sacramento action, and the resulting charges of trespassing and conspiracy lodged against twenty-four of the protesters. The *Black Panther Black Community News Service* was used to rally support for those Panthers under arrest and to raise money for their bail and legal defense.[16]

The second issue also introduced one of the group's enduring symbolic devices—the pig. Under a grotesque cartoon of a pig in police uniform, the caption read, "A Pig is an ill-natured beast who has no respect for law and order, a foul traducer who's usually found masquerading as a victim of an unprovoked attack." In just a month, the Panthers' rhetoric and iconography had escalated dramatically. The paper ran a banner headline screaming, "The Truth About Sacramento," to counter the stories in the national press. The Panthers had succeeded in gaining widespread coverage, but they were not happy with the results, declaring that "the mass media has indulged itself in an orgy of distortion, lying, and misrepresentations seldom equaled in the history of the racist U.S.A." Bobby Seale later contended that the party had to battle "lies by the regular mass media—television and radio and the newspapers—those who thought the Panthers were just a bunch of jive, just a bunch of crazy people with guns," thus firing the first salvo in the group's war with the media. This would be a lasting paradox for the group: they could not control the media attention they so avidly sought. This made the *Black Panther Black Community News Service* an essential part of the Panthers' revolutionary culture.[17]

Emory Douglas, who became the Panthers' Minister of Culture, was intensely attracted to the group's mix of ambitious radicalism and cultural politics. An art student at San Francisco City College, he designed theater sets for plays by Amiri Baraka (LeRoi Jones), who was a visiting faculty member. He was also part of the contingent of Panthers who provided security to Betty Shabazz during her visit to San Francisco in February 1967. It was at the Black House, established in the city by Cleaver, playwright Ed Bullins, and another San Quentin alumnus, Willie Dale, in January 1967, where Douglas and other young activists gathered. "I would hang out at the Black House on Broderick Street [in San Francisco] and Eldridge Cleaver lived upstairs," Douglas recalled. "Huey, Bobby and Li'l Bobby [Hutton] would all come there. One evening, I went over and Bobby Seale was laying out a newsletter. I had some basic experience and they were impressed with my work. They had big ideas, big dreams for a publication that would come out at least weekly." Douglas brought to the Panthers technical expertise and an uncanny ability to produce images that struck a chord with readers. He also supported the recruitment of Eldridge Cleaver, who was making a name for himself in the Bay Area. "Bobby and Huey were trying to get Eldridge Cleaver to be the editor," noted Douglas. "He had a captivating writing style. We would hang out at his lawyer's [Beverly Axelrod] house, and then move over to his [Cleaver's] place."[18]

Eldridge Cleaver took the title of Minister of Information and immediately wielded an enormous influence on the language and style of the publication and on the Panthers' relationship with mainstream media. Cleaver was considerably older than the other party leaders, having spent nine years in prison. During his incarceration Cleaver became an accomplished writer, and one of his attorneys, Beverly Axelrod, arranged to have some of his work published in *Ramparts* magazine. It was during this period that he penned the essays for *Soul on Ice*, published in February 1968, which would bring him international fame. After his release from prison, Cleaver began working for *Ramparts* and established himself as a media personality in the Bay Area with appearances in the press and on local radio. His first assignment for *Ramparts* was to accompany Stokely Carmichael on a lecture tour of college campuses in the North.

The young Panther leadership was both impressed and intimidated by Cleaver. "Eldridge's verbal ability awes me. He's not scared of saying anything," Hilliard remembered. "Damn! Who is this cat?" Newton asked Seale. "This cat is blowing, man. He's been in prison!" Newton and Seale did succeed in getting Cleaver to serve as the *Black Panther Black Community News Service*'s first editor, and in these early months it was produced in his San Francisco apartment. His writing was flamboyant and provocative; he could be simultaneously outrageous and incisive, and this became true of much of the paper's content. Newton and Cleaver were masters of hyperbole, borrowing phrases from Malcolm X, Mao Tse-Tung, and other radical icons. The newspaper routinely reminded readers that "the sky's the limit," that the Panthers stood for "all power to the people," and that revolution would arrive "by any means necessary." Cleaver insisted on crediting Newton for having the vision to get the paper published each week. "It was this concern for getting information to the people, that drove Huey practically at the point of a gun, to round us all up and stay on our backs until we would get out another issue of the Black Panther newspaper," Cleaver said.[19]

While Cleaver shaped the rhetorical elements of the Panther newspaper, Douglas made his imprint on the visual content through his cartoons and graphics. Starting with the paper's third issue, he oversaw the design and layout. He helped the Panthers shift production to offset printing, which gave the publication a more polished appearance and allowed the use of photographs and more sophisticated graphics. Not long afterward he was awarded the title Minister of Culture. Douglas coined the term "revolutionary art" to define his visual politics. He invented much of the paper's iconography: the images of exaggerated Panther warriors with massive armament, the grotesque police and government officials as pigs, the bootlickers' gallery that showed assimilated blacks prostrate before symbols of white power, and the ever-present black fist. Douglas fashioned himself as a cultural solider whose products were a "tool for liberation." "Revolutionary art . . . gives the people the correct picture of our struggle whereas the Revolutionary

Ideology gives the people the correct political understanding of our struggle," he wrote in 1968. Douglas noted with pride that "the paper became a paper that people relied on. Readers sought our political endorsements; like in the bootlickers' column, that had an impact. It was sharper than a double-edged sword. People loved those pictures. Our art, our paper was reflective of the community." The Black Panthers transformed this nascent print culture into a going concern. They purchased an old typesetting machine from the San Francisco *Sun-Reporter*, initially working with local print shops willing to produce their materials. Eventually, the Panthers put together from used parts a printing press that produced multiple formats, after facing complaints about the content of their publications from print businesses and the printers' union. "We also did outside printing jobs for community folks, for clinics, and schools," he noted. "All of this came out of necessity and need." The small staff was overwhelmed by the demands of distributing to a rapidly growing audience, and by the time the fifth issue of the paper appeared in July, they were looking for a circulation manager: "We are swamped with possible readership and we need a black revolutionary genius to deal with circulation." Sam Napier was appointed to the position and played a significant role in creating a national and international audience for the paper until he was killed in 1971.[20]

Former *New York Times* reporter Earl Caldwell, who covered the Panthers as a correspondent in San Francisco, called the Panthers' newspaper "brilliant" and said their deployment of rhetoric and art "was nothing short of shooting a gun." "I had met Emory, and at first I thought his art was so crude," Caldwell recalled. "But they [the Panthers] knew it worked in that it became a signature thing; people gravitated to it. I came to see how effective it was." The *Black Panther Black Community News Service* quickly became the paradigmatic periodical of black revolutionary politics, although there were certainly competitors. For example, the rival Black Panther Party of Northern California published its own newsletter, *Black Power: Harambee!! Umoja! Uhuru!!*, in an attempt to assert their presence in this political spectrum. Their mimeographed sheet also used the snarling black cat on its front page and featured articles on black liberation struggles around the globe. But, like many underfunded alternative publications, it lacked the visual, symbolic power of the Black Panthers' newspaper and gradually shifted from claiming an autonomous identity to announcing its solidarity with the Oakland-based Panthers.[21]

Eldridge Cleaver's influence went well beyond the Panthers' newspaper, as he devised a host of public relations strategies to increase the group's visibility. Among his most enduring projects was to set up a photo shoot for Huey Newton. One evening at Cleaver's attorney's apartment, a photographer took a series of images of Newton seated in a wicker chair with African shields in the background, a shotgun in one hand, and a spear in another. Although Newton's public commentary derided black cultural nationalists' embrace of African symbols, they appeared prominently in this and other party illustrations. Cleaver understood that positioning the Panthers within an Afrocentric context might further their appeal in African American communities. The resulting photo first appeared in the May 15, 1967 issue of the *Black Panther Black Community News Service* and became a signature image for the Panthers, appearing regularly in national media such as the *New York Times* and on posters, buttons, and pamphlets generated by the party. "So this is really what Huey P. Newton symbolized with the Black Panther Party—he represented a shield for black people against all the imperialism, the decadence, the aggression, and the racism in this country," wrote Seale. The image also became a powerful tool in Newton's struggle for survival.[22]

Cleaver and Seale and others in the party leadership could not have anticipated that this construction of Newton would be followed by his incarceration for the shooting of an Oakland police officer in October. Seale, who was serving time in prison on trespassing charges stemming from the Sacramento protest, learned about the incident from an article in the *Oakland Tribune*, underscoring the growing role of the press in transmitting party news. The *Black Panther Black Community News Service* accrued even greater influence from its role in promoting the exoneration of Newton in what would become known as the Free Huey campaign. Cleaver explained that with Newton's imprisonment, the rhetoric in the party newspaper became part of the Panthers' "psychological warfare." When headlines screamed, "Free Huey or the Sky's the Limit," "we mean that Huey must be set free or the country will be destroyed," he said. The front-page flag started carrying a photograph of the martyred Newton in full military regalia next to the snarling black cat. He was referred to as a political prisoner, and considerable space was

devoted to the details of his legal case. One issue announced the Free
Huey campaign with a front-page photo of Newton in the wicker
chair with the banner headline "Huey Must Be Set Free." The article
declared that Newton's imprisonment was a call to arms: "Huey Newton's case is the showdown case. It marks the end of history. We cannot
go a step beyond this point. Here we must draw the line." In the ensuing months, the *Black Panther Black Community News Service* rallied the
troops, attracted media attention, and solicited financial and political
support on Newton's behalf.[23]

With both Newton and Seale serving time in jail, Cleaver seized the
opportunity to further assert himself as a party authority, in the process
overshadowing Hilliard and some of the other high-ranking officials.
The party also acquired another talented member when Cleaver mar-
ried Kathleen Neal in December 1967. Kathleen Neal Cleaver, a
SNCC activist, had met Eldridge at a conference at Fisk University the
previous spring. Their romance blossomed and she joined Eldridge in
San Francisco in the fall. In a 1971 interview Kathleen Cleaver noted
that when she arrived, she, Eldridge, and Emory Douglas were "the
three functional members of the Party that began to put together a
movement to liberate Huey Newton." More recently she recalled that
"Eldridge kept telling us that he wasn't going to let Huey fry in the
electric chair. We felt we had to do something—to mobilize people."
She became the party's Communication Secretary, the first woman to
have a position on the Black Panthers' Central Committee.[24]

Kathleen Cleaver had acquired sophisticated public relations skills
during her years with SNCC, experience that was crucial for the Panthers' efforts. She took an active role in publishing the newspaper and
became an effective spokesperson at rallies and press conferences. "I
was the nuts-and-bolts media person," she explained. "We lived in
San Francisco, and a lot of days I sat at my desk answering phone calls,
doing press releases and such. We started organizing demonstrations,
and we would call media organizations and they would come and
cover us. . . . Once the media got on to the story, they loved it—it had
action."[25]

By January 1968 the paper's title was shortened to the *Black Panther*,
it was published on a weekly basis and functioned as the organization's
steadiest source of income. Attorneys' fees were a constant drain on
party funds, and Eldridge Cleaver promoted the concept of using the

newspaper and other ephemera such as pamphlets, posters, and buttons to raise money. Each Panther chapter or cadre was assigned a number of newspapers they were expected to sell, at twenty-five cents a copy. Hawking the paper was a regular task for the rank and file. Nonmembers, often neighborhood children, were also recruited to sell the paper, with the promise that they could keep ten cents for every sale. The *Black Panther* became ubiquitous in black communities across the United States. By 1968, Bobby Seale boasted that the party was selling 125,000 copies per week. A government investigation surmised that the national headquarters received about 12.5 cents for each copy sold and that the circulation neared 140,000 copies by 1970, netting the party $40,000 a month. Selling and producing the newspaper became a concrete activity for Panther members searching for some tangible result for their often symbolic efforts.[26]

The act of publishing the paper was also a process of community building. In the present age of desktop publishing and digital imagery, it is difficult to imagine the very physical, tactile nature of producing a periodical such as the *Black Panther*. It was a group endeavor that required creativity and collaboration. Former *Black Panther* editor JoNina Abron described the laborious process: "[T]he newspaper was typed and graphics were done with instant type. Rubber cement was used to paste the galleys down. Kathleen and other BPP members typed and proofread articles." Elaine Brown, who edited the newspaper in the early 1970s, recalled the rigors of the job: "You can't imagine how hard it was. People had to send in articles and they didn't know how to write. People didn't know about fact checking. We spent so much time cleaning it up; it was exhausting." Most of the writers and contributors were community residents, ranging from students to prison inmates, with little or no journalism background. Getting people together to lay out pages and prepare articles into the wee hours of the night facilitated organizational cohesiveness. Kathleen Cleaver recalled, "We put our passion into that paper—it showed what we cared about, how hard we were working." This was a mode of expression not often available to Party members, and it was a treasured experience. As one author has noted, "alternative media flourish in the wastelands left by official media." Publishing the *Black Panther* was a weekly act of resistance against the corporatization and homogenization of mainstream media, which generally demonized the Panthers as a threat to the national order.[27]

The paper deployed several symbolic and rhetorical devices toward this end. Perhaps the best-known was the use of *pig* in words and pictures to represent all forms of authority. Huey Newton is usually credited with coining the term as an epithet for police, and this slang was used widely by black and white radicals of the era. The term was extended in the newspaper to include government, business, and black public figures considered "Uncle Toms." One former Panther remembered, "We were looking for the most despicable name to call the police, and the pig is symbolically the nastiest animal. Pig caught on very naturally." An equally pervasive symbol was the gun. Throughout the paper photographs and sketches often portrayed a lone black man aiming or carrying a rifle; sometimes a black figure was portrayed as shooting a pig. The gun was represented as a necessity in the daily lives of the revolutionary, and the paper's text urged members to arm themselves, often giving detailed discussions of gun styles and architecture. The paper attempted to convince readers that guns were to be desired rather than feared. For example, during one Christmas season the paper's back page was devoted to a "Black Revolutionary Xmas List," which offered a visual smorgasbord of pistols, bullets, grenades, and machine guns. Weapons represented power and the ability to seize control of one's destiny, while inciting terror in the white populace.[28]

Heroes and martyrs were another staple of the *Black Panther*—an essential component for an invented revolutionary culture. In the first year, the paper carried regular full-page tributes to Malcolm X and Che Guevara, icons who stood for the ideals of strength, courage, and commitment to "the struggle." As the party moved toward an ideology of revolutionary intercommunalism there was a concerted effort to link the Panthers to other Third World communities. There were regular reports on protests, strikes, and wars in Asian, Africa, and Latin America, and expressions of solidarity with the Republic of Vietnam. Dispatches from Palestine, Biafra, and Mexico, among others, sought to show followers that there was a worldwide revolt against oppression in which the Panthers played an active role. As more and more Panthers were jailed or killed, they achieved martyrdom through their sacrifices—particularly the absent leader Huey Newton.

The editors sought to shape the party's internal culture through the *Black Panther*, particularly for those members beyond the home base of Oakland who might not have direct contact with the leadership. In addition to publishing the ten-point program each week, the paper disseminated rules of behavior and a value system for party members to follow. There was to be no drug use or alcohol consumption at Panther headquarters and meetings, and there were strict guidelines for carrying weapons. Although we know now, in hindsight, that many of these rules were ignored or flouted, Newton, Seale, and Cleaver understood the necessity of creating the impression of order and discipline within party ranks. This was important in creating a distinct identity for the party, which sought to differentiate itself from the southern-based civil rights movement or cultural nationalists. The Panthers saw themselves more akin to the troops marching under Mao and Castro than to those blacks celebrating Kwaanza and taking African names. The black leather jacket was linked to the urban street culture of the party's origins; it connoted sophistication and style and required considerable hustling to acquire the money to buy it. But everyone could wear their hair in a natural, put on a black beret and sunglasses, and stand in military formation. The Panthers taught party members the stern, scowling facial expressions by example; everyone wanted to be Huey, or Bobby, or Eldridge.

The *Black Panther* newspaper had an instructional quality as well. One trend centered on gender roles and gender politics. While the paper's iconography celebrated strong black women carrying weapons and functioning as dedicated soldiers to the revolutionary cause, the texts tended to argue for an assertion of masculine authority and a sexual division of labor. In one issue, for example, an article written by "A Black Revolutionary" took both men and women to task for failing to properly exhibit black pride. Black men were too interested in courting white women, while black women failed to support their men: "The Black woman should take a supportive role in bringing about the awakening of the Black consciousness of her man." The bottom of the page was illustrated with an image of a young, proud black woman with an Afro under the caption "The Sky's the Limit." Another essay, written by a woman, asked: "What is a black woman's chief function, if it is not to live for her man? The black woman must drop the white ways of trying to be equal to the black man. The woman's place is to stand behind the black man, so in the event he should start to fall, she is there to hold him up with her strength." Similar commentary appeared regularly in Black Panther publications.[29]

These arguments were standard fare among African Americans who struggled to negotiate the mores of postwar feminism and the sexual revolution with internal community demands for loyalty to the race and sexual propriety. The Panthers' intellectual and political influences all extolled a resurrection of black masculinity and patriarchal authority as a crucial step in the building of black communities. From Malcolm X to Frantz Fanon to Stokely Carmichael, black power rhetoric insisted on women's role in bolstering the black male ego to fortify the institution of the family. Fanon, for example, employed a range of psychoanalytic frameworks in his analysis of the emasculation of the black male—in his case, Algerians under French occupation. In one poignant treatise, he proclaimed, "The person I love will strengthen me by endorsing my assumption of my manhood." Fanon argued that black men and women who sought white lovers exhibited a psychopathology rooted in self-loathing and abuse. In the United States, writers such as Carmichael reacted defensively to the thesis of New York Senator Daniel P. Moynihan that proclaimed the black family dysfunctional because black men had allowed women to become matriarchs and usurp their influence as head of household. Noting the disastrous effects of unemployment in black communities, Carmichael argued this "perpetuates the breakdown of the black family structure" by forcing black men to leave their wives and children.[30]

This gender ideology was integral to the analysis of black nationalism promulgated by the Black Panthers' leadership. In the second issue of the *Black Panther Black Community News Service*, Huey Newton argued that black men suffered from a double burden of "being ineffectual both in and out of the home" and that the Black Panther Party gave them an opportunity to resurrect their manhood. In advancing this position, Newton subscribed to the insidious notion that life was easier for black women because they had already transcended the borders of the domestic sphere to work outside of the home; indeed, they were in some respects already liberated from their degraded status. Eldridge Cleaver's pronouncements on gender relations were also published regularly in the pages of the *Black Panther,* as well as in his best-selling book of essays, *Soul on Ice.* For Cleaver, the core of white supremacy was the psychological and literal castration of black men; they were prevented from assuming their rightful position as patriarchs, and they were feared and reviled as sexual predators by the dominant culture. There was virtually no consideration of the effects of slavery, racism, and inequality on black women. In Cleaver's often-cited discussion of James Baldwin's work, black homosexuality was representative of blacks' self-hatred induced by generations of oppression. Homosexuality was "a sickness" and a rejection of black masculinity, Cleaver declared, as he failed to consider the possibility of intraracial homosexual relations. This diatribe insisted that Baldwin's submission to whiteness—his homosexuality—could only be resolved through a radical invocation of the black heterosexual male subject. "We shall have our manhood," Cleaver declared in his ode to Malcolm X.[31]

Part of the Black Panther Party's mission was to produce an exaggerated black masculinity and to insist that patriarchy was essential for the building of a black nation. Ironically, these notions shared much with the Victorian ideal of separate spheres, in which women were the managers of the domestic sphere, and with nineteenth-century African American notions of racial uplift, which called for women and men to adhere to traditional gender conventions. Black cultural nationalists such as Amiri Baraka and Maulana Karenga found similar gender ideals in their theories of complimentarity, and linked them to African history and culture.[32] The Panther leadership fashioned their gender politics as part of a modern, revolutionary project. This was coupled with a rhetoric that insisted that equal rights for women and a reordering of gender roles, advocated largely by white feminists, were anathema to African American values and aesthetics. What emerged in the Black Panthers' articles, speeches, and visual culture was a contradictory gender ideology that revealed the group's struggles over how to negotiate these myriad impulses. Men and women appeared in equal numbers in the photographs of disciplined and earnest Black Panthers at marches, protests, and rallies. Emory Douglas' illustrations, such as one titled "Revolutionary Sister," fashioned beautiful black women in African garb toting a rifle—women could be simultaneously alluring, true to African traditions, and modern-day warriors. Figures including Angela Davis and Ericka Huggins were evoked as heroes to the revolution, and Kathleen Cleaver and Elaine Brown clearly wielded considerable authority in the organization. But gender relations within the Party often reverted to crudely sexist and misogynist practices, and the group's public representations promoted a conservative gender ideal. Elaine Brown, Assata Shakur, and other women have written about the range of indignities they experienced because of their gender.[33]

The sex appeal of the Black Panther men was also an undeniable part of their media visibility. The pattern of love and theft—in which whites both desired to embody the sensuality of black manhood and were simultaneously repulsed by it—partly explained the media's fascination. Newton, Seale, Cleaver, and Hilliard were all young, good-looking, muscular, and daring. "The media liked the Black Panthers; we were sexy, we did dramatic shit, and we had handsome men," said Elaine Brown in a 1998 interview. Brown wrote in her memoirs that the hypermasculine image of the Panthers was an effective recruiting tool. Shortly after the Los Angeles chapter was formed in 1968, fifty to a hundred prospective members would show up at weekly recruitment meetings. "It was admirable and 'tough,' they felt, to be a Panther," Brown wrote. "There was the uniform: Black leather jackets and berets. There were the guns. There was the manhood and the respect to be claimed. There was the heroic image of the leadership." Most of the recruits were men, but women such as Ericka Huggins played a decisive role in the chapter's organization. Indeed, women were an integral part of the Black Panther Party from its inception despite their low visibility. In one interview, Huggins said, "Women ran the party, and men thought they [the men] did." Another former member, Lynn French, told a documentary filmmaker that during her years in the party, 1968–1973, "there were an awful lot of women who were unsung heroes in the party . . . there were a whole lot of sisters out there too, and [they were] committing heroic acts." The newspaper was an arena that welcomed—even expected—women's contributions. In one issue black women were exhorted to devote their clerical skills to the party. "Jive Sisters—don't read this. the *Black Panther* needs typists. If you can type well and want to work for black liberation, call." Generally, women were left to negotiate their position within the Panthers' masculinist culture, either by accepting a secondary role or by quietly forging an alternative path. But their presence was undeniable.[34]

Some have asserted that the Panthers undermined their goals of nation building by disseminating representations that were intentionally heterosexist and homophobic. "Rather than reconstructing black masculinity in terms that would have truly disturbed white power, the

Panthers aided in codifying the obviously still current cultural demonization of both black male youth and political radicalism," argued Erika Doss. The Panthers' dangerous self-fashioning clearly contributed to their undoing, as this commentary suggests. But their revolutionary culture reflects the limited frameworks within which African Americans operate. They were intent on rejecting the emerging icon of the token assimilated, successful black male—as in the novel *The Spook Who Sat by the Door*—choosing instead to appropriate and reformulate the threatening, violence-prone black male image. In so doing the Black Panthers, like the zoot-suiters before them and the hip-hop generation that followed, engaged in risky, sometimes dangerous acts of cultural resistance that could come back to haunt them.[35]

The *Black Panther* also addressed strategies for indoctrinating individuals beyond the party's central membership. Children were considered members of the revolution and were expected to develop an early social and political consciousness and to consider themselves as soldiers in training. This rhetoric was clearly intended for adults as part of the reification of the black family. The "Black Child's Pledge" was published in the pages of the newspaper as much for the strategic ability to incorporate children into the revolutionary culture as it was an actual directive:

I Pledge allegiance to my Black People.
I Pledge to develop my mind and body to the greatest extent
    possible.
I will learn all that I can in order to give my best to my people
    in their struggle for liberation.

In 1969 these discourses were furthered with the implementation of the Free Breakfast Program and the Liberation Schools.[36]

The *Black Panther* newspaper, the only medium completely under the party's control, was essential to the construction of the party's imagined community as well as shaping its public representations. Newton wrote in the first issue of the paper, "Lacking access to radio, television, or any other mass media, we needed an alternative means of communication . . . a way of interpreting events to the community from a Black perspective." The Black Panther Party was as much at war with the nation's symbolic culture as it was with law enforcement authorities. Dominant mass media circulate "traditional icons, its [the nation's] metaphors, its heroes, its rituals and narratives," providing the mechanism for a collective national identity. The Black Panther Party was intent on producing and maintaining a dissident symbolic culture. If national media are oriented toward the creation of moments of national communion—a sense of national unity—then radical media such as the *Black Panther* seek to induce a sense of common outrage and grievance among the disenfranchised. "It is absolutely essential that we develop our own media," Cleaver said in a 1969 interview. "Political movements and political organizations need media both for ideological reasons and for the interpretations of events. In this regard, the establishment press is unreliable and must be viewed as an enemy." Such commentary emphasized that the Panthers' struggle over representation was inextricably tied to the group's calls for material change in the lives of black Americans. The national press, with little direct access to black communities, would rely heavily on the content of the newspaper to find information, quotes, and images.[37]

The Black Panther Party created numerous spin-off publications, generated from the central headquarters in Oakland and from the growing legion of chapters around the country. As the Free Huey campaign picked up steam, Cleaver and his cadre produced occasional newsletters called the *Black Panther Ministry of Information Bulletin*. These two-paged mimeographed flyers were cheap to produce quickly and were used to disseminate information that would be dated by the next issue of the weekly newspaper. The *Bulletin* carried unsigned pronouncements, illustrations, and appeals for readers to attend demonstrations and other events. They were distributed for free at rallies and on the street, supplementing the more elaborate material in the *Black Panther*. Many chapters also started their local versions of the party newspaper. Party members in Los Angeles, for example, published the *Black Panther Community Newsletter* on a weekly basis in 1969–1970. The paper established its own style and discussed issues specific to the southern California chapter, thus establishing its autonomy from the Bay Area leadership. But the project was short-lived, folding in 1970 with the announcement that all pertinent information would henceforth appear in the *Black Panther*.[38]

By 1969, several Bay Area labor unions took up the Black Panther name and published a periodical that employed similar strategies. The Black Panther Caucus of the United Auto Workers Local 1364 issued

FOCUS, which featured images of black rank-and-file laborers struggling against unfair practices of the automobile industry. They were
joined by Local 250-A of the Transport Workers Union, as black power
ideology and the Panthers' influence helped to shape African American's labor organizing and political practices. The Black Panthers' rhetoric was readily apparent; the minutes of one union meeting concluded
with the phrase "All Power to the Workers."[39]

Rhetoric, articulated in the party's print and oral culture, was at the
core of the Panthers' appeal. No element of the Panthers' culture was
more prized than the leaders' ability to engage in righteous rapping, to
combine street vernacular with social theory, to call on the classic black
jeremiad in their defiant harangues demanding radical resistance. The
black jeremiad had its origins in the nineteenth-century black church,
where ministers and activists warned whites of the dire consequences
of continued racial oppression. This political tirade, modernized by
significant public speakers including Martin Luther King Jr., Malcolm
X, and Stokely Carmichael, was a staple of the protest discourses of the
era. And no one was more adept at this rhetorical strategy than Eldridge Cleaver. David Hilliard remembered Cleaver's enormous talent
in this area: "I listen to him give interviews and think: I want to speak
this clearly, make my points so forcefully." A vivid example was how
the tale of how Cleaver managed to get an audience of nuns to recite
"Fuck Ronald Reagan" at a rally in San Francisco. Huey Newton
called Eldridge Cleaver the "master of the word," but he called himself the "master of the gun." The Panthers' rhetoric was classically militant; it called for force through threats, harassment, and disruptions,
noted one scholar. This style of rhetoric was customarily most effective with elites who have some authority to respond to their demands,
rather than the general public. But in the case of the Black Panthers,
the reverse seems to be the case: their militant cries elicited a negative
response from those with authority, but it was appealing to those who
lacked power—the "lumpen" they sought to recruit.[40]

The rhetoric of black power, as articulated by Eldridge Cleaver,
Huey Newton, and others, was intended to provide multiple layers of
understanding. Their open defiance of white power, their threats of
armed self-defense, and their ridiculing of polite, middle-class interaction were calculated to inspire the disenfranchised and strike fear into
the hearts of the privileged. When Cleaver would stand ramrod straight,

pointing his finger in the air, and offer the following rapid-fire delivery,
he was guaranteed to attract national attention: "One of our revolutionary comrades is being hunted by professional mad-dog assassins and is
to be wantonly murdered on sight because the racist power structure of
San Francisco has branded the black liberator as a dangerous killer."
Cleaver's verbal choices painted the Panthers as victims of the state who
had no choice other than to defend themselves. They were innocents
merely protecting their own. One can read the Panthers' rhetoric as a
call for justice—a call uttered outside law and government because they
have no access to these institutions and indeed are terrorized by them.
Behind the fury of this language lies the intention of forcing a moral
decision on the national culture. The rhetoric of black power becomes
the only strategic choice available. The Panthers' rhetoric offered members an insider status that wielded some authority in their communities;
as part of the "vanguard party," they saw their job as guiding the black
masses to liberation. The rhetoric defined who were friends and who
were enemies; individuals offended by the Panthers' obscene language
or threatening harangues were immediately outsiders under suspicion.
The Panthers insisted that what they delivered was a political rhetoric
that addressed the poor and disenfranchised. In a 1969 television interview, David Hilliard explained that when he advocated killing President
Richard Nixon in one of his speeches, it was intended to be a rhetorical rather than direct threat. "We can call it metaphor. It is the language
of the ghetto. This is the way we relate. Even the profanity, the profanity is within the idiom of the oppressed people," he said. [41]

Not surprisingly, the outrageous hyperbole and iconography that
were staples of the Panthers' newspaper and oratory attracted intense
scrutiny from law enforcement authorities. Indeed, entire government
reports investigating the revolutionary activities of the Black Panther
Party relied heavily on what they published. The newspaper was an effective location through which the Black Panthers' opponents could
contest their politics and their very existence. Bobby Seale remembered numerous instances in which the newspaper's future was threatened, such as when the local printers' union complained that the paper
was being typeset and packaged by nonunion Party members and they
threatened a boycott. On another occasion, half the staff at their San
Francisco printer's outfit refused to work on the paper because of its
inflammatory content. Distribution of the newspaper was essential for

the development of a national and international readership, but this left the Panthers open to further disruption. The *Black Panther* was shipped around the country on commercial airlines, and Party members accused the FBI of collaborating with the airlines to interfere in this process. Newspapers were lost or unaccounted for, and printing negatives were delayed, throwing off the entire production schedule. For example, in December 1969 the Panthers filed a claim with United Airlines for $9,000 to compensate for seven missing crates of newspapers. These incidents happened across the country, including Winston-Salem, North Carolina, New Haven, Cleveland, Philadelphia, and Detroit. Panther leaders also charged that the FBI sprayed noxious chemicals and inks on bundles of the paper to make them unusable.[42]

Within a year of the Party's founding, the central leadership in Oakland had put in place a growing media machine that engaged in a complex relationship with the mainstream media. Each had a powerful motivation to interact with the other—the Panther story was a saleable commodity, and increasingly the Black Panthers viewed their media visibility as a means of survival as government agencies tried increasingly repressive tactics to silence them. "In general, we figured being in the news kept us from being killed," explained Kathleen Cleaver. "As long as the press was there, the police wouldn't go after us." The Black Panthers—particularly Newton, Cleaver, and Seale—would be central to an ever-evolving news story that offered action, conflict, moral dilemmas, and charismatic personalities to audiences increasingly curious about and frightened by black power activism.[43]

5

FREE HUEY: 1968

[O]f all the things that you've heard in the press, of all the derogatory statements that's been made in the press about Brother Huey P. Newton, and I . . . of all these derogatory statements is to guide you away from seeing this basic platform that Huey was talking about for his own people. We have to learn to look through the white press. We have to learn to see what's going on.
                                        —Bobby Seale, speech made February 17, 1968,
                                                                  Oakland Auditorium

The year 1968 is embedded in the national memory as a time when social and political unrest exploded around the world. Mass media, particularly through the rise of global television broadcasting, enabled activists to witness and be part of this extraordinary series of events regardless of their location. Protests, riots, and bombings on college campuses across the United States and in Paris, Berlin, and Mexico City registered young people's anger over the Vietnam War, social inequality, and their own sense of opposition to their governments. In many instances, their dissent was met by intense police repression. The cold-blooded assassinations of Martin Luther King Jr. and Robert F. Kennedy, the daily carnage in Vietnam (the Tet offensive and the My Lai massacre, among others), the brutal backlash against youthful protest as typified by the Democratic National Convention in Chicago, the ascendancy of conservative Republicanism as embodied in Richard Nixon and Spiro Agnew, and the endless urban uprisings that reflected drastic economic inequalities filled many Americans with a confusing mix of dread, indignation, and despair. The Black Panther Party was both a protagonist in and influenced by this volatile mix. The group inspired many of the protests during this era and was overwhelmingly affected by the backlash that emerged.

The editors of the *Oakland Tribune* summarized the year and noted that the two biggest stories of 1968 were the murder trial of Huey Newton and the campus revolts in the Bay Area, events that placed the Black Panthers on the front page for weeks at a time. The *Tribune*'s retrospective—which spanned three pages and featured some of the most famous photographs from the era—almost reveled in the tension and excitement these stories generated.[1] The presence of the Panthers in the Bay Area media during 1968 was unprecedented—never again would they receive such consistent and widespread attention. The *Tribune* responded to the keen local interest in the trial of Newton for killing an Oakland police officer. But once the Panthers were fixtures in the paper's routine, any topic related to African American militancy was also played prominently. The Panthers had shifted from being an occasional topic of interest to being an embedded part of journalistic practice, due in large part to their successfully staged media events and their constant encounters with the law. The Panthers also fulfilled an important symbolic function as stand-ins for all disaffected African Americans who took the turn into radicalism. While there were numerous groups engaging in black radical politics, such as the Revolutionary Action Movement, the Republic of New Africa, Maulana Karenga's US organization, or Amiri Baraka's Congress of African Peoples, they were rarely singled out for sustained media attention. By the end of the year, the words "Black Panther" would be ubiquitous in headlines across the country, enabling the group to attract widespread support from multiple constituencies, while attracting the attention of government intelligence investigations.

The abundance of newsworthy stories—ones that enabled repeated, continuing coverage; that offered sensational or exciting content; that highlighted conflict and crisis—were the result of several intersecting events that ensnared the Panthers' most influential and best-known members. During the year, Newton, Cleaver, and Seale were all in the headlines because of related court battles, and Cleaver was one of several catalysts for student unrest at UC Berkeley. Other, lesser-known members of the group were also facing assorted criminal charges or were involved in the flurry of student protests that erupted during the year. The combination of demonstrations, violence, tragedy, and politics that the Panthers offered proved irresistible for the media. As they felt increasing scrutiny from law enforcement, their public relations campaigns were carried out with greater intensity. The year's reportage on the Black Panthers was dominated by the trial of Huey Newton on murder charges stemming from the death of Oakland policeman John Frey in the shoot-out the previous October. Kathleen Cleaver noted that the Newton case fit the prevailing frames of blacks in the news. "They had already covered the shoot-out and the arrest. In their minds, Huey was just another black criminal," recalled Cleaver. "So we capitalized on that; we held rallies and press conferences all during his trial because Eldridge believed that was the way to save Huey, so they couldn't kill him while he was in prison, or convict him in a rigged trial."[2]

The *Oakland Tribune*, the Panthers' "hometown" paper, turned the case into a courtroom soap opera and played an important role in framing the issue for the national press. When Newton attended a routine hearing at the Alameda County courthouse in January to request a postponement of his trial, the *Tribune* headline was "Panthers Back Newton" with a two-word kicker, "Clenched Fists," translating one of the group's popular iconic devices into language.[3] The image created by the headline was far more compelling than the accompanying story. The reporter focused on the group of Panther supporters who jammed the courtroom, and the subsequent rally on the courthouse steps after Newton's request was granted. The purpose was to provide a vivid visualization: "The demonstrators were orderly, but fervent. About two-thirds were Negroes. They chanted as they marched: Huey will be set free. Free Huey now. Down with Gestapo pigs. Black power."[4] This represented the elements the *Tribune* repeatedly chose to highlight: the racial makeup of the crowd, the group's use of organized marching and chanting, and its rhetoric. The newspaper assumed there was a high level of interest among its readership—those supporting the Black Panthers, those anxious to see Newton convicted of the policeman's death, and those looking for the next indication that the city might go up in flames.

The Panthers built on the momentum of each event, exhorting friends and followers to expand their numbers and make their presence known. After the January 11 rally, they issued a *Ministry of Information Bulletin* that outlined the logic of the Free Huey campaign in clear and compelling language and advertised another rally for January 26: "We believe that Huey P. Newton is innocent, that he has committed no crime, that his imprisonment is injust [sic], and that his life must be saved!" The bulletin declared, "We will continue to come out in force to support Huey every time he appears in court," and it publicized a phone hotline number so readers could obtain up-to-the-minute information. The Panthers fully expected local television and radio to serve as a conduit for information; they told supporters to watch the rally on TV if they were unable to attend, and the flyer advertised an interview with Seale and Cleaver on the local CBS affiliate station.[5]

The *Oakland Tribune* played into the Panthers' media strategy, as it paid ample attention to the Free Huey campaign, and the Panthers gambled that having a visible and vocal contingent at the courthouse would help win his exoneration. When a later story in the *Tribune* reported that Newton won the postponement of his indictment, it recalled earlier courtroom scenes, referring to how "[d]emonstrators last week invaded the courthouse and put on a massive demonstration." Such reports inferred that Newton's supporters were intruders on the judicial process. The paper noted that in contrast to previous events surrounding Newton's case, order was restored at the most recent hearing with the help of forty sheriffs who limited access to the courthouse, leaving some demonstrators to circle the building outside in the rain.[6]

The national press had little interest in the minutiae of the Black Panthers' legal troubles. Outlets such as the *New York Times*, the newsweeklies, and the television networks still considered the Black Panthers a regional California story with limited resonance for a national audience. But an alliance between the Peace and Freedom Party and the Black Panthers that was forged in the fall momentarily captured the attention of the *New York Times* and set the stage for future reportage. The Peace and Freedom Party (PFP), a coalition of Bay Area activists identified with the New Left, sought an alternative to the political establishment by placing its own candidates on the California ballot for the November 1968 elections. Months earlier the *Berkeley Barb* had reported that a "militant alliance" had been formed and that the group voted to vocally support the Free Huey effort. Eldridge Cleaver is generally credited with making the initial overtures toward the PFP. It sought the Panthers' help in registering voters in black neighborhoods, and Cleaver agreed on the condition that this would be a Panther-only enterprise. Bobby Seale wrote that an initial $3,000 donation from the Peace and Freedom Party was used to pay part of the retainer for Newton's defense attorney, Charles Garry. The PFP also agreed to loan the Panthers their sound truck, which could be used at large-scale rallies and press conferences. Cleaver negotiated with and cajoled the Peace and Freedom Party leadership until they came up with the funds and agreed to campaign for Newton's release. The two groups also placed Newton on the ballot for a congressional seat, and the subsequent press releases made national headlines. Historian Joel Wilson concluded that the alliance was mutually beneficial, allowing the Panthers to enter the realm of "legitimate" politics and the PFP to enjoy "a priceless opportunity for their party to prove its solidarity with people of color."[7]

In February Huey Newton reappeared in the pages of the *New York Times* in a story that reaffirmed his burgeoning celebrity status. Beneath a headline that announced "Negroes Press Nomination of Indicted Militant" was the increasingly familiar photo of Newton in the wicker chair, as the *Times* relied on the Panthers' self-representations to provide a visual reference. Newton's voice was absent, since he granted few interviews while in jail. Instead, the reporter talked with Kathleen and Eldridge Cleaver, a representative of the Peace and Freedom Party, and California election officials. The Black Panthers now qualified as public affairs news, but the article mocked the Panthers' foray into national politics. The first third of the article offered some background through a litany of Panther outrageousness: Newton had founded the organization that "showed up at the California Legislature last summer, armed with shotguns, rifles, side arms and knives." Now he was in jail, the article continued, having been drafted by Panther Communications Secretary Kathleen Cleaver, whose husband, Eldridge Cleaver, spent nine years in prison "after his conviction for assault with intent to kill." Implicit in this list was the pronouncement that such criminals had no business in the political sphere. The *Times'* blanket description of the Panthers remained within the frame of condemnation: "The party . . . is militantly anti-integration and eschews passive tactics to the point where other black militants have criticized it for overly provocative actions." The charge seemed especially ironic since the *Times* recently reported on the Panthers' coalition with the white Peace and Freedom Party. At the same time, however, the newspaper seemed captivated by Newton, as exemplified by the following description: "Mr. Newton, a handsome young man with finely drawn features, was graduated from junior college in Oakland and spent a year in night law school in San Francisco before devoting himself to the Black Panthers." He might be an anti-social thug, but he also offered an irresistible charisma and appeal that the press sought to exploit.[8]

Not to be outdone, the *San Francisco Examiner* published a profile of Newton three weeks later that responded to the growing attention to the Free Huey campaign. This article was also illustrated by an image created by the Panthers, one that was used regularly on the front page of the group's newspaper. The photo of a black-jacketed Newton, with his finger on the trigger of a shotgun and an ammunition belt around his torso, offered a classic pose of military might and defiance. Newton's cocky bearing was enhanced by a caption that read "Anger his goal." The headline sought to explain his identity as an "angry black," announcing, "Newton: Angrier and Angrier as He Grew," along with a kicker that stated, "His Family Supports Him." The story recounted, in fairly flat prose, the details of Newton's rise to prominence and why he became a radical. A minor but telling component was that the reporter attempted a false level of familiarity by referring to his subject as "Huey" rather than by last name, as was customary journalistic practice. Relying on Newton's brother and defense attorney Charles Garry as sources, the text suggests that there were no clear reasons for his militancy. At the same time, the reporter reiterated the growing popular discourse about the Black Panthers—they bore "overt hatred for whites," "rejected integration and cooperation with white liberals," and promoted guns and violence. One can only imagine the *Examiner*'s editor telling reporter George Dusheck to write a story that explained the Panther conundrum to white readers. The reporter professed his own position when he wrote, "The depth and width of black alienation from white America is nowhere more evident than in the astonishing (at least to most whites) slogan: 'Free Huey Newton Now.'" This reporter wanted to suggest a familiarity with "Huey" while plainly stating that the demands for his release from jail were ludicrous. In this and many other instances, the press conflated the frames of condemnation, ridicule, and celebrity in a confusing mix of ideological positions. Increasingly, the media struggled with the desire to embrace and commodify the Black Panthers without appearing to endorse them. Like the performers in nineteenth-century minstrel shows, appropriating their subjects enabled journalists to reconcile their love and envy of blackness with their revulsion.[9]

The Bay Area press followed the alliance with the Peace and Freedom Party with considerable interest. The Pacifica Radio station KPFA broadcast a dialogue between Bobby Seale and Bob Avakian of the PFP, while newspapers sought to make sense of their agenda. The *Oakland Tribune*, relying on a press release, reported that the Peace and Freedom Party was considering whether to adopt the Panthers' ten-point program. The front-page story in the Sunday edition suggested that there was no formal coalition between the PFP and the Panthers but that the two groups found overlapping areas of agreement. What seemed most salient was the printing of the Panthers' ten demands— for control of black communities and an exemption of black men from military service, among others—under a photograph of President Lyndon Johnson reviewing troops on their way to Vietnam. Meanwhile, the *Examiner* reported that Kathleen Cleaver had the PFP endorsement to challenge San Francisco's Willie Brown for his state Assembly seat, while Bobby Seale would run for an Assembly seat in Berkeley. PFP candidate Paul Jacobs announced that the Panthers' involvement was a clear contradiction of the idea circulated by the press that they were racists unwilling to work with progressive whites.[10]

The self-fashioning of the Black Panthers shifted once they were no longer isolated black militants but rather activists on an evolving political stage. The PFP resources and national networks were a boon to the Free Huey campaign and added significantly to their media visibility, but the alliance cost them "a significant loss of credibility within many Black communities." Cleaver addressed the founding convention of the Peace and Freedom Party with a talk titled "Revolution in the White Mother Country and National Liberation in the Black Colony." Much of his talk offered a rationale for the party's alliance with the PFP. The address was republished in pamphlet form and disseminated to constituents in both organizations. Excerpts were published in an editorial in the *Black Panther* in an effort to defuse criticism of the group's association with white activists. He wrote that creating a movement for Huey Newton's defense was a top priority and that the PFP offered a broad base of support. He gave readers a political lesson as well, declaring, "The Black Panther Party welcomes all sincere efforts to create new politics, because we know that we are into a war for our National Liberations and we want all the help we can get, because we need it."[11]

The PFP connection greatly enlarged the Panthers' media efforts— the groups appeared jointly in press conferences, joined forces to distribute leaflets and other materials, and capitalized on the PFP's contacts to attract press coverage. For example, PFP senatorial candidate Paul Jacobs attracted considerable press throughout California during his campaign, including appearances on television stations in Los Angeles and San Diego and invitations by numerous radio stations. In these addresses he always included some materials or references to the Black Panthers. The PFP also blanketed the Bay Area and other strongholds in California with literature that championed Newton's cause and instructed white activists on why their engagement with the Panthers was a necessary revolutionary commitment. One pamphlet produced by PFP chapters in San Francisco and San Mateo County was titled *Why Free Huey?* It argued that whites could not hope to understand black oppression and rage, but the Peace and Freedom Party should be "unwavering in its support of self-determination freedom struggles everywhere." Much of the pamphlet was devoted to dispelling arguments advanced by members uncomfortable with the Panther alliance: that freeing Newton meant circumventing the judicial system, that the Panthers advocated violence, that PFP should focus on anti-war activism, and that the Panthers would alienate potential members. This was a sticky organizational and public relations dilemma for the PFP leadership—they wanted to be connected to what they called "the most vital anti-establishment force in America" and break down the racial barriers in New Left activism without losing their base. The Black Panther connection also helped build the PFP beyond the ranks of white leftist activists by encouraging African Americans to register to vote, and by reminding them that a vote for Newton and Seale on the PFP ticket furthered the Panthers' political reach. These outreach strategies seemed largely successful, as the PFP delivered a sizeable and faithful cadre of white leftist activists who routinely appeared at Free Huey events in large numbers and did fund-raising on the Panthers' behalf. Meanwhile, the two groups mustered enough primary votes to get Newton and Seale on the California ballot.[12]

The Panthers were also working on a coalition with SNCC that was designed, in part, to capitalize on the national visibility of the organization and its leaders. Stokely Carmichael and H. Rap Brown continued to command headlines as fearsome purveyors of militant black nationalism. This was aided by J. Edgar Hoover's accusations, reported in *U.S. News and World Report* and other national media, that the pair used "the 'black power' slogan to stir racial trouble." In his memoirs, Carmichael said SNCC's relationship with the Panthers was more a "flirtation" than a coalition and that both groups thought they had something to gain from the association. Carmichael was impressed by Newton during several jailhouse conversations and said, "I know that Huey, at least, saw SNCC members as elder statesmen, experienced fighters who had maintained a cohesive, functioning organization under heavy fire." In the summer of 1967 Newton symbolically "drafted" Stokely Carmichael to serve as the Panthers' Field Marshal with the goal of broadening the Panthers' base beyond California. In Carmichael's view, this was a largely honorary position.[13]

Cleaver and Seale devised a plan to appropriate some of SNCC's notoriety to enhance the Free Huey campaign and build the party's base. The centerpiece of this effort was a gala birthday celebration for Newton at the Oakland Auditorium, where Carmichael would be the featured speaker and a Black Panther/SNCC alliance would be announced. Seale was aware that SNCC was undergoing its own political turmoil, as supporters of Carmichael, Brown, and executive secretary James Forman were splitting into factions. Nevertheless, he and Cleaver traveled to Washington, D.C., to invite Carmichael personally and to secure his commitment. According to Seale, they also met in Los Angeles with Forman, who expressed his discomfort with Carmichael receiving an appointment in the Black Panther Party. Seale and Cleaver decided to avoid any discord by giving each SNCC figure a leadership position. "We thought that would give us a good group of black revolutionary leaders to unify the black liberation struggle across the country," Seale recalled. Clayborne Carson suggests that SNCC's leaders initially welcomed the overtures from the Panthers "because they believed that the younger, more dynamic organization could bring new vitality" but that the relationship was ill-considered and only exacerbated SNCC's decline. The SNCC connection offered instant benefits, as the *Oakland Tribune* gave the Panthers free publicity when it published a preview of the event accompanied by a photo-graph of Carmichael visiting Newton in jail. Carmichael attracted a large media contingent wherever he went in the Bay Area, including the courthouse jail, where he told reporters, "Brother Huey P. Newton is going to be freed—or else."[14]

Newton's birthday rally attracted over more than five thousand spectators, and David Hilliard wrote about the occasion in glowing terms—the auditorium filled to capacity with a diverse, exuberant crowd who cheered on Newton's behalf. "You can't find a seat in the place," he recalled. "Yet there's no sense of tension, only celebration. The outpouring vindicates everything Huey, and we have stood and worked for."[15] The rally had multiple purposes—to raise money, to en-courage more local residents to support the Free Huey campaign, and to present a unified black power front as SNCC's leaders appeared on Newton's behalf. Amid the pomp of the event, H. Rap Brown was named the Panthers' Minister of Justice, James Forman was anointed Panther Minister of Foreign Affairs, and Cleaver bestowed the title of Honorary Prime Minister on Carmichael. Cleaver also announced that there was to be a merger between SNCC and the Black Panthers, in the process exaggerating the nature of the alliance between the two groups.

James Forman wrote in 1972 that he was attracted to the Black Pan-thers because of the goals of the ten-point program, the group's calls for armed self-defense, and "the emphasis on recruiting street brothers, young people from the 'ghettos' rather than college students." But Cleaver had taken the idea of a merger between the groups too far, and during his speech Forman struggled to explain that no such merger was in the works. Nevertheless, word of the supposed merger traveled fast, and headlines in the leftist press—including the radical newspaper *The Movement* and the *Black Panther*—fueled the story.[16]

During the rally Bobby Seale gave a long, stirring speech outlining the history of the party, Newton's political philosophies, and why the audience should care about Newton's incarceration. "Black people, we are organizing to *stop* racism! You dig it!?" he told the crowd. "When you stop racism, you stop brutality and murder of black people by the racist occupying army in our community. That's what we going to stop—what's being done to us. You dig it!?" On several occasions Seale exhorted the audience to show their support by attending Newton's court appearances or by volunteering for the Huey Newton Defense Fund. Berkeley city councilman Ron Dellums, now Mayor of Oakland, sat on the dais and announced he would introduce a resolution to that body asking for Newton's release. But the most memorable speech may have been the one given by Carmichael, who spent little time on Newton or the Black Panthers. Instead, he gave a wide-ranging lesson on black nationalism, revolutionary movements, and the needs for solidarity among oppressed groups. Perhaps most controversial was his unabashed racial separatism, in which he issued a thinly veiled threat to unreconstructed whites. "The major enemy is the honky and his institutions of racism. . . . And whenever anybody prepares for revolutionary warfare, you concentrate on the major enemy. We're not strong enough to fight each other and also fight him. . . . There will *be* no fights in the black community among black people. There will just be people who will be offed. There will be no fights, there will be no disruptions. We are going to be united!"[17]

According to Seale, the event raised $10,000 for Newton's defense fund. The Panthers' public relations efforts faltered when the television network affiliates declined to cover the event after being told they must pay $1,000 for the privilege—a story gleefully recounted by the *Tribune*. Local news coverage was limited to the *Tribune,* the black press, and alternative media. While the *Tribune* reported on the PFP-Panther alliance on the front page of the Sunday paper, news of the rally was buried inside. The article, without a byline, focused on the speeches by Carmichael, Brown, and Forman, all national figures, while barely mentioning Seale or Cleaver, indicating that the newsworthiness of the story was based on the national prominence of its subjects. The *Tribune* was fairly clear about its allegiances and priorities: no one in the Oakland Police Department or city hall wanted to see the Panthers glorified, and the *Tribune* consistently placed the Panthers within the frames of lawlessness and violence, or else did its best to ignore them.[18]

The next day, however, the *Oakland Tribune* seemed to take delight in the fact that a similar rally in Los Angeles drew far fewer people than the sixteen thousand expected, despite a broad coalition of Los Angeles activists behind the event. In addition to the Panthers, the Free Huey rally was sponsored by the Southern California Mobilization Committee to End the War in Vietnam; Maulana Karenga, head of the cultural nationalist US organization; Betty Shabazz, widow of Malcolm X;

and Chicano movement leaders. A photo illustrating the story featured Carmichael, Brown, Forman, and an unidentified Panther from southern California, but the Oakland leadership was visibly absent. Yet in Elaine Brown's account, ten thousand people attended the event at the Los Angeles Sports Arena with "hundreds more outside, involved in circus-like pandemonium." Eldridge Cleaver delivered another riveting speech that helped throngs of young blacks, including twenty-five-year-old Elaine Brown, to commit their lives to the party and helped add to the L.A. chapter's roster. Nevertheless, the *Tribune* chose to downplay the event.[19]

Pacifica radio station KPFA was also on hand to tape the birthday rally for later broadcast. KPFA, based in Berkeley, was founded in 1949 as the nation's first listener-supported independent station. It was organized by pacifists seeking a forum for a radical exchange of ideas free from commercial influences, and was the first among a group of alternative radio outlets that would fall under the umbrella of the Pacifica Foundation. By the 1960s, KPFA and its sister stations in Los Angeles and New York were deeply entwined in the radical activism of the New Left. KPFA provided an important media vehicle for the Panthers, and in the process the station captured an invaluable record of the Black Panthers' public appearances. Radical, underground newspapers that flourished in the Bay Area also paid close attention to the Oakland rally, including the *San Francisco Express Times*, which published Carmichael's speech in two issues. Abe Peck, a student of the era's radical press, notes that "[t]he Panthers were bidding to become the Movement's vanguard, an idea the nearly all-white underground papers increasingly supported." Widely read alternative periodicals such as the *Berkeley Barb* and the *Guardian* also reported on the Oakland rally and the proposed Panther-SNCC merger.[20]

Three filmmakers from a group called San Francisco Newsreel were also present at Newton's birthday bash, producing the only filmic record of the event and extending to the Panthers access to a medium previously beyond their reach. Newsreel was a collective of activist media workers—filmmakers, photographers, journalists—who organized in 1967 in New York with the goal of circumventing mainstream media. One chronicler described them as "the SDS-oriented makers of movies on Movement themes." Early collectives were based in New York, San Francisco, and Boston. A founding Newsreel member, Roz Payne, recounted their aspirations: "The only news we saw was on TV and we knew who owned the stations. We decided to make films that would show another side to the news. It was clear to us that the established forms of media were not going to approach those subjects which threaten their very existence." Newsreel historian Cynthia Young explained that this largely white and male group saw themselves as a "politically engaged combat unit," producing raw, grainy films that exuded "battle footage aesthetic." Thus they were perfectly in tune with the Panthers' militaristic, confrontational style. The presence of San Francisco Newsreel at the rally meant that the Black Panthers could engage with media producers more sympathetic to their mission rather than relying on the output from television network affiliates. In this sense, Newsreel fulfilled its desired role as "the news service of the New Left."[21]

Several films using Newsreel's footage from the event were created and circulated to sympathetic audiences. One of these films, titled *Black Panthers: Huey Newton, Black Panther Newsreel,* was made under the auspices of a radical group called American Documentary Films, which had its roots in the labor movement of the 1930s. From the sound track of African drumming, gunshots, and radical rhetoric to the murky images of the rally intercut with scenes of menacing armed police, the film disseminated a powerful alternative narrative of a movement destined to right the wrongs of American racism. The film also introduced audiences to the Panthers' ten-point program and to the rhetoric of Newton, who was interviewed from his jail cell. This was a useful propaganda piece—one that showed the Panthers ascending to greatness while in reality they were struggling for survival on multiple fronts. Within six months the film had been widely distributed; one of the filmmakers reported that it was screened at the 1968 Leipzig Film Festival in Germany, "copies were circulated throughout Europe, a copy was given to the Vietnamese delegation, to the Cubans, and to a guerilla cinema group in South America," he wrote to David Hilliard. The film's sound track was also "broadcast on Radio Internationale in East Berlin to the U.S. troops stationed in West Germany." This was among a growing number of media texts that helped to bring worldwide attention to the Black Panthers and the Free Huey campaign. San Francisco Newsreel distributed its version of the footage from the event under the title *Off the Pig (Black Panther)*, and the film was used as an essential recruiting tool across the country.[22]

For a time the local press shifted attention away from Huey Newton to chronicle Bobby Seale's latest run-ins with law enforcement. A week after Newton's birthday rally, the Oakland police went to Seale's home at 2:00 A.M., searched the premises, found a sawed-off shotgun, and arrested the Panther official and his wife for conspiracy to commit murder. Four other Panthers were arrested for carrying concealed weapons as they left Seale's house. Seale contended that the police burst into his home and searched it without a warrant. Meanwhile, Panthers around the Bay Area were being stopped, searched, arrested, and sometimes physically assaulted in what appeared to be an orchestrated campaign by the police to contain the group. Kathleen Cleaver immediately issued a press release condemning Seale's arrest and the general state of "police repression, cop aggression, police lawlessness, and 'pig rule,'" and announced a press conference for the following day. Panther attorney Charles Garry taped a phone interview with Seale from jail that outlined his grievances, and played it at the press conference. The story received minor attention except in the *Oakland Tribune*, which noted that the police quickly dropped the conspiracy charges for lack of evidence. After Seale was freed on bail, Stokely Carmichael joined him on the steps of the courthouse for another press conference to denounce the arrest as police harassment. That night, an angry Bobby Seale led a group of four hundred supporters into a Berkeley city council meeting to demand he be allowed to read a statement critiquing the police. A photo in the *San Francisco Chronicle* showed a tired but defiant Seale speaking before an array of press microphones; the photo carried the caption "I want you to disarm the police department: Bobby Seale demanded a Negro police force for the Negro community." This was a clear example of how the Panthers used the press as a crucial intermediary between themselves and law enforcement. The blow-by-blow coverage by the Bay Area press made public the police department's tactics, and gave a broad platform for the Panthers' dissent.[23]

The *Black Panther* newspaper continued to be the main venue for venting the group's grievances, but the lag time between the occurrence of events and the publication of a weekly newspaper meant that the paper generally addressed these issues after the fact. Two weeks following Seale's arrest, the paper's front page was adorned by the headline "Pigs Run Amok!" accompanied by an Emory Douglas graphic of pigs in police uniforms searching a house in utter confusion. The article, signed by Huey Newton, was another Executive Mandate, in which he ordered all members of the party to obtain "technical equipment to defend their homes and their dependents" on threat of expulsion from the party. This was a sign of Newton's frustration as he watched these developments from his jail cell; this directive offered members no tangible strategy for responding to the police, but clearly registered the Panthers' sense of anger and desperation.[24]

Newton found other outlets, however, as an increasing number of journalists sought jailhouse interviews as his star continued to rise. Early in March he agreed to one such session, attended by his attorney Charles Garry; Eldridge Cleaver, who represented the Panthers and *Ramparts* magazine; Joan Didion, representing the *Saturday Evening Post*; and reporters from KPFA and the *Los Angeles Times*. The presence of Didion was prescient—she was a young and influential writer who contributed to numerous national magazines and had recently published a book of essays, *Slouching Towards Bethlehem*, which chronicled the West Coast of the 1960s and its counterculture. Didion was part of a growing legion of writers working in the "New Journalism," a hybrid of muckraking and literary journalism in which writers blended their observations, political sensibilities, and contemporary vernacular with interviews, research, and a flair for vivid imagery. Perhaps the most famous practitioner of the genre, Tom Wolfe, declared this was a movement that both harked back to the European tradition of literary realism and looked forward to transform the moribund practices of the press. The New Journalism was explicitly political, current, and growing in popularity, and the Black Panthers provided drama and vivid characters that perfectly fit this narrative form.[25]

By the winter of 1968 the Black Panthers had made the tactical decision to drop the phrase "for Self-Defense" from the organization's title. The interview gave Newton an opportunity to explain this shift in a wide-ranging conversation that was his ideal format. He explained that the name was changed because people misinterpreted the party's use of self-defense "even though in our program we described or defined ourselves as a political party." Newton also addressed the charges,

circulated in some media, that the Panthers were anti–white and racist.
"We're subject to the tactics of racists by the white establishment, but
it's a very common thing for the people who are in control of the
mass media to define the victim as a criminal, or to define the victim of
racisms as a racist," said Newton. "This is just a propaganda device that's
used by the power structure so that they will gain support throughout
the white community." Cleaver published excerpts from the interview
in the *Black Panther* and wrote an article on Newton for *Ramparts*, while
KPFA broadcast the interview with Newton on March 7. But it was
Didion's piece in the *Saturday Evening Post* on May 4 for her column
"Points West" that elevated Newton and the Black Panthers to a new
level of renown.[26]

Didion's essay began with an outline of the shooting incident that
left police officer John Frey dead and Newton in jail, and she offered a
brief background on the Panther organization. Her powers of description and evocation were put to work as she described how the group
of journalists "signed the police register and sat around a scarred pine
table" as they waited for the interview to begin. Newton was "an extremely likable young man, engaging, direct," and she wrote that "I did
not get the sense that he had intended to become a political martyr."
By contrast, Didion described Cleaver as Newton's scribe, who wore
"a black sweater and one gold earring and spoke in an almost inaudi-
ble drawl." For Didion, everything about the interview underscored
the constructed nature of Newton's rhetoric and his symbolic role in
the Black Panther Party. Cleaver wrote down the phrase "To be black
and conscious in America is to be in a constant state of rage," and Didion saw the words "emblazoned above the speaker's platform at a rally,
imprinted on the letterhead of an ad hoc committee still unborn." She
was both deeply cynical and sympathetic at the same time, writing that
"almost everything Huey Newton said had that same odd ring of being a 'quotation,' a 'pronouncement' ready to be employed where the
need arose, whenever the troops faltered." Yet, in the true fashion of
the New Journalism, she acknowledged, "I had always appreciated the
logic of the Panther position, based as it is on the notion that political
power begins with the barrel of a gun . . . and I could appreciate as
well the particular beauty of Huey Newton as 'issue.' " Didion gave
voice to what author Tom Wolfe would call "radical chic"—the commodification of revolutionaries such as the Black Panthers to satisfy

the desire to be somehow included in the action of the era. Readers of the *Saturday Evening Post*, mostly white, upper-middle-class, and well-educated, found the Panthers demystified. At the hands of skillful writers such as Didion, these weren't frightening black thugs out to kill whites, but rather thoughtful and deeply attractive messengers of social change.[27]

For black readers, the Bay Area's leading African American newspaper, the *Sun-Reporter*, also followed the Panthers' courtroom battles and political developments as they happened. The *Sun-Reporter* provided straightforward reporting of the events while making plain its solidarity with the black power movement. If the mainstream press registered its dismay over the Panthers' quest to vindicate Newton, the *Sun-Reporter* reminded its readers that the case was rooted in African Americans' historical struggles for racial justice. An article reporting on Newton's preliminary hearing added some important historical context when the writer noted that "[t]he Newton trial seems destined to be a sort of Scottsboro trial of the 1960s. . . . Organized labor supported the Scottsboro boys, but it seems that Newton will receive most of his support from the disadvantaged."[28] The delay of Newton's trial was considered front-page news in the *Sun-Reporter*, and when Carmichael arrived for the events in Oakland he was hailed as a community leader who conveyed pride to African Americans. "We welcome Stokely Carmichael back to California and the Bay Area from visits abroad with statesmen and leaders high in public life and international affairs," announced an editorial. The paper also gave the Newton birthday rally ample publicity and encouraged readers to attend, noting that it promised to "clarify and expand the multifarious elements of Black Power." When Bobby Seale was arrested in February, the paper's front page announced, "Cops Harass Oakland Panthers," and the story lead reported that the charge of conspiracy to commit murder was dropped within a matter of days.[29]

The *Sun-Reporter* was careful not to endorse the Panthers' methods; rather, it alerted readers that these were pertinent issues to be watched. The *Sun-Reporter* also performed surveillance of blacks' troubling relations with the police, often prefacing official accounts of criminal activity with the phrase "according to the police version." The editors of the *Sun-Reporter* took note of the bias in mainstream media coverage of the Black Panthers. Tom Fleming, the paper's best-known writer and an

influential member of San Francisco's black community, wrote an ex-
pansive profile on Newton that took the Panthers' critics to task.
"Newton has an awareness of social responsibility which differs sharply
from the negative image of the Black Panther Party which the daily press
has created in the minds of thousands of readers," Fleming asserted. The
article was a point-by-point refutation of the government and press arguments against the Panthers: the group did not advocate armed conflict
with nonblacks, nor did it see hope in appealing to whites' moral con-
science as a means for social change. This was the only news account that
discussed the conditions of Newton's imprisonment as he awaited trial:
"He is now in a cell alone, where he is held around the clock. There is
no exercise; the only time he gets out is for the weekly shower period or
when he sees his lawyer or visitors. Huey spends his time reading every
book he can get his hands on, or writing."[30]

These varying perspectives on black radicalism took a back seat to
a new national crisis—the assassination of Martin Luther King Jr. on
April 4. Members of the Black Panthers were stunned by the news but
not surprised by the violent outcome of King's activism. Kathleen
Cleaver remembered that shock overtook sadness when she heard about
the assassination on television. "His leadership appeared antagonistic
to the self-defense we advocated, and most immediately, I sensed a powerful opponent of our movement was gone," she wrote in 1998. "I did
not then recognize his assassination as an explosive turning point, nor
could I see the personal tragedy of his death." The death of the civil
rights icon produced yet another moment of crisis for black American
politics and reinforced for the Panthers the belief that nonviolence
could never overthrow white supremacy. Bobby Seale had had little
time to digest the news when he saw his house and his neighborhood
flooded with police anticipating an outbreak of rioting. When David
Hilliard learned of King's death, he turned to Eldridge Cleaver for his
assessment; "Nonviolence has died with King's death," Cleaver told
Hilliard. The prediction was prophetic as cities including New York,
Chicago, and Detroit, still reeling from the riots of the previous summer, exploded with African Americans' expressions of mourning and
rage. The Panthers attempted to circumvent a rash of violence in Oakland by distributing leaflets and taking to the airwaves to encourage
calm. "Speaking to the press, Bobby [Seale] emphasized that the Black
Panther Party opposed rioting as both futile and self-destructive, for

black neighborhoods were always harmed worst," recalled Kathleen Cleaver.[31]

But the Panthers were also deeply preoccupied with what they believed to be a plot to destroy them formulated by the Oakland Police Department. Rumors had been circulating among party members and their friends that an assault was forthcoming, and they feared that the discord created by King's death would be an ideal cover under which this could take place. Two days after the assassination, on April 6, the tension peaked and several carloads of Black Panthers exchanged gunfire with the Oakland police. According to the official Panther position, the police pursued and ambushed them, but later accounts by David Hilliard suggest the incident was the result of a failed assault masterminded by Eldridge Cleaver. Seventeen-year-old Bobby Hutton, one of the Panthers' first recruits, along with Cleaver, ended up trapped by a fusillade of police bullets in an abandoned house on Twenty-eighth Street in Oakland. Cleaver was wounded and Hutton was killed as he attempted to surrender. In a 1998 interview, Cleaver admitted that he and the other Panthers "started the fight" with the police, and he maintained that the police "murdered him [Hutton] right there on the spot." Cleaver, a parolee, was spirited back to prison, and eight other Panthers were arrested in the incident. Spurred on by the madness of the moment, the Black Panthers had plunged into one more tragedy—another leader was in jail, and there was a deep sense of mourning for Hutton's untimely death.[32]

A national day of remembrance for Martin Luther King Jr. was held on April 7, but in the *San Francisco Examiner,* the front page that day was dominated by the headline "1 Killed, 4 Shot in Oakland." The *Examiner,* an evening paper, beat the morning *Tribune* to the story with a sketchy description of the events that was packaged with articles about rioting in Chicago and Baltimore, where "Negro violence again seared scattered sections of the nation." The paper linked the shoot-out in Oakland to the national rash of violence, noting that an "unidentified Negro was killed" as "violence exploded in West Oakland." The only connection to the Black Panthers was an erroneous reference to Cleaver as the party's Minister of Education.[33]

The Panthers marshaled their public relations apparatus and held a press conference on the same day to denounce the killing of Hutton. Seale and attorney Charles Garry were joined by representatives of the

Peace and Freedom Party on the steps of the Oakland Hall of Justice. Garry issued a stinging indictment against the Oakland police, accusing them of circulating photos and documents on the Panthers and issuing orders to eliminate them. "There is a concentrated and concerted effort on the part of the police department to harass, kill, and destroy the militant leadership of the Black Panther Party," Garry told reporters.[34] As the story unfolded two days after the shoot-out, the links to King's assassination and the riots continued as the *Examiner* sought to incorporate the Bay Area into the larger national race-relations crisis. Now the Panthers and the topic of black revolution were brought into focus, with a front-page headline announcing "Silence on Killing of 'Panther'" beneath a somber photograph of Coretta Scott King, the Reverend Ralph Abernathy, and the Reverend Andrew Young as they marched to a memorial in tribute to the slain civil rights leader. The *Examiner's* coverage of the Oakland shoot-out focused on the lack of information supplied by law enforcement authorities, and the immediate political fallout of the assault. The paper repeated Garry's charges that this was a "deliberate attempt to liquidate the Black Panther Party." The *Examiner* also posed the question of whether Hutton was surrendering to police when he was shot. A photo illustrating the story showed Hutton holding a rifle with the caption "Hands in the Air?" The conclusions were inscribed in the image—that this defiant, young, armed radical was unlikely to have yielded as the Panthers claimed. In a sidebar, the *Examiner* attempted to explain the ideology of Eldridge Cleaver, who was the central character in this episode. It began with a nod to American liberalism, stating that "the underlying causes of racial violence—disenfranchisement and despair—are now recognized by a fair share of the American people." But, noted the *Examiner*, few understood the thinking that fueled "the young apostles of violence," as the Panthers were characterized. The article quoted extensively from a recent issue of the *Black Panther* newspaper in which Cleaver argued that black Americans must see themselves as an internal colony, that black consciousness was central to the process of liberation, and that the United Nations should serve as a mediator for the black freedom struggle. This was one of the first efforts by a mainstream publication to provide some context for the conflicts between the Panthers and the police. But by selectively reproducing Cleaver's comments and by employing the frame of the Panthers as violent and misguided, it accomplished little other than to reinforce the standard journalistic positions. Meanwhile, the article demonstrated that the *Black Panther* newspaper was the main vehicle for the group's theories and methods for the press, as well as for party members and supporters. The newspaper had a large audience, but the Panthers had no control over how its content would be used. As the months passed, the *Black Panther* also became the primary source for law enforcement agencies investigating their activities.[35]

The front page of the *Oakland Tribune* was also filled with the image of Martin Luther King Jr.'s widow, Coretta Scott King, leading a civil rights march in Memphis, juxtaposed with the headline "8 Held in Wake of Panther Shootout." The article was a lengthy account of the incident based on police reports. There was no mention of the Panthers' press conference, which might have occurred after the article went to press. The article noted that two police officers had also been injured and that the police considered the killing of Hutton justified. The paper reported that Hutton and Cleaver were armed with two 9 mm automatic pistols, two AR-15 and one M-14 military rifles, and a large supply of ammunition. A police official maintained that Hutton was wearing a coat when he ran from the house and toward the officers. "He said that Hutton was crouched over and the officers could not see his hands," reported the *Tribune*. The police argued that when Hutton failed to stop under police command, he was shot. This was an important set of details because the Panthers maintained that Hutton was surrendering when he died in a hail of police bullets. The alternative scenario did not appear in the story, however, and no Black Panthers were consulted or quoted. An accompanying photograph depicted an armed policeman firing his gun from the rear of a patrol car, indicating that at least one journalist was on hand to witness the mêlée. Another showed an injured Eldridge Cleaver guarded by a police officer at a local hospital. The Bay Area press emerged with distinct roles in this case—the *Oakland Tribune* was a mouthpiece for the police department, ignoring much of the Panthers' responses, while the *San Francisco Examiner* gave voice to the Panthers' claims of discrimination and police harassment from a skeptical distance.[36]

On the day of King's funeral, workers throughout the state of California stayed home in observance of "Black Tuesday," while civil rights groups organized memorial events. An article on an inside page of the

Oakland Tribune reported on the varied commemorations of King's life, bringing attention to the fact that Oakland mayor John Reading would be attending the funeral in Atlanta as California's representative. The paper was at pains to demonstrate a concern for King's legacy as it systematically denounced black power activism. The most stirring image from this occasion was the photograph of a march sponsored by the Panthers and the Peace and Freedom Party down Telegraph Avenue from Berkeley to the Alameda County Courthouse. For as far as the eye could see, a phalanx of marchers ten deep spread through the city, led by a banner proclaiming, "Free the Black Panthers." Labeled militants by the paper, the group nevertheless stole the publicity thunder from civil rights groups such as the NAACP and CORE, which hoped to use the occasion to reinforce King's calls for nonviolence.[37]

Part of the developing defense strategy for the Panthers was to attract the attention and support of figures beyond the Bay Area. This was particularly effective in the case of Eldridge Cleaver, whose book *Soul on Ice* had just been published in February. Cleaver's editor at McGraw-Hill and a group of ten New York writers immediately issued a statement requesting that the Oakland police be supervised while Cleaver was in custody since "they have made no secret of their plans for extermination of the Panthers." This was reported in the *Examiner* and helped catapult the story into the pages of the national media.[38] The *New York Times* reported on the incident under the headline "Oakland Police Kill Negro in Gun Duel," buried on page 30. For the *Times*, the shoot-out in Oakland constituted yet another example of the violent racial discord moving across the nation. The article was packaged with stories of the continued rioting in Chicago and Washington, D.C., with photographs of National Guard encampments and Senator Robert F. Kennedy touring the destruction in the nation's capital. The *Times* presented the general contours of the shoot-out story, including a sidebar noting that Charles Garry intended to file murder charges against the Oakland police in the death of Hutton. Huey Newton was discussed, although he had no role in the incident: "Newton . . . has become a symbol of both black and white militants in the area as a candidate for Congress of the Peace and Freedom Party." Bobby Seale, who also was far from the gunfire, was due in court on illegal weapons charges, the article reported.[39]

The emerging celebrity of Eldridge Cleaver as an author and Black

Panther spokesman helped to capture the attention of the East Coast publishing establishment. The most salient feature of the *Times'* story, along with the theme of racial violence, was his reputation as an author. It was noted early in the article that he had recently published *Soul on Ice*, and the newspaper highlighted the expressions of concern about Cleaver's safety from the writers, including Susan Sontag, Lawrence Ferlinghetti, Warren Hinckle III, and Christopher Lehmann-Haupt, as well as a similar statement from *Ramparts* magazine. The paper quoted McGraw-Hill editor in chief Frank Taylor, who praised Cleaver's literary talents and maintained that "[h]e must be assured of every protection for his person and his rights." Cleaver was now included among a community of writers who could claim freedom of expression and who had the kind of visibility that might protect him from retribution from the state.[40]

The next week, actor Marlon Brando showed up at Bobby Hutton's funeral, guaranteeing the story prominent play in the *New York Times* and *Time* magazine as well as in the Bay Area press. Hutton's death was used as a backdrop for the national press' developing preoccupation with the Panthers as popular-culture icons, and the presence of a bona fide Hollywood celebrity added credibility to that frame. The *Oakland Tribune* and the *San Francisco Examiner* gave the story modest coverage, reporting on the crowd estimates of twelve hundred to fifteen hundred attendees, the appearance by Brando, and the incendiary speeches by Bobby Seale and the presiding clergy. The *Tribune*, seeking to temper the story, did not include a photograph and placed it next to one reporting on the arrest of four Panthers on armed robbery charges. Days later, the *Tribune* would report that three of the four Panthers had been released without charges due to lack of evidence. In contrast, the *Examiner* devoted considerable space to comments by Bobby Seale made during a press conference before the funeral, during which he accused the police of murdering Hutton in cold blood. Included were a head shot of Brando and a photograph of Black Panther pallbearers, resplendent in their leather jackets and berets, carrying Hutton's coffin.[41]

The weekly black newspaper, the *Sun-Reporter*, featured the Hutton funeral on its front page, and reporter Thomas Fleming was unflinching in his description of what occurred on the night of Hutton's death. In the *Sun-Reporter*'s account, Hutton was "slain by a hail of bullets fired by Oakland police, when Hutton and two other Black Panthers were

driven out of a tear-gas-filled, bullet-hole-studded house on the evening of April 6." There were no qualifications to the story, no use of
the word *alleged*. For the *Sun-Reporter*, the Panthers' version rang true.
Fleming also reported on the throngs of reporters who showed up for
the Hutton funeral. They included cameramen from every television
station in northern California, another from Los Angeles, and even one
from the BBC, further evidence of the Panthers' global reach. The paper took notice of Marlon Brando's appearance, featuring him in the
front-page illustration, but Fleming also acknowledged the presence of
college students, activists, and numerous local residents who felt compelled to attend. The *Sun-Reporter* was less concerned with the presence
of a white celebrity at the funeral than with the enormity of the event
and its ripple effect in the black community.[42]

The *New York Times*' account of the funeral was far more detailed,
providing background on the Panthers and their assorted legal travails.
The lead paragraphs gave a broad forum for the Panthers to air their
grievances: "White racism and the Oakland Police Department were
bitterly denounced today," the article began, and speakers at the funeral
called Hutton's death a "political assassination." The Panthers had
skillfully appropriated the rhetoric of Martin Luther King Jr.'s assassination to represent the death of one of their members. The Panthers
were described by *Times* writer Lawrence Davies as "a defense group
assertedly to protect the Negro community from intimidation," a soft-
ening of the harsh condemnation the *Times* delivered a year earlier.
Evident in the account was the weight of white spokesmen, who expressed outrage on behalf of the Panthers. Marlon Brando, who functioned as the self-appointed representative of white guilt, told the
mourners, "You've been listening 400 years to white people and they
haven't done a thing. . . . I'm going to begin right now informing
white people what they don't know. . . . I've got a lot to learn." The
composition of the photo illustrating the story put Brando in the foreground, with a line of Black Panthers standing in military formation
behind him, symbolizing an uneven black–white alliance. The article
also reported that a group of university faculty in the Bay Area called
for an investigation of the Oakland Police Department. The *New York
Times*, situating itself as the nation's political and cultural agenda setter,
enabled white supporters of the Black Panthers to appear courageous
and fashionable at the same time. The Peace and Freedom Party played

an influential role in this process: they sponsored rallies to commemo-
rate Hutton, including one in Oakland featuring comedian Dick Gregory. They donated considerable manpower and financial resources as
well; one receipt showed they incurred over $4,000 in expenses for a
memorial meeting for Hutton in Merritt Park, followed by a bus pro-
cession to Vacaville prison, where Cleaver was being held. The white
PFP activists were close partners in the crusade to hold the police ac-
countable for Hutton's death.[43]

This public outpouring of sympathy and the presence of a multiracial coalition in support of the Panthers, coupled with the group's
growing skill at handling the media, also backfired on numerous occasions. *Time* magazine relied on the well-established frames of fear and
condemnation to report about the Hutton funeral. Using the same
photograph that appeared in the *New York Times*, the caption read,
"Brando at Black Panther Memorial Service in Oakland: Hatred Is an
article of faith." Yet *Time* had little interest in Brando's celebrity beyond his visual representation—he was barely mentioned in the article.
Rather, the idea that the Panthers were the embodiment of racial discord and rage was the central theme. The ghettos of Oakland were
"hate-filled," the Panthers were "armed and angry" and "defiant," and
"hatred of law officers is an article of faith." *Time*'s customary use of
tropes and metaphors went to the extreme when Eldridge Cleaver was
described as the Panther spokesman "whose jarring eloquence bares
the pent-up rage that inspires the Panthers' snarling intransigence."
Time tried ineffectively to explain the Black Panthers to its readers. It
reported that the group had fewer than 150 members, although no
support for this assertion was provided. They were "a strutting band of
hypermilitants" who were more style than substance, according to the
magazine. Ironically, *Time*'s reportage on the Panthers suffered from
the same disability—an emphasis on colorful, quirky language with
virtually no background, interviews with sources, or other material to
flesh out the story.[44]

Paul Jacobs, the Panthers' white ally from the Peace and Freedom
Party, used the Hutton funeral to reach intellectuals and the literary
elite in the *New York Review of Books*. Jacobs' essay, published as a "Letter from Oakland," described the intensity with which young black
Americans identified with the Panthers' cause. Black youth who have
daily unpleasant encounters with the police "are not as concerned as

are most whites with whether the police fire the first shot at the Panthers or whether the Panthers fire the first shot," he wrote. "That is reality to them as it is to the Panthers, and in Oakland they are very close to the truth." Jacobs provided an overview of the Panthers' brief history and explained their recent entry into politics, using his discussion to fill in the gaps left by the media. "Most of the white community in California is unaware of the Panthers' political position; all they can see are the guns which are played up by the press and on television." White Americans needed to suspend their fears and inform themselves about the roots and realities of black militancy, Jacobs exhorted.[45]

In the aftermath of Bobby Hutton's funeral, Eldridge Cleaver's incarceration made him the subject of widespread concern in leftist literary circles, driven in part by his long-term relationship with *Ramparts* magazine. Cleaver recorded a jailhouse interview for the magazine that was published a month after the shoot-out. The Panthers' Minister of Information was particularly eloquent as he blasted President Lyndon Johnson and other power brokers for the state of unrest in America. "[G]reedy, profit-seeking businessmen," "conniving, unscrupulous labor leaders," and "unspeakable bootlickers" were his targets. Cleaver declared that "the blame is everywhere and nowhere." Next to Cleaver's manifesto was an article written by *Ramparts* editor Gene Marine, outlining the events of April 6 and establishing the necessity of white leftist support for the Panthers. He argued that on the day of the shoot-out, the Panthers were trying to quell the possibility of a riot in Oakland, not start one. "Eldridge Cleaver and the Black Panthers are not wild racists with guns," said Marine. "The Black Panthers are, in fact, the one black militant group which has reached out to the white radical community for help in the struggle for black liberation." The article compared Cleaver to dissident writers and intellectuals in the Soviet Union and challenged American progressives to shift their views of the Panthers. "If Eldridge Cleaver goes back to jail, it should outrage not only those interested in our national literature, but those who fear for the state of our nation's soul." In a similar article written by Marine for *Commonweal*, titled "Shooting Panthers Is Easy," he not only lambasted the Oakland police for "lying outright" about the circumstances surrounding Hutton's death but also critiqued the Bay Area press for regurgitating the police's story. Marine's goal was to tell the Panthers' side of the story and to inspire a sense of moral outrage in whites who

championed other social justice causes but shrank in fear when confronted with the Black Panthers. He complained that "white America
can be shocked by a murder in Memphis and ignore one in Oakland"
and that "white America can express horror when Mayor Daley talks
about shooting, and demonstrate only apathy when the Oakland police . . . actually do shoot to kill—and succeed." Marine's desire to
connect the assassination of King with the death of Bobby Hutton was
a stretch, but he was impassioned in his self-appointed status as the
translator and white ambassador for these alarming black radicals. In
particular, he wanted to reframe Eldridge Cleaver as a literary genius
and black-power elder statesman who was single-handedly transforming the organization. As if responding to white anxieties about black
male youth run amok, Marine described Cleaver as offering "mature
leadership" and as having helped "to turn the Panthers from a bunch
of angry kids into a closely knit and carefully organized group with a
genuine political program for the ghetto." Gene Marine continued to
write about the Panthers for multiple venues, eventually publishing
one of the first of many "insider" books about the organization.[46]

The *Guardian*, a leftist weekly newspaper published in New York,
took up the cause of vindicating Eldridge Cleaver as well. Robert L.
Allen, one of the few African Americans writing for the white underground press, published an interview with Cleaver just days after the
shoot-out, which extended the Panther leader's political credentials to
a more established leftist audience. Cleaver presented a quasi-Marxist
framework, arguing that capitalism was the foundation of African
Americans' problems. If the Black Panthers were to be the vanguard
of the American left, Cleaver understood that attention to political
economy was essential. "We recognize the fact that we have been oppressed because we are black people even though we know this oppression was for the purpose of exploitation," he argued. Later that
year, Allen published a pamphlet titled *Dialectics of Black Power* that explored the future of black radical politics and bemoaned the lack of
coherence and direction among the various factions. In particular, he
critiqued the separatist black nationalists who failed to recognize the
dual nature of black America: that it is simultaneously part of the national body and outside it. The Black Panthers, he declared, "is perhaps
the only militant group to recognize this contradiction and to attempt
to deal with it in their program." They were "far from perfect" and

faced the possibility of being wiped out. Nevertheless, it was Allen's project that they be understood by the white left in America. At the end of Allen's discussion, a facsimile of the Panthers' black cat strolled off the pamphlet's page, solidifying the group's grip on the iconography of black power. The Panthers' efforts to solicit and solidify support from the white left was increasingly productive: the Peace and Freedom Party, Socialists, Students for a Democratic Society, and other entities were told that true radical change in America meant embracing the Black Panthers despite their contradictions.[47]

Numerous media outlets leaped at the opportunity to add the Black Panthers to their inventory. In late May, a photographer contacted Charles Garry hoping to do a photo essay for the London *Sunday Telegraph* magazine. His request demonstrated how journalists' understanding of the Black Panthers could be entirely shaped by media representations. He wanted to photograph the Panthers "in meetings, conducting discussions, taking part in demonstrations . . . and in training," suggesting this was the sum total of their activities. He expressed no interest in exploring dimensions of the group that had not been previously depicted—their engagement with black community residents, publishing their newspaper, political campaigning, and so on. Rather, he wanted to document the threatening paramilitary group he had read and heard about. The underlying framework of the photo essay was to be conflict; the photographer noted that "we would want to show graphically the militancy of the group and the state of hostility that does exist between it and Oakland authorities." The *Sunday Telegraph* succeeded in publishing a feature story on the Panthers in its August 18 "Close Up" section. The paper's correspondent used Newton's trial as a backdrop, describing how the Alameda County courthouse felt like an armed fortress and the heated fervor that characterized the daily demonstrations on Newton's behalf. With requests such as this the Black Panthers confronted the stark reality that the revolutionary culture they so carefully crafted was largely out of their control; rather, it was being reproduced uncritically to fit the frames established by dominant media. According to Todd Gitlin, the elite media, including the *New York Times,* serve their constituencies by providing a kind of "early warning system" that maps out the general terrain of social problems. This was followed by a constant thunder of distant media outlets in the United States and abroad—newspapers, magazines, television and radio stations—which based their fundamental knowledge about the Black Panthers on the intelligence provided by the *Times'* surveillance, which was delivered in narrow and selective frames. Many were simply responding to an unspoken competitive imperative: *If those people have pictures of the Black Panthers, we want them too.*[48]

The events of the previous months made the telling of "Panther stories" a part of the daily news cycle for media outlets in the Bay Area, and this was spreading to the elite national organizations as well. Shorthand references such as "Panther," "Newton," or "Seale" were all that was required to make the necessary association for readers; the Black Panthers were regular players on the political stage of 1960s protest. Journalistic routines structure reporting and, in the process, impose their own logic that works against alternative frameworks. The logic of "Panther stories" was that they contained elements of violence, racial discord, defiance, or dissent; otherwise they might not be deemed newsworthy. The obsession with Panther news relieved the group's public relations operations to some extent—no longer did they have to constantly solicit media attention, since it was now part of an accepted routine. Instead, they were negotiating inquiries and offers from myriad media who all wanted to capitalize on and use their notoriety in some way. In a few short months, the Black Panthers had become convenient and readily available tropes for the dual sociopolitical dilemmas facing America—racial discord and radical political discontent. Their image and rhetoric were quick and convenient stand-ins for broader, more complex articulations of the roots of the black power movements. These tropes served the interests of a press wholly ignorant about black life in the United States and deeply ambivalent about how to address African Americans' grievances.

6

A TRIAL OF THE BLACK
LIBERATION MOVEMENT

The rapid spread of revolutionary consciousness among young
blacks could not have happened without network television. . . .
This it not to say that television coverage was accurate. In fact,
it thoroughly distorted the nature of the changes in black consciousness by concentrating on the superficial.

Kathleen Cleaver, "How TV Wrecked the Black Panthers,"
Channels of Communication (1982)

The Black Panther Party emerged during this period as a well-oiled
publicity machine, even in the absence of Minister of Information
Eldridge Cleaver. Press conferences were held on an almost daily basis.
The *Black Panther* newspaper was a regular fixture in the Bay Area, and
increasingly in other cities with nascent Panther chapters. Pamphlets
and flyers were churned out with regularity to explain the particulari-
ties of a legal case, such as "Release Eldridge Cleaver," written by
Kathleen Cleaver. Party representatives were increasingly armed with
the group's speaker's kit, rather than pistols and rifles. The thirty-page
guidebook offered a thorough history of the party, biographies of
Newton and Cleaver, the details of their legal complaints, and a discussion of their importance to African American communities. An important strategy was to highlight how the police harassment leveled
at the party affected the rank and file as well as the celebrated leaders.
The speaker's kit enumerated more than a dozen instances in which
Panthers had their rights violated in the course of their party activities.
In one incident, for example, an unnamed Panther and his girlfriend
were arrested for "disturbing the peace" after attending a rally, and
were beaten in jail. In another item, two female Panthers were putting
up "Newton for Congress" posters when their car was stopped and
searched, while other Panthers were prevented from distributing

leaflets and buttons. These transgressions were reported to supporters during rallies and press conferences but were only occasionally covered by the news media. When the Panthers sought a court order to prevent county officials and the Oakland police from harassing them, local reporters were on the scene. But what the press wanted was more sensational headlines that conformed to the frames of violence and racial discord that made their arrests a self-fulfilling prophecy.[1]

Throughout the spring and summer of 1968, the Bay Area news media maintained a steady spotlight on Newton and Cleaver's struggle to stay out of prison. When a grand jury was impaneled to investigate the April 6 shoot-out, the story was rigorously pursued. It was front-page news in the *Oakland Tribune* when a grand jury handed down eight indictments for attempted murder in the case and exonerated the police in the death of Bobby Hutton. Accompanying the article was a lengthy denunciation of the Black Panthers by Oakland police chief Charles Gain, who called them "a threat to the peaceful persons, both black and white, in this community." The next day the *Tribune* devoted an unprecedented five pages to excerpts from the grand jury transcript, with a skyline head that announced, "Grand Jury's 3-Day Story of Terrible Night," and illustrated with photos of many of the policemen involved. The *Tribune* signaled to its readers that this story warranted all of the attention of a national disaster or war, as the paper capitalized on the drama of the police's testimony. The blow-by-blow script presented from the police's perspective offered excitement, pathos, and danger. The *San Francisco Examiner* also carried the stories about Chief Gain and the grand jury, paraphrasing the findings but focusing instead on the circumstances surrounding Hutton's death. A sidebar, titled "How Hutton Was Killed: Officer's Story," quoted the testimony of a policeman who maintained that Hutton was fully clothed and refused to stop when ordered by the police. The *Examiner* added that the indicted Panthers refused to testify, suggesting that without their input the case was hopelessly one-sided. The story also appeared on local television news, prompting Bobby Seale to assert that Chief Gain "went on TV and lost his cool."[2]

The *Examiner*'s sister newspaper, the *San Francisco Chronicle*, was equally absorbed with the Cleaver case and Hutton's killing and came up with several scoops of its own. Reporter Charles Howe produced a front-page story describing Charles Garry's insistence that there was an alternative narrative to the one promulgated by the grand jury and the district attorney. An enormous skyline head cried, "Hutton Shooting: The Panther Side." Garry declared that two witnesses saw Hutton being tripped by a policeman and then shot repeatedly, and that at least one witness was prepared to testify. The article was accompanied by a damning photograph of Panther Glen Stafford being arrested after Hutton's funeral. The beret-wearing Panther is handcuffed and surrounded by four uniformed police, one holding a rifle, while the defendant was bent and grimacing from the Mace used to subdue him. The photo, produced by Garry, could be viewed as visual evidence of police excesses in dealing with the Black Panthers or as reassurance that the police were clamping down on black militants. For several days, the *Chronicle* continued this front-page scrutiny. One article proclaimed a "Secret Agent's Analysis of the Black Panthers" under another screaming skyline. This time, an unidentified agent of a national intelligence service reported on his success in infiltrating the group. The article generally deflated much of the hysteria about the Panthers, insisting that there were only some two hundred members in the Bay Area, that they were poorly trained and had inadequate weapons, and that they were not receiving money from any foreign power, as was suggested by the FBI. The agent professed some understanding for the Panthers' overarching goals and told readers that their membership was confined to the "disenfranchised black teenager, unsure of himself, already with a police record, and with a feeling of utter desperation." The agent argued for increased federal funding in urban communities as the best antidote to the Panthers' brand of activism. The informant could have been Earl Anthony or any number of others who operated undercover in the group. By publishing the unsubstantiated commentary of this source, the *Chronicle* delivered the message that the Panthers posed a threat only to themselves.[3]

In contrast, the San Francisco *Sun-Reporter* registered a vigorous protest over the April 6 shoot-out between the Panthers and police, and challenged the Bay Area's black community to end a "conspiracy of silence" that enabled the police to carry out a "systematic and apparently purposeful drive to cut down the black militant groups." In an editorial titled "Protect the Panthers," the paper lashed out at the black elite, reminding them, "The fate of all people is one." The area's major black newspaper was also blatant in its view that the police practiced "a studied, methodical strategy . . . without legal authority, to harass, intimidate, physically attack and even murder proclaimed members of the Black Panther Party." This was the only media organization other than the alternative press to find credence in the Panthers' claims; the editors of the *Sun-Reporter* hewed to standard journalistic principles in its news stories, but on the editorial page it announced its solidarity with its black brethren who were clearly under siege. The editorial concluded with an elegant call to arms: "If we are silent now, we lend aid and comfort to those vicious practices of the police establishment which will erode and destroy the very fabric of our legal system of government."[4]

A week later, the *Sun-Reporter* published an op-ed piece by Tom Fleming, titled "Black Containment," in which he issued a withering indictment of law enforcement authorities. He argued that regardless of who fired the shots in the Panthers' various conflicts, it was the Oakland police who were ultimately responsible for the discord. Fleming, asserting that he spoke for many African Americans in the Bay Area, accused the Oakland police of harboring "aggressive contempt for blacks" even before the days of more militant black politics. At the root of the problem was white officers' fundamental racism, he argued. "It is one of the departments in the state that has conducted vigorous recruitment programs in the Southern states where promises of good wages, better than offered in the South, induced poor whites to migrate to Oakland," he wrote. "This job also gave them an opportunity to vent their prejudices against black people." To support his argument, Fleming recounted the experiences of one of many black San Francisco residents who were routinely harassed by the police. In the victim's deposition, he said that the policeman beat him brutally while he was handcuffed, all the time shouting racial epithets such as "Why don't you black ass nigggers go back to where you came from." The irony of the incident was that the complainant's brother was a member of the San Francisco Police Department. In June another *Sun-Reporter* writer reinforced this critique of the police, writing, "An officer I know on the police department has told me that at one time he reckoned 'nigger' was the most common word in the police vocabulary." The article concluded that if the police disliked the "pig" nomenclature, "then stop being pigs and stop using derogatory labels when you refer to black Americans." The *Sun-Reporter* took an increasingly hard line as it covered the Black Panthers during the ensuing months; the newspaper considered its purview to include not only reporting the news but conveying a critical perspective. That standpoint revealed a deep sense of identification with the Black Panthers' complaints emanating from the region's black communities. In late May, the *Sun-Reporter*'s publisher, Dr. Carlton Goodlett, became Bay Area co-chair of the International Committee to Release Eldridge Cleaver, indicating that the paper was now firmly in the Panthers' corner. In this respect, Goodlett had answered his newspaper's appeal to the black elite to support black activists. Others on the committee included such celebrities as actor Ossie Davis and novelist James Baldwin.[5]

In the aftermath of the indictments, the Panthers waged a tireless campaign to raise funds for their rapidly escalating legal defenses while protesting the outcome of the hearings. With Cleaver in jail, the main party spokespersons were Bobby Seale and Kathleen Cleaver, who appeared at rallies, press conferences, and other staged events, including a benefit in New York City featuring the poet-activist LeRoi Jones (Amiri Baraka). An Associated Press report of the event recounted only Jones' comments and mentioned that the audience of two thousand was half white and "many were middle-aged or older." This focus represented a new frame for the Panthers that followed the Bobby Hutton funeral—their appeal to segments of white America. Support for the Black Panthers in the Bay Area was both racially and politically polarized, shaped by residents' personal relationships with the police or the Panthers and by their experiences within the region's diverse political culture. In places such as New York people formed their opinions about the Panthers based largely on what they read, saw on television, or heard at a public event. The wire service report omitted Bobby Seale's pronouncement at the rally that "we hate you white people." In his memoirs, Seale explained that he made the statement without providing a context; he intended it to be a parody of black cultural nationalists who made blanket statements of racial hatred. In the past, such commentary would have been a central theme of the story, even announced in an inflammatory headline. But on this occasion either the reporter was very careful not to misconstrue Seale's remarks or the press was beginning to tire of the fear frame (or perhaps both). Seale recalled that the New York audience was keenly aware of assorted crises facing the Panthers: the jailing of Eldridge Cleaver and Huey Newton, the death of Bobby Hutton, and Newton's approaching trial.

Their media blitz was bearing fruit, since there had been few public appearances of the Panther leadership on the East Coast. According to Seale, "Cops attempting to attack and wipe out the Party had caused the Party to grow, and when we left New York, on May 22, 1968, their first chapter was forming."[6]

While the Panthers' violent actions warranted front-page attention, their quieter tactics were considered of minor interest. When they returned to Sacramento in May on the one-year anniversary of their first successful media event, the local press acknowledged the occasion with bureau reports buried deep inside the Oakland and San Francisco papers. Each article registered the irony of the occasion: it was a subdued protest with no guns or scuffles with police. Instead of the words of intrusion and insurgency used by the press a year earlier, the Panther presence was characterized as a "peaceful demonstration and leaflet passing." The *Tribune* noted, "Except for the buttons, the Panthers and their sympathizers could well have been mistaken for any of the busloads of tourists who routinely come to the capitol every day," and the paper also paid close attention to the demographics of the delegation, which was "about evenly divided between Negro Panthers and white members of the Peace and Freedom Party." The news frame was built around the multiracial quality of the Panthers' appearances and their increasingly nonthreatening posture. The Panthers faced a dilemma—toning down the rhetoric of confrontation and militance might deflect a larger backlash, but this newer, gentler Black Panther was unlikely to be a sensational attraction that would further their visibility.[7]

Ramparts, the periodical that launched Cleaver's career and claimed him as one of its own, focused zealously on the Panthers in the spring and summer of 1968. Shortly after his arrest, the magazine published an essay by Cleaver called "Requiem for Nonviolence" that ruminated about Martin Luther King Jr.'s assassination. As the title suggested, the Panther leader proclaimed the end of King's dream and declared, "The violent phase of the black liberation struggle is here, and it will spread. From that shot, from that blood, America will be painted red." Minutes after dictating the piece into a tape recorder, he left his home in San Francisco and ended up in the fatal shoot-out with police. The essay was Cleaver's call to arms, and while it appeared in print weeks after the incident, it still had a chilling ring. Accompanying the article was a photo of Hutton and Cleaver in calmer days and an article by Gene

Marine, who described seeing the elder Panther as he was transferred from an Oakland hospital to police custody. Marine sounded pained and outraged by what he characterized as Cleaver's harsh treatment at the hands of law enforcement officials. Two months later *Ramparts* featured an article titled "A Letter from Jail" by Cleaver that offered an intimate account of his early days in the Panthers. The article was a paean to the organization, beginning with the oft-cited line "I fell in love with the Black Panther Party for Self-Defense immediately upon my first encounter with it; it was literally love at first sight." According to the magazine, the piece was written by Cleaver and smuggled out of his cell in Soledad prison, adding further romance to his saga. Cleaver, like Newton, was emerging as a modern-day Antonio Gramsci, turning a grueling period of incarceration into a collection of writings meant to explain and theorize social conditions. Gone was the fury of his earlier piece on King's murder, replaced with a quieter, more introspective rhetoric. He quoted Frantz Fanon and Che Guevara as he laid down the gauntlet for white Americans: "Do you side with the oppressor or with the oppressed? The time for decision is upon you."[8]

But *Ramparts* was just beginning to campaign on behalf of the Panthers. Two weeks later Gene Marine prepared a wide-ranging article on the history of the Panthers that moved from the Sacramento protest to the killing of Hutton. Ten pages were devoted to the piece, which mimicked a theatrical script divided into acts. It was illustrated with stunning, full-page photographs of Kathleen Cleaver, Huey Newton, and Bobby Seale and their opponents Bill Knowland, editor of the *Oakland Tribune*, Oakland mayor Reading, and Oakland police chief Gain. Marine systematically made the argument that the police waged a vendetta against the Panthers, not the other way around. His impassioned writing was set to a hysterical pitch; he seemed to share the Panthers' frustration that no one believed their claims, and he was determined to convince the magazine's left-leaning audience otherwise. "Few people seem willing to believe that the Black Panthers are opposed to initiating violence in Oakland at this time and that the Oakland police are trying to start it," he lamented. If the denial continued, he predicted, Newton would be executed, Cleaver would be imprisoned for life, and "the cops will go on, steadily and inexorably, trying to bust, and if necessary kill, every Panther in Oakland."[9]

Amid this constant media chatter, Cleaver's bail was reduced, and through an appeal he won at least a temporary release from prison. This made the front page of the *Oakland Tribune* two days in a row, as large headlines announced, "Superior Court Judge Orders Cleaver Freed" and "Order Releasing Cleaver Appealed." The ruling judge stated that Cleaver's jailing on parole violations "stemmed from . . . his undue eloquence in pursuing political goals which were offensive to many of his contemporaries." The newspaper's disproportionate attention to this relatively minor story highlighted the sense of outrage at Cleaver's release felt by those at the paper's helm; they were anything but enamored of Cleaver's rhetorical skills. On the day he was released, Cleaver held a press conference that was reported on by the *Berkeley Barb* with an alternative discourse that celebrated the Panther leader. "Cleaver Cleared on All Counts; Jailers Condemned," read the headline, and Cleaver was quoted championing his First Amendment rights: "I would never allow anyone to place restrictions on my freedom of opinion or expression," he told the crowd of reporters.[10]

Meanwhile, Newton's lawyers filed multiple motions to have his trial postponed. Much of this was buildup for what would be the Bay Area's biggest story of the year, as Newton's trial date in July approached. "Black Panther leader Huey P. Newton will go on trial for murder here tomorrow in a case attracting international attention," the *Oakland Tribune* reported. In the early days of the trial the paper seemed particularly interested in the throngs of journalists—numbered at over a hundred—who sat in the press gallery, for this event was a measure of Oakland's national visibility. Coverage of the first day warranted front-page placement in the paper, with a large photo of Newton's supporters amassed in front of the Alameda County courthouse holding "Free Huey" placards. There was little to report about the actual minutiae of the courtroom proceedings, but plenty of spectacle to be seen. As the lawyers and judge haggled over legal details, the Black Panthers produced some of their most stunning visual imagery to date. The dialogic nature of the event was unmistakable—the Panthers were invested in creating a symbolic role in the case, and the news media were looking for a story to tell amid the boring details of the trial. Thus, the *Tribune*, which routinely expressed hostility toward the Panthers, continued to be one of their most useful venues. One front-page photograph showed cadres of male and female Black Panthers standing at attention, their backs to the camera, and framed by the vertical structures of the courthouse building. The image was of a seamless black phalanx determined to assert their presence throughout the proceedings. Another memorable photograph, also published by the *Tribune*, showed the party faithful facing the camera with their arms crossed in front of their chests in quiet determination. The image, shot from the bottom of the steps, gave the illusion of power and control that the Panthers so avidly sought. Instead of the armed, disorganized fanatics portrayed by the police and prosecution, the visual construction of the Panthers was full of order and patience—part of the larger rhetorical strategy that would be part of Newton's defense. The visual field is not a blank slate but is itself a racial formation. These photographic representations enabled a racialized and politicized reading of the Panthers that merged the coon figures of minstrelsy origins—the black who mimics whiteness but cannot hide his basic inferiority—with the black brute and the civil rights demonstrator.[11]

The *Sun-Reporter* offered a different lens through which to view the opening of Newton's trial, in the process subverting the framing strategies used in the mainstream press. Reporter Thomas Fleming described the police as overreacting to the presence of Panther supporters at the trial: "Scores of riot helmeted police and deputy sheriffs prowled the courthouse armed with riot sticks and guns," he wrote. He noted that even the press had to negotiate a two-and-a-half-hour process to get into the courtroom, and that they towed away several reporters' cars because of their heightened anxiety. The article also underscored Charles Garry's motions arguing that it was impossible to find a jury of Newton's peers. "Black people have been systematically excluded from jury duty by the district attorney's office," Fleming wrote, citing a recent court ruling. When Newton's jury was finally seated, Fleming pressed his case that the jury selection process was discriminatory. The lead paragraph of his report, barely masking his disdain for the judicial process, began, "A predominantly white and middle class jury of seven women and five men were sworn in Tuesday to try Huey P. Newton." In later reports, the *Sun-Reporter* did not always side with the Panthers' arguments, but the paper played an important role in calling into question the assumptions presented in the Bay Area press—that local law enforcement's handling of the trial was appropriate and without bias.[12]

For all of the hoopla, the early days of Newton's trial were fairly routine, with jury selection and assorted motions taking more than two weeks. The *San Francisco Examiner* reported on much of this activity, but it was relegated to inside pages with no illustrations. The predictable news coverage was briefly interrupted by the appearance of a tabloid called the *Oakland Tribunal* that was both a parody and a blistering critique of the daily newspaper. The paper was published by a group of three hundred Bay Area residents, including labor organizers, college professors, attorneys, doctors, and clergy, who pooled their resources and distributed it in their neighborhoods. The four-page newspaper used many of the techniques of the *Black Panther* and other underground publications: the front page was dominated by the headline "Why Huey Newton?" followed by the warning, "Beware the extremist voices from high places. They are trying to get you into a lynch mob." Oakland's mayor was indicted for pronouncing Newton guilty at a public meeting, the police chief was criticized for making "inflammatory accusations" designed to prejudice Newton's trial, and the *Oakland Tribune* was singled out for "misrepresenting and smearing" the Panthers. Eschewing the incendiary rhetoric employed by many activists, the paper went on to systematically refute the state's case against Newton and to alert local residents—particularly whites—that they were being enlisted in a project to deny the Black Panthers their rights. In particular, they pointed out that the main tactic in Oakland's campaign against the Panthers was to provoke racial anxieties. "No matter how many times the *Oakland Tribune* states otherwise, the Panthers are not anti-white and are doing nothing more than defending themselves and challenging racist politics," they explained. This was a valiant effort to shake the complacency of citizens who uncritically believed what they heard from public officials and the press, and they reminded readers that the *Tribune*'s publisher, William Knowland, "was, until the voters turned him out of office, a national leader of reactionary politicians who fought unions, black people, and other ordinary citizens." The impassioned critics who published the *Oakland Tribunal* were a product of their era—in a time when government lies about Vietnam, the CIA, and other affairs were being uncovered daily, skepticism toward any official version of events was deemed prudent. Not surprisingly, the local media generally ignored this attempt to challenge the prevailing discourse surrounding Newton's case, except for a couple of small weeklies. If a tribunal acts as arbitrator among dissenting factions, this effort failed, as the *Oakland Tribune* and the rest of the press continued with their coverage of the Panthers unabated.[13]

The *New York Times* picked up an account of Newton's trial from

United Press International, which filed a report that focused on the estimated twenty-five hundred demonstrators at the courthouse, and the armed sheriffs guarding the trial. The story, buried on page 14, was accompanied by another dramatic photographic image—this time a group of female Panthers was in the foreground, unwavering in their commitment to stand in witness to Newton's trial, and flanked by a male in dark glasses and beret holding a "Free Huey" flag. The photo told a national audience that something big was happening in Oakland: young, defiant black people were gathering to express their support for the martyred Newton, and they were not in a conciliatory mood.[14]

The opening of the trial set the stage for a wide-ranging meditation by the *New York Times* on the meaning of African American militancy. For the first time, the nation's newspaper of record devoted front-page space to the Black Panthers and the problems of racial discord. The title, "Black Panthers, White Power: Violent Confrontation on Coast," laid out the article's themes: the struggle between black and white, the Panthers' advocacy of violence, and how this was a particularly Californian phenomenon. This feature story highlighted the primacy of storytelling in journalistic practice: the article opened by setting the scene of inner-city Oakland, as if creating an establishing shot for a motion picture. Oakland's "Negro slum" was described as a place where "slum dwellers clash and quarrel, seeking more room to live and breathe, seeking ego satisfactions, pleasures, hope." Next, the story set up the main characters: *Oakland Tribune* publisher William Knowland, Eldridge Cleaver, and police chief Charles Gain. Much of the article recounted the birth of the Black Panthers, the Huey Newton case, and the shooting of Bobby Hutton. While Newton's photo was used, he was clearly supplanted by Cleaver, who was given several columns to expound on his favorite topics. Cleaver rattled off his standard position on Newton's trial: "We say we'll go down with Huey and we meant that. . . . We will not allow them to murder Huey. And that means doing anything within our power to see that it does not happen." He also offered his own detailed version of the April 6 shoot-out, as he described how Bobby Hutton, blinded by tear gas, was shot as he stumbled from a shove by a police officer.

Despite this significant commitment of space, the newspaper evinced deep confusion and ambivalence about how to frame the Panthers.

Cleaver was identified as "an ex-convict, an anti-capitalist, a bitter critic of the police, a Black Nationalist," and simultaneously as "a very effective leader, a brilliant writer." In the elevation of Cleaver as a celebrity, it was also important to remind readers that his book, *Soul on Ice*, had been published recently. The reporter, Wallace Turner, failed to convey the complexity of the issues swirling around the Panthers. Instead, he ended up simplifying his investigation by setting up opposing camps: it was the Panthers versus a white establishment as exemplified by Knowland, "a vocal opponent of the Panthers." The *Oakland Tribune* publisher lambasted the group for making unreasonable demands and for employing unorthodox tactics. When asked about the Panthers' picketing of a market in Oakland, he replied, "Well, this I felt was in effect coercion—a form of extortion—you either accept our political beliefs or we close you up," he said, likening the Panthers to Nazis, Fascists, and Communists. Nowhere did the *Times* register the irony that a newspaper publisher, whose job was to guide objective recitation of news events, was obviously deeply biased against his paper's favorite villains. Police chief Charles Gain, described by his fellow officers as a "liberal policeman," was virtually invisible in this dialogue, as he declined to comment on the assorted criminal cases in which the Panthers and police were involved. Gain, who agreed it was a good idea for black police officers to patrol black neighborhoods, also acknowledged that the Panthers' growing membership was due to black residents' dissatisfaction with city government. But he offered little insight into how the Oakland police planned to respond to the city's racial crisis. Readers of the *Times* were provided with the fundamental elements of a superficial story—one that reproduced the standard journalistic practice of describing an issue rather than explaining it. There were no logical links between Oakland's impoverished black ghettos and Cleaver's insistence that Newton be freed from jail or Knowland's hostility; it was enough simply to report on the opposing camps. The sound bites the Black Panthers delivered to the press guaranteed they would get attention, but media attention was not enough to foment change.[15]

The Panthers also trickled into the pages of other leading newspapers, including the *Washington Post*. In late July, the paper published an extensive article titled "The Making of a Martyr" on the front of its Sunday "Outlook" section. The piece rehashed much of the Panthers' history, from their origins in Oakland to the circumstances that brought Huey

Newton to the brink of martyrdom. The information—old news to Bay Area residents—cast Newton respectfully but distantly. He "talks slowly and softly, long lithe fingers playing with a cigarette," and in his courtroom appearances he was "natty in a variety of turtleneck sweaters, rarely smiling." Gone was the menacing Huey Newton, armed to the teeth and taunting white America. Instead, the article was illustrated with a year-old photo of Newton, stripped to the chest, handcuffed to a hospital gurney, and guarded by police after the shoot-out that left officer Frey dead. The article focused on Charles Garry's courtroom strategy of critiquing the impartiality of potential witnesses, and the ambiguity of Newton's arguments. "If the mother country refuses to have a revolution, then the Panthers—and those white radicals who wish to join in—will inflict consequences on it. The last is left deliberately vague . . . violence is neither ruled out, nor ruled in. The burden of the interview is that black power is not the question; revolution is. It is only the fist that is black." The New York Times had failed in its initial attempts to get beyond the details of events and their limited construction of what the Panthers meant, but this Washington Post piece refused to rely on easy definitions, instead highlighting their contradictions.[16]

No matter how influential the New York Times or Washington Post may be in the universe of public affairs, to achieve national recognition one must appear on national television. While newspapers and newsmagazines set the agenda for how the Black Panthers would be discussed in public discourse, television provided the crucial visual context. Without television, the image of the Black Panthers would lack the immediacy and a sense of presence that moving images provide. The early television coverage of the Black Panthers, while sporadic, showed audiences how they looked and sounded, and conveyed the dramatic energy of their confrontations with police and other authorities. In 1967, the year that the Black Panthers gained national visibility, seventeen million Americans watched NBC for news, fourteen million watched CBS, and six million watched ABC. This was an audience that most activists desired—without it any social movement would be relegated to invisibility.[17]

The trial of Huey Newton finally secured this kind of attention, which the Panthers so avidly sought. The network affiliates in San Francisco and Sacramento had covered the Panthers sporadically for months, and the networks relied heavily on their stock footage. For example, KPIX, San Francisco's CBS affiliate, filmed and broadcast at least twenty stories on the Panthers during the first six months of 1968. But beginning in July the television networks, all based in New York City, broadcast more than thirty news stories that capitalized on the symbols and theatrics supplied by the Free Huey campaign. In fact, one of the first broadcasts appeared on national television two days before the *Times* article, suggesting that the venerable newspaper may have responded, in part, to the competition. Television was an ideal site through which to spread the now familiar images of the Panthers standing at attention and holding banners aloft in a display of solidarity with their embattled leader. But if the print media failed to provide a coherent analysis or context to the group's rise, television presented little more than a confusing mix of images and tropes. On July 18, the *ABC Evening News* tried to capture the tense atmosphere in Oakland, broadcasting scenes of a crowd of Panthers and white "hippie" supporters listening to Bobby Seale condemn the Oakland Police Department as a "terrorist organization." For the first time, a vast audience was introduced to the Panthers' symbolic universe; viewers across the country heard the group's rhetoric, learned the name Huey Newton, and saw throngs of supporters carrying "Free Huey" signs. But there was little point to the story other than to introduce viewers to these standard representations—they were little more than a curiosity in the evening news sideshow.[18]

Kathleen Cleaver would later write that television's selective attention to the Panthers, more than any other medium, fueled the organization's explosive growth by presenting pictures that "were so extraordinary that belief in the feasibility of revolution grew." The Free Huey campaign attracted television coverage, and broadcasts of the Panthers' demonstrations and press conferences helped mobilize supporters and build the group's membership in a mutually beneficial exchange. "Frequent television exposure subtly legitimized the image of the Black Panthers," Cleaver argued. "But its sensationalizing made the Panthers loom far more glamorous and ferocious than they actually were."[19]

As Newton's trial got under way, the Panthers employed another part of their public relations arsenal—their growing membership in chapters outside California. David Hilliard recalled that the Oakland headquarters received daily requests from places as far-flung as Des Moines, Atlanta, and Virginia Beach, where groups wanted to start local chapters. The Panther leadership's response was to require prospective chapter founders to spend time in Oakland, learning the rules, selling newspapers, and becoming indoctrinated in the party's politics before launching satellite groups. But in Brooklyn, New York, a renegade Panther had already set up a chapter and given himself the title of Captain. This was cause for consternation, although the nascent chapter was raising the Panthers' visibility on the East Coast. The Oakland leadership had to accept a certain level of independence among their growing legions, and other New York–area chapters quickly appeared.[20]

The new chapters came in handy when the Panthers decided to take their grievances to the United Nations. For months Newton and Cleaver had been arguing that the Panthers should gain an audience at the UN to win support for their contention that the U.S. government was complicit in the genocide of African Americans. Members of SNCC also supported this agenda. According to James Forman, they wanted to "create favorable public opinion before the [Newton] jury was picked," and they planned multiple press conferences in the New York area to accomplish this goal. They also hoped to win an audience at the United Nations to draw international attention to Newton's case. Forman circulated announcements to the new Panther chapters in Harlem, Brooklyn, and Newark asking members to attend the rallies scheduled at each location, distribute leaflets, announce them at church services, blast the "Free Huey" message in communities with sound trucks, call radio stations, and seek support from sympathetic organizations. The news conference at the UN was cancelled when the Panthers failed to show, the by-product of their infighting with SNCC. But they did hold a joint news conference with a group of white activists in an office across the street from the UN Secretariat attended by a handful of reporters. ABC sent a film crew to one rally and broadcast a brief report featuring Bobby Seale, who declared that if Newton was not freed, "[t]here will be open armed war on the streets of California." This story lacked the visual color of previous reports, but it helped to disseminate classic Black Panther rhetoric and to solidify their place in the television news repertoire.[21]

The newly formed southern California branch of the Black Panthers also helped expand the group's notoriety. The Los Angeles Panthers was organized by Alprentice "Bunchy" Carter, a former head of the Slauson Avenue gang, who became politicized while serving time in Soledad prison, where he met Eldridge Cleaver. Under Cleaver's tutelage, Carter joined the Panthers and rose to prominence in the Los Angeles chapter, which was formed in January 1968. Elaine Brown, an early recruit to the chapter, recalled that "the combination of those thousands of gritty young Brothers from the Slausons, who still saw Bunchy as their leader, with the ideals of the Black Panther Party had sent chills through everybody." For several months, two groups in the city struggled over which would carry the Black Panther name, with Carter's followers finally winning out. By that summer, the southern California Panthers had been in several shoot-outs with the Los Angeles Police Department, one resulting in the deaths of three Panthers on August 5. The Los Angeles media followed their northern counterparts by elevating the story to urgent status. The war between Panthers and law enforcement was now a local reality. Network television affiliate KNXT, for example, followed the story for several days, reporting that the local Panthers disputed police accounts of how the gunfight had occurred. Bobby Seale joined the local leadership at a press conference to denounce the Los Angeles police and warn that a Newton-like case would be the result.[22]

The Los Angeles shooting coincided with the Watts Summer Festival, an annual event inaugurated after the devastating riots in 1965 to memorialize the uprising while remaking the community's image. NBC used the festival as a backdrop to stoke national anxieties that there was a resurgence of urban violence in Los Angeles, this time instigated by the Panthers. The three-minute feature, which aired on the network evening news, reported that "three Negroes were shot to death, and four Negroes and two policemen were injured . . . in separate shooting incidents in Los Angeles." Only later in the story do we learn that the three who were killed were members of the Black Panthers—the only reference to the organization. The incident in Watts was described as an "aimless flurry of shots" in which no whites were involved, and the network proclaimed this to be the worst violence in the city since the riots. Footage in a hospital showed the injured policemen; nothing was portrayed of the dead Panthers, their friends, or family. The broadcast made no attempt to explain the shooting or to provide any background on the state of race relations in the city. Most of the story concerned the possibility that the festival

might be halted, as the camera focused on community members painting fence posts to the strains of James Brown's "Say It Loud, I'm Black
and I'm Proud." In the end, there was little point other than to link it
to the ongoing racial discord across the country, and the Black Panthers
played a relatively minor role.[23]

That the networks even attempted such a feature story was remarkable for the summer of 1968. Television news was dominated by stories of strife and mayhem—the deepening quagmire in Vietnam, the
Democratic National Convention, and Richard Nixon's ascendancy to
the Republican presidential nomination, among others. The network's
coverage of the Vietnam War was a significant test of the medium's
journalistic enterprise: correspondents relied heavily on military information, anchors read bland wire service bulletins, and station managers
strove to keep the nightly visuals bloodless. Historian James Baughman
wrote that "television reportage of the war between 1965 and 1968
was anything but critical." Broadcasters were equally inept in dealing
with race relations. The National Advisory Commission on Civil Disorders, appointed by President Johnson to analyze the rash of racial
uprisings in American cities, released its findings that spring. The commission investigated many of the core issues of the nation's racial
crisis—unemployment, ghettoization, economic exploitation, and conflicts between police and community. The news media were held up
for particular scrutiny, with the commission asserting that both print
and television generally failed in their fundamental duty to give a representative accounting of events:

> The media report and write from the standpoint of a white man's
> world. The ills of the ghetto, the difficulties of life there, the Negro's
> burning sense of grievance, are seldom conveyed. Slights and indignities
> are part of the Negro's daily life, and many of them come from what
> he now calls "the white press"—a press that repeatedly, if unconsciously,
> reflects the biases, the paternalism, the indifference of white America.

This critique slowly trickled into the consciousness of the national
news media, which began making awkward attempts to do "race stories." The Panthers were, to some extent, the beneficiaries of this new
interest in the inner city because they were available and familiar subjects for a press that had few contacts in black communities. The

Black Panthers captured the limelight because they were convenient tropes for African American militance, unlike many white activists who in some ways conformed to the agenda of elites in American society. It was the ever-escalating manifestations of African American anger and disenfranchisement that pushed the news media to respond— black people had to burn down cities and build radical movements before the national media took notice. Yet the rush to cover the nation's race relations problems occurred without introspection or attention to changes in journalistic routines and techniques; the press still turned to official sources—police, government, business—for much of their information, and they selected stories based on the traditional news values of conflict, proximity, prominence, and the unusual occurrence.[24]

Watching this footage, one is reminded that television was a black-and-white world, not only in the actual absence of color but also in the general absence of otherness except as distant, easily definable news subject. All the newscasters were white, as were the authoritative sources, and even the actors and actresses in advertisements. This familiar world was occasionally interrupted by images of strange and distant people of color—Vietnamese soldiers, victims of the Biafra famine, or black militants—underscoring the Kerner Commission's assessment that the press "repeatedly, if unconsciously, reflects the biases, the paternalism, the indifference of white America."[25]

Independent media provided an increasingly vital alternative to the output of corporate-owned outlets. The intensified activities surrounding Newton's trial attracted independent filmmakers such as Agnès Varda, who is considered one of the founders of the French new wave film movement. Varda was trained in art and photography and had been making both fiction and documentary films since the 1950s. In August and September she spent time in Oakland, interviewing Newton from his jail cell, filming a Panther rally held on a beautiful Sunday afternoon, and capturing the quality and texture of the moment with the eye of an outsider. The resulting film, *Black Panthers*, was the antithesis of what appeared on commercial television. The twenty-eight-minute film focused heavily on the Panthers' symbolic culture, the camera panning from the image of clenched fists to the ubiquitous buttons, the faces of children at the rally, and a group of random members holding copies of Chairman Mao's quotations. "This is the Black

Panther style," intoned the narration, "black leather, black berets, black sunglasses, return to African dress, natural hair." As one scholar has explained, the film's goal was to "explain and vindicate the Panthers," and Varda was unabashed in her support of their cause and in her vilification of their enemies. The narration noted, "The Oakland police, well known for their reputation of brutality, never miss an opportunity to harass the Black Panthers." Near the film's end, the voice-over makes a bold, poetic statement in defense of the group:

> It is because they are an endangered minority that the Black Panthers have to express themselves violently and warn their immediate enemies—the Police. Their war cries exasperate the white racists who consider them black fascists, forgetting that they are much less dangerous than the police and much less fascist.

While the opening sequences emphasize the potency and fervor of the Panthers and their supporters, intercut with commentary from Newton, William Lee Brent, and Kathleen Cleaver, among others, the closing is a stark and violent exposition of the group's demise. The camera lingers on posters of Huey Newton and Eldridge Cleaver, riddled with bullet holes after their headquarters were shot up by the police. The devastating image foretold a tragic ending that is appropriate for the filmmaker's critique of American society.[26]

Agnès Varda's *Black Panthers* functioned in opposition to the sensationally violent and threatening Panthers that had become the standard trope for the mainstream media. They were ennobled rather than denigrated, romanticized rather than condemned. Yet, as David James has argued, Varda was unable to avoid her whiteness and Eurocentric perspective, in the process "almost producing them [the Panthers] as the exotic natives of an ethnographic documentary." Varda, an early feminist, also romanticized the role of women in the organization, celebrating the "promotion of women to the political and military life of the party." One scene showed Panther women drilling in formation and marching along Oakland's Lake Merritt. The voice-over was of Huey Newton proclaiming that "the role of women in the Black Panther Party is exactly the same as the man." An interview with Kathleen Cleaver and comments from other women accentuated this point. But Varda clearly spent little time learning about the complex, and often contested, gender dynamics of the organization—her extended interviews were with male Panthers, including Newton and Brent. What was on the surface was enough. Like other sympathetic white writers, filmmakers, photographers, and artists, she saw her role as giving the Panthers a voice and an audience. In so doing, Varda constructed an alternative but no less narrow framing for the group, one that unequivocally accepted their self-representations as the vanguard party while advancing their celebrity.[27]

A bevy of alternative voices kept the Free Huey campaign at a high and often frenzied pitch. The Communist Party provided another faction of white supporters for the Panthers' efforts. David Hilliard noted that one senior Communist Party member, William Patterson, pushed the idea of setting up a formal defense committee for Newton to "raise funds and propagandize about the trial." The Communist Party weekly the *People's World* provided coverage of Newton's trial and published a pamphlet titled *Black Liberation on Trial: The Case of Huey Newton*. The tract, sold at rallies and lectures for fifteen cents, offered a sympathetic overview of the proceedings. The author, Celia Rosebury, who covered the trial along with the throngs of reporters, argued for the importance of the Newton case, declaring, "It is a trial of the black liberation movement in the United States." In the preface she admitted that she had been inclined to believe in Newton's guilt, but as the evidence was presented her opinion shifted. Rosebury also argued that many journalists covering the trial "had accepted their assignments with preconceived notions of Newton as a 'cop-killer,'" and that they too had been won over to Newton's side. Rosebury created vivid verbal images of the occurrences both inside and out of the courtroom as she tried to convey the political importance of the case. "Newton's supporters kept up a loud, determined vigil under the hot sun," she wrote, while across the street "a line of nearly 100 Panther brothers stretched the length of the block, and they stood there, facing the courthouse, all day." Such details were important in conveying the role of the trial in the lives of the Black Panthers—no mainstream media recounted the stamina or commitment required to stand watch day after day. A deep admiration for the rank-and-file of the party was evident in this narrative.[28]

The activist San Francisco–based periodical *The Movement* also churned out regular commentary on Newton's case. The publication, with a circulation of twenty thousand subscribers and a national distribution, conducted a long-ranging interview with Newton from his jail cell, in which he laid out the principles of the Black Panthers to a white activist readership. The article was reprinted in a booklet titled *Huey Newton Talks to the Movement* that was distributed widely to muster continued support for his defense. In this manifesto, Newton sounded bright, articulate, and patient, rather than the prosecution's image of an irrational and trigger-happy murderer. The cover of the booklet, which was published by SDS, showed Newton behind bars flashing a V-for-victory or peace sign. Other versions of the pamphlet were also distributed with a cover featuring a cropped version of Newton in the wicker chair and the snarling black cat emblem. Newton explained his critique of black cultural nationalism by stating that "as far as returning to the old African culture, it's unnecessary and it's not advantageous. . . . We believe that culture itself will not liberate us." He told the SDS membership that the Black Panthers were deeply concerned with the connections between capitalism and racism, and that their role as "white mother country radicals" was to "aid black revolutionaries first by simply turning away from the establishment, and secondly by choosing their friends."

Newton's emphasis on the reclamation of black masculinity was central to his manifesto; he declared it was "penis envy" that prompted the white slave master to psychologically castrate the black male. In his view, black women failed to respect black men because of this emasculation, and white radicals were unable to recognize that "the black man has a mind and that he is a man." Newton was appealing to the masculinist impulse of the New Left at the same time that he articulated his own feelings of emasculation as he languished behind bars. He echoed, even imitated, the discourse of the "new black man" articulated by Eldridge Cleaver in *Soul on Ice*. Cleaver too reduced the problem of white supremacy to the male member: "The black man's penis was the monkey wrench in the white man's perfect machine," he wrote. Both Newton and Cleaver present themselves simultaneously as the castrated prisoner and the revolutionary leader who forged a movement through the power of the black male body and the rejection of the feminine. This was a dangerous scenario—the exaltation of black male sexual power might appeal to aggrieved African Americans but simultaneously feed into the mythologies of the black brute, thus exacerbating whites' fears. By making black male heterosexuality at the core of the politics of racial justice, Newton insisted that white radicals accept the presence of the hypermasculine black male as the price for being allowed to claim an alliance between blacks and whites.[29]

As Huey Newton's trial approached its denouement, the 1968 Democratic National Convention in Chicago provided the press with another dramatic example of political discord. The convention, held August 25–28, became a mediated event that exemplified the perils of social protest and the extent of police violence. Prior to the convention, the Panthers told the press that they would not demonstrate at the convention, but Bobby Seale was present on one night to address the crowds. The protests during the Democratic Convention "were media events tailor-made to crack any lingering image of politics as usual," explained Todd Gitlin. He argued that the media exaggerated the polarization between the protesters and convention participants, giving Mayor Richard Daley justification for authorizing the brutal police attacks on the demonstrators. The appearance of Seale at the demonstrations, organized by members of Students for a Democratic Society, Abbie Hoffman's Yippies, and other groups, was proof that the Panthers had been anointed as the black radical darlings of the white left. While the Democrats debated whether to nominate Hubert Humphrey, Eugene McCarthy, or George McGovern in Chicago, the Peace and Freedom Party held its own convention in Ann Arbor, Michigan, which made the *CBS Evening News*. The juxtaposition of the two disparate events further underscored how embedded the Panthers had become in national politics. The report noted that Dick Gregory and Black Panther leader Eldridge Cleaver were vying for the presidential spot, and Cleaver announced, "All Americans are aware of our existence." These events shifted the Panthers away from the frames of threat and black lawlessness and into the frame of extremism in left-wing politics constructed around SDS and the largely white anti-war movement.[30]

In this climate of heated politics, the Bay Area news media kept a steady eye on the Newton trial. From July 15 until early September, the *Oakland Tribune* published more than two dozen front-page articles that gave readers a blow-by-blow description of the proceedings. From the jury selection to the testimony of assorted witnesses, from Newton's day on the witness stand to the detailed ballistics analysis, readers were presented with a narrative filled with sports metaphors and high drama. When the prosecution agreed to drop kidnapping charges against the defendant, the headlines read, "Newton May Win Round in Kidnapping." As the trial came to a close, the paper reported, "The difference between life and death for Huey Newton could depend on an instant in time—a brief limbo unclear in the memories of three people." The *Tribune* virtually ignored the ongoing Free Huey protests after the first few days of the trial, instead providing a sterile recounting of the courtroom developments. The *Tribune* continued to privilege the testimony and perspectives of the perceived victims of the case. The memory of the slain police officer, John Frey, was invoked almost daily, as was the police officer wounded in the shootout and the bystander who was allegedly kidnapped by Newton. Typical headlines reproduced the charges of Newton's guilt: "Witness Saw Frey Killed" or "Witness Saw Newton Kill, Says Jensen" lent credence to critics' claims that he was being unfairly tried in print. When Charles Garry began Newton's defense, the headline read "Defense in Newton Trial Fires Back"; the metaphor of the trial as a reenactment of the original shooting was a convenient way to sustain interest in the trial coverage. The *Oakland Tribune* left it to the competition to provide interviews with members of the Black Panthers, Newton's family and associates, or any other of the city's black citizens.[31]

The *San Francisco Examiner* also avidly covered the trial, frequently putting the day's developments on the front page. By contrast, the newspaper across the bay spent considerable time and space exploring the personal and political dimensions of the case. In one article, for example, the *Examiner* acknowledged the symbolic nature of the trial and that race relations was at its core: "For many people Newton's trial is only part of a larger issue—whether the police do or do not serve the same function in the ghetto as they do in the white community." A front-page interview with Oakland's mayor, John Reading, exposed the dramatic transformation in local politics spurred by the Panthers and other black activists. Reading lamented that when he was elected, "the emphasis was on civil rights," but that "a militant, articulate extremist Negro minority has seized leadership of the black community from more moderate leaders." Deeply frustrated by this state of affairs, Reading noted he would not seek another term, and he predicted that an African American could wind up mayor of Oakland in the near future.

Newton's attorney, Charles Garry, was furious about Reading's interview, arguing that it created "an atmosphere of hysteria" that made it
impossible for his client to receive a fair trial. The *Examiner* reported on
Garry's complaint, noting that his motion for a mistrial was summarily
dismissed by the judge. What the newspaper ignored were the merits of
Garry's concerns: had the media frenzy so influenced public opinion
that a fair trial was impossible?[32]

The *Examiner* also devoted considerable space to the human-interest
aspects of the case with the reportage of black journalist Rush Greenlee. He began his career as a correspondent for UPI before moving to
the Bay Area where he worked for the *Oakland Tribune*, and later for *the
San Francisco Examiner*. Greenlee's writing on the Black Panthers stood
out amid the multitude of stories in the local press for their insight,
depth, and inclusion of African American's perspectives. In an interview with Newton's mother, Greenlee elicited from her numerous anecdotes about the defendant's childhood and his character. "He's the
most sympathetic and tender-hearted kid we have," Amelia Newton
told the newspaper. The article included reminiscences of Newton
playing a leading role in a Sunday school convention, and his mother's
assertions that his trial was tarnished by racial bias. The paper also profiled Newton's father, the Reverend Walter Newton, who lambasted
the press, saying, "All that ever come out is lies. One of you even came
over to my house and all that came out was lies." Another story profiled Newton supporter Earl A. Neil, a minister who was identified as
the Panthers' "spiritual advisor." He defended his decision to allow the
Panthers to hold meetings in his church and argued that "it is the
church's mission to be part of the community." In giving a voice to
African Americans beyond the Panther leadership, the *Examiner* re-
futed the assertions that the Panthers lacked community support, and
put a human face on the demonized militants.[33]

As the case was poised to go to the jury, Greenlee recognized that it
would be impossible for the jury to isolate the facts of the case from
its political ramifications, noting that during his testimony Newton
"made it clear . . . that he wishes to stand or fall on the validity of his
cause." The article also pointed out that the Newton trial had global as
well as national implications and that it had been widely reported in
the international press. In summing up the case, Greenlee wrote, "The
testimony inside the courtroom and the evidence outside show all too

plainly that the case is at least in part one of people who feel they have been discriminated against and who are not willing to take it any longer." Thus, the *Examiner* was considerably more receptive to the Panthers' framing of the trial as a test of the courts and as a referendum on race in America. Most news organizations refused to work within this frame. Instead, by highlighting police accounts and the prosecution's case, they relied on the familiar theme of law and order within which the Black Panthers easily fit. In this way, they still conformed to their constructions as a threat to be contained, and the criminal justice system could be seen as meting out fair retribution for the Panthers' outrageous acts. Huey Newton, cast as martyr by the Panthers, could be framed as an anti-hero or a victim of the excesses of a police state, depending on the media organization's leanings.[34]

The *New York Times* displayed minimal interest in the case, as the upcoming presidential election, the Soviet occupation of Czechoslovakia, the Vietnam War, and an impending school strike in New York City dominated its pages. Ironically, when the nation's newspaper of record did report on Newton's trial, it focused on the most sensational elements it could find: the prosecution's promise of a surprise witness, and the fact that marijuana fragments were found in Newton's pocket when he was arrested. It wasn't until a verdict was anticipated that the Panthers reappeared in the national news agenda. As the case went to the jury, CBS and ABC both broadcast reports on the potential effects of a guilty verdict for Newton. The Panthers' television presence was also elevated by the growing activism of chapters beyond the West Coast. The networks were prompted by a local incident in which more than two hundred off-duty New York City policemen beat up a group of Panthers trying to enter a courthouse in Brooklyn. For the first time, the networks could not deny that the remote problem of black militancy in California had reached their doorstep. One *CBS Evening News* account offered only a brief overview of Newton's trial, with the bulk of the report focused on a statement by Mayor John V. Lindsay condemning the policemen's behavior. ABC broadcast a four-minute feature that captured much of the Panther iconography and reproduced footage from the 1967 Sacramento protest and a Free Huey rally. Viewers were treated to close-ups of guns in holsters and the menacing stares of Panthers in military formation. The reporter described them as "a paramilitary organization whose members carry guns, wear a uniform of sorts, and openly speak out for black power." Eldridge Cleaver was introduced to national television audiences as the "best-known Panther" and was filmed declaring, "The oppression of black people started four hundred years ago in this country. Anything we do to the oppressor is categorized as self-defense." While the story was ignored by the *New York Times*, the *San Francisco Examiner* made the assault by New York policemen front-page news, just beneath an article about the closing arguments in the Newton trial. The wire service report noted that many of the officers were wearing "Wallace for President" buttons, signaling their support of racial segregation, and that they attacked the black bystanders with rubber truncheons. This was an alarming prospect for Bay Area readers who may have known little about the growth of the Panthers on the East Coast. The story provided further evidence that the conflicts in Oakland and San Francisco were part of a national crisis in which law enforcement agencies, unused to having their authority challenged, were striking back.[35]

Time magazine devoted two pages to assorted news about black power activism, including a story on the tense anticipation of Newton's verdict. The article was accompanied by a photo of Newton, characterized as "cool, composed, sardonic." The Panthers were "the cop-hating Negro militant organization" whose supporters saw them as "a dedicated band of black Robin Hoods," while according to their detractors they were "hate-mongering, crime-prone psychopaths." Despite the magazine's effort at balancing the opposing positions, the representation of the Panthers as hating white authority prevailed. *Time*'s overview of the case was tinged with skepticism as it claimed it was "predictable" that Newton's supporters would focus on issues of race relations rather than his guilt or innocence. The magazine seemed critical of the fact that Newton's case received such publicity, at the same time that it contributed to the phenomenon.[36]

When Huey Newton was found guilty of voluntary manslaughter rather than murder—a verdict that satisfied neither his supporters nor his opponents—the news was rapidly transmitted across the country. The *New York Times*, as well as the Bay Area press, put the story on its front page. Beyond the details of the case, the *Times* focused on the Panthers' rapid rise to fame, asserting that the group "has rocketed to national prominence far beyond its numerical strength or actual influence in the affairs of Negro militancy." The newspaper offered no accounting of the Panthers' membership or commentary from other black activists that might support this assertion. The *Oakland Tribune* added that Newton faced anywhere from two to fifteen years in prison when sentenced. An accompanying *Tribune* article, headlined "'I Want to Forget It'—Newton Jury Foreman," provided a lengthy account of the jurors' experience; the only response from Newton's supporters was depicted in a photograph of his sister being comforted by a black clergyman. The *San Francisco Examiner* headlined the decision "A Compromise on Conflicts in Testimony," reporting that the "puzzling verdict" was based on the jurors' determination to convict Newton despite the lack of evidence. One source told the paper that the jurors wanted to avoid a hung jury because that would make it more difficult to convict Newton in the future. The constant presumptions of Newton's guilt became a self-fulfilling prophecy.[37]

A coda to Newton's trial occurred the following day, when two drunken Oakland police officers shot up the Panthers' headquarters to express their frustration with the manslaughter verdict. The national news media capitalized on the irony of the event, which elicited further journalistic commentary about the violent conflicts between the police and black radicals. According to one NBC News correspondent, "The Panthers were expected to lose their cool, but it was the police who lost theirs." This was a story that could be built on the police and National Guard excesses at the Democratic National Convention and during the assorted urban uprisings. But rather than condemn the signs of anarchy in law enforcement, journalists commiserated. In all of the news accounts from this period, the police were constructed as an aggrieved group. In addition to the now familiar Panther narratives, replete with the black cat emblem and the marching cadres, broadcasters produced features sympathizing with the difficulties of police work. An NBC story reported that "there has been almost open war between the police and the Black Panthers" as the camera showed the shattered glass and walls riddled with bullet holes at the group's Oakland headquarters. The Panthers maintained that this action merely reinforced their claims of police lawlessness and brutality, but the press presented an alternative picture.[38]

NBC and CBS each devoted an unprecedented seven minutes to feature stories on the issue, structured around the daily lives of the police. NBC's report was based in Oakland. It began with a portrayal of the racial disparity in the city and the claim that the Black Panthers "hit back at that society by baiting the police." The reporter talked of the Panthers' behavior as "abuse" hurled at the police, as the camera recorded the daily roll call in a police station. Several officers were interviewed, complaining bitterly about being a "whipping post" for blacks' grievances while working for a public and court system who failed to support them in "the fight against crime." One officer bemoaned that he was so tense that he spent the day eating antacids, while another described Oakland's black residents resenting "anything that keeps them from doing what they want to do, right, wrong, lawful or unlawful—if we try to step in their way, then we are at fault." The CBS story was almost identical, except that it took place in New York City. Again, the camera followed policemen from morning roll call to the patrolling of their assignments in Bedford-Stuyvesant, Brooklyn, identified as a "rough beat." The reporter claimed that only 10 percent of the community's residents supported "the militants'" critiques of the police as a foe. Unlike the Oakland story, CBS also interviewed local Panther spokesman Jourdan Ford, who sneered as he used the word *pigs* to describe the police, claiming they "wallow in the mud of hypocrisy and oppression and death and murder."[39]

The intent of the news media was obvious—to create sympathy for embattled police departments, in the process repudiating activists who targeted the law enforcement establishment. In many of these stories, the crisis of African Americans' relations with law enforcement was discussed through the metaphor of the Vietnam War. The phenomena were clearly linked: in both instances, bleeding-heart liberals were making it increasingly difficult for the hardworking, dedicated enforcers to do their jobs, be it in the Southeast Asian jungles or in the inner city. The news media framed these issues as a contest between right and wrong and between order and chaos, echoing the government rhetoric that rationalized the war effort. In a follow-up story on NBC, the crisis was transported to New York City, where a patrolmen's organization formed to take a hard line against groups such as the Black Panthers. The footage of a police roll call, this time in a Brooklyn police station, was a familiar strategy to reinforce the image of law enforcement and restore their position as disciplined defenders of the public. The story ended by mentioning that attorney William Kunstler had filed suit against the New York police, claiming there was an organized "vendetta against black militants in the city." Kunstler, an activist attorney who would defend the Chicago 8 a year later, provided another indication that East Coast cities were becoming key players in the conflicts between black radical activists and the state.[40]

The weekly newsmagazines underscored the trope of an embattled nation. Under the subhead "State of War," *Time* magazine argued that the Panthers' conflicts with the police were rapidly spreading across the country. The report enumerated recent clashes in Seattle, Brooklyn, and San Francisco in which Panthers carried guns and allegedly took pot shots at the police. It was not surprising, according to *Time*, that "police get tough with Panthers," although it recognized that there was "more menace than reality to the Panthers' bloodthirsty bluster." The tone of the article did little to relieve white anxieties, as it warned whites that "moderate" blacks are intimidated by the Panthers, and "quite a few like the way they stand up to white authority and foster black pride." The dominant framing continued the themes of threat and extremism. Similarly, *Newsweek* covered the Panther-police standoff by evoking their mascot in the headline "Oakland: On the Prowl." The article regurgitated a host of clumsy metaphors, as it found considerable humor in the chaos in Oakland. In the magazine's playful language, "[t]he Panthers stayed holed up in their lairs" after the police shooting of their headquarters and "left the prowling" to the police. The "pack's Defense Minister" pleaded for calm, as another Panther said, "This will mean more cats will join the party now." The Black Panthers failed to win much sympathy from the media establishment in this instance; instead it was suggested that the harried and abused Oakland police were justified in striking back at their enemy. The Panthers had promised that if Newton was convicted there would be a tumultuous response to demonstrate black Americans' anger. Instead, Newton pleaded for calm and the Panther leadership kept a low profile to protect them from further police backlash, and some media took the opportunity to subject them to further scorn and ridicule.[41]

With the exception of the San Francisco *Sun-Reporter*, black-owned newspapers and magazines tended to hold the Black Panthers at arm's length, lending credibility to the claim that the group had little support in mainstream black America. These periodicals often catered to a decidedly middle-class audience and aligned themselves with the nonviolent principles of the civil rights movement. African American sociologist

E. Franklin Frazier accused the postwar black press, particularly magazines, of having little political edge or race consciousness, focusing instead on an isolated and insular "Negro social world." By the late 1960s,
many of these publications avidly covered the race relations crises in
their own communities while maintaining a cautious distance from radical black power activists. The most prominent periodicals in this category, the newsweekly *Jet* and the monthly *Ebony*, both owned by
Johnson Publishing, virtually ignored the Panthers during their highly
publicized escapades. Although *Ebony* published several feature articles
on varying aspects of black militancy, there was no mention of the Black
Panthers. In January 1968, *Ebony* saw black power in terms of the successful elections of Carl Stokes as mayor of Cleveland and Richard
Hatcher as mayor of Gary, Indiana.[42]

Aside from some news briefs, *Jet* waited until Newton's trial had
ended to provide an overview of the group. The ten-page article presented the Panthers to its black readers as if they were a recent
phenomenon—there seemed to be little familiarity between the group
and the audience, although it noted that there were chapters in Port-
land, Seattle, Washington, Los Angeles, and Chicago, among others.
The piece, written by *Jet* editor Luis Robinson, reiterated the history
of the group, Newton and Seale's biographies, the ten-point program,
and other basics, followed by an overview of Newton's trial. There was
no new information here; most of the photographs were from the wire
services and mainstream newspapers, and the article considered the
Reverend Earl Neil's support as a "startling aspect of the Panther's acceptance" in Oakland. *Jet* had managed to avoid addressing the Black
Panthers, allowing the white, mainstream press to shape their representations while standing on the sidelines. It wouldn't be until late 1969
that the Panthers became more routine subjects for the magazine, long
after the group had gone through several transformations.[43]

More surprising was the coverage in African American newspapers
that had active Black Panther chapters in their own cities. The *Los Angeles Sentinel* published a few brief articles about the Newton trial, but
readers would learn little about the local chapter until the next year. By
contrast, the New York *Amsterdam News* paid no attention to Newton's
trial or other Panther travails until the Brooklyn confrontation with the
off-duty police officers occurred in September. This incident prompted
the paper to give front-page coverage to the incident and to the New

York Panthers' lawsuit, which was co-sponsored by several organizations. A sidebar on the aftermath of Newton's conviction hinted at the *Amsterdam News*' condescension toward the group, noting that the manslaughter verdict "has sparked a propaganda campaign by his [Newton's] double or nothing militant associates." Like its Los Angeles counterpart, the *Amsterdam News* found little reason to pay attention to the national Panther organization, even while they were being discussed by network television and the *New York Times*. There were no expressions of racial solidarity emanating from these publications; indeed, the Panthers' invisibility could be read as a clear repudiation by some segments of the African American establishment.[44]

But one black journalist who had broken into the all-white media establishment took a keen interest in the Black Panthers as news subjects—a young black reporter named Earl Caldwell. In the early 1960s Caldwell had worked his way from a small newspaper in Pennsylvania to jobs at the *New York Herald Tribune*, the *New York Post*, and then the *New York Times*. In the wake of Newton's trial, he played a significant role in the framing of the Panthers' mediated image. Much of the *Times*' reportage on the Panthers up to this time had been carried out by Wallace Turner, a white journalist who was the Bay Area's chief correspondent. Years earlier Turner used "a panoply of denigrating techniques" when he reported on a series of 1965 anti-war marches in Berkeley, according to Todd Gitlin. Turner relied on "entirely antagonistic statements by authorities" when discussing the student and faculty protesters, while he overtly defended the University of California in the midst of the demonstrations. In his coverage of the Panthers, Turner used the same frames of extremism, deviance, and threat that he had employed in writing about SDS and the new left. His July 20 front-page feature on the Panthers was an awkward attempt to provide some insight into a world about which he knew little—Oakland's racial conflicts and black radical activism. The leadership at the *New York Times*, perhaps for the first time recognizing the importance of the Panthers' story, was ready for a change. "The *New York Times* editor in San Francisco said, 'We have to have a black reporter out here,' and that's how it started," Caldwell recalled.[45]

In a few short years Caldwell had reported on some of the crucial episodes in the racial crises of the decade. He was one of the few African American reporters covering the urban uprisings during the summer of 1967, he was the only reporter on hand when Martin Luther King Jr. was shot in Memphis, and he was fresh from covering the Democratic National Convention in Chicago. Caldwell was intimately aware of African Americans' wariness toward the white press. As a reporter for the *New York Herald Tribune*, he recalled how black audiences at rallies and meetings would protest the presence of white journalists, shouting, "White reporters out. White reporters out." He was also part of the new generation of journalists influenced by the critical culture that surrounded them; these reporters confronted authority with a new level of skepticism and sought to integrate interpretation and investigation into their news work, like in the tradition of the muckrakers. Caldwell was excited about his new assignment and immersed himself in the Panthers' revolutionary culture. His job was to bring an insider's perspective to this increasingly vital story.[46]

"When I first went to California, I was struck by the Panthers' program," said Caldwell. "I'd go to a church in the middle of the night and there would be all of these people working for them. It was truly wonderful; it was a genius model program." Caldwell reminisced how he enjoyed staying up all night with the Panthers in their headquarters or in their homes, listening and talking about politics. "You truly thought you were caught up in something revolutionary," he said. "Their efforts were magical; I was fascinated by it."[47]

Caldwell's first dispatch explored the immediate aftermath of Newton's guilty verdict. While Wallace Turner reported that the Panthers were starting a "propaganda campaign" to win Newton's release, Caldwell spent time in San Francisco's black neighborhoods, measuring the mood among the party faithful. The headline for Caldwell's article, "Angry Panthers Talk of War and Unwrap Weapons," seemed at first glance to conform to the dominant framing strategies—the words *angry*, *war*, and *weapons* were the prevailing signifiers in journalistic commentary. But the article quickly moved beyond these narrow categories to consider the interior life of the Panthers—how they felt, what they thought, and how these thoughts were expressed. Caldwell used the real and metaphorical street as the device that signaled his privileged access into this environment. The lead paragraph opened with a description of the "cluttered storefront they occupy on Fillmore Street" in San Francisco and noted that "in the streets talk of violence persists." The article offered a range of Panther archetypes, from the "tall, lanky youth" who threatened a war if Newton remained in jail to Eldridge Cleaver, who "stayed clear of the war talk that was so prevalent on the streets." Caldwell portrayed the back room of a "slum" apartment, where "a bearded youth in an Afro hair style uncovered a stack of rifles." There was no shock or alarm registered at the presence of the guns; rather, the article presented the weaponry as a fact of inner-city life. He also presented the grim surroundings in which this revolutionary culture festered: "On abandoned buildings and in grimy storefront windows there were old signs advertising a 'Free Huey' rally." In the article's conclusion, he captured street vernacular, quoting one young man who read a newspaper account of Newton's conviction and proclaimed, "Ain't this a bitch?" There was little news in this feature story, but it provided insight about the Panthers without the mocking, condemnation, or thinly veiled fear of black men that was the norm.[48]

Days later, Caldwell's byline appeared again in the Sunday *New York Times* under the headline "Panthers, Treading Softly, Are Winning over Negroes on Coast." This article represented yet another significant shift in the media discourse swirling about the group. For the first time, they were announced with a muted headline that avoided the language of violence and confrontation that usually heralded their appearances. Similarly, Caldwell's prose was measured and deliberate, his intent seemingly to interrupt the frenzied, often hysterical, accounts that followed the Panthers and their exploits. This second article picked up where the first one left off—Caldwell continued to survey the Panthers' territory in Oakland and San Francisco to assess the responses of black community residents. He found that the Panthers were an established presence and that they devoted considerable time to building positive relationships with black churches and community institutions as well as with white activists such as members of the Peace and Freedom Party. He quoted one Panther leader who explained, "We're letting the people see us. We're trying to get people over the fear that we're some kind of monsters." The commentary from ordinary blacks was far from monolithic; one "Negro moderate" remained skeptical about the Panthers' agenda, while one older black Oakland resident expressed outright support following the police assault on their headquarters. Caldwell described the "disillusioned street youths" who were at the core of the party's membership: "They aggressively sell the party's newspaper in the street," he wrote. "They talk its ideology, and they proudly wear the Panther uniform." In so doing, Earl Caldwell was carrying out the edicts of the National Advisory Commission on Civil Disorders—to give average black Americans a voice. He talked with people who would never have confided in a white reporter. Much of the information in the article had been reported previously. The difference was in its matter-of-fact delivery that told audiences that the presence of militants in black communities was not unusual and that black political ideologies could not be conveniently rationalized or defined. Yet Caldwell also conformed to the framing of black activists as either "moderate" or "militant," in effect helping the *New York Times* shift its representational strategies. Gitlin notes that in late 1968, the national news media emphasized a "moderation-as-alternative-to-militancy" frame for anti-war activists as an emphasis emerged that posed respectable movements against those deemed unrespectable. The *Times* seemed to be engaged in a similar struggle over how to handle the Panthers: was their demonization simply fueling their rapid growth, and should their more sensational aspects be downplayed?[49]

Caldwell's Sunday article set the stage for an opinion piece published in the same edition. The editorial was written by another African American reporter, Thomas A. Johnson, who was the first to work as a foreign correspondent for a major daily newspaper. His particular focus during this period was on the black soldiers based in Vietnam, and he brought this perspective to his essay on the Panthers, titled "Black Panthers: Angry Men 'At War' with Society." Johnson recapitulated the refrain "Who are the Black Panthers and what do they want?" and repeated the standard themes used to represent the group: they were "angry young Negroes rejecting 'moderate' approaches to racial problems," and "their primary opponents are local police forces." Unlike Caldwell, Thomas Johnson wrote about the Panthers from a distanced and jaded point of view. He used quotation marks liberally to emphasize his doubts about their claims: Were they really "protecting" their communities? Did they really have "chapters" across the country? Were "white attitudes" responsible for bringing more recruits to the organization? While Caldwell admitted his fascination with the Panthers, Johnson took the position of the worldly black elder who had seen this all before. He presented a compelling argument when he noted the similarities between the young, uniformed Black Panthers and black troops he observed in the elite units in Vietnam. "The appeal of the Panthers to Negro youths is to their manhood, status, pride and the need to protect one's own," wrote Johnson. This argument underscored the prevailing notions—advanced by Newton and Cleaver, among others—that black activism was a result of black masculinity in crisis. He noted that much of black America did not rush to embrace the Panthers, citing an editorial from the NAACP's *Crisis* that condemned "rash rhetoric and guns" as a strategy to confront police violence. The editorial's last words followed the subhead "A Danger," as Johnson argued that the Black Panthers had the potential for "sharpening racial conflicts and leading to more racial shoot-outs between Negroes and the police and perhaps between Negro and white groups." This opinion piece offered the credibility of black authorship while reifying the dominant frames of the Panthers as a threat to be contained by more moderate activism. Earl Caldwell sought to counter the prevailing frames introduced by the *New York Times* eighteen months earlier, and Thomas Johnson aided in their reinforcement.[50]

When the Panthers reappeared in the *New York Times* two weeks later, it was to report that Huey Newton had been sentenced to at least two years in prison for voluntary manslaughter. The article by Wallace Turner conflated Newton's sentencing with a state appeals court decision against Cleaver that might revoke his parole. The remainder of the report discussed the decision by the judge to deny Newton's motion for bail, and Charles Garry's angry declaration: "I think it's a dirty, rotten way to handle this whole matter." For the last time, the Newton trial provided a spectacle that Turner recounted dryly. When Newton was led from the courtroom, he gave a black power salute; "[h]is supporters replied, "Power to the people! Free Huey!' " while Newton's mother "sobbed loudly" in the background. The accompanying photo showed Garry with Eldridge and Kathleen Cleaver looking concerned as they discussed the sentencing. Earl Caldwell's interventions were nowhere in this account.[51]

The image on the front page of the *San Francisco Examiner* more accurately represented the shock that swept through the Black Panthers when Newton was sentenced. The page-filling headline announced, "Newton Sent to Prison." The photo below showed a half-dozen Panthers and their supporters looking stricken and grim-faced as the news was handed down that Newton had been denied a new trial, probation, and bail. The defeat was etched in the expressions of the young black men and women, some wearing the Panthers' signature beret. They had failed to win Huey's release. The *Oakland Tribune* also deemed the Newton decision front-page news, but the only photograph was a head shot of a defiant Newton. The lengthy article included no comments from Newton or his supporters, but it described one woman who "held up a picture of Newton and shouted obscenities at the sheriff's deputies guarding the door when the decision was announced." Thus, the picture presented by the *Tribune* was of an efficient judicial system that "whisked away" Newton to Vacaville prison while his ineffectual attorney stood by. The article also provided excerpts from Newton's probation report, noting it considered him "intense and volatively re-active to social conflicts." The information presented was in careful support of the court's actions; the tone of the *Tribune*'s account was one of smug satisfaction.[52]

After Huey Newton was taken to prison, he disappeared from the news media for several months. The protracted saga of his trial was over and there was nothing more to report. The Black Panthers would resurrect the Free Huey campaign, but it would never again have the vigor of its early days. Yet Cleaver, the Panthers' Minister of Information, would offer plenty of his own exploits to keep the news media interested.

Black Power Erupts At a 1966 Greenville, Mississippi, rally, SNCC (Student Nonviolent Coordinating Committee) leader Stokely Carmichael tells supporters and journalists that Black Power is the new rallying cry for black activism. (© Bob Fitch Photo)

"The BLACK PANTHER PARTY is going forth to make sure the desires and needs of the people are answered."

OCTOBER 1966

BLACK PANTHER PARTY

PLATFORM and PROGRAM

WHAT WE WANT

WHAT WE BELIEVE

FREE HUEY

What We Want The cover of a brochure containing the Black Panthers' ten-point platform and program, which was distributed widely. (Courtesy of University Archives, The Bancroft Library, University of California, Berkeley: 86/157 c 5:2)

The Iconic Huey Newton One of the many posters and illustrations derived from the 1968 photograph that became synonymous with the Black Panthers' image. (Courtesy of University Archives, The Bancroft Library, University of California, Berkeley: 1982.034—E)

Above left: **The Black Panther** A young man reads the party newspaper at a September 1968 rally at Bobby Hutton Memorial Park in Oakland, California. (© 1997 the estate of Ruth-Marion Baruch)

Above middle: **Ministry of Information Bulletin** The Black Panther Party championed numerous activist causes in their publications, including the case of jailed anti-war activists dubbed "The Oakland Seven." (Courtesy of University Archives, The Bancroft Library, University of California, Berkeley: 86/157 c 5:7)

Above right: **Revolution and Education** Pamphlet written by Eldridge Cleaver and sold as an educational and fundraising tool. (Courtesy of University Archives, The Bancroft Library, University of California, Berkeley: 86/157 c 5:3)

Print Culture Panther members sell posters, buttons, flags, and the *Black Panther* newspaper at a 1968 rally at De Fremery Park in Oakland, California. (© 2007 Ilka Hartmann)

(clockwise, from top left)

Woman Warrior A classic graphic image by Minister of Culture Emory Douglas that idealized weaponry while suggesting that women could also be revolutionaries. (San Francisco African American Historical and Cultural Society)

Hutton as Martyr The Black Panther Party and the Peace and Freedom Party joined forces to memorialize Bobby Hutton at events like this one featuring comedian Dick Gregory. (Courtesy of University Archives, The Bancroft Library, University of California, Berkeley: 70/186 c)

The Death of Bobby Hutton Alternative media like the *Berkeley Barb* joined in an angry requiem for the slain Panther. (Author's collection)

(clockwise, from top left)

Bobby and Huey for Office Peace and Freedom Party flyer for 1968 California elections. (Courtesy of University Archives, The Bancroft Library, University of California, Berkeley: 86/157 c 5:2)

Vote for Eldridge Los Angeles Peace and Freedom Party campaign poster. (Courtesy of University Archives, The Bancroft Library, University of California, Berkeley)

Speak to the Masses Bobby Seale atop Panthers' mobile sound unit, flanked by members of the Los Angeles chapter, addresses a "Free Huey" rally at De Fremery Park in Oakland, California, July 1968. (© 1968 Pirkle Jones)

Female Leadership Kathleen Cleaver, Communications Secretary of the Black Panther Party, on the steps of the Alameda County Courthouse in Oakland, California. (Jonathan Eubanks, courtesy of African American Museum and Library at Oakland)

(clockwise, from top left)

"Free Huey" Literature *Black Liberation on Trial,* published at the height of Newton's courtroom saga, argued that his case had become a national referendum on black power. (Courtesy of University Archives, The Bancroft Library, University of California, Berkeley: 86/157 c 5:3)

Soul on Ice The cover of Eldridge Cleaver's celebrated book of essays, published in 1968 to critical acclaim. (Author's collection)

Cover Art The Black Panthers became popular visual subjects for periodicals, including this 1968 issue of *Seattle* magazine. (San Francisco History Center, San Francisco Public Library)

(clockwise, from top left)

Minister of Education Black Panther George Murray, a catalyst for the student strike at San Francisco State University, teaches the *Autobiography of Malcolm X* to an English class in October 1968. (© 1997 the estate of Ruth-Marion Baruch)

Global Figures *The Black Panther* newspaper featured Kathleen and Eldridge Cleaver with their newborn son during their exile in Algeria in 1969. Note stamp at lower left indicating that the newspaper was collected by the San Francisco Police Department. (San Francisco History Center, San Francisco Public Library)

Spectacular Fiction San Francisco artist Ovid Adams conceived of a comic book, titled *The Adventures of Black Eldridge*, to address a youthful audience. (Courtesy of University Archives, The Bancroft Library, University of California, Berkeley: pDT546.262.C541 1971)

Huey Is Free The press mobs Huey Newton and his attorneys, Charles Garry (left) and Faye Stender (right), after his release from prison in August 1970. (© 2007 Ilka Hartmann)

Media Memories Eldridge Cleaver in Paris in 1974 in front of a collection of photos, clippings, and memorabilia. (© David Graeme-Baker)

FROM CAMPUS CELEBRITY
TO RADICAL CHIC

The disquieting news never gets on the air: *Every non-white man, woman and child in America is a Black Panther*. We do not all wear black leather; we do not all boast "Free Huey" buttons, but every one of us is a Black Panther. . . . The "uniformed" Black Panthers proclaim the same rage the rest of us feel but, for one cop-out or another, do not show. Eldridge Cleaver is skilled in exhibiting that rage; I, for one, am skilled in suppressing it.
                                        —Gilbert Moore, *Rage* (1970)

Life magazine reporter Gilbert Moore was one of many Americans—black and nonblack—who found a certain resonance, even reassurance, in the Black Panthers' expressions of social and political rage. From college campuses to northern urban communities, the Black Panther Party tapped into a simmering desire to lash back at power and authority. The most direct evidence of the Panthers' influence was in the organization's monumental growth, which was aided greatly by the news media. The selective framing that cast the group as stylish, gun-toting, menacing, and anti-white struck a receptive chord among budding black radicals around the country. By September, less than two years after the official formation of the group, the *Black Panther* newspaper reported twenty-five chapters in cities across the United States. There were Panthers in Denver, Omaha, Des Moines, Indianapolis, and Philadelphia. In Chicago, a bright, ambitious young activist named Fred Hampton was recruited to the Party by Lennie Eggleston, a member of the Los Angeles chapter. Hampton joined forces with former SNCC member Bobby L. Rush to form the Illinois Black Panther Party in 1968. Today, Rush is a congressman representing Illinois. Chapters in Los Angeles, Seattle, and New York had already engaged in violent encounters with the police and had achieved independent notoriety, such as the September melee between New York Panthers and the police at a Brooklyn courthouse that was covered by the network.[1]

On the other side of the country, Seattle's nascent Black Panther chapter was also attracting publicity. In October, the region's main cultural and newsmagazine made the local Panthers their top story. The whimsical cover featured Captain Aaron Dixon in full Panther garb sitting at the wheel of a Seattle police cruiser. The caption read: " 'Hey Chief, I hear you're looking for black policemen,' " a jibe at the group's struggles with area law enforcement. Seattle's Panther leadership was made up of black student activists from the University of Washington who formed their chapter after attending Bobby Hutton's funeral in Oakland. Bobby Seale flew to Seattle to formally acknowledge the group and give his blessing. The *Seattle* magazine article interviewed several members, told the group's history, described their setting, and attempted to explain their politics. The reporter argued that while their rhetoric and iconography—such as the cartoon depictions of police as pigs—were devastatingly inflammatory, the Panthers were neither racists nor criminals. Rather, they were mostly middle-class youth with a burning desire to improve the conditions of Seattle's relatively small African American community. The Seattle Panthers cataloged numerous instances of police harassment and unlawful imprisonment, and the publicizing of these transgressions seemed to bring a steady stream of new recruits. A black law student interviewed for the article maintained that Seattle's police hoped to break the back of the Panthers and wipe out black militancy in the city. "What they don't realize is that without the moderating influence of these few leaders—especially Aaron Dixon—things would be a lot worse." Seattle, like Oakland, Los Angeles, New York, and other urban centers, seemed to be on a steady course toward a worsening racial climate.[2]

As if to acknowledge and embrace this national scope, news of the Black Panthers beyond California became a regular component of the *Black Panther* newspaper. "We have attracted a cross section of our generation—political activists, warriors, intellectuals," David Hilliard proudly recalled. But Eldridge Cleaver later regretted the rapid recruitment of members and the establishment of far-flung chapters during the frenzied days of the Free Huey campaign. "We knew who the Panthers were, but in order to maximize the number of people we pulled in, we did not argue with people if they put on a black leather jacket or black berets, or said that they were Panthers. They just walked in and said they support Huey Newton and they wanted to join our organization," he told an interviewer in 1969. The fact that these new recruits were drawn by the mass-mediated constructions of the Panthers was troubling. Some of the new Panthers were anxious to emulate their ideological mentors by devoting themselves to the betterment of black communities, while others simply wanted to look and behave like the images they'd seen on television and in the press. "As membership boomed, many recruits fatally confused their [the Panthers'] flamboyant tactics with the substance of their goals," Kathleen Cleaver lamented years later. "Few Panther recruits understood that the theatrical actions were primarily a way of dramatizing a revolutionary message, only the initial step in organizing a movement for social change."[3]

The goal of the Oakland leadership—to maintain a high visibility as a form of strategic protection—was a double-edged sword. The Panthers were caught in a kind of perpetual motion of public relations: they carried out an unrestrained quest for media attention that ultimately allowed the media to control the discourse within which they would be discussed. The Free Huey campaign attracted young adherents and supporters but failed to sway the courts or mainstream opinions in Newton's case. The publicity around Eldridge Cleaver's plight initially kept him out of jail but was quickly overturned. The rapid growth may have been gratifying to the Party leadership and a repudiation of those who condemned their tactics, but it was also dangerous. The new chapters, often beyond the control of the central committee, were left open to state-inspired repression without the protective celebrity of a Newton, Seale, or Cleaver. As Stokely Carmichael remembered in his autobiography, by allowing the media to determine how the Panthers were constructed in mass culture, the membership became "black cannon fodder." The assaults were not only by law enforcement officials brandishing guns but also by covert operatives on the inside of the organization.[4]

During this period it became increasingly apparent to the Panther leadership that they were the objects of an orchestrated surveillance and destabilization plan carried out by the federal government in concert with local police. In the summer of 1967 the FBI received permission from the Johnson administration to focus its attention on the

rise of black radicalism in the United States. This was a logical extension of the surveillance, disinformation, and harassment encountered
by civil rights activists in the South, which, as Julian Bond recalled, included systematic efforts to plant inflammatory material in the press.
Indeed, by the early 1960s, the FBI's counterintelligence agenda, ostensibly targeting the Communist Party, included a Mass Media Program devoted to leaking negative information to the news media. A
Senate Committee investigating the excesses of the American intelligence community noted that "leaking information based on non-
public information to media sources" was a central part of the FBI's
counterintelligence program, known as COINTELPRO. "The FBI has
attempted covertly to influence the public's perception of persons and
organizations by disseminating derogatory information to the press, either anonymously or through 'friendly' news contacts," concluded the
committee, headed by Senator Frank Church. In August 1967 the FBI
launched a new project under the category "Black Hate Groups,"
which sought to "expose, disrupt, misdirect, discredit or otherwise
neutralize" SNCC, the Nation of Islam, the Southern Christian Leadership Conference, and the Revolutionary Action Movement, among
others. This initiative was based on the Cold War rationale that much
of the black power movement was inspired and financed by Communists. Yet, as Kenneth O'Reilly notes, "J. Edgar Hoover focused on the
black menace and not the Red menace during the last of the Great
Society years." SNCC historian Clayborne Carson found that the FBI
had received reports on SNCC meetings as early as 1960, and that
Carmichael, H. Rap Brown, Floyd McKissick, and others were included on a "Rabble Rouser Index," making them targets of intense
espionage activities. It would not be long before the Black Panther
Party would fall under FBI scrutiny as well.[5]

An FBI memo distributed in the winter of 1968 became the death
knell for radical black nationalists, including the Panthers. According
to the memo, COINTELPRO was intended to prevent black power
activists from forming coalitions, to prevent the rise of a leader, such as
Carmichael, who could become a "messiah," and to discredit these
groups before the American public. By September, Hoover had identified the Panthers as "the greatest threat to the internal security of the
country." Two months later the FBI chief called for regional FBI offices to engage in "imaginative and hard-hitting intelligence measures

designed to cripple the BPP." According to one researcher, "Hoover's pursuit of the Black Panther party was unique only in its total disregard for human rights and life itself."[6]

In the San Francisco Bay area, the FBI's Division Five began to scrutinize the Panthers intently, and formulated strategies to foment opposition among the region's black populace. FBI correspondence reported that the division produced a steady torrent of anti-Panther mailings, and starting in September they concentrated on preparing negative reports for "referral to appropriate news media representatives." The local press was already predisposed to critique the words and actions of the Black Panthers. Now they received ready reinforcement from government operatives. It is likely that reporters and editors, like their peers in the southern press earlier in the decade, rebuffed much of the FBI's smear campaigns. But evidence suggests that at least some of the government's fictions sneaked into the media, where it carried the authority of objectively gathered news.[7]

Another of the COINTELPRO strategies was to prevent and disrupt coalitions among radical groups. This tactic had a particularly disastrous effect on the fragile Panther-SNCC alliance, and the news media were an instrument in its undoing. Tensions had been simmering between the leadership of the two groups ever since their association was announced in February 1968. Carmichael was at odds with Cleaver over the Panthers' relationship with the Peace and Freedom Party; he maintained that white activists would only co-opt the black power movement and that the alliance worked against black autonomy and self-reliance. The Panthers were also disappointed with James Forman's efforts to build an audience for their UN appearance in New York. Unbeknownst to all of the actors involved, the FBI planted a stream of rumors and innuendo to worsen the relations. According to Carson, the FBI made anonymous calls to Forman alleging the Panthers were out to "get him." Similarly, Carmichael's mother received calls that the Panthers planned to kill her son, which some believe led to his flight to Africa. The Church committee on U.S. intelligence found an FBI document that boasted about the "pretext phone call" to Carmichael's mother that was part of their larger plan to destabilize the relationship between the groups. When the UN press conference disintegrated, a group of West Coast Panthers allegedly menaced James Forman at gunpoint. Stokely Carmichael recounted this incident as being the final straw leading him to leave the party. "It signaled the beginning of the end for me and the Panthers," he wrote. But Carmichael also noted that the incident was suspicious: "We all understood that these particular Panthers were Cleaver's enforcers, acting on some beef or another between Forman and Cleaver. But, given the disinformation and dirty tricks, who knows for sure? They could easily not have been Panthers at all but hoods in black leather jackets sent in by the COINTELPRO criminals." The SNCC Central Committee ended their association with the Black Panthers shortly after the incident. A month later, the *New York Times* reported that Carmichael had also split with SNCC.[8]

The author of the *Times* piece was another of the newspaper's tiny corps of black reporters, C. Gerald Fraser. Like Earl Caldwell, he had worked his way up the journalism hierarchy, starting at the *Amsterdam News*, then moving to the New York *Daily News* and finally the *New York Times*. Fraser's article on the Carmichael-SNCC split was buried on an inside page and was based on a press release issued by SNCC's program director. The writing was dispassionate, noting that SNCC took pains to praise Carmichael, but that they were "moving in different directions." The end of the article suggested that SNCC was in severe decline, with a membership far below the height of its popularity in the mid-sixties. The cause was implied in the final sentence: "Earlier this year the organization merged with the Black Panthers of California." This statement both contradicted the vigorous denials by Forman, Carmichael, and others that there was no agreed-upon merger, and took as fact the statements made by the Black Panther leadership. Several weeks later, Fraser followed up on this theme with a feature story headlined "S.N.C.C. in Decline After 8 Years in Lead." The title set the tone for the story, which posited a competition for control of the black liberation movement between SNCC and the Black Panther Party. According to the *Times* article, Stokely Carmichael's decision to join the Black Panthers and support their more radical politics spelled the death of SNCC. He joined the civil rights movement in 1961 and served as SNCC chairman in 1966–67. "He [Carmichael] came to believe, it seems, that the Panthers—wise to the ways of the slums, politically sophisticated and organized around the gun—had the nerve and the ability to carry on the struggle in America's urban communities." The article sought to dispel the notion that SNCC was somehow less militant than the Panthers; rather, it had lost its direction once the focus was organizing urban youth in the North rather than rural blacks in the South. The Panthers, in Fraser's narrative, were the real villains.[9]

In the third paragraph, Fraser gave an account of James Forman's violent encounter with the Panthers:

> Members of the Black Panthers walked into James Forman's office at the committee on Fifth Avenue in late July, according to Federal authorities. One of them produced a pistol and put it into Mr. Forman's mouth. He squeezed the trigger three times. The gun went click, click, click. It was unloaded.

The unattributed sources used by Fraser were undoubtedly FBI or police agents, and in telling this story authoritatively, the *New York Times* had played into the hands of COINTELPRO. In his memoirs, James Forman vigorously denied the story. Calling it a "vicious lie," Forman tried in vain to convince Eldridge Cleaver that he was not the source and that this was part of a FBI plot. "It was obvious, I told Cleaver, that the federal government had decided to escalate the conflict between SNCC and the Panthers," he wrote. "The *Times* story was a lie." Cleveland Sellers, another former SNCC leader who was close to Foreman, also denied that the incident with the Panthers ever happened. But at least one scholar has suggested that Foreman was merely covering up the incident in his autobiography. The FBI was also highly successful in turning Panther members into informants. One of the earliest was a high-ranking officer, Earl Anthony, who helped organize the Los Angeles chapter. Anthony wrote two books recounting his experiences, and he maintained that the incident with James Forman did happen, that Eldridge Cleaver was present and party to the acts of intimidation, and that the FBI had it all on tape because Forman's office was bugged. Afterward, the FBI agents allegedly bragged to Anthony that their efforts to goad SNCC and the Panthers into a fight were bearing fruit.[10]

Surveillance of the Panthers was carried out by local officials as well as national law enforcement agencies. For example, San Francisco's Mayor Joseph Alioto collected regular police reports on the Panthers and maintained careful files that monitored their activities, no matter how minor. In one instance, a source told the Mayor's office that the

Black Panthers were trying to recruit high school students, and they provided as evidence a newsletter from a student organization that espoused black power themes. The principal of the junior high school sent Alioto a copy of the *Black Panther* that had been confiscated from a student, with a note complaining that "this is what we are up against in some cases." San Francisco operatives kept track of every rally, press conference, meeting or speaking engagement that even remotely involved the Panthers.[11]

Fraser's article in the *Times*, a lengthy feature written in a languorous style, was based almost entirely on unnamed sources. Indeed, the only person referred to by name was Eldridge Cleaver, who called SNCC members "black hippies" in a statement that had appeared many times previously in print. It was not at all apparent that the quote came from a direct interview with Cleaver. That Carmichael and others close to the organizations initially believed the rumor indicates that it was circulating long before the *Times* article. The *New York Times*, perhaps unwittingly, was the conduit of government information intended to discredit the Panthers and undermine the organization.[12]

A new frame emerged in the representations of the Black Panthers: they were to be seen as the heirs to the black freedom struggle, having supplanted SNCC in the national arena. This was an underlying argument of the *New York Times* article, but it was also reflected in other media. The Bay Area press relegated most stories about the civil rights struggle to inside pages while devoting massive space to the conflicts closer to home. The Black Panthers increasingly dominated the content of many alternative periodicals as well. In *The Movement*, which was founded in 1964 as the newsletter of the Bay Area Friends of SNCC, there was less and less news about SNCC and events in the South, while Newton, Cleaver, Seale, and the various Panther travails filled the paper's front pages. A sign of the Panthers' ever-expanding reach was the extent to which they were taken up as revolutionary models by student activists. Nowhere was this more apparent than on college and university campuses across the country.

Although the Black Panthers' origins were rooted in their identification with the black underclass, they also had ties to the student movements in the Bay Area and beyond. Newton and Seale formulated the Panthers' programs while members of the Soul Students Advisory Council at Merritt College in Oakland. Sproul Plaza at the University of California at Berkeley was where they sold copies of Mao Tse-Tung's *Little Red Book* and gave some of their earliest speeches. These ties intensified during the spring and summer of 1968. The alliances with the Peace and Freedom Party and with SNCC—both student-based organizations—meant that a significant proportion of their support and manpower came from college-age activists. Students had carried the Free Huey campaign beyond northern California, chanting Panther slogans at anti-war rallies and displaying posters of Huey Newton in their dorm rooms and apartments. The Panthers were poised to appropriate higher education as another forum for their message. Academia would give them new intellectual and political legitimacy and might bridge the void between marginalized, inner-city youth and their peers on college campuses. In particular, these activities would further Eldridge Cleaver's celebrity status; he already had a reputation as a journalist and a best-selling author. Being a college instructor and popular figure on the lecture circuit added to the promotion of Cleaver as an organic intellectual.

The Panther leadership was cognizant that college students represented a vast, potentially receptive audience. In the early part of the decade, brave and determined black college students confronted southern segregation through sit-ins and marches beginning with Greensboro, North Carolina. By the 1960s, the focus had shifted from integrating public institutions in the South to the internal politics of academia. The Afro-American Association, founded in 1960 at UC Berkeley, was one of the first groups to address the particular experiences of black college students and to demand a transformation of the curriculum. Huey Newton and Bobby Seale were politicized, in part, by the association's activism on the Merritt College campus. The Free Speech Movement at Berkeley emerged in October 1964 when the university denied students the right to solicit support and funding for civil rights workers on campus property. The subsequent protests and sit-ins at the campus's Sproul Plaza set the stage for militant student critiques of institutional authority. A year later, students at Berkeley were holding round-the-clock anti-war teach-ins as legions of youth around the country became intent on rejecting the Cold War consensus that had bound the country together in the previous decade.[13]

However, it was black power theorists Malcolm X and Stokely Carmichael who laid a different groundwork by arguing that the path to black liberation lay, in part, with learning black history—the narratives of intellectual, political, and cultural development that were largely ignored in western education. Black nationalists such as Maulana Karenga and Amiri Baraka cut through the integrationist rhetoric that infused liberal education—they extolled African-based knowledge and imagined separate, autonomous communities that would operate independent of the white world. The link between black power and the study of the black experience influenced the increasing numbers of black Americans attending college as well, inspiring a nationwide movement to institute Black Studies and Third World Studies programs into the curriculum. According to William Van Deburg, "black students' expressions of rage at 'the system' reflected their membership in a vital, militant youth culture that sought self-definition and power for all college-age Americans." By 1968, black students led protests at historically black institutions such as Howard University and at majority-white schools including the University of Massachusetts and Cornell. They demanded black professors, black student organizations, separate black housing facilities, a voice in campus affairs, and permanent courses about black America and the African Diaspora.[14]

The Black Panthers capitalized on and were part of this fervor in the Bay Area, and the local news media often conflated them with the rise of student militancy. The party's leaders were regular speakers at area schools during the Free Huey campaign. In the spring of 1968, for example, Bobby Seale gave an incendiary talk at San Francisco State College. According to the local press, Seale exhorted a mostly white, cheering crowd to contribute money to Newton's defense. The *San Francisco Chronicle* emphasized the predictable Panther rhetoric: Seale referred to whites as "honkies" and the police as "pigs," and declared that blacks "must unify around the gun," the paper reported. The story was illustrated with a photo of Seale speaking behind a podium adorned with a poster of H. Rap Brown. The caption read, "Black Panther Chairman Bobby Seale: 'Honkies' heard some tough talk." This narrative, and others that followed, argued that the Black Panthers had invaded another space once reserved for the nation's elite—first the state legislature, then the courts, now the halls of higher learning.[15]

Increasingly, the Panthers were using their access to higher education as a platform to reach a different audience. Harry Edwards, a sociology instructor and former student at nearby San Jose State College, had earned a reputation as a black power activist as the organizer of United Black Students for Action on that campus in 1967. The group was formed by black students, many former athletes, who were dismayed by the institution's racial climate. "It suddenly dawned on us that the same social and racial injustices and discrimination that had dogged our footsteps as freshmen at San Jose were still rampant on campus," he wrote. Edwards led a successful student protest that culminated in threats to halt the university's opening football game. The school's administration agreed to meet with the students and concede to their demands, including an end to housing discrimination on campus and denouncing racism in the university's fraternity system. Governor Ronald Reagan criticized the school's president, accusing him of yielding to student intimidation. In the summer of 1968 Edwards, as one of the founders of the Olympic Project for Human Rights, urged black athletes to boycott the Olympic Games in Mexico City.[16]

Edwards also announced that he was joining the Panthers during a carefully orchestrated press conference at the offices of the San Francisco Sun-Reporter. He used the venue of the black press to urge other black professionals to follow his lead, declaring, "You can no longer ignore the Black Panthers." The San Francisco Chronicle covered the story and devoted a paragraph to a physical description of Edwards, painting a fearsome image of this black scholar, who was completing a doctorate in sociology at Cornell University. He was "at six-foot-eight a former basketball star" wearing the Panther uniform of beret and dark glasses, and his voice manifested an enormous range of emotions, "[i]mpassioned, sarcastic, sorrowful, angry, anguished and finally desperate." These were not the usual qualities associated with the stereotype of the tweed-jacketed white male professor, who was expected to exude an erudite confidence. Edwards was quoted as repudiating nonviolence in the wake of Martin Luther King Jr.'s assassination, telling reporters, "I personally encourage violence, until somebody shows me a better way. Non-violence essentially has not worked." In this statement, Harry Edwards gave a new face to the Black Panther Party. Here was a scholar who was deeply politicized and committed to transforming the racial climate of the university. Edwards, like many of his contemporaries, saw no contradictions between his advocacy of black power and his role as an academic. Indeed, the academy was the staging

ground for some of the era's radical politics. Edwards, who was emerging as a media figure in his own right, helped to insert the Black Panthers into the university arena. While Edwards was speaking in San
Francisco, a group of white university professors staged a press conference at nearby Stanford to criticize the police and judicial harassment
of the Black Panthers.[17]

On the heels of the black student protests at San Jose State College,
conflicts involving the Black Panthers erupted at UC Berkeley and at
San Francisco State. In early September, as the Panther faithful awaited
the verdict in Huey Newton's trial, a brief notice in the *Oakland Tribune* announced that Eldridge Cleaver had been invited to teach an experimental course at Berkeley that was developed by a student group
and approved by a committee of the academic senate. The course, titled "Humanization and Regeneration in the American Social Order,"
was to be led by regular faculty and feature ten weekly ninety-minute
talks by Cleaver on "the meaning of blackness." One of the graduate
students who developed the course argued that it was a direct result of
the struggles of the Free Speech Movement, which culminated in students having the right to propose experimental courses for the Berkeley campus. The San Francisco press also decided that the prospect of
Eldridge Cleaver as college lecturer was newsworthy, even sensational.
The *Examiner* reported that Cleaver was to be involved in the course—
"[t]hat is, if he can find the time between court dates and can manage
to remain out of jail," the article noted. The paper's thinly veiled contempt for Cleaver, and for the university for developing experimental
courses, helped to elevate this relatively minor matter into a statewide
controversy.[18]

This issue typified the nation's polarization as depicted in popular
media: the black militant celebrity Eldridge Cleaver pitted against the
rising star of American conservativism, Ronald Reagan. The former
actor had been elected to the California governorship in 1966 and inaugurated an agenda of government cutbacks and zero tolerance for
anti-war and student protests. Reagan was the personification of the
conservative backlash of the 1960s, reacting against Johnson's Great Society programs and arguing for a return to law and order. In this view,
the urban riots and student uprisings were evidence of an immoral,
criminally inclined youth culture rather than of underlying social problems. Part of Reagan's election platform was based on cleaning up the

University of California campuses, seen as hotbeds of protest and countercultural excess. During his election campaign, Reagan singled out Berkeley as bringing shame to the state's university system. The idea that Cleaver would lecture at Berkeley played into Reagan's hands as a direct challenge to his authority as the protector of state institutions. The stage was set for a protracted battle.

Within a week, state officials were in an uproar. Bay Area newspapers published stories that Reagan and the state senate vowed to halt the course, and they threatened to censure the University of California Regents if it was allowed to proceed. The *Examiner*'s story, headlined "Reagan Protests: UC Ban Asked of Cleaver," noted that the governor held a press conference to denounce the decision to hire Cleaver as a lecturer, calling him an "advocate of racism and violence" and saying his potential lectureship was "an affront, an insult to the state of California." The press highlighted the notion that Reagan was using this issue as a means to flex his political muscle and assert his influence over the state's university system. When the governor was reminded that state funds were not being used to teach the experimental class, he responded: "I don't really care if they are printing the money in the basement. It is on the university campus." This attempt by Berkeley students to exercise their influence, and by Cleaver to find a new forum for his political agenda, quickly became a media event. It satisfied the media's need to keep the Black Panthers in the public eye, and to provide tie-ins to state politicians in an election year. As the issue played itself out, it became increasingly clear that the press was milking it for any sensational outcome, giving prominent coverage to the inflammatory rhetoric coming from the key actors. Both Cleaver and Reagan seized on this opportunity to gain more visibility and further hone their reputations— as a fearless foe of the white establishment or as a conservative politician capable of holding radical forces at bay.[19]

The issue burst onto the front pages of the Bay Area press, which anticipated a dramatic confrontation. The *Examiner* used the language of conflict when it announced, "Crisis at UC over Cleaver: 2 Sides Face Showdown." The article summarized the reasons why it deemed the issue so important: on one hand, "taxpayers and Sacramento legislators condemned the hiring of a 'jailbird' and agitator to teach UC students," while on the other hand, "students and faculty saw it as a threat to academic freedoms hard won during the Free Speech Movement."

Cleaver's name appeared in boldface type at the top of the *Chronicle*'s front page the next day as well, with the headline "Assembly Raps UC Regents on Cleaver." The paper devoted substantial space to a story on the close vote by the state assembly to censure the Regents. In the adjacent column, the paper featured a story about a bloody battle between students and Army troops at the National University in Mexico on the eve of the Olympic Games. The Mexican crisis, which was the culmination of a lengthy student strike, suggested the possibility that such violence might occur closer to home.[20]

The *Oakland Tribune*, in a succession of front-page articles, also followed every nuance of Cleaver's confrontation with the University of California. Headlines such as "Monetary Problems, Cleaver Issue Occupy U.C. Regents" and "Cleaver Problem Confronts U.C. Regents at L.A. Meet" promised to further the mediated Panther drama, with state officials providing a barrage of provocative rhetoric. Reagan declared that Cleaver "[s]hould not give even one lecture" for the university, while the chairman of the Alameda County Board of Supervisors told the Regents that Cleaver was "totally incompetent to lecture at Berkeley," according to the *Tribune*. The Regents' meetings were filled to overflowing, and Cleaver's supporters and detractors bombarded the committee with letters. The meetings were dominated by technical discussion of administrative matters, but they gave Cleaver considerable visibility as his fitness to teach was examined. Some Regents argued that Cleaver's criminal record immediately disqualified him from appearing in the classroom, while others countered that he showed considerable talent and eloquence in his book *Soul on Ice*. One Regent declared the book to be a work "of great mastery, of great significance and of great sensitivity," the *Tribune* reported. A Berkeley student attending the meetings told reporters that rejecting Cleaver's lectureship would galvanize students and faculty into a new spirit of protest.[21]

The front pages of both the Saturday *San Francisco Examiner* and the *Oakland Tribune* announced that after three days of heated debate the Regents had voted to limit Cleaver to one lecture rather than the scheduled ten. The body also censured a faculty committee at Berkeley for improperly structuring the course, and instituted a rule that guest lecturers offering more than one talk must have a formal faculty appointment. Reagan's efforts to prohibit Cleaver's appearance were only partly successful, and the governor hinted at possible retaliation through state funding for the university. Cleaver held a press conference to announce that the Regents' decision was a partial victory in that it defied the governor's goal of denying him the opportunity to speak at Berkeley. The Panthers' Minister of Information was uncharacteristically muted in his response, but the Regents' decision elicited an outcry from several faculty groups, who said it undermined faculty authority and squelched free speech on campus. The press' avid coverage of this controversy signified their interest in keeping the Black Panthers in the limelight. The story itself was relatively tame: there were no violent encounters with police, no courtroom maneuvers, and no massive protests by uniformed Panthers with fists held high. But the news media clearly expected it to explode into a storm of student demonstrations.[22]

Only the *Sun-Reporter* addressed the broader implications of the debate over Cleaver's role as instructor. In a terse editorial, the black weekly newspaper argued that Reagan and the state administration sought to interfere with academic freedom and "assert political control upon the great University." The paper argued that students were able to sort the issue out by themselves, and that higher education had a responsibility to air a range of views. Eldridge Cleaver received the *Sun-Reporter*'s endorsement as well. The editorial declared that he was a fine candidate to give authoritative lectures on racism and that Cleaver's presence would help educate young people about the nation's core social problems. This made it apparent that the governor's tactics did not impress many in the Bay Area's black establishment.[23]

During the next few weeks the issue dragged on, pitting conservative state officials against students and faculty at the university, with the Regents caught in the middle. The state superintendent of public instruction, Max Rafferty, threatened a full investigation of the University of California, and he announced his intention to cut the terms of the Regents. Meanwhile, public figures such as Dr. Benjamin Spock, as well as assorted faculty, vowed to fight the decision. It was a page-one story when two thousand Berkeley students gathered on the campus to demand that the Cleaver decision be rescinded. They held a press conference during which they declared their intention to defy the Regents and have Cleaver lecture as originally planned: "We will offer the course as approved notwithstanding the actions of the Regents," one professor told the local press. There were vague promises of protests,

emergency meetings, circulating petitions, and threats from the speaker
of the state assembly, Jesse Unruh, that voters would overturn a bond
measure designated for construction on university and college campuses across the state. Unruh repeated the charges against Cleaver popularized by the news media: he was someone who preached violence
and racial hatred, and Cleaver's student and faculty supporters were
"irresponsible agitators." Reagan charged that Cleaver and the student
committee that designed the course were "deliberately provoking an
altercation between the Regents and state government," the *Tribune*
reported.[24]

The *Oakland Tribune* added its voice to the debate by siding with
Reagan and his administration. A lengthy editorial called the Berkeley
students and professors "doctrinaire" and claimed their main objective
was to spur confrontation with authority. "Many of the activists have
the avowed purpose of overthrowing 'the establishment,' educational,
political or economic, existing in our country today." The editorial declared the university was "a place for learning and not for continual
churning" and described Cleaver by excerpting several sentences from
Soul on Ice that revealed his history as a convicted rapist. The *Tribune*
expressed further outrage that "another self-appointed advisor to the
students on the Berkeley campus," Black Panther leader Bobby Seale,
had encouraged students to take over the university. "The only way
they can stop you is by sending pigs into the classroom," the editorial
quoted Seale as saying. The Black Panthers were a backdrop to this
scenario; the only affront they had committed was to have garnered the
endorsement of students and professors. Nevertheless, the *Tribune* re-
asserted the frame of condemnation that first had been articulated by
the news media nearly eighteen months earlier. In the view of the *Tribune* editorial, the eventual outcome of the Cleaver issue was a referendum on the university, the government, and the state's character. These
were high stakes, and the newspaper was determined that the Black
Panthers not win. The *Sun-Reporter* responded with an editorial of its
own, arguing that the Regents' acquiescence to the governor's political
agenda was a "flagrant invasion of academic freedom." As with its earlier commentary, the *Sun-Reporter* was far more perceptive about the
implications of this debate than the mainstream press was willing to
admit. The editorial noted that while many might be wary of defending the rights of a controversial figure such as Cleaver, this was exactly

the point. "The test of greatness, even for a university, depends upon its capacity to defend freedom," the *Sun-Reporter* maintained. The region's prominent black newspaper kept up the critique for several weeks. Carlton Goodlett, publisher of the *Sun-Reporter*, participated in the California Negro Leadership Conference that condemned the actions of the University of California. The *Sun-Reporter* ran a lengthy editorial that reproduced the conference's assessment, denouncing the university for continuing to practice "racism in higher education," especially in its employment practices.[25]

The day after issuing this declaration, the local press had different news to report—Huey Newton was sentenced to two to fifteen years in prison after being denied probation. The front-page headlines brought back into stark relief the real, life-altering issues facing the Black Panther leadership. As Newton was whisked away to the state prison at Vacaville, Eldridge Cleaver had reason to worry about his freedom as well. The state district court of appeals was about to rule on whether his parole was to be revoked. If so, Cleaver too would wind up in prison. He didn't wait long. Just hours after Newton's sentencing, the appeals court ruled that Cleaver had violated his parole in the April shoot-out with police. The news was announced on the front page of the *Oakland Tribune* in an article headlined "Court Cuts Off Freedom for Cleaver." The order would not be enforced for sixty days, and Cleaver vowed to fight it. But time was running out for another Panther leader, as the *Tribune* made clear. One of the national newsmagazines also made a point of noticing that both Newton and Cleaver could be out of circulation for a long time. *Time* magazine's headline, "Penning the Panthers," was a characteristic use of alliteration and pun. The article was a straightforward account of Newton's trial, noting that the Black Panthers "promised violent vengeance if he were convicted," but his attorney's planned appeals "helped mute their wrath." The photo illustrating the story showed a handsome, clean-cut Newton in sport jacket and black turtleneck as he sat in the Alameda County jail. Newton appeared calm and composed in the photograph, but the caption repeated the phrase "with muted wrath," as if to warn readers not to be fooled by his demeanor. The article also reported on the court of appeals ruling to reverse Cleaver's parole. He was described as "a jail-educated militant of abrasive eloquence," and suggested the court decision was an embarrassment given Cleaver's high visibility. Increasingly, the news media seemed to breathe a collective sigh of relief that the threat of the Black Panthers was being contained by the courts. Yet *Time* ended its report on an ambiguous note: "For the Panthers, with two of their leaders on ice, it was a time of barely throttled fury." The Panthers may have toned down their angry rhetoric, but *Time* registered the fear that their expressions of black rage continued to simmer and had yet to fully erupt.[26]

Despite the disappointing news, Cleaver continued his critique of the University of California with relish. He appeared on a panel at the Irvine campus, where he lambasted state officials to the delight of the audience and the press. The *Examiner* headlined the event "Cleaver Rants at Whites in Irvine." The Panthers' Minister of Information made fun of Governor Reagan and the Regents, saying, "The buffoons said I could deliver only one lecture. I am going to deliver twenty," according to the *Tribune*. On this occasion, the Oakland newspaper devoted an entire page to assorted developments in the story. Cleaver's defiant attitude toward the university was highlighted, accompanied by an Associated Press photo of the panel discussion, which attracted two thousand onlookers. Two sidebar articles offered a clear repudiation— one, headlined "Cleaver Course Homeless," noted that the Berkeley academic senate had not requested a room for his lectures, while another, "Turndown: Court Bars Cleaver as Candidate," reported that the California Supreme Court ruled him ineligible to be on the Peace and Freedom Party ticket because he did not meet the state requirement of being at least thirty-five years of age. The *Oakland Tribune* appeared to respond to each of Cleaver's acts of insubordination with prominently placed stories that undermined his positions and exposed his lack of power.[27]

During the month of September 1968, the *Oakland Tribune* published fourteen front-page articles on the Cleaver controversy, while the *San Francisco Examiner* put out seven. The publicity helped make Eldridge Cleaver an increasingly popular draw on college campuses. Stanford University invited him to give a series of weekly lectures during the fall term. He read poetry at San Francisco State College, spoke at a conference at Santa Clara University, rallied crowds at Sacramento State College, and warned students at American University in Washington, D.C., that America was on the brink of becoming another Nazi Germany. As Cleaver's star rose, inviting him to be a campus speaker was a way for students and faculty to register an immediate and recognizable voice of protest. His appearance at Stanford finally attracted momentary attention from the national news media as well. The *New York Times* reported that Cleaver "derided" Reagan and presidential candidates Richard Nixon, Hubert Humphrey, and George Wallace during his speech. The *Times* reproduced Cleaver's incendiary rhetoric, which had been heard often in the Bay Area but had the ring of novelty for East Coast readers. According to the paper, Cleaver said, "Ronald Reagan is a punk, a sissy and a coward, and I challenge him to a duel to the death or until he says Uncle Eldridge." The newspaper also reported that a group of black community leaders in the Bay Area, headed by the *Sun-Reporter*'s publisher, Carlton Goodlett, was demanding that the University of California hire black and other minority administrators and employees. This was an expression of concern about racial discrimination at the university uttered by individuals not easily labeled as militant provocateurs. The material was deemed newsworthy by the *New York Times* but not by the *Oakland Tribune*.[28]

At the same time that the *Times* article appeared, a meeting of the University of California academic senate set off another round of student protests and public appearances by Cleaver. Berkeley's Afro-American Student Union and a group of black faculty and administrators staged a protest in Sproul Plaza, home to the Free Speech Movement, during which they accused the university of using token efforts to increase their numbers, and they called for the creation of a Department of Afro-American Studies. They also maintained that the Regents' ruling had less to do with Cleaver than with squelching black dissent. "It has only to do with the way white folks feel about black folks," the group said in a prepared statement. The next day, Cleaver appeared in the same location to give a speech that was widely covered by the local news media. "Could this be a classroom out here? I always say that when they shut you away from the regular channels, when they lock the doors, when they won't let you into the building, you have no other recourse than to take it to the streets, take it to the plaza," Cleaver declared to a cheering throng. These words exemplified Cleaver's utility in this era of heated conflict between universities and their students. In his case, institutional authorities had literally locked the doors to prevent his appearances. But the lockout was metaphorical as well. College students, particularly African Americans, felt excluded from the nation's

200 FRAMING THE BLACK PANTHERS

sites of authority—the government, the military, and education, among others—and often their greatest power lay in their ability to threaten discord and disruption. The nation's young people were demanding a voice in the body politic, and in this instance Cleaver was both an enabler and a symbol. If the principles of free speech in the academy had any meaning, he suggested, then radical voices such as his should be heard even in the face of fierce opposition from the governor and his allies.[29]

Even the national black weekly *Jet* could not resist reporting on the war of words between Cleaver and Reagan. The magazine, which had paid scant attention to the Panthers, took delight in the idea that "the drumbeat of ridicule Cleaver heaped upon the governor" found a broad audience. Speaking before a crowd of five thousand at the University of California at Los Angeles, Cleaver challenged Reagan to a duel with any weapon, "ranging from a knife to a marshmallow." *Jet* noted that at the end of the address, students in the audience joined him in his favorite chant, "[F]——k Ronald Reagan."[30]

The *Oakland Tribune* made the Cleaver case a cause célèbre, giving it a high profile with an almost frantic tone. Letters to the editor consistently supported the paper's critiques of the Regents and lambasted Cleaver and the Black Panthers, and the paper sought every opportunity to reinforce its stand. One particularly telling instance was the publication of an editorial from the *San Diego Union*, which declared that the Regents' decision to allow Cleaver to give one lecture was a move in support of "the forces of destruction." The editorial likened the conflict to a "high noon" confrontation in which the Regents were weak-kneed and Cleaver's supporters were purveyors of blackmail and harassment. Cleaver was a "racist," a "convict," and a "self-styled rapist" who uttered "language too foul to print or broadcast." In the *Union's* view, this was disastrous for the state's university system, which might have "hell to pay" if it failed to stand up to militant forces. The message was clear: the university must serve as a bulwark against radicals such as the Black Panthers. SDS and other antiwar advocacy groups had already overrun higher education. Now black militants were a powerful threat. David Hilliard recalled that despite the wails of consternation emanating from newsrooms across the state, students were clearly enamored by the defiant representations of Cleaver. "The students adore him. It's fall 1968, and every-one is jumping on the revolutionary bandwagon . . . a model for re-volt emerges: revolutionary action, rebellion in the black community, support actions in the student/youth areas that surround the great universities, cities coming to a halt, working- and middle-class peo-ple becoming radicalized."[31]

In the end, the University of California found a compromise to stave off the possibility of violent protests, in the process robbing the news media of more sensational material. Max Rafferty, the state su-perintendent of public instruction, who was also a Republican senato-rial candidate, used the Cleaver issue as a political platform; he raised the level of hysteria by threatening to take away faculty credentials and state funding if Cleaver was allowed to teach for the university. This all made the front page of the *San Francisco Examiner*. The university's president and Berkeley's chancellor stepped in to quell the crisis, per-suading the campus' academic senate to back off from a confronta-tional outcome, and they eventually convinced the students to do the same. The officials argued that the Cleaver controversy was costing the university the support of moderates, who were joining with right-wing conservatives over the matter. Thus, the Cleaver course was con-tinued so as not to violate academic freedom, but it would not carry any course credit. This did not entirely mollify the students, some of whom threatened to seize a university building for the course. But they eventually backed down. The start of the course was anti-climactic, al-though played up by the press. A skyline head on the front page of the *Examiner* shouted, "Cleaver Gets a Poor Turnout at UC." According to the report, the classroom was only two-thirds full, and Cleaver's lecture was dry rather than polemical, suggesting this was a phenomenal disap-pointment. For the press, it was also a self-fulfilling prophecy. Bay Area newspapers beat the drums of student dissent and hoped that Cleaver would deliver more controversial rhetoric during the course, so as to continue the discord. Instead, the issue gradually faded.[32]

But Eldridge Cleaver's ability to integrate humor and satire into his biting commentary on race and power in the United States continued to make him an irresistible news subject. The fall election season was winding down, and in the final days the national media turned its at-tention to the numerous minor-party candidates. Among the most photogenic and articulate of the group was Cleaver. An article in the Sunday *New York Times Magazine* offered a survey of the colorful figures who were independent presidential candidates. While Hubert Humphrey, Richard Nixon, and George Wallace dominated the news media's political conversation, the *Times* writer noted that the general climate of dissent and dissatisfaction had produced nearly two dozen people who sought a national platform. Right-wing candidates were in short supply, as most groups threw their support behind Wallace's campaign. The Socialist Workers Party, the Universal Party, the Prohibition Party, and the Berkeley Defense Group were only some of those representing alternative points of view. The Peace and Freedom Party candidates were among the most visible—and legitimate—and Cleaver was the anchor for this category. The writer supported Cleaver's right to use the electoral process to state his positions: "the war in Vietnam is an imperialist venture which must be liquidated and that the black people of America demand 'liberation.' " Notwithstanding the use of quotation marks that questioned the viability of black American's oppression, the article was evenhanded in its quest to represent the views of the individuals discussed. Cleaver was compared to his Peace and Freedom Party competitor Dick Gregory, whose followers were described as "middle-class liberals." By contrast, Cleaver attracted the support of "upper-class and lower-class radicals," certainly a broad spectrum. The generally lighthearted piece was designed to both inform and entertain; the underlying thesis was that only the nation's most disenchanted voters might throw away the franchise on such marginal characters. It could all be summed up in the headline: "If You Don't Like Hubert, Dick or George, How About Lar, Yetta or Eldridge?" Once again, Eldridge Cleaver was a symbol of the political disarray of the late 1960s, which allowed an ex-con radical black nationalist to have such a public voice.[33]

The networks also found considerable humor in the minor-party candidates vying for the presidency. The *CBS Evening News* broadcast a five-minute feature story, designed to lighten the otherwise deadly serious commentary on the upcoming elections, and Cleaver received substantial airtime. After a brief introduction, the opening sequence showed Cleaver at a podium delivering his characteristically sarcastic evaluation of the main presidential candidates. "You have a choice between oink, oink, and oink," he told a group of cheering supporters.

The voice-over gave viewers a quick impression of his resume—most salient was that he opposed the war in Vietnam, that he had served time in prison, and that he was author of *Soul on Ice*. "His speeches drip contempt for the white power structure," noted the reporter, "but un- like some black militants, he believes in working with sympathetic whites." The report included a thirty-second interview with Cleaver, dressed in a dark suit, who appeared charming, erudite, and eminently cynical before the camera. Like the *New York Times*, this television broadcast was particularly interested in highlighting the differences be- tween Cleaver and Dick Gregory, who were conveniently constructed as the "bad Negro" and the "good Negro." "Where Eldridge Cleaver denounces police as pigs, Dick Gregory advocates increasing the salaries of police," the reporter narrated. ABC News also did a five- minute report on the minority candidates, as if obliged to make a sym- bolic nod to the political diversity they represented. Once again, there were several shots of Cleaver, with a brief reference to his platform. The report ended cynically, noting that in the previous presidential election, minor-party candidates garnered only 0.4 percent of the vote. No news story considered the possibility that the appearance of Cleaver and Gregory on the Peace and Freedom ticket would attract African American voters previously lost to the electoral process. Nor was there any mention of the community-based voter registration drives conducted by the Panthers and PFP workers across the country. What was salient and salable was the specter of Cleaver upstaging Ronald Reagan or ridiculing Hubert Humphrey, making him the black militant audiences might both laugh at and fear. Projecting him in a humorous light helped to dismantle his construction as the fear- some black buck, thus containing whatever political and cultural power was under his control. The commodification of Eldridge Cleaver was almost complete.[34]

Cleaver failed to earn more than a handful of votes in the election, but he continued to win popular attention and praise. An article in the mass-market *Saturday Evening Post* once again recounted the Panther narrative with a focus on the charismatic Cleaver. The author de- scribed accompanying Cleaver on a transcontinental flight during which the Panther Minister of Information charmed the flight atten- dant and belied the apprehensions of the all-white passengers. "You don't have to like him, but if you care about the division that is tearing us apart, you must know him," wrote Don Schanche. "For one thing, he is the only genuinely militant black extremist in the public eye today who deeply and honestly likes white men, and believes the two races can get along." Cleaver had managed to usurp the legions of black power activists alongside him by capitalizing on white Americans' fear of black anger. He was conveniently elevated to serve as the reliable and authoritative source on all African American grievances. Perhaps the biggest tribute to Cleaver's power to captivate segments of white America came when it was announced that *Soul on Ice* had made the *New York Times'* top ten list of outstanding books.[35]

While Eldridge Cleaver was advancing his career at the University of California, an institution across the San Francisco Bay was on the verge of a similar crisis, one that satisfied the journalistic yearnings for conflict and violence. A brief article in the *San Francisco Examiner* reported that George Murray, the Panthers' Minister of Education, had been rehired by San Francisco State College as a teaching assistant in the English Department. Murray, a graduate student, had worked the previous year in the same capacity. The short piece, buried on page five, emphasized that Murray had recently returned from an unauthorized trip to Cuba and that the hiring of Murray was routine. This article made two things clear: the local news media had multiple informants who reported on any minor occurrence involving the Panthers, and the press expected that Murray's presence, like that of Cleaver, was going to erupt into a bigger story. Three days later, it seemed apparent that the news media were instigating discord when the *Examiner* published an article with the headline "Militant Black: S.F. State Puts Admirer of Mao on Teaching Staff." According to the *Examiner*, Murray held a press conference during his trip to Cuba, and told the national newspaper *Granma*, "Our thinking is inspired by Che Guevara, Malcolm X, Lumumba, Ho Chi Minh and Mao Tse-tung." In a Red-baiting gesture, the *Examiner*'s reporter made sure to note that *Granma* was "the official organ of the Central Committee of the Communist Party of Cuba." The discourse generated by this minor story was clearly intended to inspire outrage among readers and university officials.[36]

The reporter covering this developing saga at the *Examiner*, Phil Garlington, had an ideal vantage point from which to gain access to sources inside San Francisco State. Just a year before, he had been the city editor of the college's student newspaper, the *Golden Gater*, while posing as an undergraduate. In fact, Garlington was already on the staff of the *Examiner*. This reporter carried out an ongoing political vendetta against the Panthers' supporters at the college while ensuring a steady stream of copy for his employer. According to *The Movement*, in the spring of 1967 Garlington ran for student body president on a conservative slate of candidates that was endorsed by the *Gater*, a clear conflict of interest. Garlington was profiled in the *Golden Gater* with a headline that called him a rogue politician. Part of his platform, according to the campus newspaper, was criticism of liberal professors at the college. He won the election, which empowered a conservative alliance of students to run the campus government and the newspaper. *The Movement* contended that this group of students had close ties with conservative state politicians such as Max Rafferty and that they focused their energies on repudiating the anti-war and black power movements on campus. Thus, the local news media's crusade against Black Panther George Murray was led by a reporter with clear and public biases whose expressed goal was to bring down the radical student revolt.[37]

Within a week, the press' sensational attention to Murray's teaching status had inspired an uproar in the state government. The chairman of the State College Board of Trustees told an investigating committee that the body had been unaware of Murray's status at the college until they read about it in the *Examiner*. The trustees held a six-hour debate behind closed doors and voted to ask San Francisco State president Robert Smith to take Murray out of the classroom and assign him to other duties. But Smith refused on the grounds that there was a signed contract with Murray that could not be broken without flouting the institution's procedures. This set the stage for a showdown, and the *San Francisco Examiner*, which was the catalyst for the story, now covered it avidly. The paper reported that there was "widespread public outcry" after the college hired Murray, but that the English Department's chairman had praised the Panthers' Minister of Education for his "ability with students from a ghetto background." The trustees' opposition to Murray continued to be deeply politicized. They argued that he was unfit to teach because of his unsanctioned trip to Cuba and his controversial public statements. But the main issue was that Murray was on probation following a battery conviction stemming from an incident in November 1967 during which he was charged with physically attacking the editor of the student newspaper, the *Golden Gater*.

This made George Murray the prototypical Black Panther—violent, unpredictable, and prone to expressing "the exaggerated rhetoric of black militancy." The *Examiner*'s story was packaged with an article titled "Cleaver Rants at Whites in Irvine" and another reporting on a Stanford University resolution criticizing the UC Regents' position on Cleaver. The George Murray case at San Francisco State promised to build on the Cleaver controversy, keeping the Panthers and their forays into academia in the public eye.[38]

Embattled and emboldened, Murray used his newfound celebrity to carry the Panthers' message to multiple audiences. Students across California quickly embraced him as a symbol for black radical activism within higher education. A month after the trustees' decision, Murray was invited to make a speech at a rally at Fresno State College on the same day that the trustees were meeting nearby. The press anticipated a confrontation, reporting that SDS members from San Francisco State also planned to attend. The *Oakland Tribune* reported on the event, with the headline "Panther Prof's Job in Jeopardy Again" to highlight the continuing nature of the story. Murray used "four-letter obscenities" as he told a crowd of eighteen hundred, "If the students want to run the colleges—if the administration won't go for it—then you control it with a gun." He reportedly exhorted the audience to "burn the flag to a crisp" and said, "We are slaves. The only way to become free is to kill the slave masters." To the press' apparent delight, the report noted that the audience dwindled and Murray "received only scattered applause," confirming that his provocative rhetoric did not appeal to most of those in attendance.[39]

The next week, Murray allegedly held forth in the cafeteria at San Francisco State, where he said that black and brown students should "bring guns to campus," according to an article in the *Examiner* written by Garlington and another reporter. This story was based entirely on hearsay; no sources were quoted who heard Murray's comments, and the press was not present at the impromptu gathering. Nevertheless, the allegation, which was trumpeted in the news accounts, was sufficient to prompt the state college's chancellor to push for Murray's suspension. Within days, the *Oakland Tribune* reported that state officials were looking for a legal rationale to suspend Murray from his teaching post, because he advocated the use of guns and violence on the campus. It was a front-page story when San Francisco State president Robert Smith "grudgingly" agreed to suspend Murray after facing intense pressure from the chancellor and Governor Reagan, who said Smith "should be rebuked" for not acting on the matter sooner. "S.F. State Suspends Murray" read the skyline head on the front of the Saturday *Tribune*, with the terms "Black Panther" and "tough-talking Negro militant" used to describe Murray in the first paragraph. According to the *San Francisco Examiner*, Murray maintained that his words had been misinterpreted and that he was advocating that "black students carry guns to protect themselves from racist administrators." Most of Murray's speech that day was devoted to a critique of the college's black studies program and the lack of African American faculty. A student journalist who was in the cafeteria later wrote that Murray decried the inequality of college admissions, noting, "There are four and one-half million black and brown people in California, so there should be five thousand black and brown people at this school." But the news media failed to put any of this in their reports, focusing instead on the customary Panther rhetoric of "picking up the gun."[40]

The *Examiner* also reported that San Francisco mayor Joseph Alioto had gotten into the act and was seeking evidence that Murray had committed a crime; the mayor was quoted as describing Murray as "an old-fashioned Marxist." In a sidebar headlined "No Crime in Murray's 'Gun' Comment," the paper reported that no grounds for a criminal charge had been found. The piece also noted that there were no witnesses to Murray's commentary, suggesting that those present were being intimidated by the Panthers. "At this point no one has been found who is willing to testify to what Murray actually said in his campus speech on Monday," stated the *Examiner*. Even a local judge became involved when he sent a letter to another judge advocating that Murray's parole be revoked. This was also given prominent coverage on the *Examiner*'s front page, as the newspaper sought to follow the paper trail that singled out the Black Panther for extraordinary scrutiny. The local press was clearly engaged in a heated competition with each other to gather every iota of information that might further the sensational nature of the story. The inflationary reporting, coupled with the way state and local officials jumped into the political fray, set the stage for a major student insurgency.[41]

Students of color at SF State were encouraged in their protests by the examples of their peers at San Jose State and by the confrontational rhetoric uttered by figures such as Eldridge Cleaver and George Murray. Activist students on the campus had been at odds with the college's administration for over a year. SDS had led a boycott of the school cafeteria in late 1966, and in December 1967 there had been a violent encounter between students and the police after the college banned an underground student publication for featuring indecent material. The November 1967 fracas at the *Gater*, in which George Murray was a participant, was prompted by the paper's criticism of the Black Student Union, which angered some black students. In February 1968, San Francisco State's president resigned after eighteen months on the job, declaring that the governor and state authorities were engaging in "political interference and financial starvation" at the state colleges. In May, police were once again called to the campus to halt a student sit-in against the Air Force ROTC campus recruitment program. The protestors seized the campus administration building and locked administrators in their office, demanding that more students of color be admitted for the next year and that more minority faculty be hired. Sixty students and faculty, some badly beaten by police, were arrested. Kay Boyle, a novelist and English professor at the college, recalled that this was a pivotal moment. "That night in May marked the moment when San Francisco State ceased to be a place that I went to for the purpose of meeting with students. . . . Almost without warning, it became a concerned state of mind."[42]

Despite the history of discord on the campus, the Bay Area news media were quick to reduce the new crisis to one culprit—the Black Panthers. "As of October 31 Black Panther George Murray, Minister of Information [*sic*], became the main (and oversimplified) issue for the media in its reporting on the growing tensions at San Francisco State," Boyle wrote in an essay published in the *Evergreen Review*. On November 4 the *Examiner* reported that the Black Student Union at the college called a one-day strike to protest Murray's suspension. The article made no mention of the students' other demands. Yet at a press conference on the campus, the students and two black administrators presented a list of ten issues that included the creation of a degree-granting black studies program, the admission of all black students who applied to the college, and the promise that no disciplinary action would be taken against the strikers, in addition to restoring Murray's teaching status. The *Examiner* ignored these concerns but did highlight that white students were barred from the news conference, that Latino and Asian students were encouraged to participate in the strike, and that President Smith responded that the college faced a budgetary crisis. A student journalist present at the press conference disputed the report that whites were forced to leave, noting that anyone without press credentials was excluded—including both black and white students.[43]

The strike began the next day, led by black students who marched across campus and went into classrooms to urge students and teachers to join them. Another student group, the Third World Liberation Front, voted to support and participate in the protest as well. That day, Stokely Carmichael spoke to nearly all of the estimated eight hundred black students attending the college at an event that was kept secret from the press. Carmichael, who was making only rare public appearances, arrived at the San Francisco State campus flanked by Black Student Union leaders and Black Panthers. He fired up the young crowd, giving them a lesson in radical resistance: "You sustain the struggle by first deciding what your aims and goals are. And you decide that nothing can stop you from achieving those aims and goals." Carmichael also warned the students against the fetishism of celebrity, noting that their growing notoriety should not be an end in and of itself. "[I]f it became your goal and end that you want to be the most notorious, you're in trouble, you're in trouble," he said. Nevertheless, Carmichael told them, they would not be able to control their mediated image. "Your biggest fight will be television. . . . Because Mayor Alioto can call a press conference anytime he wants to and put on any program he wants and can bring any Negro he wants to fight you on television." This commentary, outside of the view of the news media, provided inspiration for the students as they embarked on their campaign to challenge the racial climate at the college. Some sporadic violence on campus led President Smith to halt classes that afternoon. The college reopened the next day, but the strikers continued their quest to shut the classes down. There was scuffling between pickets and opponents of the strike, occasional shouting matches, and some property destruction—a shattered glass door and small fires set in wastebaskets. When the strike entered its third day, the protesters accelerated their tactics to force a closure of the campus, increasing the number of random acts of vandalism. The *Gater*, now headed by a student sympathetic to the strike, published supportive editorials and estimated that as many as 50 percent of the classes on campus were halted or disrupted.[44]

At the end of the strike's first week, the *San Francisco Examiner* published a front-page assessment written by Garlington that predicted a long standoff between the students and administration. Both parties "took a hard line yesterday, thus offering the prospect of more strife and disruption," he wrote. There was no reference to the Black Panthers in the text, but the accompanying photograph relied on their symbolic devices. A classroom of white students was shown being interrupted and challenged by black students, all of whom were wearing Afros and paramilitary garb signifying radical black power. The article broke the student body down into definable factions: the black students, who were the clear villains; the white liberals, who were sympathetic to the demands of the strikers; and the radicals—mostly members of SDS—who were general troublemakers. Garlington made no reference to the students who opposed the strike and its aims. The article also offered a harbinger of worse to come—members of the San Francisco Police Department's tactical squad were assembled nearby and ready to intervene at a moment's notice.[45]

Those who lived through the ordeal remembered November 13 as "Black Wednesday" at San Francisco State. Shortly after the Black Student Union held a press conference to update the strike news, the police were ordered to go after the students. *Gater* editor Karagueuzian recalled "the tall, thin sergeant had placed fourteen members of the Tactical Squad in front of the office and eventually had ordered them to charge on the students who were taunting them. The officers had indiscriminately hit everyone in sight and singled out blacks for arrest." Observers described a frightening specter of policemen "waiting in formation, clubs readied, for whatever violence they could manage to incite," while bruised and bloodied students were hauled off to jail. The faculty senate called an emergency meeting with President Smith, who was persuaded by faculty and students to close the college "until tranquility was restored."[46]

The melee was reported on the front page of the *Examiner*, which captured little of the drama and mayhem that had occurred. The lead paragraph recounted that the faculty had voted to suspend classes after "a brief but violent ruckus on the beleaguered campus." Much of the article was about the faculty meeting, and attributed the outbreak to "the beating of a television cameraman by a black student." The college newspaper provided a quite different account the next day, stating that there was an altercation between a newsman and a campus guard that preceded the violence, and that "a KGO–TV cameraman allegedly clubbed two students with his camera, knocking one unconscious." It is not surprising that multiple versions of a complex incident circulated in different venues, but the *Examiner* also fell into the pattern of giving the benefit of the doubt to the police rather than the protestors. The events of the day were a significant turning point for the strike—it showed a San Francisco police department willing to use excessive force on a college campus, it further enraged the student protestors and garnered them support from the faculty, and it showed an additional weakening of the school's administration.[47]

The *Oakland Tribune*, which consistently showed a penchant for supporting police strong-arm tactics, also downplayed the police role in the crisis at San Francisco State. A front-page article reported that the campus troubles "included only one or two isolated incidents of violence, but resulted in the appearance of police tactical squad units and a confrontation between students and President Robert R. Smith." Thus, the violence was dissociated from the presence of the police. In a lengthy recounting, the *Tribune*, like the *Examiner*, also attributed the violence to an attack on a television cameraman by a "Negro youth," and said the police quelled the trouble quickly and efficiently. The accompanying illustration was more telling. The caption read: "A demonstrator at S.F. State decided to tackle a member of the police tactical squad, with this result." This disciplining language ran underneath two photos of police in riot gear brandishing their batons as a student clung to one officer's legs. In the second photo, the student was pinned to the ground with the officer's knee in his back. The press had anticipated this kind of action at UC Berkeley, but particularly aggressive intervention by the San Francisco police satisfied the need to pose black militants as losers in their struggle against the state.[48]

San Francisco State was now in a full-fledged state of emergency. The local news media followed every development of the story, but it failed to capture the interest of the national press. Perhaps it was considered only a regional concern in an era in which violent protests were erupting on college campuses throughout the United States, in Europe, and in Mexico. The connection to the Black Panthers, who

had demonstrated their ability to garner national attention, was fleeting
at best. San Francisco State's striking students and faculty kept the issue
of George Murray in the forefront of their demands—his presence on
the Black Panther Party central committee and his use of black power
rhetoric made him the target for state officials angry about the culture
of dissent, particularly among students of color. The Black Panthers
were also a less visible component of the San Francisco State crisis, one
that was not easily translated into evening news reports. The black students who were the catalysts for the campus protests were profoundly
influenced by the symbolic power of the Panthers; they watched and
participated in the Free Huey campaign, heard the speeches from the
leadership, read the *Black Panther* newspaper, and had party members in
their midst. The aggressive, in-your-face tactics of the Panthers were
put to use by the Black Student Union and Professor Nathan Hare, a
sociologist who lobbied forcefully for a bona fide black studies department on the campus.

At the end of this chaotic week, the college's president was under intense pressure from Reagan and the speaker of the state assembly, Jesse
Unruh, to reopen the campus. Reagan accused Smith of "capitulation to
the militants when the school was closed Thursday," according to the
Oakland Tribune. The faculty senate voted to ask the president to support
some but not all of the student demands—to commit eleven faculty positions to the black studies program, get the program under way within
a year, and rescind George Murray's suspension. The chancellor of the
California State College system, Glenn Dumke, refused to consider the
proposals. At the faculty meeting, a professor named S.I. Hayakawa
emerged as a figure who would further polarize the campus and acceler-
ate the crisis. Hayakawa denounced the closing of the college, proposed
a faculty-student committee to negotiate a peaceful settlement, and declared, "If that does not work, call in the police. One way or another, education must go on." His other remarks, published in the local press,
were racially and politically inflammatory. Hayakawa accused the black
student protestors of engaging in "the intellectually slovenly habit, now
popular among whites as well as blacks, of denouncing as racist those
who oppose or are critical of any Negro tactic or demand." Hayakawa
set the tone for an uncompromising indictment of the student activists:
they were to be broken, and order was to be restored. After the meeting,
Smith announced that the school might reopen after a weekend break,

and that he wanted to form a task force including black students and faculty to help solve the campus' problems.[49]

While the faculty were meeting, the college's Third World Liberation Front took the local media to task for using "distortion and outright lies" in their reporting on the student strike. They assembled outside the offices of the *San Francisco Chronicle*, marching and carrying placards to protest the media coverage and Murray's suspension. A student spokesperson asserted that, among other inaccuracies, the press reported that the strike was ineffective and that student attendance was actually far less than what was being reported by the college administration. The San Francisco newspapers made no mention of the critique, leaving it to the *Tribune*. When the *Examiner* took the pulse of student attitudes toward the protests, they found widespread support for the black and Third World students' demands, but discomfort with the politics of confrontation. The paper used the term "silent majority" to characterize the students who remained on the sidelines of the strike but nevertheless had opinions. This man-on-the-street technique of gathering quick quotes from available subjects gave the aura of a survey of student sentiment, but the tiny sample was far from being representative.[50]

On the day when Smith hoped to reopen the campus, the Black Panthers displaced San Francisco State as the dominant story. The *Examiner* used a skyline head in huge black print to announce, "3 Police Shot Here by Black Panthers." After several months of relative calm, the Panthers were once again the central players in a violent encounter with the police. The headline noted that two police officers were critically wounded and that the Panther culprits had been "captured," as if to ease any public anxiety that they might be at large. Two front-page photos showed a helmeted police officer hauling away a black suspect in the shooting, while another showed emergency medical personnel treating one of the wounded officers. The coverage was immediate and frenzied, giving a general account of the incident based on early police reports. The shoot-out occurred around noon in downtown San Francisco, when the police were summoned to an $800 holdup at a gas station. They pulled over a panel truck that had just left the station, with the *Black Panther Black Community News Service* logo on the side. "Witnesses said a rain of bullets came from the blacks' panel truck," reported the *Examiner*, highlighting the race of the assailants. When more police arrived on the scene, the occupants of the truck attempted to flee. More photos on an inside page showed the Black Panther truck surrounded by police and reporters, a damaged patrol car, and two officers subduing a black man whose face was partially obscured. The event made for a high-profile police drama, and serious trouble for the Panthers.[51]

The next day's account by the *Oakland Tribune* identified the Black Panthers involved in the incident. Several of those arrested were high-placed and influential members of the organization. Among the arrested were Sam Napier, the circulation manager of the *Black Panther* newspaper; Raymond Lewis, the paper's editor; and William Lee Brent, a squad captain close to Seale and Cleaver. According to the paper, a grand jury would investigate whether the Panthers were involved in a conspiracy to commit murder, and San Francisco mayor Joseph Alioto demanded an inquiry into "any organization which advocates the killing of a policeman." The only silver lining for the Panthers was that both wounded policemen were expected to recover from their wounds. The *Tribune* also made note of a curious element of the robbery, reporting that the main witness, the gas station attendant, was accosted by a passenger of the truck, who "asked for change for a quarter and when the cash box was open drew a gun and took the money. Then, strangely, the bandit peeled off two $1 bills and paid for the gas from the loot."[52]

The answer to the mystery would not come for thirty years, when Brent finally explained the incident in his memoirs. According to Brent, he and several Panthers were taking the van from Oakland to San Francisco to pick up some members for David Hilliard. Over the course of the day, Brent had consumed copious amounts of alcohol, Dexedrine, and an unidentified pill that left him in a dazed, nearly hallucinatory state. At the gas station, he approached the cashier, unaware that a gun was visible in his waistband. "The attendant looked down at the gun and up at my face. Whatever he saw there made him scoop up all the bills in the cash box and hand them to me. Without thinking, or even glancing at the money, I stuffed them into my jacket pocket, walked back to the truck, and climbed in." When the police arrived, Brent started shooting wildly. Two police officers were seriously injured. This momentary, drug-induced, reckless mistake cost the policemen, Brent, and the Black Panther organization dearly. With Newton appealing his conviction and Cleaver struggling to stay out of jail, this was not the kind of publicity they were seeking.[53]

The shooting allowed the press to reprise the themes of the police as victims and the Black Panthers as homegrown terrorists. The final edition of the next day's *Examiner* used another skyline head, "Panther Battle Cop Fights for Life," to highlight for readers the salient elements of the story—this wasn't just any gunfight but a "Panther battle," with all the attendant racial connotations. The article began with a poignant tale of Mayor Alioto visiting the injured police officer in the intensive care unit. "They looked at each other, neither saying a word. Then the mayor turned and walked away," the reporter wrote. This offered little actual news, but situated the mayor as justified in his sense of outrage toward the Black Panthers. On an inside page, a single photograph signified the troubled status of the Panthers—six of the group who were arrested the day before were lined up on a bench in the city jail, looking dejected and exhausted as they stared at the floor. Gone were the determined expressions of defiance—both verbal and nonverbal—that signified the Panthers during the Free Huey campaign. In this image, they were captured and defeated.[54]

The television networks also picked up on this story, giving it brief but nonetheless sensational coverage. Both NBC and ABC squeezed in reports that San Francisco police officers were shot during a botched robbery attempt, and that the suspects were members of the Black Panther Party. The NBC report noted that the police stopped a truck marked "Black Panther Black Community News Service." The coverage was brief—no more than thirty seconds—and neither network provided any film footage. But the presence of the Panthers as the perpetrators of the crime elevated it from a routine regional story to something of national importance.[55]

Despite the excitement and dramatic potential of this new episode of Panther violence, the troubles at San Francisco State still captured the local media's attention. In the same edition of the *Examiner*, reporter Phil Garlington noted that although the college had reopened, the strike continued. A group of faculty organized a campus-wide convocation that was broadcast on the college's close-circuit television. "Plainclothes policemen were in evidence everywhere on the campus, but there were no disorders," the newspaper reported. A front-page photo showed a multiracial panel of faculty addressing the students, suggesting that a sense of harmony prevailed at the college.

Accompanying this report was a brief article stating that a fund-raising party for Eldridge Cleaver to be held in the Hall of Flowers in Golden Gate Park was cancelled because the permit had been revoked. The placement of the story on the front page seemed to celebrate this small defeat for the Panthers. The short article was based on a press release issued by the city's Recreation and Park Department stating that the sponsors of the Cleaver benefit had no permit to host the fund-raising event on city property. Among the collected papers of San Francisco mayor Joseph Alioto is evidence that the decision was purely political. The Park Department claimed that another group had already reserved the Hall of Flowers and that fund-raising was not the stated purpose on the original application for the permit. However, the published rules for using the Hall of Flowers did not prohibit fund-raising and similar activities, and the applicants for the original permit, the radical weekly the *Guardian* and its San Francisco bureau chief, Robert L. Allen, were undoubtedly associated with Cleaver's supporters. So the charge that the Cleaver benefit violated such rules was dubious at best. These inconsistencies did not escape the attention of a local civic group, the Council for Civic Unity of the San Francisco Bay Area, which publicly denounced the permit denial and framed the city's action as a violation of free speech rights. In a press release, the organization argued that "all views—popular and unpopular—may be presented to those who care to listen" in public venues. The blatant infringement on Cleaver's rights had clearly outraged members of the city's political establishment, and in their view threatened to further polarize the community.[56]

Undaunted, the fund-raising event sponsored by the International Committee to Defend Eldridge Cleaver was held at another location. As attorney Charles Garry continued to file court appeals to keep Cleaver out of prison, the Black Panther leader's friends and supporters held parties, wrote checks, filed petitions, and spoke on his behalf to shape public opinion around the country. The International Committee to Defend Eldridge Cleaver was headed by Robert Scheer, an editor at *Ramparts*, and included a list of progressive political and cultural luminaries including James Baldwin, Allen Ginsberg, Norman Mailer, LeRoi Jones, Susan Sontag, Ossie Davis, Ruby Dee, and Jean-Paul

Sartre. The organization, based in San Francisco, frantically worked to cover Cleaver's mounting legal bills and to influence the courts and state government. The event featured the author Jessica Mitford as the mistress of ceremonies, comments by James Baldwin, music by folk legend Phil Ochs, and an art auction with works by cartoonist Jules Feiffer and the Panthers' Minister of Culture, Emory Douglas. The *Examiner* and other news organizations made no effort at follow-up on this story; the only documentation was made by the Pacifica Radio station KPFA, which broadcast Cleaver's speech the next day. The media's interests were in controversies and conflict; to acknowledge that more than two hundred prominent intellectuals and political figures supported Cleaver's defense worked against his demonization.[57]

In Los Angeles, a similar group called the Newton-Cleaver Defense Committee was also busy at work, circulating the word that Cleaver's freedom was in doubt. "At stake for us all is political and intellectual freedom, and for Eldridge Cleaver political intellectual and *actual* freedom," stated a letter from the committee's director, Milton Zaslow. "He will be returned to jail within 3 weeks unless something is done to prevent it." As with the Free Huey campaign, the Panthers orchestrated a well-organized and elaborate public relations effort to counteract the power of the state and news media. Huey Newton was enshrined as a martyred warrior, and the campaign for his liberation relied on the symbolic presence of a youthful, paramilitary black armada. Eldridge Cleaver was a best-selling author, rising public intellectual, and political candidate, and he was surrounded by a multiracial coalition of well-heeled and influential public figures. Neither constituency could counteract the increasing fervor to silence the Black Panthers, as they were both proclaimed "the most important national leaders of the Black Liberation movement." Newton and Cleaver had come to embody what author Tom Wolfe would later call "radical chic": to be seen or associated with the Black Panther celebrities offered a connection—real or imagined—to the inner sanctum of currency and hipness. But this also emboldened their enemies.[58]

The convergence of the San Francisco State protests and the shootout with police provoked the local press into a state of pure outrage. The *Oakland Tribune* focused its attention on the student strikes, in an opinion piece that vehemently denounced the protests. Once again, a news media organization used the metaphor of the "silent majority" to argue that most college students were conventional, law-abiding citizens who would never participate in such actions. The paper juxtaposed the crisis in San Francisco with a vote by Stanford University students to "condemn coercive tactics in student disputes." By contrast, "a small group of San Francisco State College troublemakers were discrediting and closing down their campus." The *Tribune* made a thinly veiled reference to the influence of the Panthers, noting that "a climate of coercion and violence, of intimidation and guerrilla warfare, is as repugnant and unacceptable to responsible, mature students as it is to the general public." The editors of the *Tribune* wanted its readers to be reassured that this influence had been contained.[59]

The *San Francisco Examiner* was far more direct in its critique. In an editorial titled "The Violence of the Panthers," the newspaper enumerated the group's "record of violence" in a list beginning with their 1967 Sacramento appearance in which "[t]wenty Panthers armed with loaded rifles, shotguns and pistols invaded the State Assembly chambers." With these words, the *Examiner* transformed a dramatic expression of dissent into an act of violence. Clearly, the memory of the Panthers at the state capitol was still vivid and infuriating for the city's establishment, whom the newspaper represented. The editorial's position was straightforward—a grand jury should investigate the Panthers' role in the most recent shooting, with the goal of stopping them in their tracks. But the newspaper, which took for granted the privileges of the First Amendment, advocated revoking those same rights for the Black Panthers. The *Examiner* questioned whether "[d]emocracy, free speech and freedom of dissent include tolerating the open advocacy of assassination." According to the paper, the Panthers were "utterly in variance with the democratic concept of orderly change and a contemptuous challenge to the public safety." The *Examiner* proclaimed that "[t]he people are entitled to protection from terrorists" even if that meant stifling free speech, foreshadowing the kinds of rhetoric that would be used to justify the extreme measures following the September 11 attacks more than thirty years later. The *San Francisco Examiner* took the lead in articulating a "moral panic," in which it was imagined that the Black Panthers posed a grave threat to social order and stability, thus rationalizing the suspension of civil liberties.[60]

But on the same day that the editorial was published, it became apparent that the newspaper had jumped to an extreme conclusion. A news report on the front page of the *Examiner* noted that only one Black Panther, William Lee Brent, was charged with a crime in the shoot-out with the police. Two others were charged in the gas station robbery, but Brent was identified as the "sole triggerman." The remaining Panthers were released. Hence, there was no evidence pointing to a larger conspiracy, as had been suggested by the paper's editorial board and Mayor Alioto. The grand jury in San Francisco refused to conduct an investigation of the Panther organization, instantly deflating all of the heated rhetoric circulated by the news media. Nevertheless, Alioto continued to press his case, stating, "The public has the right to know whether this is an organization along the political lines of another Murder, Inc., or a bunch of thugs." Alioto also lambasted the grand jury, accusing them of being "timid" and possessing a "play-it-safe attitude." Despite—or perhaps because of—law enforcement's frustration at failing to catch the Panthers in a wide net, the frames of condemnation and threat continued. This began the discourse of the Panthers as thugs or criminals that remains widely in use today. Bobby Seale added to the inflammatory language with his own ethnic slurs. In one media account he claimed that the Panthers were not involved in the holdup and that the calls for an investigation were "a conspiracy on the part of Italian Alioto and the Irishman [Thomas] Cahill," chief of police, to destroy the Panthers. Both Seale and Cleaver argued the arrest and prosecution of the Panthers in the case was a "frame-up."[61]

As the evidence against William Lee Brent was compiled, however, the Black Panther leadership switched their rhetoric and publicly denounced his actions. Their developing theory was that Brent was a police or federal agent whose assignment was to stir up trouble and make the Panthers look bad. Cleaver called a press conference to repudiate Brent, and the *Examiner* published his comments: "I was suspicious of Brent from the time he joined the party, but I didn't have time to check him out and the persons who are supposed to are inexperienced in security matters, we all are." Cleaver said a Panther delegation was sent to the jail "to ask Brent why he had done such an unbelievably stupid thing," according to the paper.[62]

Federal investigators also got into the act when representatives of a Senate subcommittee commissioned to investigate riots and student demonstrations set their sights on the Black Panthers. Two investigators for the McClellan Committee spent a week in the Bay Area, meeting with police and the district attorneys in San Francisco and Oakland, to scrutinize the Panthers, the Black Student Union at San Francisco State, and "similar militant groups, including the radical Students for a Democratic Society," reported the *Examiner*. A Senate counsel denied any connection between their investigation and Mayor Alioto's quest for a grand jury probe. Nevertheless, the Panthers' high profile in the local press curiously coincided with the arrival of the federal agents.[63]

Just as the excitement over the shoot-out was beginning to die down, another Panther spectacle emerged—Eldridge Cleaver's refusal to return to prison. A huge banner headline in the *San Francisco Examiner* announced that "Cleaver Won't Surrender" if his last appeal failed. The reporter, Rush Greenlee, who covered much of Huey Newton's trial, snagged an exclusive interview with Cleaver at the offices of *Ramparts* magazine. The Panthers' Minister of Information admitted he would not return to prison because it was unlikely that he would win a release again. The profile painted a picture of Cleaver as a defeated and frightened soul, rather than a belligerent critic of the nation's leaders. "His voice was husky, but he said he did not have a cold," wrote Greenlee. "He was slumped wearily in the chair behind his desk. A cornered look broke through the distant calculations in his eyes." The article added to the *Examiner*'s discursive annihilation and rehabilitation of the Black Panthers. They were now beaten, caged animals who could simultaneously evoke both sympathy and disdain.[64]

Cleaver's crisis also drew the attention of *New York Times* reporter Earl Caldwell, who sought to gain some personal insight into the Panther's dilemma. The article in the *Times* was given minimal play, buried on page 23 and packaged with stories about the trial of H. Rap Brown and black student protests at South Carolina State College. Caldwell reported on the defense team's efforts to petition the courts on Cleaver's behalf and said that Cleaver "refused to say what he would do" if the appeals failed. Later in the article, however, Caldwell said that "Cleaver conceded that prison was not his only option" and that he might leave the country. Caldwell interviewed Cleaver in his home, making note that "Cleaver himself appeared edgy." The Black Panther was far less open than he had been the day before with Rush Greenlee of the *Examiner*, Caldwell indicated that their conversation was difficult, and wrote, " 'I'm going to jail Wednesday,' he snapped. 'I don't have any time for interviews.' " The article described the loyal band of Cleaver's supporters who maintained a vigil on the Black Panther's doorstep. "Late this afternoon about a dozen demonstrators, mostly whites, sat on the wooden steps and walked back and forth in front of Cleaver's home." The group distributed leaflets saying they would continue "until Eldridge is no longer in danger," and they maintained concern that the police planned to "murder Eldridge when they go after him." For Cleaver and this small band of the faithful, his imprisonment was a life-or-death matter. The Black Panther was also using the news media to notify law enforcement authorities that he planned to escape.[65]

The next day's *Examiner* front page was dominated by a headline that announced the realization of Cleaver's worst nightmare: "Cleaver Loses in High Court." U.S. Supreme Court justice Thurgood Marshall had denied Cleaver's petition to stay out of jail, dashing any hopes of a reprieve. Cleaver's attorney, Charles Garry, said he had no indication that his client planned to ignore the order. "He's supposed to turn himself in at 9 A.M. tomorrow," Garry told the *Examiner*. In stark contrast to Cleaver's plight was the main front-page photo, of a handsome, smiling O.J. Simpson upon hearing that he had won the Heisman Trophy, given annually to the best collegiate football player. The caption celebrated Simpson's roots in San Francisco, in the process constructing a "good Negro" to contrast with Cleaver's "bad Negro" persona. In another thirty years, O.J. Simpson would have a similar experience at the hands of the news media.[66]

The bad news also appeared in the *New York Times*, again buried on an inside page. The headline "Cleaver's Wife Says Panthers Won't Let Him Go to Prison" placed Kathleen Cleaver in the center of the story as "one of her husband's chief lieutenants." This unusual acknowledgment of women's role in the Black Panthers was only possible through the Cleavers' marital relationship; Kathleen Cleaver could appear as her spouse's representative but not as the Party's. The Panthers' reaction to the court decision was painted as angry and direct, unlike their pained and muted response to Huey Newton's conviction. Caldwell reported that Bobby Seale hurled a vituperative string of criticisms at Justice Marshall, whom he called "an Uncle Tom, a bootlicker, a nigger pig, and Tonto and a punk." Kathleen Cleaver pledged that "the Panthers would use guns" if the police attacked them. Caldwell emphasized the extent to which Cleaver embodied the radical chic of the times, noting that actor Gary Merrill and a group of writers picketed outside the Hotel Pierre in

New York, where president-elect Richard Nixon had offices. Merrill told the *Times* that "Cleaver's been railroaded," and Caldwell added that Merrill had been "looking over some plays" when he heard about the demonstration, as if to enhance the protestor's artistic credentials. Another participant in the pro-Cleaver protest was author Susan Sontag, who said, "I don't think picketing is a very serious activity, but it's one of the last nice things people can do, and I support Cleaver." As Cleaver sweated out his last day of freedom, members of the New York literati made it known that they were part of his fan base.[67]

In this spate of renewed press attention, Eldridge Cleaver appeared in a new category—the celebrity fugitive. Just three days earlier, the *New York Times* had included *Soul on Ice* in a list of the year's most influential books. On the day he was to turn himself in, Cleaver disappeared amid a cloud of speculation and mystery. The press reported that an "all-points bulletin" had been issued for his arrest after he failed to surrender, and they participated in the chase by distributing a description of his car and license plate number. One reporter estimated there were a hundred journalists waiting at the state building at 9:00 A.M., when Cleaver was to arrive. Eldridge Cleaver, the master of media relations, had been successful in creating a news story through his avowal not to return to prison. The press took him at his word and anticipated a juicy story about his resistance. The tone of the coverage was breathless and excited. "No one knows—or at least no one is saying—where the Black Panther leader is," proclaimed the *Examiner*. The front page was dominated by the story; in the center was a photo of Kathleen Cleaver, stylish in her Afro, dark glasses, and knee-high boots, accompanied by Charles Garry. The caption noted that Cleaver's wife showed up at the state building, "but not her husband." A head shot of a smiling Cleaver taunted readers with the question "Where is he?" Kathleen Cleaver and Charles Garry told the press they had no idea of Eldridge's whereabouts and that neither had seen him for several days.[68]

The throngs of reporters and cameramen followed the pair to the Cleavers' home, where they held an impromptu press conference outside. Kathleen Cleaver seized the opportunity to highlight her innocence and the logic of Eldridge's escape. Calmly and defiantly, she told the assembled press that she "hoped her husband would oppose efforts to return him to prison . . . by any means necessary." The scene at the Cleavers' home added drama to the press' vivid fascination with the story. An *Oakland Tribune* reporter took readers on a virtual tour of their abode under a skyline head across the front page that announced, "Inside Cleaver's Fortress—He's Gone." The report noted that despite the flanks of heavily armed guards, there was no sign of Cleaver. Garry explained the presence of the bodyguards: "We don't want any excuses for the police to come in here and have any trouble." This story was purely for dramatic effect, not news, since officials had already deter-mined that Cleaver was not at home. But it was a bold public relations move by Garry and Kathleen Cleaver, as they invited journalists to see for themselves that Eldridge had disappeared. The story also height-ened Kathleen's visibility once again, as the reporter described her as "strikingly beautiful, and herself a Panther leader," simultaneously ac-knowledging her profound influence in the organization while dimin-ishing her authority with references to her physical appearance. Kathleen Cleaver was a conundrum for the press: attractive, well edu-cated, and self-assured, she fit none of the prevailing mythologies of black womanhood. Kathleen and Eldridge Cleaver were poised to be-come a black version of Bonnie and Clyde.[69]

The flight of Eldridge Cleaver also contained an irresistible visual el-ement that was exploited on network television. That night, NBC News broadcast a story that relayed the scene in front of the Cleavers' doorstep for a coast-to-coast audience. The voice-over, by network anchor Chet Huntley, described the setting, noting that "members of the Black Pan-ther Party, Peace and Freedom Party, and hippies gathered outside Cleaver's house this morning" with the goal of "trying to stop the police from taking Cleaver away." The camera panned across posters outside the Black Panther Party offices and then to a motley group of supporters gathered on the street. The visual context fit the prevailing frames of deviance and extremism, while naturalizing the fugitive Black Panther by showing his home and surroundings. This was furthered when Kathleen Cleaver and Garry took the film crew on a tour of the house in the same fashion as the *Oakland Tribune*, with cameras gazing on the dark, empty rooms and the heavily armed Panther bodyguards. Kath-leen Cleaver was shown pushing through the throng of reporters as she announced that during the last twenty-four hours she had received over a hundred threatening telephone calls. The three-minute story concluded by constructing Eldridge Cleaver as a kind of Robin Hood figure, simultaneously a hero of the oppressed who evaded imprisonment and a common criminal in the eyes of the state. "And so the mystery remains. Where is Eldridge Cleaver?" asked Huntley. "He is now a political refugee in his own country or abroad. But to the law he's simply a fugitive from justice." The Bay Area news media, in concert with local politicians, were invested in a narrative that reduced Eldridge Cleaver to the black rapist, irresponsible militant, and violent criminal that parts of his background suggested. But in the media center of New York, where Cleaver also registered as a celebrity, the press picked up on the Black Panthers' central argument that black Americans existed in a state of internal colonialism. The excitement surrounding his flight to freedom had the ring of a fairy tale.[70]

The thrill of the hunt kept the news media on Cleaver's trail in the ensuing days. The front page of the *San Francisco Examiner* announced, "Cleaver Eludes Police: Wife, Friends Remain Mum." Despite its prominent placement, there was little new to the story—the police were searching for Cleaver, and "[n]one of his friends could—or would— provide any leads." The front page of the *Oakland Tribune* speculated that Cleaver had left the United States. Cleaver's parole officer expressed tacit support for the fugitive's decision when he told the newspaper, "I think he would be very foolish to remain in this country, because methods of detecting parole violators are pretty good." The story also appeared on the front page of the *New York Times* reiterating much of the same information, emphasizing that even members of the Panthers' leadership were surprised by Cleaver's escape. Earl Caldwell recaptured the visual and rhetorical tropes that constructed the Panthers during the Free Huey campaign: "Panthers, wearing black leather jackets and black berets, stood on the steps of the gray-and-white three-story wooden frame house and turned away all visitors." The corps of Cleaver's supporters carried signs that said "On Watch Against Murder by Police" and "Support Eldridge, Defend the Leaders of the People," he wrote. Once again, Kathleen Cleaver's presence was a significant element of the story. According to Caldwell, she "scoffed at the idea" that Eldridge had left the United States. She told Caldwell, "In the first place, I don't think he has had the time, and in the second place, he gave no indication that he was leaving the country." Kathleen Cleaver's commentary was intriguing and added to the mystery being primed by the press; was she trying to throw Eldridge's pursuers off his trail, or was she an abandoned wife who had no idea of her spouse's whereabouts? When the story jumped to an inside page, it was accompanied by a photo of Kathleen Cleaver and Charles Garry surrounded by microphones and reporters. The image of Kathleen Cleaver—serious and calm in the midst of a nationwide manhunt—left an indelible impression. She was the stoic, fearless female warrior exalted by the Black Panthers' revolutionary culture.[71]

The Bay Area and national press continued to cover the Cleaver-as-fugitive story as they followed tips and sightings. Even the African American–owned *Jet* magazine, which seemed to ignore the Panthers in recent months, ran an article headlined "Massive Search on for Black Panthers' Cleaver." The magazine article recapitulated what had been reported in the daily press, featuring photos of Kathleen Cleaver talking to the press, a head shot of Eldridge Cleaver, and one of Supreme Court justice Thurgood Marshall, who "ruled, in effect, that Cleaver isn't a political prisoner." The *Tribune* noted, with some irony, that stories of Cleaver sightings were "rampant" in the Bay Area. Local newspapers reported that federal authorities suspected Cleaver had flown on a chartered flight from Los Angeles to Montreal, "a jumping off place for Cuba," and that the FBI might be called into the case if a federal fugitive warrant was issued for his capture. The press based their speculation on unnamed "federal and local sources," suggesting that FBI agents fed them regular information about the Black Panthers. The *Examiner*, in particular, wove an elaborate theory that Cleaver might be in Montreal, which was hosting a major anti-war conference. "As the Peace and Freedom Party candidate for president and a black militant celebrity, Cleaver would be among friends at the Canadian conference." The next day, the *Tribune* said that the hunt for Eldridge Cleaver "was still centered in the Bay Area" despite assorted rumors otherwise. In yet another dispatch to the *New York Times*, which was reprinted in the *International Herald Tribune*, Earl Caldwell ensured that the Cleaver story maintained a high visibility. The *Times* noted the "growing speculation" that Cleaver was headed to Cuba, but added a new wrinkle: "he has been a close associate of Stokely Carmichael . . . [and] Mr. Carmichael has developed significant ties with revolutionary forces in many countries." Thus, Cleaver could have found refuge in

any number of locales sympathetic to the Black Panthers' cause. Caldwell quoted Charles Garry as empathizing with Cleaver's decision. "I
can understand it. I don't blame the guy for being despondent and dis-
gusted," Garry told the *Times*. Eldridge Cleaver had committed perhaps his greatest act of defiance to date, in the process capturing an
international audience. His ability to escape imprisonment in the
United States suggested that he had influential assistance along the way,
and that he preferred life in exile to life as a criminal at home. Beyond
this conjecture, it was clear that the press had lost touch with one of
their favorite subjects, as they wallowed in the minutiae of the Panther's
comings and goings. Years later, both Eldridge and Kathleen Cleaver revealed that he did travel clandestinely to Cuba after Bay Area radicals
negotiated his asylum. He stayed there until May 1969.[72]

On December 1, a Panther spokesman told the *San Francisco Examiner*, "Eldridge Cleaver will reveal where he is when he is ready." With
this pronouncement, the frenzy over Cleaver's mystifying escape lost
steam. Any hope that law enforcement might capture him, in the process generating dramatic visual material for the evening news, had dis-
sipated. The vigil at the Cleavers' home was over, and the *Examiner*
reported that their house was empty. The paper said "it was learned"
that Kathleen Cleaver had withdrawn $11,500 from the couple's joint
bank account, indicating that anonymous police or federal agents continued to feed information to the press. Adding to the suspense was the
fact that Kathleen Cleaver had apparently disappeared. An op-ed piece
in the Sunday *New York Times* seemed to close this chapter of the
Cleaver drama. Writer Steven V. Roberts recounted the popularly
known aspects of Cleaver's public life and described him as "the angry
young black who is fed up with half-measures and is determined to
grab power, by violence if necessary." Roberts mused that despite his
fugitive status, Cleaver was unlikely to relinquish his carefully nurtured
state of rage. Cleaver's rise to celebrity was meteoric—within two
years he was transformed from a writer-convict to a nationally recognized author. "Suddenly, Cleaver was fashionable—at least in certain
circles," wrote Roberts. He also reminded readers that despite his
stature as "an angry black," the Panthers' Minister of Information advocated "a form of interracial tolerance." His departure transformed
Cleaver into a different kind of icon: he could not continue to garner
center-stage attention from afar, and his influence in the Black Panther

Party and in leftist political circles would eventually wane. But Eldridge Cleaver left in his wake a powerful collective memory of African American radical resistance that would be sustained by cultural industries—the press and book publishing, among others—looking to capitalize on his radical chic.[73]

While the Cleaver manhunt dominated the pages of the Bay Area press, the crisis at San Francisco State continued. On November 27, the day that Cleaver became a fugitive, the *Oakland Tribune* reported that Robert Smith resigned from his post as the college's president, and S.I. Hayakawa took over the helm. At a meeting of the state college trustees, Smith faced a barrage of questioning regarding the closure of the campus; the trustees, with the backing of the governor, Ronald Reagan, demanded an unequivocal commitment from Smith to open the campus and suppress the radical students and faculty. Unable to withstand the pressure, Smith suddenly resigned, leaving San Francisco State leaderless. The trustees immediately appointed Hayakawa, who in recent days had organized a group called Faculty Renaissance to halt the student protests. The *New York Times* also reported on the transition, referring to it as "the violence-ridden San Francisco campus." The article noted that Reagan "had left no doubt about his vexation at the campus situation" and that he had expressed great enthusiasm for Hayakawa's appointment.[74]

Hayakawa, who had a scholarly reputation as a semanticist, was suddenly elevated from part-time English professor to college president, and he took to the position with relish. As a federal follow-up study found, perhaps his greatest talent was in public relations rather than college administration. One observer noted, "He had no constituency on the campus, he moved off campus, through television and speeches, to create one off campus so he could come back with some power." But as the editor of the student newspaper recalled, many on the campus were dismayed by his selection. "Hayakawa's appointment was bleakly humorous to many professors and students at San Francisco State. It seemed to them that during a faculty meeting over a week earlier he had exhibited a complete lack of understanding about the crisis at the college."[75]

San Francisco State's acting president managed to appear on the front pages of the Bay Area press for weeks at a time. His appointment did not offer the hoped-for salve the trustees expected. Student protests continued, and while many faculty supported him, a vocal contingent expressed their strong opposition to his leadership. By December, he had completely alienated the Black Student Union on campus, which had turned itself into a close facsimile of the Black Panthers. During a press conference, Hayakawa "reaffirmed the trustees' policy of keeping the campus open," and he insulted black students when he offered suggestions to them on how to make demands. "He said society was willing to offer much more than the very little the blacks were asking for," recalled the student newspaper editor. After that, the Black Student Union leadership saw themselves as a "military group." "There would be days, after Hayakawa took over, when as many as fifty black students came to school armed with revolvers just in case the police used their firearms." Hayakawa managed to alienate a coalition of local black spokesmen, including San Francisco *Sun-Reporter* publisher Carlton Goodlett, Berkeley councilman Ron Dellums, and Assemblyman Willie Brown, who supported the black students' goals. At one tense negotiating meeting Hayakawa stormed out, prompting the *Sun-Reporter* to publish a story titled "Hayakawa Stalks Out of Black Meeting in a Huff." The new president at San Francisco State managed to further polarize the region's already tattered race relations, aided by a press that seemed to cheer him on at each stage.[76]

Meanwhile, the Bay Area press continued to target George Murray as the main symbol of the campus crisis; rarely did other student or faculty activists see their names in the headlines. The *Oakland Tribune* ran the headline "Murray May Land in Jail" when a municipal court judge set a date for a hearing during which Murray would have to demonstrate why his probation should not be revoked following his suspension from San Francisco State.

The Panthers remained as visible news subjects in other arenas as well. The trial had begun for the Black Panthers involved in the April 6 shoot-out in Oakland—without the featured defendant Eldridge Cleaver. The trial of Panther Warren Wells, one of six arrested in the shoot-out, never attracted front-page attention despite the efforts of attorney Charles Garry to foreground issues of police harassment and the black power movement. Indeed, the possibility that Eldridge Cleaver had hijacked a TWA flight to Cuba, which was featured prominently on the front pages of the *Oakland Tribune* and *San Francisco Examiner*, was seen as considerably more newsworthy than

Wells' testimony, which was buried on inside pages of the same news-papers. The trial, which moved through the court quickly, ended in a hung jury, which could not deliver a sensational ending. Unlike the Free Huey campaign, the press did not find throngs of uniformed Pan-thers surrounding the courthouse. Warren Wells was just another black man in trouble. The subject of the November San Francisco shoot-out and the case of William Lee Brent was also in the news, but never deemed front-page material. Perhaps more important, the Wells and Brent stories were never positioned as national items to be picked up by the New York Times or the broadcast networks. In early December a grand jury indicted Brent and two other Black Panthers in connection with the shooting and gas station robbery, but it turned the investiga-tion of the case over to the police department. The matter would go on well into the next year.[77]

As 1968 came to an end, the Bay Area news media tried to squeeze the last bits of attention out of Eldridge Cleaver's disappearance. The Black Panther newspaper contributed its own perspective to this discur-sive universe with the December 7 issue. The front page was filled with a photograph of Cleaver in a defiant pose, with the gleeful head-line "Eldridge Cleaver's Free! Damn Pigs and Prison." The newspaper that Cleaver had founded and transformed into a vital forum for the Panthers now celebrated his escape from the clutches of the state. Sev-eral inside pages focused on a photographic essay in tribute to Cleaver titled "Eldridge Cleaver Takes Revolution Underground." The cap-tions under the assorted images asked the same plaintive question, "Where's Eldridge?"—rhetorically professing that even his comrades in the organization knew nothing of his whereabouts.[78]

The Oakland Tribune and San Francisco Examiner both reported on their front pages that a federal fugitive warrant was issued on 10 De-cember, bringing the FBI into the "hunt" for the escaped Black Panther leader. The metaphor of an animal under pursuit was used regularly. Two days later, the Examiner speculated that his wife had met surrepti-tiously with Eldridge in New York after withdrawing more funds from their bank account. A front-page headline announced, "Kathleen May Face Fugitive Aid Charges," over a story that drew on information from a San Francisco–based FBI agent. The romance and excitement of this story were hard for the press to abandon. The New York Times joined the Bay Area press in reporting on a $59,000 tax lien levied against the Cleavers' property, and noted that Cleaver would forfeit his $50,000 bail bond if he failed to appear in superior court. Journalists were fascinated by the Cleavers' finances—particularly the fact that Cleaver had earned generous royalties for his book *Soul on Ice*. "The large tax lien indicates the IRS believes Cleaver's income for the year may be well over $100,000," said the *Examiner*. According to Earl Caldwell, the IRS targeted Cleaver because he was also "a high paid lecturer," and their goal was to "determine what assets he may have left in the Bay Area in order to insure payment of taxes." If Cleaver could not be punished for his use of guns or his incendiary rhetoric, his success as a cultural figure could at least be taxed. Three days after Christmas, the $50,000 bail money was lost when Cleaver failed to reappear. Some of Cleaver's supporters who had underwritten the bail bond—including comedian and actor Godfrey Cambridge, *Ramparts* founder and attorney Edward Keating, and Peace and Freedom Party leader Paul Jacobs—held a press conference saying they would ask the public for help to pay the debt. They hoped that Cleaver's celebrity would continue to generate attention from rich and influential supporters, capitalizing on the Panther's "radical chic" image.[79]

A high-profile interview with Eldridge Cleaver, conducted before his disappearance and published in the December 1968 issue of *Playboy* magazine, proved that the Panthers would continue to be celebrated commodities regardless of their whereabouts. *Playboy* published serious intellectual and critical commentary alongside playful, sexually loaded material—including the popular nude centerfolds—designed to appeal to "today's man." The fourteen-page article devoted to Cleaver, subtitled "A Candid Conversation with the Revolutionary Leader of the Black Panthers," emphasized his salience among the East Coast liberal intelligentsia. The author, jazz and cultural critic Nat Hentoff, who had championed Malcolm X and Lenny Bruce in other influential articles, now anointed Cleaver as "a writer and theoretician of major dimensions." Indeed, Hentoff directly compared Cleaver to the fallen black nationalist leader who had had such a profound influence on the early Black Panthers. "I remembered, as we talked, the conversations I'd had with Malcolm X; both were intrigued with ideas and their ramifications, but both were impatient with theoretical formulations that did not have application to immediate reality," he wrote. Hentoff had been worried that Cleaver's parole was about to be revoked, and he'd traveled to San Francisco to personally talk with and observe the Panthers' Minister of Information. He noted, with some irony, that Cleaver was the "most articulate and controversial spokesman for the Black Panthers—and the only one free to talk, as we go to press."[80]

The *Playboy* interview was probing and incisive—Hentoff did not avoid pressing Cleaver about the contradictions of his positions or about the violence he seemed to routinely advocate. The length and depth of the interview allowed Cleaver to move beyond the homilies and clichés that had become the rhetoric repeated in newspapers and on television. Gone were the scatological outbursts, the comical allusions, the outrageous rhetorical flourishes. He argued that black Americans were fed up with racial repression and might resort to violence if they found no relief. "How long will they endure the continued escalation of police force and brutality?" he asked. Yet Cleaver acknowledged that violent resistance was a last resort: "Let me make myself clear. I don't dig violence. Guns are ugly. . . . If our demands are not met, we will sooner or later have to make a choice between continuing to be victims or deciding to seize our freedom." Cleaver expressed faith in the radicalization of young whites and put the onus for the structural transformation of society on white Americans: "Be Americans. Stand up for liberty. Stand up for justice. . . . Make this really the home of the free," he insisted.[81]

The *Playboy* interview was just one indicator that the Black Panthers' most celebrated figures were out of sight but not out of mind. *Jet* magazine argued that Cleaver, Newton, and Seale were part of a larger phenomenon intended to silence black dissent: "radical black militants who blossom as leaders in the war of words soon find themselves defoliated by the heat of law and order—or worse." The weekly black-owned newsmagazine included the Black Panther leaders in a long list of black male activists—Marcus Garvey, Martin Luther King Jr., Malcolm X, and Robert Williams among them—who had been harassed, jailed, exiled, and sometimes killed in their quest for social change. "The pattern is the same wherever black men rebel," declared managing editor John Britton. Just a few months earlier, *Jet* had virtually ignored the Panthers; now they were recognized as part of the larger black liberation struggle.[82]

In nine months Eldridge Cleaver and Huey Newton (with Bobby Seale, David Hilliard, Kathleen Cleaver, Emory Douglas, and other key players) had demonstrated a keen organizational and public relations prowess that brought them international attention and widespread support despite the fact that both men were accused of shooting a police officer, and that both spent most of their time fighting prison sentences. As a front-page *Wall Street Journal* article noted at year's end, the trial of Huey Newton put on the table a question central to the black liberation struggle—can African Americans expect a fair trial if they are not tried by a jury of their peers? Although Newton was convicted of manslaughter, his case not only made him a celebrity but brought into sharp relief "long-standing traditions of jury selection" that exclude blacks and other minorities. While Charles Garry hammered this home during Newton's trial, other legal teams were using similar arguments to whittle away at discrimination in the legal system. A spokesman for the NAACP told the *Journal* that the organization had twenty to thirty pending cases that disputed jury selection practices. Similarly, Eldridge Cleaver's quest for a public forum—as either college lecturer, political candidate, or journalist and author—highlighted the perils of being outspoken and controversial, and brought him a range of supporters concerned about threats to free speech. These contradictions—between their personae as dangerous, violent criminals and as intellectuals and talented political strategists—are what enhanced their appeal as cultural icons.[83]

8

SERVANTS OF THE PEOPLE: THE BLACK PANTHERS AS NATIONAL AND GLOBAL ICONS

> As a reporter, I try to be sympathetic to anything I want to understand and write about. But the more I work on the subject, the more I know that sympathy is not my primary feeling. Deep in my white, possibly racist, probably unrevolutionary heart, I am afraid of the Black Panther Party.
>
> Gene Marine, *The Black Panthers* (1969)

By the end of 1968, numerous journalists, authors, and photographers were engaged in the task of memorializing the Black Panthers and the past tumultuous year. They sought to capitalize on the enormous popularity of the Black Panthers, and to somehow capture the uniqueness of the times—to convey to current and future audiences the complexity and chaos that engulfed much of the nation. The texts they produced often transcended the constraints of daily journalism to provide insight, texture, and analysis to the barrage of news stories that had been generated. Many of these cultural products were also the result of a political mission; they hoped to further the Panthers' agenda of critiquing the police, the state, and racial ideologies. If the Panthers remained tied to certain narrow frames—threatening black males, criminals, deviants, terrorists, and celebrities—this emerging material would reinforce the alternative frames of revolutionary heroes, victims of state repression, and servants of the people.

One genre of Panther literature that emerged during this period was the "insider" account of the organization in the form of memoir. The media had generated an enormous popular curiosity about the Black Panther Party; news stories gave only glimpses into the thoughts and personalities of these charismatic rebels, while making them irresistibly attractive. Many unanswered questions abounded: Who were they? How did they come up with the idea? What did they want?

What went on behind the stern-faced, paramilitary façade seen on television? These personalized narratives satisfied the Panthers' need to vindicate themselves, to explain their ideas and actions to a national audience that formed much of its opinions based on the mainstream press. They also filled a market demand for texts that enlarged the debates on social unrest, political dissent, and race relations that were in the forefront of American mass culture. The cultural entrepreneurs who understood the marketability of the Black Panthers also guessed— shrewdly—that the same throngs of urban black youth, New Left activists, and university students who attended Panther rallies and lectures would willingly pay a few dollars for a book that might provide them with lasting inspiration. In the process, the Black Panthers had moved from relying on hand-lettered mimeographed flyers to disseminate their ideas, to having major publishing companies at their disposal.

The editors at *Ramparts* magazine, who played a major role in promoting the idea of the Black Panthers as the vanguard of the black liberation movement, were a major force in this process. In the fall of 1968 they encouraged Panther co-founder Bobby Seale to create an oral history of the organization on tape. Immediately, this was envisioned as a book project. In the October 26 and November 17 issues, *Ramparts* published "Selections from the Biography of Huey P. Newton by Bobby Seale," which were edited excerpts from the taped recordings. Eldridge Cleaver also claimed some credit for helping Seale with the project during his last speech before fleeing the United States. "Bob Scheer [a *Ramparts* editor] and I took Bobby Seale down to Carmel-by-the-Sea. But we went away from the sea. We went into a little cabin, and we got a fifth of Scotch, a couple of chasers, a tape recorder and a large stack of blank tapes. We said, 'Bobby, take the fifth, and talk about brother Huey P. Newton,'" Cleaver recalled. The magazine noted that the selections were part of Seale's forthcoming book but did not acknowledge that *Ramparts* staffers were involved with the process. Thus, the illusion was created of an authentic, unvarnished narrative penned by one of the Panthers' chief architects. The language was clipped and conversational, full of the vernacular of the black inner city. The style was unmistakably Panther-like—bold, scatological, and confident in the righteousness of their program. In the second set of memoirs that appeared in the magazine, Seale remembered an early Panther confrontation with the police:

The people began to line up and brother Huey told me to go ahead and start blowing. So I start blowing to the brothers there, running down to them about the ten-point platform and program, what kind of organization we had now, and the fact that brother Denzil Dowell had been killed by some racist dog Gestapo pigs.

The strategy behind this project was twofold: to memorialize the Party's origins and leadership, and to further martyr the jailed Huey Newton. Although Seale was a co-founder of the Black Panthers, his narrative often placed him in a secondary role, while Newton was cast as the all-sacrificing servant of the people and as the Party's primary theorist. As the title indicated, Seale was delivering not his own biography but that of Newton. The next year, while Seale sat in the San Francisco County jail, he completed the tape-recorded history. The material was edited by a former *Ramparts* editor, and it was published as *Seize the Time: The Story of the Black Panther Party and Huey Newton* in 1970 by Vintage Books, an imprint of Random House. The narrative ends, rather abruptly, during Seale's trial for conspiracy as part of the Chicago 8. Although *Seize the Time* was ostensibly to tell Newton's story, the book's cover featured a courtroom rendering of Seale bound and gagged on the judge's orders; this became one of the most memorable images from the case. This book was immediately seen as the definitive story of the Panthers and to this day remains an authoritative source. A short statement at the end of the book notes, "Mr. Seale supervised the preparation of the final manuscript and every word is his."[1]

Unlike Eldridge Cleaver, Seale's first foray into publishing was not hailed as a literary event. Christopher Lehmann-Haupt reviewed *Seize the Time* for the *New York Times*, giving the book a thrashing. He argued that while Seale ably mapped out the Panthers' history, the book was "badly written, lacking both Eldridge Cleaver's brilliant rhetorical fire and the irresistible funkiness, of say, a Julius Lester." Lehmann-Haupt recognized that *Seize the Time* was yet another marker in the Panthers' quest for visibility and recognition rather than a distanced study with thoughtful analysis. Seale was convincing when proving the case of the Panthers' misrepresentation by the media and government. But the reviewer held Seale responsible for the anti-Zionist slant of the *Black Panther* newspaper and for Cleaver's embrace of the Arab guerrilla movement al-Fatah. *Seize the Time* got its hearing in the *New York Times* but was not poised to become a best-seller.[2]

Other memoirs were slower to appear. Eldridge Cleaver had also devoted considerable energy to maintaining a public memory of and reverence for Huey Newton. During the Free Huey campaign, Cleaver wrote and published a pamphlet titled *The Genius of Huey P. Newton* that offered a history of the Party and of Newton's central role in formulating its ideologies. The thirty-three-page book, published by the Panther Ministry of Information, included reprints of Newton's speeches, articles, and photographs with a personal narrative by Cleaver, who endlessly revealed his admiration for Newton. This was an important public relations tool that helped raise funds for Newton's legal defense while keeping his voice and image visible. But it was also Cleaver's way of paying homage to the young rebel who had inspired him to devote his life to the Black Panthers. "Huey was always conscious of the fact that he was creating a vanguard organization, and that he was moving at a speed so far beyond where the rest of Afro-America was at, that his primary concern was to find ways of rapidly communicating what he saw and knew to the rest of the people." Cleaver's skills as Minister of Information were central to the fulfillment of this agenda. But it wouldn't be until two years after his release from prison that a book authored by Newton would hit the market. *To Die for the People*, a compilation of Newton's writings published by Random House and edited by a young editor named Toni Morrison, appeared in 1972. However, this was not an insider's narrative of the Black Panther Party but rather a polemic that signaled Newton's reappearance on the political scene. It would take twenty years before prominent Black Panthers—Assata Shakur, Elaine Brown, David Hilliard, Geronimo Pratt, William Lee Brent—would write serious autobiographies that interrogated the organization, their experiences, and the group's legacy. They needed time to heal and time to reflect.[3]

In the Panthers' early years, however, numerous publishers welcomed sensational material that sold to an audience fed a steady diet of the conflict and mayhem dominating the headlines. The proliferation of memoirs and biographies, once out of the hands of the Panther leadership and their allies, shifted from a political enterprise to a strictly economic one. Many of these texts had little redeeming value beyond their desire to capitalize on the group's popularity. Indeed, it seemed that anyone who purported to have been a member of the Panthers could get a book contract. Some of the less memorable projects included the tales of "a young boy who joined this militant black group" but who declined to reveal his identity. The book, *I Was a Black Panther*, published by Doubleday, was an adventure tale for young readers by a ghostwriter named Willie Stone. The protagonist could have been a pirate, an explorer, a medieval knight, or a football player. The book was part of a series that offered teens the stories of "real-life" adventurers, and included biographies of model minorities such as Arthur Ashe, Shirley Chisholm, and Cesar Chavez.[4]

I Was a Black Panther told the story of a high school student in New York City who became politicized after experiencing racism in the Deep South. After joining SNCC at a tender age, he was drawn to the Panthers' bravado and aggressive resistance to the police. A crucial motivation for this protagonist is revenge. In a particularly chilling chapter, the young Panther and one of his comrades decide to ambush a police officer to attract publicity. "More and more, the newspapers were running stories of 'shoot-outs' between Black Panthers and the police. There were no reports of shoot-outs in New York, however. As far as the public was concerned, the Black Panthers were still a West Coast group." Fueled by this warped and juvenile logic, the pair shot and wounded a lone patrolman, in the process building notoriety for the local chapter. The narrator expressed mild regret as he looked back on his actions, but the book's emphasis on violence muted these reflections. *I Was a Black Panther* was intended to explain why young African Americans were attracted to the group, according to the author's note, but it did more to reinforce their public persona as a violent, immoral, lunatic fringe engaged in deeply anti-social behavior.[5]

Similarly, former Panther Earl Anthony penned two memoirs that presented a scathing indictment of the organization and the law enforcement agencies that pursued them. His first book, *Picking Up the Gun*, was put out by another prominent publisher, Dial Press, in 1970. Anthony tells the story of joining the Panthers in early 1967 after a 360-degree political switch from his membership in the Young Republicans at the University of Southern California. He quickly fell in with the Panther leadership and represented the organization at numerous events. He was part of the group of Panther bodyguards who protected Betty Shabazz in February 1967. Elaine Brown recalled that

Anthony was a founding member of the early Los Angeles chapter after serving on the Panthers' Central Committee and working for the Huey Newton Legal Defense Fund. Indeed, Brown notes that Anthony was influential in bringing her into the Party. Anthony also became an FBI operative after being recruited by two agents who were former acquaintances.[6]

Anthony's memoir presents a harrowing tale of intense pressure from the FBI, and suspicion and harassment from his Panther colleagues. He asserted, many years later, that James Baldwin helped him secure a book contract but that Panther officials forbade him to write the book. He claims that after he ignored the Black Panthers' warnings and signed the book deal, his life and those of his family was threatened. The book has no footnotes, references to interviews, or other evidence to support Anthony's recollections. Readers are left to decide the degree to which they believe his story. Once again, the publishing industry found an informant who offered sordid, frightening accounts of the internal workings of the Black Panthers. The *New York Times* published an article in its news section that announced the book's publication amid a torrent of threats from the Panthers. Anthony told the reporter that he had written most of the book while in exile in Sweden and that he was still committed to the principles of black nationalism. *Picking Up the Gun* reached a global audience; it was translated into French the next year, titled *Prenons les armes!: Les Black Panthers*, and may have appeared in other languages as well. In 1990, Anthony published his second account of his years in the organization, this time with a small publisher. Sensing that, once again, the Black Panthers were a saleable commodity, Anthony recycled his tales in *Spitting in the Wind*. The book's subtitle boldly announced his spin on the organization: *The True Story Behind the Violent Legacy of the Black Panther Party*, as if this was enough to prove the veracity of his claims. The book provided endless descriptions of weapons, blatant charges of Panther killings, and assertions that Panther activities were financed by the Communist Party, suggesting a never-ending thirst for dark and troubling narratives about the group.[7]

Black Panther supporters also sought to capitalize on the potential market for books about the group. Shortly after Cleaver fled the United States, his colleague at *Ramparts*, Robert Scheer, compiled an assortment of his letters, articles, affidavits, and speeches into an anthology. It also included an edited version of the recent *Playboy* interview. This book, also published by Random House in collaboration with *Ramparts*, was simply titled *Eldridge Cleaver*, with the subtitle *Post-Prison Writings and Speeches*. In the introduction, Scheer validated his close relationship to Cleaver as he told the story of their last dinner together in a San Francisco restaurant. The account also defended Cleaver's right to avoid imprisonment as he recalled how Cleaver was menaced by four San Francisco police officers when they left the Chinatown eatery. Cleaver told him "had he been walking alone he would have been killed, and from what I had seen of those swollen faces I knew he was right," Scheer wrote. They bid farewell, Cleaver disappeared, and Scheer reflected the sorrow of many activists of the period.[8]

Cleaver is evoked as a hero and celebrated as the black radical who invaded white America's sacred territory and "managed to put whites on the spot." "Cleaver was particularly troubling because he was outrageously public, perhaps the most upfront man alive," Scheer proclaimed. Their celebrated icon of black rage was gone, and no one knew if he would ever resurface or return. This anthology proceeded to memorialize Cleaver as if he had been in exile for years, rather than one month. The book capitalized on Cleaver's reputation as an author, functioning as a fund-raising tool in the event that he surrendered to the authorities and needed enormous sums of money for a legal defense. The marketing of Cleaver was instructive: his image on the cover of *Soul on Ice* was menacing, as he scowled outward with a deeply furrowed brow. By contrast, the *Post-Prison Writings* anthology fashioned Cleaver as a gentlemanly scholar: the jacket photos are of a softer, more pensive black man, seated before a typewriter on the back.[9]

Gene Marine, another *Ramparts* editor who had written a powerful defense of Eldridge Cleaver in the magazine as well as numerous articles on Newton's trial, turned this material into a book within a year's time. *The Black Panthers* appeared in June 1969, published by New American Library. A blurb announced it was "[a] compelling study of the angry young revolutionaries who have shaken a fist at white America." The cover graphic, subscribing to the dominant mythologies of the Panthers, showed a nude black male figure with a muscular arm raising a clenched fist. The publishers used an anonymous visual metaphor to the sell the Panthers as raw, powerful, defiant, and deeply erotic, while the author conveyed a similar sensibility through words.[10]

Marine's goal, it seemed, was to scare white readers much as the Panthers had done. In the liberal white discourse of the era, Marine professed his white privilege as he capitalized on the Panthers' story. The introduction cast the Black Panthers as white America's problem—one that average readers would rather ignore or deny. *The Black Panthers* traced the backgrounds of Newton, Seale, and Cleaver, the rise of the Party, and the controversies swirling around their violent clashes with the police. The book ended in the middle of the story, as the Black Panthers expanded across the nation and the influence of its founders waned. Marine reserved judgment until the final chapter, where he expressed a combination of support for and revulsion toward the Panthers' core principles. "I have been accused, because of my magazine pieces, of being an apologist for the Black Panther Party. I am not," wrote Marine. "I am frightened by them, and I am fascinated by them. I find myself stirred to admiration and stricken with apprehension." In particular, Marine critiqued the Panthers' overt misogyny and poor treatment of women, and the notion that "Panther rhetoric is based on the simple necessity to kill." Ironically, Gene Marine, a smart and politically savvy writer, was prey to the popular discourses insisting that violence and death were central to the Panthers' program. Had Marine actually listened to the speeches by Newton, Seale, and Cleaver, or closely read their newspaper, he would have found a clear disjunction between the abundant images of guns and weapons and the articulation of their political project. But their symbolic deployment of violence, coupled with their run-ins with the police, shook him—like most of white America—to the core. While Marine argued that the Panthers were not racists, he deeply feared the specter of the armed and angry black militant; the black brute lingered somewhere in the background. *The Black Panthers* was a success for the author and his publisher. It went into a second printing, and was translated into foreign languages and distributed in Europe.[11]

Writers and artists also rushed to inscribe Huey Newton's trial as a pivotal moment in American history. The first full-blown text memorializing this event was edited by Mona Bazaar, a Bay Area activist who had compiled several books about the peace movement and black activism. *The Trial of Huey Newton*, published at the end of 1968, was a project designed to provoke both nostalgia and outrage by recounting dramatic moments in the trial along with impassioned analysis by observers outside of the mainstream. The one exception was *San Francisco Examiner* reporter Rush Greenlee, one of the only African American reporters covering the Panthers for a mainstream newspaper. He provided photos and articles from the *Examiner* archives and expressed a more personal perspective in which he saw the Panthers subjected to racially coded media discourse. As a reporter for the daily press, Greenlee was an anomaly among the other contributors, who worked for alternative periodicals, including *The Movement, San Francisco Bay Guardian, Progressive*, and *People's World*. Greenlee's contribution, titled "Equal Justice the Issue in Huey Newton Case," was a recapitulation of an article he had written for the *Examiner*, but with a stinging rebuke of the institutions he worked for. He wrote that many whites considered the Panthers to be the equivalent of the Nazis. A parenthetical commentary added that "this is a result of the deliberate distortions both by the news media and the Police Department." *The Trial of Huey Newton* was an amateurish product—the pages were typewritten and copied rather than professionally typeset, and it was inexpensively bound. The photos and drawings from the trial were sometimes poorly reproduced. But it accurately reflected the sense of moral imperative felt by the Panthers' supporters. The introduction likened Newton's case to the trial of Sacco and Vanzetti and to the Salem witch hunt, noting that "Newton had his roots deep in the tradition of the struggle of the oppressed people's quest for freedom." It was not only the trial that was being remembered but the surrounding display of devotion to Newton and the issues raised by the trial. Bazaar and her colleagues urged readers not to forget the spectacle of marching Panthers, banners waving, with fists held high. "There was an unmistakable note of jubilation in the tremendous chanting of the marching thousands, and this may well have been because most people there had, until this moment, lived their entire lives as outsiders. . . . For this one time, they were strong enough in numbers and conviction to be heard." This was a victory to be savored and stored for the future.[12]

A member of Newton's legal defense team, Edward M. Keating, published his reminiscences of the trial almost two years later. In *Free Huey!* Keating, founder of *Ramparts* magazine as well as an attorney, admitted that his explicit purpose in writing the book was to prevent Newton from sinking into obscurity. Keating had been instrumental in promoting Eldridge Cleaver's career as an author. In the dedication to *Soul on Ice*, Cleaver thanked Keating for being "the first professional to pay any attention to my writings." Keating worried that the nation's collective memory was brief, particularly during the tempestuous late 1960s. "Unfortunately, because of the wild events of the last year and a half, Newton himself has fallen into the background," he wrote. *Free Huey!* begins with a recounting of the day Oakland police officer John Frey and Newton had their fateful encounter in October 1967. There were no footnotes or acknowledgment of his sources; Keating relied on his access to Newton, depositions, trial records, and other materials to flesh out the story. Much of the book is a detailed review of the trial, with numerous asides to evaluate the prosecution's evidence and witnesses. But Keating was an activist at heart. The final paragraph revealed at least part of his motivation: "It is my contention that the Oakland police and the District Attorney's office are harboring secrets. Huey Newton didn't kill Officer John Frey or shoot and wound Officer Herbert Heanes. The people should demand an end to the mystery that shrouds the killer and that allows the world to believe that Huey P. Newton, an innocent man, carries the brand of cop killer." Keating sought a reevaluation of the trial, in the court of public opinion if not in the California appeals court. He also hoped for some financial rewards, but his timing was poor. *Free Huey!* would have been "a huge seller, but then Huey was freed," said Keating's son after his father's death. Nevertheless, a year later Ramparts Press donated fifteen hundred copies of the book to the Panthers, at Newton's request, to help raise funds for his defense.[13]

No words could substitute for the powerful visual imagery that surrounded the Panthers during 1968. The photos in daily newspapers and the footage on the evening news were fleeting—once the day's story concluded, they receded into memory unless resurrected for later use. But independent photographers sought to capture the visual impact of the organization and install it more permanently. A week before Christmas that year, the de Young Museum at Golden Gate Park in San Francisco mounted a photographic exhibition that celebrated the manner in which the Panthers had transformed the visual culture of the era. Two white photographers, Ruth-Marion Baruch and Pirkle Jones, had gained unprecedented access to the Panthers, producing a portfolio of sensitive and often breathtaking images that showed their subjects from multiple perspectives. The pair, students of Ansel Adams,

Dorothea Lange, and Edward Weston, were well-known artists in the Bay Area. Baruch wrote that they were drawn to the Panthers after attending a meeting of the Peace and Freedom Party. They were sympathetic observers—Baruch noted that as a Jew, she too had experienced a lifetime of prejudice—and their artistic impulses were also political. "Slowly, we began to comprehend how severely maligned they were by all the communications media," Baruch wrote in 1969. "The urge to correct this unjustice grew rapidly within me." In a 2004 interview, Pirkle Jones confirmed that he and Baruch saw themselves as activist photographers. "In the back of our mind, what we were doing was a response to the negativism around these people—we wanted to show that there's another side to the Panthers besides what was being presented in the press."[14]

Baruch and Jones first established contact with the Cleavers, who supported the idea. Next, they attended a Free Huey rally at DeFremery Park in Oakland in mid-July. "From that moment on, we both became deeply involved and committed to the project," recalled Baruch. They attended several events and photographed Huey Newton in jail the day before he was convicted of manslaughter. The collection of images that they amassed included tender portraits of Black Panthers with their children, the bullet-riddled window of their national headquarters in September, and attentive faces at assorted rallies, as well as stern-faced, rifle-bearing troops. In exchange, they routinely gave prints to Eldridge and Kathleen Cleaver, who used them in the *Black Panther* newspaper and on posters and flyers. During their quest, Baruch and Jones had to negotiate skeptical colleagues, hostile Panthers, and an FBI agent who came knocking at their door. The art director at the de Young museum initially balked at opening the show because of the negative press swirling around the Panthers. But, according to Baruch, an unnamed art critic at a local newspaper intervened, and the show proceeded.[15]

None of the Bay Area press covered the exhibit; in fact, the mysterious local critic admitted that her employers "wanted to keep this out of the paper." But it captured the attention of *New York Times* reporter Earl Caldwell, who wrote a brief article more notable for the illustrations than the prose. The headline was tempered and neutral: "A Photographic Exhibit in San Francisco Tells Story of the Black Panthers." The article noted that the exhibit attracted a largely white audience, who seemed to be moved by the images. Two of Jones' photographs used with the story had far greater impact—one of an angry-looking Bobby Seale thrusting his fist before a microphone, the other of four male Panthers standing at attention and bearing Panther flags. The *New York Times* selected images that conformed to the dominant framing of the Panthers—male, enraged, uniformed, and defiant—and that also relied on collective memory. These photographs endured as the exhibit appeared in numerous venues across the country. Nine months later, Baruch and Jones published a book titled *The Vanguard: A Photographic Essay on the Black Panthers* that ensured a greater permanence for their images and for their vision of the Panthers.[16]

Not all of the published projects about the Black Panthers were intended to memorialize or glorify them, however. Conservative watchdog groups quickly mobilized to produce books and tracts that would counter what they saw as the group's subversive threat and Communist ties. One of the earliest was *The Black Panthers in Action*, published in May 1969 by the Church League of America. The thirty-page book introduced the Panthers as "owing allegiance to the alien Marxist politics of Red China's Mao Tse Tung and forming political alliances with such diverse militant radical groups as the Students for a Democratic Society, the Socialist Worker's Party, and the bizarre Yippies as well as with the Communist Party, USA and the Peace and Freedom Parties." The text's goal was to signal alarm; from the list of thirty branch chapters to the overview of the Panther ten-point program, *The Black Panthers in Action* capitalized on and enlarged their framing as a threat to social order and national security. The influence of the FBI or other law enforcement agencies was also apparent: the book had no listed author and noted that the material was compiled from other sources. The language was analytical and distanced, with particular attention to the Panthers' political philosophy and to their paramilitary organization. The book included numerous photographs, including a two-page spread of Panthers rallying outside the Alameda County courthouse in the summer of 1968. Yet there were no photo credits, and their layouts seemed more akin to police exhibits—each figure in the photos was carefully labeled or numbered, sometimes highlighting individuals' political affiliations with organizations such as the Communist Party. The concluding paragraph was a call to arms to the nation's more conservative forces: "The Black Panthers and their many militant radical supporters must be stopped before they can do serious harm to our society."[17]

Others soon joined in the chorus of unabashed anti-Panther publications. Among them were a book titled *The Black Panthers: Are These Cats Red?* from the Conservative Society of America, and *The Black Panthers Are Not Black . . . They Are Red*, published by Christian Crusade Publications. These throwbacks to the McCarthy era were written for a limited audience—readers readily convinced that the Panthers were a Communist front. But by the dawn of the 1970s, mainstream publishers also found critical sentiments marketable. The Popular Library, based in New York, published an edited anthology titled *The Black Panther Menace: America's Neo-Nazis*. The book's essays universally indicted the Panthers through a range of arguments—they were anti-Semitic, authoritarian, and undemocratic, part of an international Communist conspiracy, and following in the footsteps of the Nazis. The book's editor, Norman Hill, reassured readers that he was not anti-black: "The editor and reporters who created this book have the profoundest admiration and respect for the black race," he declared in the foreword, but the Black Panthers were "the worst enemy the black man has in America." In particular, Hill criticized the press for doing "a woefully inadequate job of informing the public about the Black Panthers," and he also blamed the influence of the "fiercely rabble-rousing books about and by Panther leaders that have sold millions of copies in America." Thus, *The Black Panther Menace* was an effort to counter this trend—to stridently oppose the Panthers' popularity and their visibility in mass culture and to lessen their political influence. The preponderance of anti-Panther publications were evidence of their iconic influence.[18]

On January 4, the *Black Panther* newspaper proclaimed 1969 "the year of the Panther" on its front page. The graphic by Emory Douglas portrayed a fearsome black man wearing the signature beret, his mouth open as he shouted out a grievance, a muscular arm holding a machine gun aloft. The cover captured the sense of anger and outrage felt by many Black Panthers following Huey Newton's conviction, Eldridge Cleaver's exile, and the pending troubles for Bobby Seale and David Hilliard. It also conveyed a desire for retribution. Despite the defiant bravado of this image, the Panthers were under siege from without and within, prompting them to avoid high-profile confrontations with the police. The press increasingly looked elsewhere for sensational stories of racial conflict—there was little to compare with the breathless symbolism of the Free Huey campaign or the drama of police shoot-outs of 1968. But the Black Panther Party was now an enduring part of popular culture, and they would reappear frequently as both villains and victims. Even though Cleaver had disappeared, his saga as a fugitive from justice was one of the primary vehicles that maintained the Panthers' national visibility. By 1969, his celebrity status was firmly ensconced, fueled by his literary success. The *New York Times* had anointed *Soul on Ice* one of the ten most important books of 1968, and ten months after its publication, Cleaver's prison memoirs had sold a half million copies, exceeding all publishing expectations.[19]

Look magazine started the year with a special issue called "The Blacks and the Whites: Can We Bridge the Gap?" The cover, illustrated with the silhouette of an Afro-coiffed woman, signaled the media's interest in the signifiers of black power, if not the substance. Senior editor William Hedgepeth wrote an article titled "The Radicals: Are They Poles Apart?" based on conversations with Georgia white supremacist Roy V. Harris and with Eldridge Cleaver. Both interviews constructed their subjects in personal terms—Harris was a "disarmingly amiable old radical with kindly eyes," while Cleaver was "lean, mean, tall, bearded, and black-jacketed." *Look* represented Cleaver as "the hottest piece of radical merchandise on the market," and they were anxious to get a share of this commodity. The article revealed little new in Cleaver's thinking; rather, it was yet another source for whites to learn something about the Panthers' established platform. Hedgepeth presented numerous unsupported assertions, such as "Just the sight of a Black Panther—representing, as he does, the elite among militant groups—sounds a strong gong of racial pride in most black breasts." He clearly had little idea that some black Americans kept their distance from the Black Panthers' aura. Cleaver's commentary sounded relatively tame against this backdrop, as he argued that blacks must have "an equal and proportionate share" in the affairs of the United States, and for "a Yankee Doodle Dandy form of socialism . . . to take the wealth away from a few and make it the property of all." On the facing page, segregationist Harris maintained that there is "a larger percentage of lower IQ's in the Negro race than any other," and that "the highest ambition of every Negro is to be a white man—which they can't be." By juxtaposing the two figures as opposite sides of the racial divide, *Look* perpetuated the same myth as the *New York Times* in an editorial two years earlier. These influential media organizations found it easy to equate the Black Panthers with racist white supremacists even as they published evidence to the contrary. Interestingly, the *Look* article failed to mention that Cleaver had fled imprisonment and was in exile, perhaps assuming that this was common knowledge among readers.[20]

Other media organizations had a change of heart regarding Cleaver. *The Nation* had excoriated the Black Panther Party in the spring of 1968; a year later the magazine published an interview with Eldridge Cleaver that gave him another open forum to address white America. The interview, conducted by a law student at UC Berkeley, was introduced with the kind of hero worship that had become customary. "As I entered Eldridge Cleaver's house on the 24th of November and watched the double-bolted door close behind me, I was more than ever impressed by the fact that Cleaver had made a leap that is characteristic of the true revolutionary. He had put his life on the line for his beliefs," wrote Henry E. Weinstein. Throughout the four-page article, the interviewer asked Cleaver to explain or clarify the work of the Black Panther Party, and Cleaver obliged with apparent good humor. He addressed the usual objects of criticism—the police, the mass media, and middle-class "black capitalists." He proclaimed that the Black Panther Party had been attempting to unite various strands of the black liberation movement and that its goal was to change the system rather than to assimilate into it. Cleaver also showed a remarkable willingness to critique some of the Party's weaknesses. For example, he bemoaned that the *Black Panther* newspaper lacked the funds and qualified staff to produce a well-edited product, and he expressed concern that "there have been many contradictions in the positions taken in the paper." He gave his earnest interviewer a rhetorical pat on the head, noting that student activists were well ahead of their parents' generation, although they fell short of exercising "revolutionary action." But he chastised Weinstein as well, telling him, "It has been like an extended field trip to upset their elders and it has not gone far enough. The students have stopped short of what is needed. They probably won't be willing to take up guns and execute the Regents, as they deserve." Then the lesson was over.[21]

Similarly, the *New York Times* devoted more space to praising Cleaver's *Post-Prison Writings* than to covering the crises in African American communities that were the focus of his polemics. In February, *Times* staff book reviewer Christopher Lehmann-Haupt wrote a glowing review of the Cleaver anthology, calling it "a powerful and persuasive book . . . and a testament to the editorial skills of Robert Scheer." Just nine months earlier Lehmann-Haupt had been one of the signatories of the letter demanding that Cleaver's parole status be reinstated. The review further expressed his concern and admiration for the Panthers' Minister of Information. Lehmann-Haupt noted that the book consisted of "hastily written journalism and speeches" but was nevertheless useful in answering the many questions surrounding its author. The review traced Cleaver's life from criminal to activist intellectual through his writing—from *Soul on Ice* to his "Farewell Address," included in the anthology. He found that the book resolved "apparent inconsistencies between his visions of violence and his fundamental faith in human rights." For Lehmann-Haupt, this was the legacy of "a humane, brave and wise man."[22]

Another assessment of *Post-Prison Writings* appeared two months later in the *New York Times Book Review*, written by Lindsay Patterson, a novelist and scholar of African American literature. For Patterson, Cleaver was an articulate spokesman for the rage engulfing black America and for "the American malaise and its relationship to current work affairs." He called the collection "astonishing," likening Cleaver to other recently lost political figures including Robert F. Kennedy and Malcolm X. "Our history fairly bulges with the names of the right men at the right time who rescued America from the brink of disaster," Patterson wrote. "Lately, however, we seem bent on destroying these saviors before they can accomplish their mission." Cleaver had not been assassinated, but his forced exile was comparable, in Patterson's view. What this review so poignantly revealed was the way that Cleaver's thoughtful, scathing, and controversial musings touched a chord with many readers in the late 1960s. Patterson deeply identified with Cleaver's assessments of the race problem in America, if not with all of his solutions. "But reality is here and now, and the white man must stop playing games with the black man," he asserted. In the pages of the *New York Times*, Eldridge Cleaver was now a visionary, a sage, and the answer to the nation's racial crisis. The longer he was away, the more America seemed to embrace him.[23]

Even the *Wall Street Journal*, which presented a conservative perspective on its editorial pages, was compelled to review Eldridge Cleaver's writing in early spring 1969. A combined review of *Soul on Ice* and *Post-Prison Writings* found insight, hope, even redemption in the Black Panther leader's work. In particular, the reviewer made it clear why white America rushed to embrace a convicted rapist and black revolutionary who delighted in frightening his enemies. Cleaver did not hate white people after all, or so his books seemed to reveal. There was even a place for whites in the coming social revolution. "It would be an oversimplification to dismiss Cleaver as a black racist," wrote the reviewer, Grier Raggio Jr. "[H]e emphasizes class rather than race, and he does seek help from white Americans in making the system more benevolent for poor people, black and white, abroad and at home." The *Wall Street Journal* called Cleaver an optimist, noting that his writing allowed for the hope that reason rather than violence might produce social reforms. The reviewer also recognized what many media organizations refused to see—that the Panthers' rhetoric was strategic. "Cleaver recognizes that the American social organism is very durable and that no one is about to storm the White House. But he feels that violent talk may force those in power to listen when modest petitions fall on deaf ears." Clearly, many were hearing his message.[24]

As the national fixation with Eldridge Cleaver continued, the Central Committee of the Black Panther Party shifted the organization's focus by instituting new programs and initiatives. The FBI and law enforcement activities designed to destabilize the organization were already having an effect, creating dissension and suspicion among its members. The Central Committee, led by Chairman Bobby Seale, decided to publicly acknowledge their awareness of the COINTELPRO activities and to denounce those who were infiltrating the ranks of the Party. At a press conference, Seale explained that the announcement was intended, in particular, to distance the Panthers from William Lee Brent, whom he termed "either a provocateur agent or an insane man." Seale, who was furious about Brent's holdup of a gas station and subsequent arrest, was convinced that Brent was a police informant whose job was to discredit the group. "The Black Panther Party doesn't advocate roving gangs of bandits robbing service stations and taverns," Seale declared. Brent's supporters were busy raising funds for his legal defense and arguing that he was being framed by the police, and the Panthers wanted no connection to their efforts. The get-tough policy was a warning to others in their midst who were blatantly violating Party rules and regulations—problem members would be repudiated and expelled. Seale told the press, "We are turning inward to tighten security, get rid of agents and provocateurs and to promote political education."[25]

The *Oakland Tribune* reported on the directive without comment, giving the Panthers a wide-open forum. Seale declared that while the Party defended the right to bear arms, the use of weapons in committing "crimes against the people" was a clear violation of Party rules, according to the *Tribune*. The alternative press also showed considerable interest in Seale's announcement and the controversy regarding Brent. Robert Avakian, a leader of the Peace and Freedom Party, wrote about the issue at length in the January 1969 issue of *The Movement*. The article, illustrated with a photograph of uniformed male Panthers marching in formation, laid out the details of the November service station holdup and the subsequent actions by the police. He argued that there were numerous discrepancies that lent credence to the idea that Brent was working for the police. Avakian argued that Brent was "an experienced armed robber" who was unlikely to pull off a botched job in a marked Black Panther vehicle, and that it was strange that the police suddenly dropped the charges against five men arrested for the incident. "But if, as is far more likely, Brent was merely a black man, convicted of armed robbery, whom the authorities could blackmail, he might well have acted as a police agent, without feeling any allegiance at all to the pig," he wrote. Avakian's purpose was to reassure white activists that the Black Panthers were still intact despite this breach of security, and that they continued to be worthy of support. In June, Brent would create another sizeable headache for the Panthers when he hijacked a TWA jetliner to Cuba. Although he had been expelled from the Party, headlines from the *New York Times* to the *Oakland Tribune* labeled him as a member.[26]

In late 1968, the Panthers began what became known as Survival Programs in communities where there were active chapters. One of the earliest and best-known of these was the Free Breakfast for School Children Program, which started at St. Augustine's Church in Oakland

and then spread to other Bay Area locations, Seattle, New York, and elsewhere. In a 1997 interview, Bobby Seale told a historian that he came up with the idea after talking with some local teachers who wanted to set up a free lunch program for their students. But he recalled that Eldridge Cleaver called it a "sissy program," and had to be convinced of its utility. This softer, gentler Black Panther Party may have rubbed against the grain of Cleaver's revolutionary impulses, but it was a clever strategy for building community support by providing a badly needed service. "We started the Free Breakfast for Children Program by asking businessmen in the black community and outside of it, to donate food and money," Seale wrote in *Seize the Time.* "We also moved to get as many other people in the community as possible to work on these programs and take over running them." By January 1969, the Panthers were actively soliciting donations through their various publications.[27]

It took a while for the story to filter into the mainstream press. The *San Francisco Examiner* published a brief story reporting that nearly 150 children were receiving a full breakfast provided by the Black Panthers as part of a pilot project. In addition to comments from Seale, a local mother assisting the program offered her own endorsement, saying that "some children would not get a hot meal before school if it wasn't for the program." Although limited, such coverage helped to counter the crisis-filled narratives that usually followed the Black Panther Party. It also put a spotlight on the problem of hunger in African American urban communities. By March 1969, Seale called for every chapter and branch of the Party to start a free breakfast program: "[O]ur children shall be fed, and the Black Panther Party will not let the malady of hunger keep our children down any longer," he declared.[28]

From this modest beginning other survival programs were developed—free food distribution, transportation to local prisons, health care, legal aid, and Liberation Schools—that gradually made an important intervention into public perceptions of the Panthers. These projects posed a challenge to the framing of the Panthers as dangerous and a threat to society. Some media organizations shifted their prevailing narrative to argue that the Panthers' goal was to lure black America's youth into their clutches. On the two-year anniversary of the Panthers' protest in Sacramento, at least one television network picked up the story of the breakfast program and conveyed this perspective.

NBC's *Huntley-Brinkley Report* devoted several minutes to a feature that started with the following voice-over: "The Black Panthers are sponsoring a program for young people in which there are free breakfasts and chants about revolution." The footage showed two vibrant young women serving food to a table of smiling black children while they chanted about being black and beautiful. "The revolution has come. It's time to pick up the gun," they sang into the microphone. The reporter's tone was cynical as he suggested that the children were also being fed propaganda, but the story was still a public relations coup for the Panthers. The children appeared happy and healthy, the program well organized, and the Panther spokeswoman told the reporter that their purpose was "for our children to eat in the mornings and be strong revolutionaries."[29]

An alternative framing—the Black Panthers as servants of the people—also began to emerge. On the same day, *Newsweek* magazine carried its own version of the story, titled "The Left: Guns and Butter." The overarching narrative in this piece was that the fearsome Panthers, constrained by police harassment, internal battles, and the absence of its leaders, were resorting to less controversial—and more benevolent—activities. The magazine's profile of the Panthers was colorful and apt: "They were all of white America's nightmares of the black revenge come chillingly to life—an armed, angry guerrilla cadre uniformed in black berets, black leather and black looks and devoted almost obsessively to guns." The Panthers had grown from a group of "ghetto coffeehouse intellectuals" into a national organization boasting twenty-six hundred members and seventy chapters. The *Newsweek* piece was filled with exaggeration and hyperbole—few observers in the Bay Area would locate the Panthers in coffeehouses, and this was a significant overstatement of the Party's size (in January Bobby Seale told the press there were forty-five recognized chapters). "But the party has lately begun running into the limits of the bellicose steel-and-leather imagery that helped it grow," *Newsweek* argued. Hence, feeding poor children breakfast was a means to "broaden their revolutionary base." Bobby Seale told *Newsweek*'s reporter, "Breakfast for children is a very socialistic program," and the magazine warned that "Panther-style hasn't lost its edge of menace." In this version, there was little concern that the Panthers would have a long-term influence on the children they fed.

Rather, it saw the survival program as a subterfuge masking the Panthers larger intent.[30]

In August the national news media returned to the story of the survival programs, giving the Black Panthers more sustained and rigorous coverage than had occurred in the previous six months. The aid programs offered an ideal human-interest angle and fulfilled several journalistic imperatives—narratives with which the audience could identify, narratives that address social problems, and narratives that repeat familiar subjects or themes. ABC News broadcast a three-and-a-half minute feature about a Black Panther health center opening in Chicago. Anchor Frank Reynolds presented a brief primer on the Panthers, while an image of a black panther overlaid with a medical symbol appeared on the screen. The dominant theme was the Panthers as paradox, calling them "an organization that seems at times to have a split personality." The voice-over continued: "They spend a good deal of time on community projects and a great deal of Panther energy is spent in the police courts defending themselves against assorted charges of arson and murder. Panther activities seem to be channeled in a positive direction." The remainder of the broadcast provided footage of a black neighborhood in Chicago, and addressed the lack of medical services available to inner-city residents. "Most Caucasian physicians are afraid to come into this neighborhood," a local Panther representative told the reporter. ABC News concluded the story with a dubious commentary: "So the Black Panthers will try it on their own, but they may be kidding themselves."[31]

The *New York Times* focused its gaze on another survival project, the Panthers' Liberation Schools, which offered education and child care. Another among the *New York Times*' growing cadre of black reporters, Charlayne Hunter, wrote a profile of a Black Panther Liberation School in the Brownsville section of Brooklyn. Hunter had earned some renown as the first African American woman to graduate from the University of Georgia in 1962, and would eventually become one of the best-known African American female journalists in the nation. She started her career at the *New Yorker* magazine and at a television news station in Washington, D.C., before joining the metropolitan staff at the *Times*. During her tenure at the newspaper, she focused on covering African American communities and for a time was Harlem bureau chief. The article's headline was blatant in furthering the demonization of the group: "Panthers Indoctrinate the Young." But Hunter's story and the accompanying photograph delivered a more complex set of images and ideas. The illustration showed a high-school-age Black Panther leaning over to talk with a small child enrolled in the Liberation School. The photographer caught a particularly tender moment and conveyed a sense of intimacy between the two; the child seemed entirely trusting of the Panther and the Panther completely devoted to the child. Hunter's article gave the sense that the Black Panthers were a familiar part of the neighborhood landscape. She described shouts of "Power to the people" coming from a local church, and the classroom of seventeen youngsters presided over by two earnest young men. "The curriculum could be described as free-wheeling, provided the teachers remain within the scope of the 10-point Panther program," wrote Hunter. She described one six-year-old who easily recited the Panther mantra, "We want freedom and the power to determine our own destinies." Hunter also related an extended classroom discussion on what constituted a "pig" and said the Panthers are "basically Marxist-Leninist and see their enemy as the capitalistic system and its exponents." The message was clearly mixed: on one hand, the Black Panthers seemed to be delivering an important community service—this chapter fed fifty to sixty youngsters breakfast and lunch each day as well as providing the classroom instruction. This belied, to some extent, the fearsome representations of armed deviants as revolutionaries. But mainstream readers were also presented with an insidious aspect of the survival programs: the larger purpose, it seemed, was to inculcate children with Panther propaganda.[32]

Not to be outdone, the *Wall Street Journal* published its own feature story on the Black Panther Party, also using the survival programs as its central focus. "The Black Panthers: Negro Militants Use Free Food, Medical Aid to Promote Revolution" dominated the front page of the August 29 issue of the *Journal*. The subhead signaled several prevailing themes: "Anti-Capitalist Indoctrination Comes After Breakfast; Many Leaders Are Jailed and Teaching Hatred of the 'Pigs.'" Like other newspaper accounts, this headline was more sensational than the actual story. The article was written by a young staff reporter named David McClintick, who would go on to an illustrious career as an investigative journalist and author. It began with a mother from Staten Island, who praised the Black Panthers for feeding breakfast to youngsters in her neighborhood. " 'The Black Panthers are doing things for us no one else has done,' says Mrs. Reynolds, who is 30 years old and black. 'If they can keep it up, a lot of people are going to cooperate with them.' " The rest of the article, spanning a full column on the front page and an entire inside page, proceeded with this theme. Much of the narrative provided yet another overview of the Panthers' three-year history, from the founding of the party to the now infamous shoot-outs—described as "bloody clashes"—as well as their court cases and infiltration by the FBI. But these crises had not dampened the organization's fervor. "Combining armed bravado, pointed social action and opportune circumstances, the Black Panther Party appears to be gaining increasing influence not only among Negroes but also among radicals, black and white," according to the *Journal.* This pronouncement was highly ironic, since it was news media outlets such as the *Wall Street Journal* that popularized the Panthers and were the prime vehicle for their increased visibility.[33]

The article also sounded an alarm that the Party was growing in size and influence despite the best efforts of the state to suppress them. But, like the *New York Times*, the assessment was ambivalent: the Black Panthers were simultaneously doing good and doing harm. For example, the reporter noted that in addition to its food and health care programs "the party is making an increasingly effective effort to curb narcotics traffic in the ghetto—often by physical intimidation of pushers and users." The breakfast program in Staten Island provided a microcosm of the Party's successes and failures. At its height it fed a hundred children each morning, according to McClintick. But the program collapsed when one of its leaders became an FBI informant and was subsequently expelled. Demoralized, the Staten Island chapter lost members and was unable to solicit sufficient food from merchants to keep the food program going. The *Wall Street Journal* article went further than other media in probing the implications of the Black Panthers' role in America. The reporter suggested that the Party seemed to be pushing other black-led organizations to become more visibly militant. It ended with commentary from black Harvard psychologist Alvin Poussaint, who declared that the Panthers were "the only group really appealing to young ghetto blacks" and that increasing numbers of African Americans were agreeing with the Panthers' critiques of capitalism and structural inequality. Six months later the *Wall Street Journal* followed with another feature story on the group, reporting that the Panthers enjoyed widespread support from African Americans based, in part, on community initiatives such as the breakfast program. The article quoted one New York resident, who told the *Journal*, "Right now, they're backing up what they preach, and that's why the man is coming down on them."[34]

The achievements of the survival programs did not fundamentally alter the ways the Black Panthers appeared in the media or were viewed by the dominant culture. Violence and controversy continued to shape their representations, particularly as the growth of the organization led to highly publicized incidents beyond the Bay Area. The prevailing news accounts of 1969 were bracketed by the murder of prominent Panther figures. In January, the Panthers lost two leaders of the southern California chapter at the hands of followers of Maulana Karenga, founder of the US organization, and in December the head of the Chicago chapter, Fred Hampton, was gunned down by the police. The deaths of John Huggins, Deputy Minister of Information, and Alprentice "Bunchy" Carter, Deputy Minister of Defense, both from Los Angeles, were particularly traumatic for the Panther hierarchy. The southern California branch of the Black Panther Party had been organized the year before under the aegis of Carter. "Bunchy had become a key Party member," David Hilliard remembered. "Bunchy exudes charisma. He's a lover, revolutionary, and warrior, a genuine tough guy who never fronts." Carter had been leader of the Slauson Avenue gang, had served time at Soledad prison with Eldridge Cleaver, and commanded considerable respect on Los Angeles streets. Huggins, Carter, Elaine Brown, and a new recruit named Geronimo Pratt had enrolled in the High Potential Program at UCLA, and the Panthers became active in organizing the school's Black Student Union. According to Brown, John Huggins hoped to mobilize UCLA's black students to work with SDS and other anti-war groups on campus. The murders were the tragic result of a turf war between the Panthers and US over who would dominate black power politics in southern California. The rivalry had been simmering for months, and it accelerated as Black Panther chapters emerged in Pasadena, San Diego, and Riverside County, significantly increasing the group's presence. The conflict was worsened by the active manipulations and coercive activities of the FBI; a study of the US organization noted that the FBI sent anonymous letters to both groups to exacerbate the tensions between them. One FBI agent wrote in a report that they hoped to fuel "an 'US' and BPP vendetta." Geronimo Pratt, a Vietnam veteran who became Carter's bodyguard, noted, "We got anonymous phone calls, letters, insults, taunts. We found hate mail in our lockers at school," all of which was part of the FBI campaign.[35]

As the new year started, the Black Panthers and US were vying over who would have a role in the selection of the director for UCLA's black studies program. In a heated meeting in Campbell Hall on January 17, members of US and the Black Panthers squared off in a debate over the matter. By most accounts, bursts of gunfire erupted out of nowhere, people fled in horror, and when the chaos was over Huggins and Carter lay dead on the floor. As word spread, Los Angeles' black community was in an uproar—armed members of the Panthers vowed revenge, US supporters expressed outrage, and the police conducted sweeps, arresting a contingent of Panthers and their friends, including John Huggins' wife, Ericka Huggins, who had a newborn child. Geronimo Pratt remembered a scene of intense police repression: "Across Central Avenue from Panther headquarters, police emerged from behind a building façade and arrested every African American in sight. . . . By midnight nearly a hundred Panthers had been herded into paddy wagons." The Black Panthers quickly mobilized their public relations apparatus, and leaders from the Central Committee hurried to Los Angeles. The day after the killings, David Hilliard held a press conference to declare that Carter and Huggins had died "courageous, revolutionary deaths" and that their loss would not "slow the Party down." The national newspapers and magazines failed to report on the incident, but one network, ABC, broadcast a story that included footage of the press conference, background on race relations in Los Angeles, and a brief on the Panthers' rise in that city.[36]

The incident quickly made the front pages of the Bay Area press. In the *Oakland Tribune*, the story was packaged as part of a new surge of campus violence across the state. On one side, an article reported that Governor Ronald Reagan "narrowly escaped a mob of students" at the Berkeley campus, while another headline announced that students were on a "rampage" at San Jose State College. Under the headline "2 Panthers Shot Dead at UCLA," a wire service report offered a dry accounting of the events, including descriptions of the weapons found following a police raid of the Hugginses' home. The next day, the *Tribune* rehashed the story under the headline "Panther Killings Stir Revenge Plot." In this retelling, the arrested Panthers were suspected of planning a violent retaliation for the murders of Carter and Huggins. Nothing was reported about the potential capture of the pair's killer.[37]

Across the bay, the *San Francisco Examiner*'s front-page headline, "Police Hunt UCLA Killers," suggested that the Panthers were victims in the confrontation. The wire service story offered the basic details and included photos of Huggins and Carter. Several days later, *Examiner* staffer Rush Greenlee, a veteran of Black Panther coverage, went to Los Angeles and investigated the story firsthand. Greenlee reported that two suspects, both members of the US Organization, had been arrested on suspicion of murder in the case. But Black Panthers who witnessed the shooting told Greenlee that another potential culprit was still at large. The story also delved into the conflict between the two groups: "The Panthers, political activists, had long been at ideological odds with US, whom they consider cultural activists, or 'pork chop nationalists,'" he wrote. After this initial flurry of attention, the Bay Area press dropped the story, which was seen as beyond its audience's sphere of interest. The national news media never blinked.[38]

Los Angeles' black-owned newspaper, the *Los Angeles Sentinel*, was able to capture the complicated community dynamics swirling around the killings. The *Sentinel* had been slow to cover the burgeoning Black Panther chapter in its own city. But a front-page story in the weekly reported that local residents were "on tenterhooks" as they waited to see how the Panther-US crisis would be resolved. The *Sentinel* recounted a press conference several days earlier in which a local Panther spokesman "literally accused the former social worker [Karenga] of murder." Unlike the mainstream press, which knew little about local African American politics, the *Sentinel* discussed the broader implications for the showdown between the two groups. In particular, the future of an umbrella group called the Black Congress, headed by Karenga, was suddenly in doubt. A sidebar article gave Karenga a chance to answer the Panthers' charges. He denied any knowledge of the shootings and implied that the Panthers might be responsible. "If you will remember, it was the Black Panther Party who brought rifles into the BSU meetings," he told the newspaper. "We have never been known to advocate violence."[39]

An opinion piece in the same issue indicted Los Angeles' black political establishment for letting the competition between the two groups get out of hand. "This black community is shot to hell," the author complained. The editorial was written by Booker Griffin, who was part of the city's civil rights establishment, a founder of the Watts Summer Festival, and an administrator at the Westminster Neighborhood Association. "The self-ordained leadership groups, both moderate and militant, have failed," he asserted. The essay was also a bold criticism of well-organized groups who "claim noble intentions but in the final analysis they mean to rule by any means feasible. That includes from the barrel of a gun." The reference to the Black Panthers' rhetoric was unmistakable—they were the group fomenting the greatest discord. The next week, the *Sentinel* reported on the funeral services for Bunchy Carter on a front page dominated by rumors that Diana Ross was leaving the Supremes. The story noted that Panther leaders Seale and Hilliard presided over the somber occasion, and that the brief service "was prolonged by the constant stream of viewers who filed past the ebony casket." John Huggins' body was sent to his hometown of New Haven, Connecticut, where another large funeral was held.[40]

The *Black Panther* newspaper was an essential tool in the group's retaliation against Karenga and the US organization. Much of the February 2 issue was devoted to articles railing against US, whom the Panthers dubbed "United Slaves." They were "cowardly snakes" who were part of a government conspiracy to eliminate the Black Panther Party, according to one headline. An editorial by Frank Jones, the Party's Deputy Minister of Information, asserted that the Panthers would fully cooperate with the Los Angeles police investigation with the goal of bringing US suspects to justice. The southern California chapter published its own edition of the Ministry of Information Bulletin, and the January 22 issue announced, "Black Pigs Assassinate Two Panther Leaders," underscoring the theory being advanced by the Party. The Panthers called US a "pork chop organization" and the

Black Congress a front group for Karenga and US. Most insidious, according to the Panther periodical, was that "a pork chop organization may be found doing the police department's job of repression."[41]

There were other continuing points of stress for the Black Panthers as well, which brought them in and out of the limelight. Shortly after the UCLA shooting, Bobby Seale received some unexpected good news—an Alameda County superior court judge ruled that his arrest the previous year on conspiracy to commit murder was unlawful, and the charges were dropped. But his troubles were not over. Less than two months later, while Seale was in Europe for a series of speaking engagements, he was indicted by a federal grand jury in Chicago on charges of conspiring to incite a riot during the Democratic National Convention the previous summer. He was thrust into what would be known as the trial of the Chicago 8, which included Tom Hayden and Abbie Hoffman among the defendants. The front page of the *San Francisco Examiner* followed the story as Seale surrendered on his return to the States, posted bail, and was scheduled to be arraigned in Chicago on April 1. Meanwhile, Huey Newton hoped to win an appeal of his conviction and gain release on bail. On May 1 the Free Huey campaign was resurrected in all its glory—the press estimated that two thousand marchers holding signs with Newton's image marched at the federal building in San Francisco. But the demonstration was only for a day, and the appeal for bail was denied. The strike at San Francisco State College dragged through the winter and spring of 1969. On January 6, Black Panther Minister of Education George Murray was arrested after the college's acting president, S.I. Hayakawa, charged him with disturbing the peace and inciting a riot. Three weeks later, Murray's car was stopped, two guns were found, and he was arrested again for illegal possession of firearms. With these two strikes against him, Murray was sentenced to serve six months in jail for violating his probation.[42]

Over the ensuing months, the news media remained fixated on Cleaver's exile. After several months of silence, it was front-page news when Cleaver was located in Havana, Cuba, in May by a reporter for Reuters. The headline in the *New York Times* suggested Cleaver's importance as a cultural icon: "Cleaver Is Found in Havana Working on a Book." Perhaps he was writing the sequel to *Soul on Ice*, the article implied, as it reminded readers of his status as a best-selling author. He was found living in an apartment that had become "a meeting place for the small Black Panther colony in exile here." The reporter devoted considerable space to the minutiae of Cleaver's life, from how he spent his time to the pictures decorating his walls. The story spread like wildfire through national and local news organizations. What readers did not know was that the reporter, James Pringle, had been tipped off by a woman who had an axe to grind with Cleaver. The historical record is unclear on the precise circumstances—one Cleaver interviewer called it "a vengeful tip from a mentally disturbed young American lady" who alleged that Cleaver tried to rape her. In 1975, Cleaver told an interviewer that the woman who "blew his cover" had "more of a conflict with the Cubans than with me." Whatever the circumstances, the U.S. news media picked up the story enthusiastically.[43]

But he did not anticipate that this scoop would threaten his refuge in Cuba. Cleaver offered varying versions of what happened next, but it is clear that the Cuban government was not happy that the world knew it was harboring the fugitive Black Panther. In the aftermath of his Cuban sojourn, he told interviewers that the Cuban government frowned on his associations with other black American expatriates, some of whom had hijacked planes to get there. He had also expected the Cubans to help him reunite with Kathleen, who was pregnant with their first child, but this never materialized. The press began to pick up on the discord, and reported that Cleaver's movements were restricted to his "luxury apartment" in Havana. When an unnamed source claimed that Cleaver was unhappy in Cuba, the story was covered on both coasts. "Black Panther in Cuba Discontented," announced the *New York Times*, as if to imply that exile in Communist Cuba was worse than imprisonment in the United States. The *Times* even took notice when Kathleen Cleaver was said to have joined her husband in Havana, although this turned out to be an erroneous story based on a report in the *Black Panther* newspaper. Cleaver's adventures offered significant entertainment value, and their episodic nature continued to attract an audience. But the media were also preoccupied with Cleaver because he had become a truly global subject, bringing an international dimension to the Panthers' visibility.[44]

The mystery deepened when a publisher of *Ramparts* told the press that he had received word that Cleaver had left Cuba and had permission to share their communications with reporters. Cleaver appeared to enjoy, from afar, the speculation and interest his travels generated. In a long, vague letter to his associate, Cleaver said that "since leaving Babylon, I have been in about eight countries. . . . And every place I've found much to love; people are beautiful everywhere, and those amongst whom I've been, including these with whom I find myself right now, are amongst the poorest in the world." Soon, the press found that Cleaver's new locale was Algiers, birthplace of one of his chief inspirations, Frantz Fanon. Here he was joined by Kathleen, who was close to giving birth and had been escorted by Emory Douglas. Cleaver later explained that the Cubans made the arrangements and took him to Algiers, leaving him with the expectation that he would return to Cuba in a few weeks. But that never happened. Thus began the next phase of Cleaver's exile.[45]

Shortly after their arrival, Eldridge granted an interview to Lee Lockwood, a photojournalist who had worked for *Ramparts*, among other publications. Lockwood described the couple living in one room in a seedy hotel with their situation uncertain. But Cleaver was determined to insert his voice back into the political discourse in the States. "It should be clear from this interview that Eldridge Cleaver, though temporarily removed from the American scene, has no intention of 'dropping out of history,'" wrote Lockwood. The press frenzy over Cleaver's presence in Cuba had created another problem—the U.S. government designated him as a Cuban national, making it impossible for him to access his funds in U.S. bank accounts, and so the Cleavers were broke. Nevertheless, Cleaver quickly developed grandiose plans for his stay in North Africa. He told Lockwood that internationalizing the Black Panther Party was a key goal: "Our struggle in the United States is not an isolated struggle. I have always been an internationalist. I think that any true revolutionary has to be an internationalist, because our oppressor has an international system," he stated. Years later Kathleen Cleaver noted that Eldridge hoped to use Algiers as "a base for Black Panther political and military action against the United States." Meanwhile, Lockwood's interview appeared in a book published by McGraw-Hill in 1970—with a British version as well—adding to the growing library of texts memorializing the Black Panther Party's most visible figure.[46]

Several weeks later Cleaver also granted an interview to Don Schanche, who had written an article on the Panthers the year before in the *Saturday Evening Post*. Much of Schanche's Algerian conversation would end up in his book *The Panther Paradox: A Liberal's Dilemma*, which also appeared in 1970. Schanche wrote that the *Saturday Evening Post* assigned him to the story because they wanted to see how a middle-class white man would react to Cleaver. The resulting book was a curious mix of white liberal angst and distanced observation of the Panther phenomenon. He blamed Ronald Reagan and the California Regents for boosting Cleaver's celebrity, and he found an undercurrent of violence amid the good-natured atmosphere of the Black Panthers' meetings. Schanche seemed simultaneously shocked and amused by the Panthers' iconography and rhetoric, and he was especially offended by the "obscene and Jew-baiting *Black Panther* weekly." Nevertheless, Schanche told readers to take the Black Panthers seriously. Like Gene Marine, he revealed his underlying fear that the Panthers' primary goal was retribution rather than social change.[47]

The *New York Times Magazine*, once the chief critic of the Black Panthers, could not resist publishing yet another feature about Eldridge Cleaver. The article, written by radical novelist Harvey Swados, was not based on an interview but rather relied almost entirely on secondary sources. Titled "Old Con, Black Panther, Brilliant Writer, and Quintessential American," this hagiography of Cleaver proceeded unabated for nine pages, each one including a breakout quote from one of his books. Swados rehashed former Cleaver interviews and dissected his writing to produce an eloquent argument that the Black Panther leader was symbolic of the American spirit of democracy and dissent. He recounted Cleaver's life history, but it was clear that he knew little about his subject's foreign adventures. He praised Cleaver for his ability to capture the attention of young African Americans, white radicals, and writers. He considered the Panthers' ten-point platform, which demanded the exemption of black men from military service and freedom for black prisoners, to be noble expressions of the quest for black liberation. What Swados failed to note was that Cleaver was not the author of the ten-point platform; in this text, Newton and Seale were erased and Eldridge Cleaver was the embodiment of the Party. In a particularly ironic passage, Swados bemoaned the media's desire to commodify black radicalism: "What I did not foresee was that publishers' eagerness to capitalize on the revolution in racial consciousness would result in the courting and publishing of untalented young men merely because they were black—or that the talented . . . would find their words distorted by the crazyhouse mirrors of the mass media." Yet the *New York Times* was complicit—perhaps even in the forefront—of this trend. Nevertheless, Eldridge Cleaver seemed to be the literary world's black hero, and they were delighted about his return to the public eye.[48]

Eldridge Cleaver was back, and anxious to use the news media. He granted numerous interviews that ended up in the *Black Panther* newspaper and other alternative media, and he began to write again. With headlines such as "Eldridge Cleaver Breaks His Silence" and "Somewhere in the Third World," and an occasional column titled "Notes from Exile," the Minister of Information had regained his platform in the newspaper he had shaped and nurtured. When the Cleavers' son was born, the *Black Panther* announced the new addition with a full-page photograph of the couple with their baby under the title "Another Problem for the Fascists." The *Black Panther* and other Bay Area newspapers reported, with great excitement, that Cleaver had accepted an invitation to the first Pan-African Cultural Festival in Algiers, and that David Hilliard and Emory Douglas also intended to attend the July event as official party representatives. Others in the Panther delegation were *Ramparts* colleague Robert Scheer, Panther Ray "Masai" Hewitt, and Julia Wright Hervé, daughter of Richard Wright. The *Black Panther* published several pages of photos of the event, cheerfully highlighting Cleaver's newfound international recognition. The *New York Times* followed with a story of Cleaver's arrival at the festival, replete with details about his actions and entourage. What seemed to delight the press was that once again they had direct access to their favorite black nationalist. Cleaver and his group established an Afro-American Information Center as part of the festival, and he used every opportunity to address the media, which included numerous reporters from Africa, the Middle East, and Europe. Cleaver held a press conference on 17 July, at the start of the festival, his first official appearance since his flight from the United States. The *Times* reported that Cleaver read a highly critical letter addressed to Stokely Carmichael, who had publicly resigned from the Panthers two weeks earlier. The press smelled controversy, noting that Carmichael said the Panthers "should be concerned mainly with the struggle of nonwhites against 'Western imperialism.'" They were amply rewarded when Carmichael told reporters that in a private meeting with Cleaver the two had agreed to disagree over the role of whites in the black liberation struggle. Never before had an African cultural event received such concentrated attention from the U.S. media. According to the *Times*, "Carmichael appeared to be having a fine time at the festival, which is being staged by the Algerian Government. 'Man, it's so beautiful,' he said." Meanwhile, Cleaver seized every opportunity to tweak the U.S. government; when he called the Apollo 11 moon voyage "a circus to distract people's minds from the real problems" at a press conference in Algiers, he fulfilled the press' expectation that he could be relied upon to say something unexpected and contentious.[49]

San Francisco Examiner reporter Rush Greenlee introduced another tantalizing angle to the Cleaver story—he was homesick and had thoughts of returning to the United States. In a phone interview with Cleaver, Greenlee told readers that the exiled Panther leader missed San Francisco and that he was willing to return to the States to stand trial if he was not imprisoned first. "I just demand a fair hearing. I'm perfectly willing to go along with the trial, but not being put up in prison without a trial," Cleaver told the *Examiner*. When David Hilliard returned from the festival, he confirmed this account, noting that Cleaver "is yearning to come back to the United States" and that the Panthers were "working on the machinery to get Cleaver home." It would be years, however, before Eldridge Cleaver came back to the United States. In December, an Associated Press report noted that Cleaver and his associates planned to remain in Algiers. According to the report, the U.S. diplomatic mission offered him a travel visa to return to the States, but Cleaver refused, saying, "We're not going to accept any documents that puts us in the custody of the Babylonian Pigs."[50]

At the Pan African Festival, Kathleen Cleaver recalled that "[t]he crowd enthusiastically welcomed the Black Panthers, and the Algerian visitors to the Center were intensely curious." Eldridge Cleaver set to work making international contacts, obtaining an invitation from North Korea to visit that country the following year; opportunities to visit Japan and Vietnam also materialized. Cleaver failed to establish a formal relationship with the Algerian government, but he used the country as a launching-off place to travel and as a locale to host visitors. These activities coincided with the establishment of a new Black Panther Party position, International Coordinator, a post first held by Connie Matthews, who had coordinated Bobby Seale's visit to Europe earlier in the year and had helped organize the Danish Committee for

Solidarity with the Black Panther Party. This was just one of a number of groups that began to crop up as the Panthers sought international support. In September, Eldridge Cleaver officially established the International Section of the Black Panther Party, although it had no official status in Algiers. Despite these ambitious goals, the time in Algiers was difficult. Kathleen Cleaver recalled there was a "lack of any clear focus for carrying out the revolutionary aims of the Black Panther Party in the Algerian context" and that language, cultural barriers, and a lack of funds made life for the exiles extremely difficult. The Algerian government was willing to give them refuge but provided little material support for their plans. "Later, the Panthers came to realize that their political presence outside the United States also allowed socialist governments to manipulate the Black Panther Party to serve ends that were extraneous to their own goals within America," she noted.[51]

The dream of a global Black Panther Party based in Algiers never materialized, but the organization had become a transnational entity. There were solidarity committees in Britain, France, Italy, Germany, the Netherlands, and the Scandinavian countries, as well as in Japan. Panther friends in Paris had helped Kathleen Cleaver reach Eldridge in Algiers, and they made contacts with radical activists in the Congo, Mozambique, and Palestine, among others. Shortly after the Pan-African Festival, Eldridge attended the International Conference of Revolutionary Journalists in North Korea, and Black Panther Party delegations visited China and Japan in the early 1970s. Publications by and about the Black Panthers cropped up in Dutch, French, German, and a host of other languages as the demand for information on the group grew. The visibility of the Black Panthers in the U.S. media spilled over into a global arena, providing a model for a race-based political activism for groups in numerous countries. Britain was the first country to establish a full-blown Black Panther Party spin-off organization, and the experience there provides evidence for how far the Panther aura had traveled.

The embodiment of American-style black power politics was brought to Britain not by Huey Newton or Bobby Seale but by Malcolm X, who visited the country in 1964 and 1965, and by Stokely Carmichael two years later. The British news media was crucial in disseminating the images and ideas of radical black nationalism to their audience, and they relied heavily on the output of the U.S. press. In 1967, for example, the British national television network, the BBC, broadcast several news stories about Carmichael's calls for black power in the United States, the legal problems of H. Rap Brown, and the urban uprisings spreading across the States. The visit of Carmichael to London in the summer of 1967 was an important catalyst for Britain's Caribbean, African, and South Asian populations, who were beginning to organize against rampant segregation, discriminatory immigrant policies, and abuses by law enforcement. Obi Egbuna, a Nigerian writer and activist, remembered that "Stokely's arrival was like manna from heaven" and that with his speech "[a] new phase of Black history had begun." Carmichael gave an address in July to the International Congress on the Dialectics of Liberation at the Round House in London, which was also attended by Angela Davis, Allen Ginsberg, Herbert Marcuse, and other celebrated activist/intellectuals. Carmichael told the audience, "Black people have no time for parlour games. The death and damage concomitant with the rebellion are a price to be paid in the revolutionary struggle." The event attracted widespread media attention. A report on BBC television noted that Carmichael represented black power by attacking white Western civilization. The British press demonized Carmichael as "highly intelligent and dangerous, the most effective preacher of racial hatred at large today." Four days later the Home Secretary rose to his feet in the House of Commons to announce that Carmichael would not be allowed into the country again.[52]

These political denunciations helped raise the visibility of black power, and Carmichael's words ignited Britain's black activists. A report by Britain's Institute of Race Relations noted that the positions articulated by Carmichael "ceased to be local American concerns and had taken on a relevance to the British situation." Within days Egbuna emerged as president of a newly formed group called the Universal Coloured People's Association (UCPA). He seized on the call for black power and pushed his colleagues to consider how it might address the needs of Britain's communities of color. The UCPA distributed a manifesto on black power in Britain that received some brief press attention. "Black Power Men Launch Credo: Time to Smash the System," read the headline in the Times, Britain's most influential newspaper. The article reserved judgment, instead reproducing the arguments laid out in the fourteen-page document. "The manifesto says the only way the black man can get real power is by smashing the system that incubates the exploitation of the black." The short article put the British establishment on alert that a new, race-based radical movement was emerging. The article also offered a tantalizing detail—that the document's cover was illustrated with the image of a black panther.[53]

Egbuna sought to exploit the media using American tactics in the quest to gain a national hearing of black Britons' grievances. He told a press conference that the UCPA had succeeded in recruiting nearly eight hundred members, and that "[t]here is only one way for it to go. And that is the way to total liberation." The British press began to pay halting attention to the activities of this group. When another civil rights organization modeled after the NAACP, the Campaign Against Racial Discrimination, underwent an internal struggle over the issue of white involvement in the anti-racist movement, the Times devoted a full page to covering the debate. The image of black power as a specific threat emerged in the press when a headline declared, "Black Revolution Needs Violence: No Alternative in Britain." This time, the Times reported on a speech given by Egbuna to the Institute of Race Relations. The second sentence proclaimed that "black power in Britain was a revolutionary movement which rejected white cooperation, and that revolutions had always involved a resort to violence." The article didn't stray from the content of the meeting; there was little about the organization or about the aggrieved condition of blacks in Britain.[54]

The 1960s were a period in which race relations in Britain were at a tinderbox stage—racially motivated riots and conflicts with police were common throughout the decade. The beginning of the era was marked by upheavals in London and Nottingham in 1958, in which months of random attacks by whites against West Indian and Asian residents culminated in several nights of rioting. The press and politicians alike aroused both sides with inflammatory rhetoric—both Tory and Labour MPs declared that blacks should be barred from immigrating to the country. Historian Peter Fryer described this period in graphic terms: "people of color in Britain watched the racist tail wag the Parliamentary dog," he stated. The Commonwealth Immigrants Bill enacted in 1962 restricted immigration to those with employment vouchers, and by 1965 the government dramatically reduced the number of such vouchers to be issued. Yet during this period 625,000 immigrants from parts of the former British Empire entered the country, fueling a widespread backlash. Immigrants experienced the full spectrum of Jim Crow discrimination in hotels, restaurants, public services, and—most important—in employment. According to a *Time* magazine article, "non-whites are not welcome in 98% white Britain." The BBC broadcast a story on the efforts to halt immigration, and noted that such efforts were likely to "generate more support for the black power movement." Amid the furor, a senior Conservative MP named Enoch Powell began writing newspaper articles protesting the expansion of Asian and African immigration and a proposed antidiscrimination bill. In April 1968 Powell made a virulently racist speech that was widely carried in the British media. He predicted that continued immigration would lead to a race war—"As I look ahead, I am filled with much foreboding. Like the Roman, I seem to see the River Tiber foaming with much blood." Powell also argued that colored immigrants, whom he referred to as "grinning pickaninnies," made Britons "feel like strangers in their own country." Powell's speech was denounced by the Tory government, but many among Britain's working class showed their support for his sentiments in demonstrations and letters. A poll by London's *Daily Express* found that 79 percent of Britain's citizens supported Powell's views.[55]

Powell's sentiments made explicit many of Britain's racial problems and helped mobilize anti-racist activists. A group calling itself the Black People's Alliance was formed and held a conference "with declarations of unity and of gratitude to Mr. Enoch Powell." The group's inaugural gathering attracted the BBC and the *Times*, as well as other media outlets. One of London's liberal tabloids, the *Daily Mirror*, denounced Powell and began to cover black protests across the nation. But unlike in the United States, the specter of racial discord was rarely in the media spotlight in Britain. Most articles in the national press, when race relations were covered at all, relegated the issue to minor status unless there was a significant outbreak of violence. Often, the British learned more about racial conflict and civil rights activism in the United States than at home. And Britain's aggrieved groups continued to be inspired by American-based movements for social change. "They have drawn upon black politics, institutions and culture, in the literature, philosophies and music of African Americans," explained

Stephen Small, "[f]rom the philosophies of Marcus Garvey and W.E.B. Du Bois, Angela Davis and Kwame Ture, to the strategies of Malcolm X, Martin Luther King, and the Black Panthers." According to two observers of the period, "blacks in Britain were watching on television the conflagrations in American ghettos, the repressive tactics of the police and the outburst of Governor Wallace. Is it us next? They asked themselves."[56]

It would be the Black Panther Party that forged the most visible representation of black power in Britain during this period, despite the fact that none of the celebrated Panther leaders set foot in the country. The Panthers' influence in Britain was indirect—disseminated by dominant media, the underground press, and the travels of a handful of British black activists. Immigrants in Britain gained inspiration from reading the *Black Panther* newspaper and other publications, and from watching the party's victories and crises on television. For example, the BBC broadcast a story on Bobby Hutton's funeral in April 1968. The footage included scenes of Marlon Brando being welcomed by Panther leaders, and Bobby Seale leading a group of uniformed men in marching formation. The next month, Britain's independent television network, ITV, devoted an episode of its *This Week* talk show series to the life and death of Bobby Hutton, including an interview with Marlon Brando, who explained why he supported the Panthers.[57]

Obi Egbuna was a product of these influences. In 1967 he spent several months in the United States meeting with a range of civil rights and black power activists, and he was deeply moved by the experience. He grew frustrated with the disunity of the UCPA, and in April 1968, while Enoch Powell was whipping up anti-immigrant fervor across England, Egbuna announced the formation of the Black Panther Movement. "Our ideological oneness and unflinching dedication to the cause became so infectious that Pantherism soon began to spread like wild-fire," he recalled. From the beginning, the small group was a hybrid of the American organization—borrowing tactics, rhetoric, and iconography but addressing the specific interests of British immigrant communities. Perhaps most contentious was Egbuna's desire to forge a black identity based on African descent, rather than the notion of blackness as a symbolic or political racial identity that encompassed numerous immigrant groups. The Black Panther Movement, as they called themselves, began a monthly magazine, *Black Power Speaks*, using some of the rhetoric and iconography of the U.S. Panthers. The first issue, published in June 1968, had a cover photo of the South African singer Miriam Makeba, wife of Stokeley Carmichael, and an extended editorial denouncing the five-year prison sentence of H. Rap Brown as symbolic of state repression against blacks. The white establishment may be silencing the "generals," but there are still unknown soldiers to wage the war, wrote Egbuna, the magazine's editor. "The unknown soldier in this case is the Black masses of the world, and nearer home, here in Britain. Do the unknown soldiers shout action to hide their own inaction? Or are we prepared to stand together and stave off the aggression of White Power?" The back page of the magazine announced the opening of a Black Panther Party office in London. By 1970 the Black Panther Movement was publishing a broadsheet newspaper called the *Black People's News Service* that was wholly reminiscent of the *Black Panther* newspaper, including the images of a snarling black cat, black figures in beret and black leather holding up defiant fists, and the liberal use of the word *pig* to refer to police.[58]

But there were some crucial differences between the U.S. and British groups. The British Panthers' own ten-point platform highlighted "the racist immigration policies of the British government," particularly the unwarranted detention in prison and illegal searches of immigrants. They also demanded an end to the "brainwashing of our children in British schools and through the mass media." The British Panthers eschewed the emphasis on guns and the use of weapons, which were staple items for their American counterparts. The symbolic and actual use of guns was not possible outside of the U.S. context—British citizens had no constitutional right to bear arms, and guns were not a core part of the social and political culture. The representational strategies deployed by the Panthers in the United States could never work as effectively in the British context, particularly because of the differences in press and sedition laws. For example, threats of retaliation against police brutality and expressions of self-defense are considered seditious. But the language of critique, the black power salute, and other manifestations of the Black Panthers had clearly traveled across the Atlantic. The organization struggled for years to build its membership, but by the early 1970s they were firmly ensconced in Britain's left political culture. Members Darcus Howe and Linton Kwesi Johnson founded an influential journal, *Race Today*, and the group organized the National Conference on the Rights of Black People in spring 1971.[59]

The British Black Panthers were virtually ignored in the national press until they were linked to a potential act of violence. The first time the words "Black Panther" were used to describe British activists was in an article in the *Times* (London) headlined "Kill Police Order Alleged in Black Panther Case." Just as in the United States, the British press was attracted to the prospect of a confrontation between the Panthers and law enforcement. In July 1968, Egbuna and two allies were arrested at a Hyde Park meeting for masterminding a plot to murder the police, based on a written manifesto that had been circulated among some members. Egbuna and his colleagues vehemently denied that they had issued a death order against the police. Nevertheless, he was held in Brixton prison for six months, repeatedly refused bail, and eventually convicted and given a three-year suspended sentence. The Black Panthers and their supporters mounted demonstrations on the trio's behalf, including a protest outside Brixton prison that was violently broken up by police. These events momentarily captured the interest of the British press, but it was short-lived. The Black Panther Movement issued a letter of protest in October 1968 that, among other things, critiqued the media's coverage. "Already the *Evening News*, the *Evening Standard*, all the morning papers and both B.B.C. and I.T.V. have presented their versions of the case in ways directly calculated to shock the public," they argued. According to the British Panthers, the media labeled them "black racialists" and "extremists" and called for blacks to denounce black power activists. "And of course, they have persistently maligned and misrepresented the Black Power movement," they complained. This critique was identical to that raised by Panthers in the United States, who constantly railed against the media's treatment of their movement. Egbuna saw this media framing as a deliberate strategy to establish "proof of the Black man's inherent inability to unite with his fellow Black man." Like its U.S. counterpart, the Black Panther Movement needed media attention to further its cause but had no recourse when the results turned out badly.[60]

Meanwhile, the British press was enthusiastically publishing wire service and locally written articles about the American Panther celebrities. The arrests of Britain's Black Panther leaders and their subsequent detention occurred almost simultaneously with Huey Newton's trial in Oakland. But British citizens were likely to learn more about Black Panther activities in California than about the Black Panthers awaiting trial in Brixton prison. British media reports discussing black power almost always referred to this movement as a U.S. phenomenon, as if to deny the presence of racial discord within its borders. Black power was deemed to be the result of a conflation of circumstances specific to the United States—the rise of the New Left, the excesses of the Vietnam War, and the legacy of slavery and Jim Crow segregation. The British press discussed black power with a tone of bemusement; for example, one story claimed black Americans were seeking their own system of apartheid. The article was sympathetic to their complaints of endemic racism but also accused them of being naive and suffering from a type of madness. There seemed to be a certain sense of glee among the British in reporting on the racial unrest in the United States.[61]

In the spring of 1968, the *Times* attempted to explore the problem of black-white race relations with a twelve-part series titled "Black Man in Search of Power" that offered a sympathetic portrait of the quest for racial justice. "This has led to efforts by the Negro to discover his own cultural and historical origins, long buried beneath white civilization," noted one article. "It involves the teaching of African languages in schools and anti-universities. It involves the bushy afro haircut, African clothing, and the adoption of African and Arab names. The range and number of Negro groups in America matches in complexity the ramifications of the white society they are challenging. The American black man remains, after all that has happened, an American." But no such sympathies would be expressed when black power was articulated on British soil. The series did offer a discussion of racial problems globally, including the Nottingham riots of 1958 and the ongoing debates about immigration. But when it came to Britain's nascent black power movement, Malcolm X, Stokely Carmichael, Russia, Maoists, and assorted African rebels were the cause. The series concluded that while problems persisted in Britain, things were not nearly as bad as they were in the United States. "Britain still has a little time," reported the *Times*. A few months later, the *Manchester Guardian* published an editorial titled "Of Pigs and Panthers" that described the group as troublesome evidence of the racial problems in the United States. "The fear and hatred already exist, part of the dreadful price America is paying for an alienated race and an alienated generation," wrote columnist John Cole. He interviewed Bobby Seale, finding him lacking in humor and full of revolutionary double-talk. While Cole expressed dismay about the rampant racism blacks encountered in the States, he was equally disturbed by the Panthers' strategies. He and Seale also discussed the Panthers' armed demonstration in Sacramento. "With all the charm of a Madison Avenue public relations man, Mr. Seale explained these as attempts to use the mass media. It certainly got a lot of publicity," noted Cole. Nowhere did the *Guardian*'s writer link the grievances or strategies of the Black Panthers in the United States with those in Britain. Was he unaware of what was occurring in his own country, or had he chosen simply to ignore it?[62]

Mass media played an essential role in transmitting the theories and tactics of black power activism across a global network. One British activist remembered: "It was often said that the Vietnam War was the first major conflict to be played out nightly on TV. It wasn't so for us. For us, it was the Civil Rights struggle and the subsequent battle between the Black Power activists and the American Government. During those years we got to know their names and faces better than the next door neighbours." Obi Egbuna agreed, also emphasizing the linked struggles of those across the African diaspora. "The enemy of the black man in North America is the same as the enemy of the black man in southern Africa, South America, and Asia . . . it is therefore absurd to suggest that a black power organization is an anachronism in a white country like Britain because to do so is to imply that black power is something exclusive to America." Nevertheless, at the close of 1969, the Black Panther Movement in Britain was often rendered invisible, while the Black Panther Party in the United States remained salient. A December editorial in the *Times* argued that the Black Panthers might be under siege, but they were gradually winning the war of public opinion. Under the headline, "The Threat of the Panthers," the *Times* issued a warning to U.S. authorities: "They may well have the effect of creating folk heroes. Indeed a sort of heroic saga of defiance is being built up that will gather black loyalties, particularly among the young, who are ardently in search of manhood and self respect." Again, the preoccupation was with the racial crisis across the Atlantic; there was no reference to the demands for affirmation or respect among Britain's black populace.[63]

The Black Panther Party had established a global presence that continued to inspire radical activists at home and abroad, aided considerably by an increasingly transnational mass media. By the early 1970s, there were hybrid Black Panther organizations in Bermuda, Israel, India, and Australia. According to Vijay Prashad, the group founded in Bombay in 1972 clearly articulated their solidarity with their black American predecessors as they fought for civil rights for lower-caste Indians. Calling themselves the Dalit Panthers, their manifesto stated: "From the Black Panthers, Black Power emerged. The fire of the Struggles has thrown out sparks into the country. We claim a close relationship with this struggle." Similarly, communities of color across the United States found a viable option in the Black Panthers' style of confrontational politics. The Young Lords, founded in 1967 to organize Puerto Rican youth; the Brown Berets, formed in 1968 by Mexican American activists; the American Indian Movement; and the Red Guard Party, started in 1968 by Chinese Americans in the Bay Area, were all profoundly influenced by the Panthers' example. Asian Americans gravitated to the Black Panther Party because they often lived in close proximity to African Americans on the West Coast, explained Prashad. "Radical Chinese youth named 1969 'the Year of the People Off the Pigs,' a salute to the style of the Panthers and against the oppression within Chinatown." The Black Panthers offered a model for Asian Americans and other disenfranchised groups to use racial politics as an organizing principle. According to Daryl Maeda, the Red Guard became particularly adept at performing blackness as it announced its own ten-point program, published a weekly newspaper, and critiqued police harassment in San Francisco's Chinatown. An article in the *Wall Street Journal* from spring 1969 noted that a growing number of American Indian activists were using the rhetoric and tactics of groups such as the Black Panthers to forge their own red power movement. The Brown Berets grew to become a significant force in the Chicano movement, and community defense against the police was its central focus. "The Brown Berets became a paramilitary organization and, because of it, developed an image as the Chicano counterparts of the Black Panther Party," noted Carlos Munoz Jr.[64]

These were not mere imitators of the Black Panthers; rather, the proliferation of these organizations suggests the extent of domestic and international unrest in an era in which radical protest was consistently met with a brutal response in places ranging from New York to Paris to Mexico City. The London *Times*' prediction that the repression of the Black Panthers would only elevate their heroic status failed to take into account their appeal beyond black America. The Panthers' insistence that they identified with and spoke for all oppressed people resonated with the downtrodden as well as those seeking radical chic. And their strategic use of mass media guaranteed that this message would be transmitted to every corner of the globe. In an early issue of the *Black Panther* newspaper, Huey Newton claimed the Panthers were continuing the tradition of the revolutions of Russia, China, Cuba, and Algeria, and the anti-colonialist struggles in Kenya, and that the mass media would be essential for the Panthers' global influence. "Millions and millions of oppressed people might not know members of the vanguard party personally or directly, but they will gain through an indirect acquaintance the proper strategy for liberation via the mass media and the physical activities of the party," Newton proclaimed. In a few short years, the Black Panther Party created a global imagined community of radical activists that proved to be astonishingly effective despite governments' efforts to silence them. But this far-flung community was not tied together by an official nationalism, with its allegiance to a nation-state. Rather, the Panthers helped to forge a global community of the aggrieved that crossed class and racial barriers. These disparate groupings, united in their struggles against imperialism, capitalism, and racism, aspired to a new "national" formation, one that embraced the underclass and the disenfranchised.[65]

Neither stardom nor a powerful public relations apparatus nor an international presence could protect the Black Panthers from a stepped-up campaign by the government to shut them down. In June, FBI chief J. Edgar Hoover pledged that his agency would do everything in its power to bring about this outcome. In his often repeated proclamation, he declared, "The Black Panther Party, without question, represents the greatest threat to internal security of the country." The statement, part of the FBI's 1969 annual report, argued that not only were the Black Panthers wreaking havoc in urban communities, but they "travel extensively all over the United States preaching their gospel of hate and violence . . . to students in colleges, universities and high schools as well." It was published widely in the press. At the same time, a Senate subcommittee under the leadership of Senator John

L. McClellan was conducting public hearings into the Black Panther Party. Over several days, the news media published reports that Panther leaders broadcast subversive threats from Cuba and that the group was bent on revolutionary overthrow of the U.S. government. An Oakland police officer was among those who testified that the Black Panthers posed an urgent and widespread threat. "This country is involved in an internal arms race," the policeman testified. The committee also heard from two disgruntled ex-Panthers who accused the group of sexually abusing young women in the Oakland office and of carrying out a host of illegal activities.[66]

The last six months of 1969 seemed to bear out Hoover's promise. With Newton in prison and Cleaver in exile, Bobby Seale was the Panther leader under constant scrutiny. With numerous charges hanging over his head, Seale was extradited from San Francisco to Chicago in September so he could face trial as part of the Chicago 8. It was front-page news in the *New York Times* when U.S. district judge Julius Hoffman ordered Seale gagged and chained to his chair, saying the defendant "repeatedly shouted accusations and insults" during the proceedings. After three days, the judge ordered the chains removed, and a group of civil rights lawyers pressed the case that Seale's civil rights had been violated. Seale appeared on the front page again when he was convicted of contempt of court and sentenced to four years in jail. An op-ed piece in the *Times* noted that the trial had been reduced to a political confrontation between Seale and the judge. The resulting courtroom drawing of Seale straining against his restraints as he sat in the courtroom was initially published in the *Times* and was reproduced in numerous venues. It became the symbolic representation of the case, defining the contestation between the courts and radical protest. The image illustrated a story in *Life* magazine titled "In a Courtroom of the Absurd," noting that "onstage the big attraction was one of the leads, Black Panther co-defendant Bobby Seale." A similar rendering appeared on the book jacket of Seale's autobiography, *Seize the Time*. Seale was never convicted of any charges stemming from the protests at the Democratic National Convention.[67]

Meanwhile, instances of police raids on Panther chapters, arrests, and shootings came fast and furious. The *Los Angeles Times*, not always known for giving the group a sympathetic hearing, listed a series of incidents that seemed to offer proof that "[t]he Black Panthers have become a special class in the eyes of the law." There was an April 28 raid on the San Francisco office, the arrest of eight Panthers in New Haven in May on murder charges, a June 3 raid of the Chicago Panther office with the arrest of eight more members, a June 4 raid of a Detroit Panther chapter, the tear gassing and arrest of ten Panthers in Denver, and similar incidents in Salt Lake City, Indianapolis, and San Diego, among others. Charles Garry told the newspaper that the police operations were taking their toll—he had at least two hundred Panther cases to defend. The *Times* also pointed to the "elaborate surveillance of Panthers" and the government requests for wiretaps as further evidence that the Panthers were under attack. In a lengthy editorial published on the Fourth of July, the newspaper warned that these tactics might backfire; the threats of prison or death might simply inspire new Panther chapters to emerge. Regardless of its effectiveness, wrote the *Times*, singling out the Black Panthers for such treatment was fundamentally un-American. "Our only protection against tyranny, or chaos, is a strict equality in the method of the law."[68]

New York Times reporter Earl Caldwell, who had gained unprecedented access to the Panther leadership in Oakland, noted that the organization had changed considerably, although this gained little notice in the mainstream press. By the summer of 1969, the Panthers had shed their paramilitary image, no longer wearing the leather jackets, berets, and heavy armament of the past. "The Panthers have changed in style, tone and language," he declared. Most significant to Caldwell was that the Panthers no longer targeted whites as the enemy; in fact, he found the group "embracing white radicals," and he noted that "more whites were visible now around the office." This reflected a significant shift in ideology as the Panthers' rhetoric, in the absence of Cleaver and Newton, focused more on class struggle and imperialism than on a contest between black and white. He pointed to the National Conference Against Fascism, sponsored by the Panthers, during which Bobby Seale publicly denounced black racism. But such findings had little effect in countering the discourses produced by the FBI and the U.S. government, which clung to the framing of the Panthers as racist and anti-white.[69]

The most controversial, and widely reported, Panther confrontation with law enforcement occurred just weeks before Christmas as another troubled year seemed to be winding down. In a predawn raid in

Chicago, the police shot and killed Fred Hampton, the Illinois chairman, and Mark Clark, who led the Peoria chapter. The latest dead Panthers were twenty-one and twenty-two years old, respectively. The national news media picked up the story and revealed a sense of outrage at this latest instance of the state's responses to the group. According to the *New York Times*, the pair "died in a hail of shotgun and pistol fire as policemen assigned to the Cook Country State's Attorney's office raided an apartment near the group's headquarters. . . . The party's leadership has been decimated in recent months by a wave of arrests and police actions." In the *Times* account, the conflagration occurred after the police pushed the apartment door open and a woman opened fire with a shotgun. The wire service report published in the *Oakland Tribune* noted that in the aftermath, police found a cache of weapons in the apartment and that Hampton was alleged to have fired first. Although the details of the event were sketchy, the deaths elicited widespread outrage.[70]

Within days the Black Panther Party had initiated a political response. Attorney Charles Garry told the press that these were the twenty-seventh and twenty-eighth Panthers killed in clashes with police during an eighteen-month period. Members of the Illinois chapter took hundreds of local residents on tours of the site of the shoot-out, maintaining that Hampton was "murdered in his bed." The *New York Times* reported that "a broad spectrum of the Negro community" witnessed the site, expressing sympathy and dismay over the death of Hampton, who was widely respected in the city. Within days, the Justice Department, under pressure from the NAACP, the Urban League, and the *Chicago Defender*, announced it would investigate the case, a decision that was announced on the front page of the *New York Times*. Attorney general John N. Mitchell, certainly not an ally of black nationalist organizations, nevertheless agreed to consider whether the Chicago police had violated any federal laws. Particularly ironic was the report that the FBI—instigators of many of the law enforcement assaults on the Panthers—would be asked to assist in the inquiry. The *Times* also noted that an independent group led by a number of civil rights organizations intended to conduct hearings in cities across the nation as part of an independent assessment of what happened in Chicago.[71]

Three days after the Chicago slayings, hundreds of Los Angeles police officers raided the offices of the southern California branch. The conflagrations that the Panthers predicted seemed to be playing out on a public stage. A page-one story in the *Oakland Tribune* reported that three police officers were wounded after trying to serve warrants at the Los Angeles offices, where three women and eight men barricaded themselves inside. The *New York Times* carried a photograph of Los Angeles police displaying the guns they seized during the shootout. But one of the most extensive reports was produced not in the United States but in the United Kingdom. A BBC broadcast underscored the Black Panthers' troubled yet romanticized status as it covered the aftermath of the LAPD raid, which led to a five-hour gun battle. The BBC sent one of their own reporters to cover the story rather than relying on footage from American broadcast outlets. The cameras panned a crowd of protestors on the steps of city hall as they shouted, "All power to the people." The British reporter noted that "[t]he Black Panthers are in a militant mood" following the shoot-out with police, which left five wounded and dozens of Panthers in jail. "The Black Panthers claim there is a general climate of repression against black people," said the reporter. "Police in a number of American cities have been accused of cracking down on Panther activities." The piece closed with comments from Elaine Brown, who did not mask her anger when asked if the Panthers advocated violence. "We say we'll do anything at all to gain liberation for our people," she retorted. "There were eleven people in our office with the average age of eighteen, and there were over 500 pigs from the L.A. pig department. . . . You can't tell me that doesn't represent violence." Such a report was both cautionary and inspirational to activists within the United States and beyond its borders; the Black Panthers had taken their grievances to the public, challenged state authority, and rallied large numbers of people on their behalf. Yet at the end of three years, many were dead, wounded, imprisoned, or exiled, and the rest were deeply angry.[72]

At the end of the year the American Civil Liberties Union published the results of a survey of police relations with the Black Panthers. The group maintained that "law enforcement as applied to Black Panthers is a pattern of provocative and punitive harassment, denying to black militants the right of free political expression." A summary of the study, which appeared in the *New York Times* and the *San Francisco*

Examiner, among other outlets, reported that the study was part of the larger independent inquiry initiated after the shoot-out in Chicago. The ACLU documented instances of police infiltration into the organization, noting that these operatives sought to induce Panther members to commit criminal acts. The report also detailed the constant arrests of Black Panthers for relatively minor infractions, although the charges were rarely upheld in courts. These included the sale of the *Black Panther* newspaper or, in the case of one San Francisco raid, using sound equipment illegally. The ACLU findings made a strong case that the Panthers' constitutional rights were constantly infringed upon: "We view this style of law enforcement, as applied with prejudice to the Panthers, as inflammatory and very susceptible to escalation into violent confrontations," quoted the *Times.*[73]

Not all media organizations registered the same alarm, however. United Press International charged that cries of genocide against the Black Panthers were inflammatory and were being used indiscriminately by such individuals as Ralph Abernathy, head of the Southern Christian Leadership Conference. The *San Francisco Examiner,* which published the UPI account, also issued an editorial that resurrected the demonization frame that had followed the Panthers for nearly three years. The *Examiner* praised efforts between the police and Berkeley residents to prevent further violence but argued that the "Panthers are an armed revolutionary element with a strong appetite for violence." The paper argued that the crackdown by law enforcement was the reasonable response to the Panthers' actions. "When they seek to blast open the route with guns, as they repeatedly have done, it is the duty of police to act," said the editorial.[74]

The *Wall Street Journal* published an editorial that asserted that the attention placed on the so-called police repression of the Black Panthers was merely evidence of the media being duped. In an editorial titled "Warped Perceptions," the newspaper argued that when the FBI cracked down on a right-wing group, the Minutemen, no one complained of political persecution. But "the chic set seems inclined to take entirely seriously charges that the Black Panthers are not the perpetrators of a conspiracy but the victims of it." In particular, the *Journal* pointed to Charles Garry's claims that twenty-eight Panthers had been killed by the police, arguing that he failed to provide convincing evidence for this assertion. The *Wall Street Journal,* which had focused considerable attention on the Panthers during the previous months, articulated the concept of "radical chic" to describe a popular culture that seemed to blindly embrace the Panthers' complaints. The *Journal* acknowledged that there was a possibility that "some members of the Chicago police force were intent on taking revenge for the killing of two policemen by the Panthers three weeks earlier," and it supported the Justice Department inquiry. But the editorial argued that the Panthers' assertion that there had been twenty-eight deaths was little more than a publicity stunt. The *Journal* also deployed a Nixon-esque notion of the "silent majority," noting that the concern for the Panthers registered in "some circles" did not reflect public opinion.[75]

Three months later, the editor of the *New Yorker* asked political scientist Edward Jay Epstein to investigate the claim of twenty-eight deaths in detail. His findings, published in February 1971, asserted there were only ten instances in which the Black Panthers were killed directly by the police, and that these deaths did not indicate a "coordinated pattern" or strategy of genocide, as the Panthers insisted. Epstein criticized the news media for uncritically reporting these claims, arguing that while police brutality in black communities should be investigated, most of the cases were the results of confrontations in which the Panthers were also shooting at the police. This assessment did little to assuage the grief and anger experienced by the Panthers and their supporters—it mattered little whether the death toll at state hands was ten or twenty-eight. But Epstein's accounting brought into question the extent to which the press could be believed, whether they were demonizing the Panthers or heeding their claims.[76]

However, this issue had a distinctly racial dimension that most media commentary failed to address. *Jet* magazine's managing editor, John H. Britton, summed up the year 1969 in a lengthy article that placed Cleaver and Newton as part of the legacy of the suppression of radical black dissent in the United States. Despite efforts by the dominant culture to single out the Black Panthers as outside the domain of legitimate black resistance, they were part of a long tradition, he argued. The headline read, "The Pattern Is the Same Where Black Men Rebel." From antislavery martyr John Brown to Marcus Garvey, Robert Williams, W.E.B. Du Bois, and A. Philip Randolph, Britton reminded readers that what happened to the Black Panthers and others is "precisely what has always happened in the past: radical black militants who blossom as leaders in the war of words soon find themselves defoliated by the heat of law and order—or worse." The *Jet* article quoted Cleaver's *Soul on Ice* at length about the tactics used to subjugate black Americans, noting that it was "perhaps a prophetic description of his own current condition." Britton linked the experiences of African anti-colonial leaders Kwame Nkrumah and Jomo Kenyatta to the activism on American soil: "History is instructive in underscoring the fact that this trend is neither a new one nor one confined to our national borders." Perhaps only an African American journalist writing for a black-owned periodical could make this bold assessment. After surveying the array of black male activists under political and legal assault—including H. Rap Brown, Stokely Carmichael, Muhammad Ali, and Dick Gregory—the reality was sobering. "As for Malcolm X . . . well, he's dead," Britton summed up.[77]

9

THE RISE AND FALL OF A
MEDIA FRENZY: THE 1970s

In the past, all the Panthers I've seen have been helpful to reporters. But now, all journalists are associated with the oozing distortions of the media. And I can't be indignant—since I've seen how often the Panthers (and most dissidents) have been lushly misrepresented.

Nora Sayre, "The Revolutionary People's Constitutional Convention," *Esquire* (January 1971)

At the start of a new decade, the Black Panther Party no longer qualified as a young organization—they were bloodied, battered, financially spent, and significantly jaded by their experiences. An Illinois State University professor found that by the end of 1969, 348 Panthers had been arrested for serous crimes, and that by early 1970, they had spent almost $5 million to bail out their members. The Justice Department estimated that by November of that year, 469 Panthers had been arrested. They were also a fully entrenched component of mass culture. A March article in the *New York Times Magazine*, for example, offered a fascinating glimpse at how the Panthers' use of black vernacular culture was taken up in middle-class suburbia. In a discussion of the group's "rapping," linguist Gerald Emanuel Stern wrote that the Panthers' speech patterns were rooted in a "Southern-ghetto drawl" combined with a rhythmic style and grammar that made their talk "a form of weaponry." The Panthers' rhetoric had become a source of fascination and mimicry far beyond the urban centers of the North. Everyone, it seemed, wanted to rap like the Panthers, further reinforcing their celebrity status. Meanwhile, the group continued to provide plenty of sensational copy to the news media in the new decade, with the focus shifting to the East Coast. The spectacularization of Black Panther protests, which stunned audiences in Oakland, Berkeley, San

Francisco, and Los Angeles, was now a routine practice in cities such as Chicago, New York, and New Haven. The Panthers received even greater sustained television coverage as they played out controversial legal cases before the national networks based in New York City. Two trials—the Panther 21 in New York and the murder/conspiracy case featuring Chairman Bobby Seale in New Haven—dominated the news media with a visual panoply of highly orchestrated marches and demonstrations. In April in New York, for example, five thousand supporters marched from Manhattan to Queens to express their solidarity with the Panther 21 defendants.[1]

Two months earlier, in February, pre-trial hearings began for the Panther 21 in what would be a lengthy and tortuous proceeding. The group was arrested in April 1969 on charges of a conspiracy to bomb police stations, five department stores, the New York City subway, and the New York Botanical Garden. Their defense attorney, William Kunstler, maintained that they were being hunted and prosecuted by law enforcement, likening the treatment of the Panthers to the harrowing experiences of Jews under the Nazis. After a contentious period in which the defendants demanded to have their grievances heard and the judge postponed the preliminary hearings, the actual trial began in September. Nine months later, in May 1971, the jury acquitted them on all charges after deliberating forty-five minutes. Sixteen members of the Panther 21 had languished in prison for two years in twenty-four-hour confinement, and they maintained that they were denied medical care and access to their attorneys. While incarcerated they wrote their collective autobiography, *Look for Me in the Whirlwind*. This text, published in 1971 by Random House, captured the motivations of rank-and-file Panthers, presenting them as earnest individuals dedicated to social justice rather than as the crazed terrorists constructed by the prosecution. The Panther 21, all active members of the New York City chapter, were a diverse group, including college students, a Ph.D., and a student nurse. Some had already served time in jail on other charges, including Joan Bird, who was under indictment for the attempted murder of two policemen. Among the others were Afeni Shakur, mother of hip-hop legend Tupac Shakur, who gave birth to him shortly after her acquittal. All were united in their belief in the principles of the Black Panther Party.[2]

Look for Me in the Whirlwind brought the New York Panthers and their defense team widespread publicity from the same reputable, mainstream publishing house that produced books by Cleaver, Seale, and Newton. The Panther 21 also used alternative routes to get out their message, including a set of audiotapes that recorded their "Panther Manifesto" while in jail. The tapes, narrated by defendant Michael Cetewayo Tabor, gave the imprisoned Panthers a voice among supporters that helped mobilize courthouse vigils, large-scale demonstrations, and fund-raising for their defense. The tapes, distributed by a group called Radio Free People based in lower Manhattan, also included Tabor's statement on the drug problem in urban America, titled "Capitalism + Heroin = Genocide." The recording, based on a pamphlet Tabor prepared for Black Panther distribution, argued that the growing use of heroin was a crisis quietly encouraged by the state—a narrative that would be revived more than twenty years later in Mario Van Peebles' film *Panther*. Members of the Newsreel Collective were also on hand throughout the Panther 21 trial, recording the events on film and in photographs.[3]

The murder and conspiracy case in New Haven had a similar trajectory. Twelve men and one woman were defending themselves against charges that they kidnapped, tortured, and murdered fellow Panther Alex Rackley after obtaining information that he was a police informant. The newspaper and television accounts were both lurid and tedious, recounting the daily events of the trial. While protestors were marching in New York, forty-five hundred attended a Panther rally in April on the campus of Yale University. The students initiated a classroom strike that dropped attendance by as much as 75 percent. On May Day 1970, New Haven was descended on by twenty-five thousand demonstrators who gathered to hear speeches on the Panthers' behalf, including ones by David Hilliard, Yippies co-founders Jerry Rubin and Abbie Hoffman, and internationally renowned French novelist and playwright Jean Genet. The rally was peaceful, but a group who later marched into downtown New Haven scuffled with the police, who used tear gas to disperse the crowd, making the city appear to be the next hotbed of urban unrest.[4]

Behind the scenes, the Panthers had contacted Genet to campaign on behalf of the defendants in both trials. Genet's insertion into the Panthers' plight brought a new level of attention to these events, particularly among intellectuals at American universities. Genet was first drawn to the Panthers while reporting on the 1968 Democratic Convention in Chicago for *Esquire* magazine, and he became involved in the campaign to release Bobby Seale during the trial of the Chicago 8. He was attracted to the Panthers because of his own experiences of incarceration, and because of his Marxist politics and identification with radical causes. In a letter he wrote to Bobby Seale and Huey Newton from Paris, he told them that the head of the *New York Times* bureau had asked him to write "about the solution of the black problems in U.S. prisons." Instead, Genet wrote an essay on the subject and sent it to Seale and Newton with the hope that it would appear in the *Black Panther*, saying he did not trust the *New York Times*. In March 1970, Genet spontaneously traveled to the United States, where he visited Seale in New Haven, and the Panther 21 in New York. He addressed throngs of mostly white college students at the City University of New York, Massachusetts Institute of Technology, Columbia University, and State University of New York at Stony Brook. After a talk at Yale, he attended the Panthers' pretrial hearing, where he loudly accosted the judge in French after Hilliard and Douglas scuffled with the police. The *New York Times* reported on the incident in an article titled "Genet Emerges as an Idol of the Panthers," noting that Genet denounced American racism and referred to the Panthers as friends rather than political allies. Genet's May Day speech was the highlight of the New Haven agitation; he challenged American intellectuals to shed their anxieties about race and take a principled stand by supporting Seale and the other defendants. The speech was quickly published by City Lights Books in San Francisco, co-founded by Lawrence Ferlinghetti in 1953 as a venue for experimental and radical literature. The book's appearance ensured a greater permanence for Genet's commentary. The Committee to Defend the Panthers also published a pamphlet by Genet titled *Here and Now for Bobby Seale: Essays*. Genet returned to France shortly afterward and continued to write and speak actively on the Panthers' behalf.[5]

The media focused as much attention on the vocal protests of the Panthers' supporters on the streets of New Haven as they did on the actual courtroom proceedings. But *New York* magazine, an incubator for the "new journalism," used the opportunity to vilify the Black Panthers beneath a veneer of liberal concern. "*New York*'s historic role as journalistic gadfly placed it in the unusual cultural position of appearing adversarial in content (or politics) even while it was truly adversarial only in style," emphasized one scholar. Writer Gail Sheehy produced a two-part story on the New Haven trial with the stated purpose of interrogating the Panthers' effect on middle-class blacks. The articles, published back to back in November 1970, attempt to superimpose a gritty, street-smart aesthetic on her reportage of the Panther phenomenon, which she dubbed "Panthermania." The articles contained few quotes or attributions and were littered with colorful, descriptive passages. The lure of the Panthers "can be strong enough even to pull a young dude back from the traditional comfort of dope," wrote Sheehy. "The demands of urban guerrilla life offer a substitute for the desperate habitual rhythm of hustling, which is the hardest thing for an addict to give up." Sheehy continues in this vein, using an assumed black vernacular and sense of intimacy to lead readers to believe that she had an inside scoop on African American life. New Haven is described as a "white-pocketbook town," and its middle-class blacks, upon whom the Panthers were wreaking havoc, go to church and "have traditionally taken their manners from the least mobile white population—that careful, myopic, mildly-spoken core of lineruppers and Sunday-besters." Her prose was certainly entertaining in its skillful deployment of racial stereotypes and mythology. An analysis of her articles noted they "constituted a compendium of every ugly cliché about blacks one could imagine," including their hypersexuality, lack of intellectual ability, and superficiality. Sheehy's main premise was that the Panther defendants in New Haven were guilty, and that the organization was ruining the lives of earnest young blacks. She heaped scorn on the Panther leadership, who were little more than charlatan entertainers, and their supporters, whom she reduced to fawning sycophants, although she admitted to having been a Panther sympathizer at one point. Indeed, her writing became a kind of self-flagellation for white liberals, who like Sheehy were initially attracted to the glamour of the Panthers with little or no understanding of the troubled, violent underside of black American resistance. Once stripped of their popular veneer, these black radical heroes were simply human, and a deep disappointment.[6]

The Panthers were furious. When it became known that Sheehy was turning her articles into a book to be published by Random House, Panther attorney Charles Garry threatened to sue for libel. In a letter to the publisher's legal department, Garry asserted that the articles contained "[m]any, many willful and malicious defamatory misstatements of fact," and he called it an "astonishingly malicious and shoddy piece of work." Garry demanded that the publisher thoroughly review Sheehy's manuscript, and said that David Hilliard's attorneys were already in the process of filing a lawsuit. The Panthers' complaints fell on deaf ears, despite the fact that Random House had also published Seale's *Seize the Time*, Cleaver's *Post-Prison Writings*, and the Panther 21's memoirs. A terse response from the publisher's lawyer noted that the manuscript "is based entirely on public records and accurately reflects their contents." More important, Random House relied on the First Amendment protections that require claimants to prove malicious disregard for the truth. *Panthermania* was published in 1971 and helped to launch Sheehy's prodigious literary career. Like the *New York* articles, the book recounts the events leading up to and including Rackley's murder in a breezy, confident manner. In the introduction she claims to have been unable to obtain the official transcripts of the trial, yet she presents a flawless narrative that reinforces the frame of the Panthers as violent and a threat to society. While Bobby Seale is giving a speech at Yale University, she writes, a group of Panthers, including Ericka Huggins, are torturing Rackley because he has confessed to being an informant. Sheehy described the events as if she witnessed the entire scene firsthand, including when they decide to kill their captive: " 'Off him,' Sams finally said. He laid the .45 in Warren Kimbro's hand and Kimbro walked Rackley a little way into the swamp and put a bullet through his head." How Sheehy could have determined these facts is never revealed, although she suggests that middle-class New Haven blacks she "befriends" are her main informants. Sheehy was so anxious to get the book into print that she didn't wait out the trial's final outcome. She reported that one of the defendants, Lonnie McLucas, was acquitted of the three most serious charges but was convicted of conspiracy to murder, and that four others were given suspended sentences. In a curious critique of the criminal justice system, Sheehy noted that Huggins and Seale spent two years in jail without bail as the process dragged on: "With its painfully antiquated and inequitable court system, the state continues to cook a violent stew." After Sheehy's book was published, Bobby Seale and Ericka Huggins were acquitted. *Panthermania* used literary invention and private, unattributed conversations to supplement the testimony at the trial, placing it squarely within the "new journalism" genre. But in many respects there was nothing new about Sheehy's reports on the Black Panthers; she was yet one more journalist committed to reinforcing the established ideologies that condemned these militants, often before they were actually tried in a court of law.[7]

Amid the hoopla in New Haven, one Yale undergraduate found a way to inject humor and parody into the situation. Garry Trudeau, creator of the *Doonesbury* comic strip, was a cartoonist for the *Yale Daily News*. He started a series called "Bull Tales" in 1968, and included commentary on the political issues roiling the campus, including the Panthers' trial. In one strip, Trudeau captured the theatrical absurdity of the proceedings as a member of the Yale Corporation lambasted Yale's president Kingman Brewster for making comments in support of the Panthers. When asked his thoughts, Brewster holds a clenched fist and utters, "All power to the people! Dig!" symbolizing the extent to which black power rhetoric had infiltrated mainstream society. In another Trudeau strip, a Yale professor brings a Black Panther to his American studies class, treating the black man as a laboratory specimen for the students' inspection. "I think it's important that we all know the Panther side of the story," says the professor. "I have a friend who said he could get me one for my class. Needless to say, 'I was thrilled.'" In the next panel, the stunned Black Panther puts his head down on the desk in a gesture of despair while the class loudly applauds. In this comedic series, Trudeau effectively captured the multiple contradictions circulating around the Panthers trials, including misplaced white liberal sympathies and the very real injustices being meted out by the criminal justice system.[8]

Trudeau was not the only cartoonist to find the Black Panthers an irresistible subject. Comic or spectacular fictional representations of the group appeared in both conventional and unconventional venues. One catalyst for these was undoubtedly the short-lived Black Panther coloring book, which was distributed to youth groups in the Bay Area to the consternation of law enforcement officials. The Panthers' established place in popular culture, their recognizable iconography, their tales of daring and adventure, and the increasing demand for heroic black figures served as inspiration for at least two Black Panther comic projects. An independent artist, Ovid P. Adams, published an elaborate, vividly illustrated comic titled *The Adventures of Black Eldridge: The*

Panther, in 1970. The main character, Black Eldridge, was an obvious tribute to the exiled Panther leader; Adams rendered him exactly both in look and in rhetorical style. The cover of the comic showed Cleaver in full Panther regalia, shouldering a rifle on one side and hoisting a white human head on the other. The story line was a classic fable of the black power era: an innocent black man driving through Utah is brutally attacked by a white supremacist. The news is transmitted across the Atlantic to Africa, where Black Eldridge decides to avenge the crime. He proclaims, "I have vowed, in the name of 'black liberation' to match that government's actions outrage, for outrage. Atrocity for atrocity. And justice for justice. Dig!" Black Eldridge determines that the head minister of the Mormon Church is the most influential white man in Utah, and he determines to make him pay. At the end of the story, Eldridge tracks down his prey, beheads him with one stroke of a sword like a knight in armor, and disappears. "Then back into the blackness of night—like a panther this black warrior did slip. And slid from these shores again, to the safety of the mother country Africa. And a deed well done. Right on." Only one issue of the comic, published by the San Francisco black-owned bookstore Marcus Books, is extant, suggesting that *The Adventures of Black Eldridge* was more useful as a polemic than a source of youthful entertainment.[9]

Marvel Comics, one of the giants of the industry, also tried a project that capitalized on the Black Panthers' popularity. A cartoon character called the Black Panther first appeared in 1966 as a minor figure in another series. Ten years later, well-known cartoonist Jack Kirby launched the *Black Panther* comic, now considered one of the first black superheroes. Unlike Ovid Adams' story, *Black Panther* had no direct connection to the political party of the same name. Rather, the comic relied on loose associations with black power activism. The lead character, named T'Challa, was the head of Wakanda, an imaginary technologically advanced African nation. "The Prince of Wakanda," as the character was known, "stalks both the concrete of the city and the undergrowth of the velt," and his first adventure takes him to the treasure of King Solomon. The Black Panther "dons the garb of the savage cat" much as his political counterparts used the Black Panther icon as the symbol of a wild animal who lashes back when cornered. If *The Adventures of Black Eldridge* failed to fulfill the role of spectacular fiction, *Black Panther* succeeded, with the muscular superhero commandeering fantastical weapons and vehicles, outsmarting villains, and displaying both courage and compassion. The Black Panther's actions were not overtly political, but the character helped to recuperate the black male image and to inscribe Africa as a place of power and authority in the modern age. The *Black Panther* never achieved the popularity of Marvel Comics stars such as the Hulk or Captain America, but it was published on and off for at least a decade, establishing yet another site through which the Panthers could be recognized and remembered.[10]

J. Edgar Hoover continued to target the Black Panthers, announcing in the summer of 1970 that they were the country's "most dangerous and violence-prone of all extremist groups," in the same category with the SDS faction the Weathermen. The FBI was particularly concerned with the Panthers' international networking, as Eldridge Cleaver publicized his travels to Vietnam and China and other controversial locales. At the same time, however, they won some vindication in the courts. In addition to the acquittals in the New York and New Haven cases, prosecutors around the country had difficulty convicting members of the Black Panthers for serious crimes. In May, the special federal grand jury investigating the Chicago police in the December 1969 raid on Fred Hampton's apartment found that law enforcement "grossly exaggerated" the Panthers' resistance in the incident. The report, which was publicized widely in the news media, noted that at least eighty-two shots were fired into Hampton's apartment, while only one shot was fired from inside. The grand jury also found that an FBI tip that the Panthers were stockpiling weapons in Chicago was the catalyst for the raid, that the police laboratory made "serious and repeated errors" with the evidence, and that the internal Chicago Police Department inquiry was "so seriously deficient that it suggests purposeful malfeasance."[11]

Even stronger criticisms emerged from a preliminary examination of police treatment of the Panthers released in January 1970. The Commission of Inquiry into the Black Panthers and Law Enforcement, co-chaired by civil rights leader Roy Wilkins, sought insight into the motivations and behaviors of police officers who dealt with the Panthers. The report, based primarily on interviews with cooperating officers, noted that local agencies were not willing to provide their records for analysis. The commission found that policemen "harbor rather pronounced negative feelings about the Panthers" and that "concepts such as justice and due process are sacrificed" because of these sentiments. The investigators characterized the police they interviewed as fearful that the Panthers "would someday invade their homes for the purpose of killing wives and children," and the officers were thus committed to eliminating the group in any way possible. The final version of the study, published in 1973, bore the apt title *Search and Destroy*.[12]

In 1976, when the Senate Committee to Study Governmental Operations looked back on the actions of the nation's intelligence agencies, it asserted that the Black Panthers had become the primary focus of the COINTELPRO program. The report found that the Panthers were the target of 233 actions that had been authorized to neutralize black nationalist organizations. "Although the claimed purpose of the Bureau's COINTELPRO tactics was to prevent violence, some of the FBI's tactics against the BPP were clearly intended to foster violence, and many others could reasonably have been expected to cause violence," said the commission. The Panthers' suspicions, which had been routinely denied by the FBI and scoffed at in the press, were confirmed by the commission's findings. The violations of the Black Panthers' civil liberties included multiple strategies to interfere with their First Amendment rights. Intelligence agencies sought to thwart or silence Black Panther publications, particularly the *Black Panther* newspaper, "to prevent Panther members and persons sympathetic to their aims from expressing their views." Disinformation projects also targeted the mainstream press. For example, in January 1970, the FBI sent a directive to nine field offices with the goal of supplying anti-Panther material to the news media:

> To counteract any favorable support in publicity to the Black Panther Party (BPP) recipient offices are requested to submit their observations and recommendations regarding contacts with established and reliable sources in the television and/or radio field who might be interested in drawing up a program for local consumption depicting the true facts regarding the BPP.

The commission revealed that several reporters, including two working for an unnamed Los Angeles television station and one at the *San Francisco Examiner*, were willing to produce news reports that fulfilled the FBI's expectations.[13]

The Black Panthers, though targeted by the government intelligence apparatus, still celebrated their biggest victory with the release of Huey Newton from prison in August 1970 after his conviction was thrown out and a new trial was ordered. A support committee posted $50,000 in bail to release the Black Panther Minister of Defense after he served nearly two years in jail on the manslaughter conviction. Newton's release was a political, cultural, and legal victory. The Panthers had won the war of public opinion both inside and outside of the courtroom. Newton's team of lawyers succeeded in pressing the case that defendants must be tried by a jury of their peers—particularly when defined by race and class. This finding would soon be recognized as an important legal precedent. But it was Newton's return to public life that shaped public discourse. His attorney, Charles Garry, told reporters that Newton's return to the leadership of the Panthers would give "tremendous impetus to the liberation movement in America." The occasion of Newton's release generated a new set of popular iconography, this time of a jubilant Newton climbing atop a car and shedding his shirt to wave to throngs of cheering supporters in front of the downtown Oakland courthouse. The media were delighted with the reappearance of a Panther celebrity and clamored to snag an interview with him. Among other engagements, he was immediately booked to appear on CBS' *Face the Nation* news program. Within two weeks after his release, the Panther leadership fielded requests for interviews with the *Christian Science Monitor*, the *National Observer*, the *Washington Post*, the *New Republic, the California Voice*, and a dozen local television and radio programs. Conservative talk show host William F. Buckley Jr. was anxious to feature Newton on *Firing Line*, and a German filmmaker made inquiries about filming party activities.[14]

The constant media attention continued to be a catalyst for the government's scrutiny of the Panthers, a fact that was acknowledged by the head of a congressional committee. In October 1969, the House Committee on Internal Security authorized an investigation of the Black Panther Party, based on the idea that "a serious threat is posed to the internal security of this Nation and to the free functioning of its democratic institutions by the activities of certain organizations." At the start of the hearings, committee chairman Representative Richard Ichord of Missouri underscored the profound influence that media representations had on the government's view of the Panthers. He noted that while "the attention it has been afforded by the press seems to me to be inordinately disproportionate to the size of the Black Panthers," politicians and their constituencies were "alarmed by press accounts of prevalency of open incitement [by the Panthers] to kill, destroy, and revolt." Ichord admitted that alleged threats made by the Black Panthers might lie in the realm of rhetoric rather than action, but he justified the hearings by arguing that the committee was only interested in "unlawful acts" and that it intended to learn about "the objectives, the numbers, the financing, and the tactics of the Black Panther Party." The congressional committee was better equipped to divine the truth than the machinations of the press, he argued, because testimonies were given under oath and the threat of penalties for perjury were ever-present in the process.[15]

By March 1970, the committee was probing several Panther chapters that had been involved in police encounters or had attracted public scrutiny, including Kansas City (in Ichord's home state), Seattle, Detroit, Indianapolis, and Des Moines. Several of these had broken away from the national Black Panther Party in the fall of 1970, and they all struggled with the imprisonment of local leaders, FBI infiltration, and violence. For example, in April 1969, the Des Moines headquarters was bombed, and the following year the core of its leadership were arrested on charges of conspiracy to blow up a police station. Taking advantage of the disarray among these groups, the federal investigation subpoenaed current and former Panthers to testify in the hope that they would reveal the group's plans to overthrow the government. A significant proportion of the questioning focused less on alleged criminal activity of the chapters and more on the Panthers' public relations apparatus. The committee's counsel carried out extensive questioning regarding the distribution of the *Black Panther* newspaper, the extent of the group's public speaking engagements, and on its political education classes. The Panthers' ability to communicate to widespread audiences was deemed to be their most dangerous weapon.[16]

When Huey Newton emerged from prison he confronted an organization that was simultaneously growing and struggling for survival. Newton reassumed the mantle of leadership with gusto, introducing new political agendas and turning the Panthers' media strategies into a serious financial entity. Within a year, Newton had established a company called Stronghold Consolidated Productions, Inc., located at a

New York law firm, which played myriad roles—overseeing the income from Panther publications, negotiating film, magazine, and book contracts, and managing high-profile television appearances among them. Newton and his staff imposed a more stringent record-keeping system that kept track of the flurry of media contacts. Stronghold also took over the financial responsibility for the *Black Panther* newspaper, guaranteeing to subsidize the paper's operations in exchange for all subscription revenues and contributions. The Panthers were managing a complex web of relations that ensured continued visibility and a steady income. The party was publishing an average of fifty thousand copies of the *Black Panther* newspaper each week; a third were sold in the Bay Area and the rest were shipped across the United States and around the globe. Fifteen to twenty chapters, particularly those in Chicago, New Orleans, Detroit, New York, Los Angeles, Washington, Boston, and Philadelphia, distributed the bulk of the papers; a handful went to foreign locales, including Canada, Britain, France, Sweden, and China. One of the Panthers' most lucrative enterprises was in book publishing; a Stronghold report from July 1971 noted that eight separate book projects were under way, written by different party members. Newton's memoir, *Revolutionary Suicide*, was signed by Random House editor Toni Morrison in July 1971 for a $10,000 advance based on one-third of the manuscript, although an editor from Bantam Books offered $50,000 for the finished product. The Oakland-based media machine worked furiously to create spin that might help when Newton came up for retrial, and to bolster its forces in the face of increasing intraparty dissension.[17]

In the summer before Newton's release, the Panthers announced a national gathering to bring their far-flung membership together with other radical activists to write a new constitution that would address the needs of the oppressed. In so doing, the Panthers hoped to make a nod toward organizational unity while reinforcing their position as the vanguard of social protest groups. The centerfold of the June 20 edition of the *Black Panther* announced a call for the Revolutionary People's Constitutional Convention, coinciding with the 107th anniversary of the signing of the Emancipation Proclamation in Washington. A small group of Panthers and their followers had gathered on the steps of the Lincoln Memorial the day before and held a banner aloft that called for aggrieved groups across the country to rethink the U.S. Constitution.

This was just a prelude, however; the actual gathering was to take place in Philadelphia a few months later. In the period leading up to the convention, the Panthers published a treatise laying out their rationale for the gathering—that the U.S. Constitution upheld lofty principles that were not enjoyed by the majority of black Americans. "We feel that, in practical terms, it is time for Black people as a whole to address their attention to the quest of our National Destiny." The essay both evoked the political rhetoric of the framers of the Constitution, and the rhetoric of black power, as the Panthers maintained that their followers were fed up and ready to revolt. Indeed, the conceptualization of this gathering, and the rhetoric that was employed to support it, asserted the Panthers' evolving identity as national subjects and citizens.[18]

In preparation for the constitutional convention, the Panthers held a plenary session in September to plan the agenda. The *Black Panther* announced that the plenary meetings "will be the first step towards a constitution that will guarantee us the right to life, liberty and the pursuit of happiness" and a "constitution that serves the people" instead of the elite. Less than a week before the plenary meeting, the Philadelphia police carried out simultaneous raids on three local Black Panther offices or "Information Centers." The Panthers contended that the police broke down the doors and came in shooting; the results included the wounding of three police officers and the arrest of sixteen Panthers on assault and murder conspiracy charges. The front page of the September 5, 1970 issue of the party newspaper carried photos of male Panthers stripped naked in a dark alley as they were searched by the police in the raid's aftermath. This image of humiliation and objectification enraged the Panthers and their supporters. The Philadelphia contingent accused the police of deliberately seeking to disrupt the convention plenary. Defiantly, the program proceeded.[19]

Radical black nationalism—or more accurately radical intercommunalism—underscored the framework of the convention as it unfolded. But one of the highlights of the gatherings was the recognition of women and homosexuals as social groups that suffered discrimination and had legitimate complaints, in the process linking them to oppressed communities of color. During the convention's plenary planning session, groups were organized around identity categories to work through the issues they would bring to the general body. "In order for us to come together around a common vision, we first have to understand each other's grievances in relation to the system which produced them," declared a program announcement. Inserting gender and gay rights into the convention's platform was a historic transition from the masculinist, heterosexist, and often misogynist discourses promulgated by Newton, Cleaver, Seale, and other Panther leaders. The August 21 issue of the *Black Panther* published a letter from the recently liberated Huey Newton calling for "revolutionary" unity. He argued that black nationalists responded violently to women and homosexuals because of their own insecurities. "We must gain security in ourselves and therefore have respect and feelings for all oppressed people," he argued. Expletives such as *faggot* and *punk* should be used against "enemies of the people, such as Nixon and Mitchell," Newton quipped. "Homosexuals are not enemies of the people." This move succeeded in attracting the involvement and support of a range of activist groups, such as the Gay Liberation Front, but also alienated parts of the Panthers' rank and file. Nevertheless, Newton held firm to his conviction that the Panthers had an obligation to "transform this whole society."[20]

Among the observers at the convention's plenary meetings was journalist and cultural critic Nora Sayre, who regularly chronicled the social movements of the era for publications including the *New York Times*, the *Los Angeles Times*, and *The Nation*. Sayre marveled that the Revolutionary People's Convention events, including a speech by Huey Newton in front of a crowd of ten thousand, were utterly peaceful. She observed that despite predictions that the Convention would dissolve into violence, "the Panthers wielded their authority in Philadelphia," and in the process "they saved skulls and probably some lives." The police harassment bestowed on the Panthers by Philadelphia's mayor, Frank Rizzo, had further angered local black and poor communities, making them "a powerful grassroots audience" for the Party's programs, Sayre concluded. Ironically, the Panthers' relentless courting of the press gave way to an increasing wariness of the media whose attention they coveted. Sayre was among a group of reporters barred from the first day's proceedings, along with representatives from the *New York Times*, television networks, and other outlets. After hours of drama and negotiations, the Panthers relented and the reporters were finally admitted. In this small struggle, the Black Panthers reminded the media that they retained a powerful political tool—the ability to say no. Sayre wrote: "In some ways, the hassle was a healthy reproof to those who control the established press: to the arrogance which has betrayed facts for too long." Sayre was keenly aware of the pitfalls of writing about the Black Panthers, and her article, subsequently published in *Esquire*, sought to provide a more nuanced and unvarnished view of the group within the context of Cold War culture. She was less interested in whether the Panthers were right or wrong and more concerned with the economic and political conditions that fueled black power activism and social unrest.[21]

Nora Sayre, later described as a writer who produced "acutely observed analyses of America in the 1950s and 60s," was something of a rarity among the hordes of journalists and essayists who rushed to write about the Black Panthers. Most knew little or nothing about communities of color or the long-standing problems of structural inequality, and they had few contacts to help facilitate a deeper understanding of their subjects. Magazine writers such as Sayre, Joan Didion, and Tom Wolfe contributed to periodicals that catered to highbrow sensibilities—their work was expected to be literate, historically sophisticated, and socially aware. These writers were given the time to research and evaluate their subjects, and many were keenly in touch with the context within which they worked. Didion, when writing about her interview with Huey Newton, noted that she appreciated the "particular beauty in Huey Newton 'as issue.'" She questioned Newton's ability to reflect on his circumstances, reaching back to another key moment in the nation's racial history, quipping that "the value of a Scottsboro case is easier to see if you are not yourself the Scottsboro boy." By contrast, daily reporters were grinding out material for the masses that relied on the predictable, sensational elements that entertain and sustain an audience. Their primary sources were the police departments, political leaders, and business establishments in the communities they served—those most likely to view the Black Panthers as a threat to the social order. And most were inevitably trapped in their subject position as middle-class and white. One New York–based reporter wrote a column in the *Columbia Journalism Review* in 1969 that argued that whiteness—and all its requisite attitudes and assumptions—still reigned in America's newsrooms. "[W]hites edit, and to a large extent, write the news," wrote Robert E. Smith of *Newsday*. "There is a white attitude in the daily press and in major

broadcasting—innocuous, or insulting, or perhaps even inflammatory."
White journalists routinely used language that demonstrated their distance from, and disdain for, nonwhites by using condescending analo-
gies, highlighting a subject's race, or being "slightly surprised when
black people behave like something other than savages," he wrote. In
particular, Smith keyed in on this "articulate syndrome," in which it
was becoming fashionable to congratulate African Americans for being
able to express themselves.[22]

The frame of whiteness at least partly explains why the media became enthralled with the personalities of the Black Panther leadership
as they simultaneously denounced them for being violent, anti-social
thugs. Eldridge Cleaver, Newton, Seale, David Hilliard, and to a lesser
extent Kathleen Cleaver, with their powerful and lucid displays of ar-
gumentation juxtaposed to their sense of fearlessness and bravado,
made themselves the epitome of the "dangerous yet intelligent black."
Newton and Eldridge Cleaver, in particular, displayed considerable genius in their ability to exploit this trend. And they were extraordinarily
effective in convincing sympathetic whites that they bore no animosity
toward them. Newton's ability to charm white journalists such as Joan
Didion during his jailhouse interviews was instructive: he presented
himself as calm, thoughtful, and brave, rather than irrational and menacing, as he was often portrayed in the press, and he showed his appreciation for their interest. In other words, in person he didn't scare
white people, and this was conveyed across the media establishment.
Similarly, Cleaver could be a fearsome character—tall, broad-shouldered,
scowling, and provocative. Yet his writings and the interviews he
granted belied this image. As the reviewer for the *Wall Street Journal*
noted with incredulity, Cleaver actually believed that whites could
fight for social justice, and he held "special scorn for the 'vicious black
bourgeoisie.'" Thus, by the end of the decade, Cleaver was deemed an
authentic American and Newton a revolutionary genius.[23]

Critics argued that this recognition of the Panthers as anything
other than criminal was simply evidence of white guilt—a national
state of masochism in which whites allowed themselves to be brutalized
by black radicals in the quest to right past wrongs. White guilt was certainly part of the motivation underscoring the media's preoccupation
with the Panthers. The civil rights movement had demanded that black
Americans be rendered visible, and the hypervisibility of the Black

Panthers was evidence that white America was paying attention. The national obsession with the Black Panther Party was emblematic of the deep political and social polarization in the country—between the Cold Warriors who longed for a return to an era of order and predictability and the rebellious generation who believed that fundamental change was necessary. The Cold Warriors had the edge in this contestation over public discourse: they largely controlled the editorial content of newspapers and magazines and made the editorial decisions of the television networks. But cultural workers and journalists who cared about or were part of the oppositional culture managed to write articles, make photographs, and take journalistic risks.

African American writers, regardless of their political perspectives, brought a race consciousness and cultural affinity to their work that overcame some of the deficiencies of white-authored journalism. James Baldwin, among the most influential African American authors of the era, had already established a reputation as a fiery social critic and advocate for racial justice. Unlike many of his white contemporaries, who viewed the Black Panthers at arm's length, Baldwin embraced them, engaged with them, and defended them. Eldridge Cleaver's homophobic ranting in *Soul on Ice* failed to alienate Baldwin from the Black Panthers' larger agenda. In a volume of journalistic essays on the sixties and early seventies, he wrote that "the Panthers, far from being an illegal or a lawless organization, are a great force for peace and stability in the ghetto." Baldwin saw the Panthers' challenges to law enforcement and their efforts at community empowerment as a brave enterprise regardless of the risks. "White America remains unable to believe that black America's grievances are real . . . and the effect of this massive and hostile incomprehension is to increase the danger in which all black people live here, especially the young. No one is more aware of this than the Black Panther leadership." Baldwin was unapologetic in his critique of the law enforcement crackdown on the Panthers, and of the continuing racial strife that rocked the nation.[24]

The small network of African American journalists did not have the literary status or celebrity of James Baldwin, however, leaving them far more vulnerable to professional and political crises. Covering the Panthers took a toll on many. Perhaps the best-known, Earl Caldwell of the *New York Times*, was rewarded with pressure from the FBI to serve as an informant, as well as a subpoena from a federal grand jury asking him to reveal all he knew about the Black Panther Party. Caldwell refused to appear before the jury, arguing that his testimony would damage the relationship with the Panthers that he had so carefully established. In the courts Caldwell contended that the news-gathering process had First Amendment protection from government intrusion, giving reporters privileges similar to those granted attorneys and physicians. His attorneys stated, "A journalist's privilege should be there not only to make it possible for a journalist to get better stories, but to contribute to the public's right to know." This position was upheld by the federal district court and the Ninth Circuit Court of Appeals. But the federal government appealed to the Supreme Court, which reversed the decision, arguing that journalists had no special privilege and that they must respond to subpoenas or other inquiries as average citizens are required to do. This landmark decision led to the creation of state-by-state shield laws to insulate reporters from the threat of having to reveal their sources. The Supreme Court also gave notice that writers and reporters seeking to go beyond the surface of controversial topics of interest to the government were at risk of contempt of court, or worse. This ruling continues to have a significant chilling effect on the media.[25]

Gilbert Moore, one of only two black reporters at *Life* magazine, underwent perhaps the most dramatic transformation in his pursuit of the Panthers' story. In June 1968, he was assigned to write an article on the group, and for the next few months he followed them in the full grip of the Free Huey campaign. Initially, Moore was a bit frightened by the volatile Panthers and concerned that he would have difficulty communicating with them. What happened was an unexpected shaking of his faith in his role as journalist. "The first thing to go was that distancing shield, the comfortable myth of journalistic objectivity," wrote Moore's biographer. "Against his will and best professional judgment he had found himself being drawn into the story." While this was an increasingly acceptable stance for reporters practicing "new journalism," it was dangerous for a young black professional constantly under scrutiny for any sign of bias. By the time he returned to the magazine to complete his assignment, he was a "changed man," questioning his racial and political identity and unsure how to proceed. Throughout his writing, Moore makes it clear that he is often unconvinced by the Panthers'

motivations and tactics—he is certainly no dupe. Yet there was a resonance in their politics, an earnest commitment to their beliefs, which
had a profound influence on the young reporter. Moore "knows he can
never again be comfortable in corporate white America," said Ekwueme
Michael Thelwell in the afterword to Moore's book. *Life* never published
the article Moore was commissioned to write, but his full-length manuscript, *A Special Rage*, appeared in 1971. Afterward, Moore dropped out
of journalism for many years. *A Special Rage* has been hailed as the most
thorough and honest look at the Black Panther Party written during the
period.[26]

By spring 1971, the Panthers were disintegrating into factions between followers of Newton and the exiled Eldridge Cleaver, as well
as groups functioning independently in their communities across the
United States. Increasingly, the Black Panther Party within Newton's
domain centered its activities in its birthplace, northern California,
while other chapters forged their own distinct identities. Internal strife
was wrenching the party, with purges and deadly retaliations the result.
Newton criticized Cleaver for the latter's alliances with white radicals,
including the Peace and Freedom Party. The Central Committee began to expel members, including several members of the Panther 21
and Geronimo Pratt, who played a leadership role in the Los Angeles
chapter. Newton was angered when members of the Panther 21 publicly criticized his leadership in a published letter. Kathleen Cleaver
recalled that Panther 21 defendant Michael Cetewayo Tabor was
threatened by Newton supporters, prompting him to join the Cleavers
in Africa. Eldridge Cleaver wielded considerable influence over East
Coast Panthers from his outpost in Algiers; he supported the Panther
21 and criticized David Hilliard for abusing his administration of the
Oakland headquarters. Earl Caldwell filed a report with the *New York
Times* that underscored the party's state of crisis. In an article titled
"The Panthers: Dead or Regrouping," he reported that Cleaver made
public statements criticizing the expulsions. Weeks later it was announced in the *Black Panther* newspaper that Cleaver and the International Section of the Black Panther Party had been expelled. Eldridge's
supporters in New York started their own newspaper and formed "a
more radical" splinter group, according to Kathleen Cleaver. Meanwhile, the number of national chapters declined. "The Black Panther
Party became irrevocably split, with the line between the two factions

drawn in blood," she wrote. At least two murders of Black Panther leaders were attributed to this internal crisis. These stories were picked up by the *New York Times, Newsweek, Time*, and national broadcasters as the violence shrouding the Panthers came no longer from outside enemies but from within.[27]

Some former Black Panthers in New York and elsewhere began to align themselves with more radical groups such as the Black Liberation Army, while the Central Committee sought to become influential in the conventional realm of electoral politics. In 1972 Bobby Seale and Elaine Brown ran for political office—Seale for mayor and Brown for the Oakland City Council. Unlike the era in which Cleaver and Newton ran for national office on the Peace and Freedom ticket, the Panther candidates saw themselves as tangible rather than symbolic candidates and they sought an active role in local governance. Three additional Panthers, including Ericka Huggins, ran for seats on the Berkeley City Council. Elaine Brown had become an influential member of the party's leadership, taking over the title of Minister of Information following Cleaver's expulsion. In her memoirs, Brown asserted that campaigning for political office was not an abandonment of the Party's ideals. "With a minor shift in style, however, we had begun a campaign that would turn the vote into a step in the revolutionary process," she wrote. She and her counterparts shed the Panther uniform of leather jackets and dark sunglasses and hit the campaign trail as they sought support from local residents. Despite months of meetings, press conferences, photo ops, and speeches, neither Seale nor Brown was successful, although they did garner about 40 percent of the black vote. This was an encouraging sign that the Panthers were intervening in Oakland's political culture, but it was far from a revolutionary transformation. Newton often stayed out of the limelight, living in an Oakland penthouse as he furiously schemed to raise money and maintain the Party's viability. According to Brown, Newton began to carry out or endorse increasingly violent and illegal strong-arm tactics to this end. "Indeed, our electoral campaign had created the illusion that Bobby and I were so separate from such rough activity, as though there were two arms of the party: the militant, dark side and the more moderate reformist side," she wrote. The dark side was taking over.[28]

Dispirited, Bobby Seale left the Party in July 1974, while Newton disintegrated into a cycle of authoritarianism, violent gangsterism, and drug use. During this period party members "witnessed numerous incidents of abuse of power resulting from Newton's centralization of authority within the BPP," noted one scholar. "This included diverting all party funds directly to him, and viciously assaulting party members and innocent bystanders." The month following Seale's resignation, Newton fled to Cuba after being charged with the murder of a party associate, and Elaine Brown inherited the party chairmanship. When he returned in 1977 he was acquitted of felony murder charges but lost much of his remaining support network, particularly Elaine Brown and the officers who had kept the party running in his absence. Brown noted that in addition to being exhausted, she too had been the victim of one of Newton's assaults.[29]

Throughout the 1970s, the media chronicled the Black Panthers' decline much as it had helped to facilitate the party's rise. In September 1977, *Newsweek* published a feature story titled "The Party's Over," with a focus on the divergent paths of Eldridge Cleaver and Bobby Seale. *Newsweek* portrayed the two as failed radicals who sought to escape their Panther pasts. Seale, described as "an engagingly unembarrassed deserter," was "broke, unemployed," and floating aimlessly. Cleaver, who returned to the United States after eight years in exile, was serving prison time, finishing another book, and launching a new career as an evangelical Christian minister. The Black Panthers had "withered back to its roots in Oakland" and these once-fiery figures were shadows of their former selves, according to the article. This obituary for the Panthers presented former black nationalist icons as denouncing their radical pasts and the era in which they were prominent.[30]

In 1978 Bay Area journalist Kate Coleman wrote a blistering investigative report on Newton and the Panthers for *New Times*, an alternative magazine. Titled "The Party's Over: How Huey Newton Created a Street Gang at the Center of the Black Panther Party," Coleman produced a devastating portrait of an organization gone bad, of a marauding gang who used the Black Panther mantle to commit a host of criminal acts. "They have, say reliable sources, committed a series of violent crimes—including arson, extortion, beatings, even murder," wrote Coleman. "Unlike the skirmishes that marked the Party's infancy in the late sixties, the recent incidents appear to have no political explanation." Ironically, another of the Panthers' vocal critics, David Horowitz, was one of the anonymous sources for Coleman's article. In an interview with Hugh Pearson, author of *The Shadow of the Panther*, Horowitz claimed that he had doggedly investigated the Panthers' illegal actions after he suspected that his friend Betty Van Patter was murdered by Newton or his associates. Horowitz passed the information on to Coleman, who, like Horowitz, has carried on a continued campaign to reveal and denounce Newton's misdeeds in this period. Coleman says she is motivated, in part, because Newton and his henchmen threatened and harassed her to prevent publication of the story. Undaunted, Coleman wrote the article and then went underground to escape Newton's wrath. The title of her article turned out to be more than a pun; what remained of the Black Panther Party was in steep decline. Indeed, while the Panther icon Huey Newton was engaged in the kinds of activities associated with the Panthers a decade earlier, the mass media mostly missed the story. By the late 1970s, they were considered vestiges of the sixties with few followers, and they were no longer a saleable commodity. In the early 1980s, the *Black Panther* newspaper folded, the Oakland Community School closed, the once far-flung network of chapters was gone, and the Black Panther Party resided only in collective memory.[31]

CONCLUSION

Articulations of Memory

Scholars, media observers, and government officials have consistently argued that the Black Panthers were a "media-made" movement, suggesting the organization was all style and little substance and that their growth was based largely on their phenomenal exposure. An early researcher of the Panthers made this claim explicitly: "If they had not carried guns, worn black berets, uttered inflammatory rhetoric, suffered a few unfortunate shoot-outs with police, and above all, if they had not been covered on TV, they would have gone virtually unnoticed," said G. Louis Heath. "But they were blessed with a theatrical sixth sense that enabled them to gain an audience and project an image." This was also a theme repeated by those inside the media such as Gail Sheehy, who stated, "Panther deaths have been tallied, retallied and distorted out of all proportion to the party's actual membership. This is because the Panther movement was created by and for the media." Similarly, a 1971 report of the House Committee on Internal Security credited the Panthers' media savvy with their early success: "the leaders compensated for many of their limitations by their flair for the dramatic and an ability to exploit the resources of the communication media."[1]

Central to this commentary is the idea that public visibility does not necessarily constitute meaningful political or social influence. Indeed, we are presented with a dialectic between whether a media subject is automatically bestowed with meaning and importance, or whether a subject must be meaningful to attract substantial and sustained media attention. The lamentation about "media-made" movements reflects the angst generated by the intense culture of mediated artifice in the 1960s and 1970s. From pop art and rock and roll to the incursions of television into America's living rooms, there was an enduring suspicion that what appeared in mass culture—even journalism—was artificial, frivolous, and temporary. In an earlier era, mass media and lowbrow culture were linked, while politics and high art occupied a different domain. But the televised debates between Nixon and Kennedy, the bombardment of media images from the Vietnam War, and the techniques of New Journalism, among other phenomena, helped to blur these boundaries. The cultural matrix of the black power movement, which integrated fashion, soul music, street theater, underground journalism, African spirituality, and urban vernacular, disrupted basic assumptions about how politics is conducted. For many observers, then, the Black Panther Party inhabited a hyperreal state in which it was unclear whether the meaning they embodied was superseded or replaced by the signs, symbols, and rhetoric that swirled around them. This lent credibility to the idea that there was nothing behind their image but Oz-like wizardry. The Panthers' very materialist perspective argued otherwise—that it was their claims of race, class, and gender prejudice, not cultural context, that encouraged most elites to deny their importance.

These statements questioning the Panthers' importance also raise a corollary issue: whether they should be discounted because they lacked the size or formal legitimacy accorded to other social movements. An underlying supposition is that in order to "matter" there must be tangible objectives to the protest project—the end of war, the passage of a civil rights law, the closing down of a nuclear power plant, the enfranchisement of black voters. While the Student Nonviolent Coordinating Committee was confrontational in its politics and evolved into a radical organization, there is little suggestion that the group did not deserve serious attention or that it existed only in the realm of popular culture. It seems that what is at issue has more to do with the nature of the Panthers' agenda and identity rather than how often they appeared in the media. The group's protests addressed police brutality and state repression in sweeping terms; they called for nothing less than a radical transformation of American society and a complete redistribution of its wealth. There was no gradualism to their demands; what they sought seemed unattainable and impractical. They were unsparing in their assessment that the nation was racist in its core beliefs and hypocritical in its policies. They were simultaneously local, national, and global. The Panthers' goal was often consciousness-raising rather than a particular set of actions; they sought to mobilize the frustrations of the black American underclass and turn these simmering emotions into a critical mass movement. They did not play the game as it was understood. As a result, they were dismissed as reckless, dangerous, crazy, or all three.

Both critics and those enamored of the Black Panthers have had difficulty reconciling the fact that they were a self-made group that grew to have a sizeable and devoted following. It is tempting to see the phenomenal rise of the Panthers as nothing more than the result of a successful public relations campaign, except that they generated a program and purpose that were a powerful enticement for many of their recruits. Young would-be activists were exposed to the Panthers through the media, and drawn to the group because of the struggles in which they were engaged and because of the confident, self-affirming and defiant possibility that they offered. Testimonials from defendants in the New York Panther 21 court case offer anecdotal evidence of this process. Joan Bird recalled:

> The first time I thought about the Black Panther Party at all, I remember reading in the newspaper—*Daily News,* mass media paper—that Panthers at Brooklyn Criminal Court were viciously assaulted and attacked by off-duty members of the New York police force . . . this incident that was happening to these brothers really caused me to want to investigate further and find out more about the Black Panther Party.

Or Jamal, who joined the Panthers at age fifteen:

> The next thing I heard about the Black Panther Party was when Bobby and the rest went into the state legislature in Sacramento. I was watching the news one night and I saw these niggers come walking into the legislature with guns. I said wow, these niggers are crazy, you know. They were cool, really committed.

Or Shaba Om, who learned of the Panthers from reading *Ramparts*:

> I was walking down the streets in midtown Manhattan and saw this magazine called *Ramparts*, and Black Panthers were on the cover of the magazine. I'd heard about the Black Panther Party before, so I bought a

copy of *Ramparts* and began reading it—and man these dudes are together and as crazy as hell. The more I learned about the party the more
it excited me . . . the day came when I met a man selling the *Black Panther*, the paper. I went wild in my pad reading that.[2]

To call the Black Panther Party a "media-made" movement is too easy;
it assigns the power of representation to media institutions rather than
their subjects. This assertion ignores the dialogic relationship—the
interdependence—between media producers and media subjects and
erases individual and group agency. Rather, we might see the great
power of the Black Panthers in their ability to create, manipulate, and
subvert mass culture. As Nikhil Pal Singh suggests, "Like black activists
past, what made them special was their ability to bring claims to a
world stage and their abiding mistrust of attempts to domesticate their
radicalism." The Panthers weren't invented by the media—Bobby
Seale, Huey Newton, Eldridge Cleaver, David Hilliard, Kathleen
Cleaver, Fred Hampton, and a handful of other actors invented themselves and delivered the goods to the mass media. Furthermore, the
Black Panther Party enabled the national media at the end of the 1960s
to have an agenda about race relations as the civil rights movement and
icons such as Martin Luther King Jr. became less salient. The Panthers
gave them something to simultaneously cover and to critique while
avoiding a deeper, more thorough analysis of the nation's widespread
discord. Yet media institutions that made enormous profits and built
audiences based on their commodification of the Panthers' image simultaneously denied the Panthers' influence to deflect the accusations
that they were being "soft" on black militants.[3]

The news media, in particular, had a conflicting social agenda—to appease the power elites of whom they were a part and to uphold societal
norms while professing some concern for the problem of racial inequality. The media had a stake both in maintaining the status quo and in promoting social transformation. This argument has been underscored by
several related studies. One scholar came to the conclusion that because
the press is primarily invested in reinforcing normative values, one
should not expect them to seriously interrogate the complexities of a
group such as the Black Panthers. A study that looked at the media coverage of the death of Fred Hampton offered a similar assessment: "when
an opposition group like the Panthers question fundamental beliefs and

institutions, the mainstream press fail to perform their watchdog function by marginalizing the critical position." The civil rights movement demanded fundamental changes in the ways African Americans' concerns were addressed in the public sphere. The National Advisory Commission on Civil Disorders made it clear that it was no longer legitimate to ignore or silence black Americans' grievances. Media organizations felt this urgency and faced the contradictions between its First Amendment mandate and its profit-making imperative. Accounts of the violent encounters between black militants and the police fulfilled the public's insatiable appetite for one historically situated stereotype—the violence-prone, irresponsible, and threatening black male figure. These representations become part of national discourse, painting the Black Panther Party with a broad brush that led many in mainstream America to believe they were out to kill white people—particularly the police—to finally avenge centuries of slavery, discrimination, and abuse. Thus, the government was authorized and emboldened to employ legal and illegal methods to halt this perceived threat. Gail Sheehy admitted that the media "spread the myth of open warfare between cops and Panthers" and that Panther sympathizers "backed up the myth," leading to a climate in which the police and the FBI "had a good excuse to attack." Most damning, perhaps, was that the media was deeply invested in the self-fulfilling prophecy it advanced. "The media need more than a string of routine homicides to become interested in black deaths," she wrote. Media workers such as Sheehy were happy to satisfy this demand.[4]

Recent analysis of the Black Panthers has offered widely divergent views about how they were covered by the media. One writer, for example, argued that the Panthers were treated in an evenhanded manner by the press until late 1969: "for more than three years, or from the inception of the party in 1966 until the winter of 1969, mainstream media representations of the Panthers had been neither particularly hostile nor especially sympathetic." This changed following the FBI assertion that they were the nation's main national security threat. In this perspective, J. Edgar Hoover's pronouncement and subsequent campaign against the group was the primary catalyst for the panic that demonized the organization and its leaders. At the other end of the spectrum, journalist Hugh Pearson maintained that the media was hardly evenhanded with the Panthers, but rather was obsessed with the idea that they epitomized the African American character. The mass media

"continued to play a major role in elevating the rudest, most outlaw element of black America as the true keepers of the flame in all it means
to be black," he wrote. The evidence presented in this study counters
these perspectives—the Panthers became national media subjects by
spring 1967, not two years later, and the anxiety that gripped the
nation about these black militants preceded, not followed, J. Edgar
Hoover's condemnation. Pearson is correct in his assertion that the
press loved to highlight black deviance and degeneracy, but he takes the
position that these were indeed the sole characteristics embodied by
the Black Panthers and that the press presented essentially truthful depictions. This study argues that none of the actors in the process was
immune to the historical constructions of blackness that shape U.S.
culture and politics; media workers and the Panthers themselves always
operated in this context. The representations produced in the 1960s as
well as those thirty years later were all informed by or in response to
the stereotypes and myths that are embedded in the nation's understanding of race and difference. These representations crossed national
and ethnic boundaries to inspire aggrieved groups seeking models of
resistance in the modern era.[5]

It is far more difficult to know what viewers and readers actually
thought about the Black Panther Party during this period. For the
most part, we can only know about what the media—both mainstream
and alternative—told them. Public opinion surveys noted that while
60 percent of whites were concerned about a threat posed by the Panthers, only about 20 percent of African Americans registered the same
concern. Similarly, news outlets such as the *Wall Street Journal* reported
an upsurge in black community support for the organization by 1970.
This suggests that white Americans were more susceptible to the demonization of the Black Panthers than were black Americans, and that
a significant number of black Americans identified with the Panthers'
cause, if not their tactics. Hence, even mainstream civil rights groups
such as the Southern Christian Leadership Conference and the Urban
League expressed solidarity with the Panthers over the question of law
enforcement's harassment of black activists and the sanctioning of state
repression in black communities. Media representations cannot tell us
how audiences interpret their messages, but they are an indicator of
what elites in both local and national environments thought about the
Black Panthers. That the FBI put considerable energy into feeding

misinformation to the media and congressional committees spent enormous amounts of time scrutinizing the Panthers' publications suggests that the state also saw this as a contestation over who had the most effective grasp on public communication.[6]

Official Memory

Forty years after the group's founding, the Black Panthers' talent in fusing radical politics with indelible images and rhetoric has been transformed into collective memories that continue the debates over race and social justice. Scholars and journalists have a privileged position in their ability to produce "official" memories through books, articles, documentary films, and ongoing commentary. Unlike the ephemeral nature of popular music and motion pictures, authoritative histories of the sixties are expected to endure and inform; they are often the catalyst for other memorializing projects such as exhibitions, Web sites, archives, and the like. Starting in the late 1980s, scholars turned to the sixties as a subject of legitimate inquiry, but the Black Panthers and other manifestations of black power activism have remained on the margins of this scholarly conversation. The proliferation of research on the era has focused on protest movements ranging from the New Left to civil rights and later to second-wave feminism. Studies of Students for a Democratic Society have dominated this work as writers seek a consensus history. In many of the recent texts on this period, the Black Panthers either are ignored or function as tropes for violence and lawlessness. These mostly white historians and journalists construct the Panthers as peripheral to their understanding of the sixties experience. Their memories conflate radicalism with whiteness and with working–class struggles; their stories are of youthful idealism, nonconformity, collectives and alternative culture, and leftist ideology in the university. The black freedom struggles in the South are an inspiration and moral influence; the black power movement in the North is a problematic.[7]

One of the most popular histories, James Miller's *Democracy Is in the Streets*, gives only passing mention to the Black Panthers. This nostalgic view of SDS maintains that the idealistic proponents of the New Left were dedicated to reinventing democracy in the United States. "What democracy ideally meant underwent such a dizzying series of metamorphoses in the minds of young radicals during the Sixties, connoting at different times everything from registering black voters in the South, to rule-by-rule consensus in small communes, to street fighting in chaotic demonstrations," he maintained. There is no room for the black nationalism of the Panthers in this narrative. Instead, they mainly function as a backdrop to Tom Hayden's rise to prominence or as symbols of urban unrest. In one section, Miller discusses the protests at the 1968 Democratic National Convention in Chicago and Hayden's arrest. "That night, Bobby Seale of the Black Panther Party, an independent black organization with links to SNCC and a commitment to armed struggle, addressed the throng in Lincoln Park. 'If a pig comes up and starts swinging a club,' advised Seale, 'then put it over his head and lay him out on the ground.' " This becomes the Panthers' sole contribution to the era. Similarly, Terry Anderson's four-hundred-page history of the sixties reduces the Black Panthers to colorful radicals who were notable for coining the term *pig*, carrying guns in the Sacramento state capitol, and being targeted by the FBI.[8]

Todd Gitlin's *The Sixties: Years of Hope, Days of Rage,* a mix of popular history and personal recollection, became one of the most influential overviews of the decade. Like Miller, Gitlin builds the idea of the sixties around the deeds of SDS, in which he held a leadership position. We learn little of the substance of black power advocates beyond how they fulfilled the New Left's desire to address the "race problem." Yet Gitlin's willingness to criticize his former colleagues is crucial. The Black Panthers were a "godsend" for the New Left because they built alliances with white leftists rather than promoting black separatism. The Panthers generated a provocative, dangerous mystique that thrilled the New Left, allowing young white activists to believe they shared the "struggle" with the black urban underclass, Gitlin explains.[9]

But while the New Left may have been naive and misdirected, their vision of collective action for democracy was admirable, notes another former activist, Meta Mendel-Reyes. Her book, *Reclaiming Democracy: The Sixties in Politics and Memory,* also relegates the Black Panthers to the symbolic realm. She argues that the nation's collective memory is divided into "good" and "bad" narratives about the sixties. On one side are the sympathetic stories that celebrate the era as a period of democratic action and progressive social change, such as Miller's. On the other side are the stories of excess and lawlessness. "To refer negatively to the sixties in political discourse is to call up memories of

young people in revolt," she wrote. "Disheveled, wild-eyed demonstrators rioting in the streets of Chicago during the 1968 Democratic
National Party Convention; Black Panthers in leather jackets and
berets, carrying rifles and shouting Black Power." Mendel-Reyes is
disturbed by these conservative, dominant memories about the sixties
that reduce activism to juvenile, reckless rebellion, and she despairs of
the way the Black Panthers have been dehumanized. She is also highly
critical of the emphasis on white male activists that is central to most
histories. Yet the black power movement doesn't fit her recollections
or the way she wants the sixties to be remembered—civil rights and
the New Left continue to dominate this framework.[10]

These journalists and scholars, all part of the baby-boom generation,
have established themselves as the authoritative community in charge
of preserving the memory of sixties radicalism. Their participant-
observer histories resonate collectively as they call upon the memories
of the millions of young Americans who lived through the era and are
now in middle age. Former members of the Black Panther Party have
written individual accounts of their experiences, but these have yet to
be integrated into the larger historical narrative. The history of black
power activism, rather than being part of the sixties historiography, has
emerged separately, largely through the efforts of African American
writers and cultural workers. What exists, then, is a deeply segregated
universe of memories and official histories—recollections that are
interdependent but also racially specific. Interpreters have a personal
and/or racial investment in interrogating these subjects and in countering prevailing myths and assumptions.

The task of paying serious attention to the history of the black
power movement of the sixties has been left almost entirely to specialists in African American studies and history. These scholars have
looked through the lens of organizations such as SNCC and the Nation of Islam, or through individuals including Robert Williams, Elijah
Muhammad, and Amiri Baraka. Several have examined the Black Panthers within the larger context of the history of black nationalism.
The group is generally understood in relation to other black militant
organizations, and fitted into a chronology of protest beginning with
the southern civil rights movement. Much of this scholarship devotes
a few pages to recounting the Panthers' history and then makes an assessment of their legacy. In one sweeping overview of black politics in

the late twentieth century, the Black Panther Party is identified as "[t]he most provocative challenge to white liberal politics" in the 1960s. Another study of the culture of black power noted that "no revolutionary nationalist group received more publicity than the Black Panther Party," due to their youth, fashion sense, outrageous rhetoric, and use of guns. This author concludes that once the media frenzy died down in the 1970s, "[i]nstead of policing the police and scream- ing 'off the pigs' they now appeared to be looking out for number one and living high on the hog." William Van Deburg noted that of all of the groups that emerged during the sixties, "it was the Black Panther Party that most effectively carried on the legacy of Malcolm X," and that their community orientation was an important example for groups that would follow. This study suggests the Panthers fell prey to the "iron hand" of the government as well as their own frailties. They were too radical, too effective at reaching the black working and mid- dle classes, and too critical of capitalism and U.S. imperialism to be ig- nored, argued Rod Bush.[11]

More recently, two scholars of the black power era have positioned the Black Panther Party as a principal actor. Jeffrey Ogbar, for instance, situates the Nation of Islam and the Black Panther Party as the most influential yet opposing poles in the black power continuum. The Na- tion of Islam occupies a conservative terrain that condemned black popular culture and sought to elevate the black masses through a strict and didactic lifestyle. The Black Panthers inhabited the progressive political terrain, with their embrace of Marxist ideology and calls for black self-defense. Though profoundly different, both organizations challenged the tenets of integrationism and nonviolence. In Ogbar's words, the Panthers and the Nation of Islam endorsed and promoted the principle of "black self-love," which transformed the way black Americans understood themselves. Another historian, Nikhil Pal Singh, distinguishes the Black Panthers for their attention to working- class, ghettoized African Americans—black subalterns—by offering them "purposeful political action." The Panthers' focus on the internal colonization of blacks and other minority groups in the United States identified a problematic that had been ignored by the civil rights estab- lishment. Singh notes that the Panthers endeavored to carve out a means of survival, to "imagine how ordinary black people could make a life on the horns of the American dilemma." Both authors demonstrate that the Black Panthers were not an aberration, as their opponents claimed, but rather standard-bearers of the tradition of black protest and resistance. "In many ways, the Panthers were simply being faithful to the brilliant utopianism of the black vernacular: they were in search of *the way out of no way*," wrote Singh.[12]

Another important contribution to the scholarly conversation surrounding the Panthers appeared in an edited anthology published in 1998. *The Black Panther Party Reconsidered*, edited by Charles E. Jones, was the first serious incursion into an arena dominated by popular culture. The book juxtaposed scholarly research with essays by former Black Panthers in a search for a middle ground between celebration and condemnation. The editor, a professor of African American studies, said the project's goal was "not to deify the Panthers, but rather to offer a critical and balanced analysis of their activities and politics." In many respects, this text was a reclamation project, putting the Black Panthers on the academic stage and opening up the topic for more intense scrutiny. Even the publisher, Black Classic Press, focuses on resurrecting lost or little-known texts by African American authors. The eighteen essays offered an uneven look at little-understood dynamics of the Black Panthers, including gender conflicts, transnational politics, and the factors that led to the party's demise. It has become an essential resource both for scholars and for those interested in the perspectives of rank-and-file members of the organization. But short articles and essays, some based on dissertations or preliminary research, cannot take the place of full-length monographs that allow a topic to be fully explored. A similar project appeared a few years later. In 2001, Kathleen Cleaver and a colleague edited *Liberation, Imagination, and the Black Panther Party*. Like *The Black Panther Party Reconsidered*, this new venture combined original and reprinted scholarly articles on the Panthers, including several by Cleaver. The collection offers provocative glimpses at important issues surrounding the Panthers but was ultimately limited in its scope. Both efforts sought to interrupt or engage with the official histories emerging in the scholarly arena, but they have received far less attention than the biographies and memoirs of individual members. In replacing the drama of revolutionary action and social protest with more abstract scholarly analysis, neither book was likely to capture an audience beyond specialists in the field.[13]

The only single-author book devoted solely to the Panthers, written in the mid-1990s by an African American journalist, was a particularly harsh appraisal of the group's impact. Hugh Pearson's *The Shadow of the Panther: Huey Newton and Price of Black Power in America* is a scathing indictment of the Panthers, whom he described as "African American leaders with criminal mindsets." In this respect, he generally conformed to the dominant constructions of the Black Panthers, whether based in popular culture or in scholarship. But Pearson had his own set of memories about the Panthers that shaped his analysis. As a black man of the post-sixties generation, he was indelibly marked by the specter of the Black Panthers from grade school through college, when he adhered to the "left-liberal notions of the day," he recalled. The book's title is suggestive of how Pearson was haunted by the memory of the Black Panthers—and Huey Newton was the ghost he must exorcise. Sociologist Avery Gordon described the haunting presence of such memories as a "constitutive element of modern social life," to which no one is immune. Part of Pearson's agenda of exorcism was to demystify and de-romanticize the Panthers for young blacks seeking idols and political role models. He takes the "radical Left and the Left-liberal media" to task for raising the visibility of the Panthers and their imitators, and in that sense refusing to let the ghost die.[14]

The book traces, in great detail, the criminal exploits of Huey Newton and other Black Panthers within the context of the organization's rise and fall. The project's methodology, however, is deeply flawed. *The Shadow of the Panther* is based on interviews with three former Panthers who broke ranks with Newton, an interview with Panther critic David Horowitz, an assortment of newspaper and magazine articles, declassified FBI reports, and the published memoirs of Panther leaders. By relying almost entirely on those who take a critical stance in relation to the Black Panthers as main primary sources, the book becomes a self-fulfilling prophecy. Pearson's own ambivalence about his subject is clear. On one hand, he notes that African Americans in Oakland in the 1960s had serious and legitimate grievances against the police and local government, and that the area was an ideal incubator for black power politics. On the other hand, he maintains that the Panthers were misguided at best, and dangerous and destructive at worst. While there were many well-intentioned Panther members, according to Pearson, the Panther leadership was corrupt, prone to violence, and primarily interested in their own self-aggrandizement. Like Mendel-Reyes and other writers, Pearson is particularly troubled by the Panthers' lasting negative image: "an image that could have been not a racist's worst nightmare but a racist's ultimate dream." The overarching angst of Pearson's analysis is that Newton, who might have been his hero, was unable to make the transition from the underworld to respectable citizenship. Pearson, like numerous other critics of the Panthers, carelessly conflated Newton with the entire black power movement. Despite its shortcomings, *The Shadow of the Panther* has been read widely, and Pearson, like others who have penned the recollections of the 1960s, has been accorded the status of an authoritative source.[15]

Critical Memory

Pearson's goal, in part, was to resist the powerful nostalgia about the Black Panthers that he found circulating in African American communities and beyond. Nostalgia is a form of remembering, a set of selective memories that emphasize the positive while forgetting the bad, burnish faded recollections into polished images. Nostalgia also provides an opportunity to rewrite history. Marita Sturken offers a vivid example of the nostalgia industry that emerged after the Vietnam Veterans Memorial was erected in Washington, D.C. The flurry of books, magazines, T-shirts, reunions, and other projects embraced by veterans and their families capitalized on the desire to find a guilt-free, celebratory engagement with the memory of the war. The post-1960s generation was particularly fascinated with Vietnam precisely because it was not part of their immediate consciousness. "This nostalgia represents a desire to experience war," noted Sturken. The contemporary crises in Iraq and Afghanistan have perhaps muted any simplistic fascination with the Vietnam War, but those memories from the sixties continue to shape how we think about militarism, patriotism, and protest.[16]

Similarly, the hip-hop generation looks to the Black Panthers as a way to feel the exhilaration of armed, radical resistance, while their parents try to block out the painful and difficult recollections of the era. African Americans, whose history has generally been obscured in dominant culture, use nostalgia as a way to erect heroes and claim a place in the national memory without airing their "dirty laundry" in public. Hence the nostalgic impulse reinvents a multifaceted figure such as Martin Luther King Jr. into a champion of integration and a symbol of nonviolence. This legacy became reified through the creation of a national holiday in King's honor, countless tributes and memorials, and his established place in history textbooks. But, as Houston Baker warns, this nostalgia can be dangerous, as it operates in the service not only of those seeking to elevate black heroes but also of those hoping to eradicate the complex memories of the rebellious sixties. "Only a colossal act of historical forgetting allows envisioning the King of 1967 as anything but *a black political radical of the first order*," he notes. Baker suggests a dialectic between nostalgia and critical remembering; the latter can be "the very faculty of revolution." While nostalgia "writes the revolution as a well-passed aberration," critical memory "judges severely, censures righteously, renders hard ethical evaluations of the past."[17]

In the last decade, African American cultural workers have generated this kind of critical memory about the Black Panthers. Their work avoids a wholesale romanticization and refuses to engage in an unfettered nostalgia at the same time that it recognizes the Panthers' importance in history. Rather, the Black Panthers are the synecdoche for the dream of collective action and the promise of black power militancy. These texts recover the memories of the Black Panthers while situating them in the context of black life in a new millennium. Roger Guenveur Smith's evocation of Huey Newton in his one-man play *A Huey P. Newton Story* can be viewed in this light. Smith, who bears a striking physical resemblance to Newton, presents a warts-and-all portrait of Newton in his final years, using the Black Panther leader's own words. Smith's interpretation of Newton is of a tragic figure—a brilliant but tormented personality who disintegrates into crack addiction. Smith performs in black shirt and pants against a stark background, alluding to the dark, prison-like circumstances of Newton's interior life. Newton is a chain-smoking, stuttering, sometimes shy personality who recounts key episodes in the Panthers' history interspersed with his own narrative. Like Pearson, Smith has no desire to cover up Newton's criminal acts or drug problems, but he is unwilling to write off the black power movement because of one individual's frailties. The play deliberately disrupted the nostalgic recollections of Huey Newton as freedom fighter. One of the play's reviewers admitted his dependence on this memory:

His [Newton's] defiance against authority made an indelible impression on the minds of young Black boys living in the ghettos of South Central Los Angeles, constantly confronted with racism and police brutality. That was the Huey P. Newton of my youth, the mythological Newton—he is the one I chose to embrace in the recesses of my memory, not Huey P. Newton the "crack head!"[18]

Smith's performance offered an alternative to the mythological Newton, a memory intent on forcing a reevaluation of the Black Panthers. Was Newton a martyr or an egotist? A hero or a tortured soul? Could Newton have cleverly invented himself as the symbolic leader of a black revolution while struggling with a violent personality prone to addiction? Smith argues through his script and performance that Newton, like many complex public figures, embodied all of these contradictions. Only a simplistic or trivial understanding of the sixties would allow one side of the dichotomy to win out.

A Huey P. Newton Story won critical acclaim, including two Obie Awards and three NAACP awards, and moved from Los Angeles in 1995 to the Public Theater in New York and then to an international tour. The play had a particularly long life for a theatrical production before it was transformed into a mass cultural product in 2000. That year, Spike Lee filmed Smith's performance before a live audience and added an elaborated musical score and film clips of episodes in the civil rights and black power movements, reminiscent of the opening sequence to *Panther*. The film version, originally broadcast on the Black Starz cable channel in June 2001, later appeared on public television during Black History Month 2002. The film's promotional campaign included full-page ads in periodicals such as *Essence*, and an elaborate Web site with the running headline "He Defied and Defined Generations." Unwittingly, perhaps, the transition of the play from stage to film and television meant marketing just the kind of nostalgia Roger Smith sought to transcend. The fledgling network Black Starz used *A Huey P. Newton Story* to attract new, young subscribers; its strategies included giving away scholarships to high school students and hosting public screenings and panel discussions in markets with significant African American populations. The process of creating a mass market appeal for this text meant that some of its critical edge was muted. Many of the obvious references to Newton's drug use were eliminated in the film version, while connections to hip-hop culture and national politics were added. The possibility of making money on the image and memory of Huey Newton was too tantalizing for a major media corporation to avoid.

Critical memory has also shaped the way the Black Panthers have appeared in popular literature. In numerous books, these black power icons crop up as historical and cultural markers. Even when the name of the organization has changed, the references to black berets, paramilitary titles, and confrontations with police are unmistakable strategies to hail the Panthers from collective memory. Walter Mosley, who has written a series of popular and critically acclaimed mysteries with the protagonist detective Easy Rawlins, employs Panther-like activists in his novel *Bad Boy Brawly Brown* to capture the spirit of revolt of the period. The story, set in the underworld of 1960s black Los Angeles, includes a group called the Urban Revolutionary Party who became tangled in a struggle between good and evil. Like many of Mosley's characters, the Urban Revolutionaries are not always what they seem: the police may be criminals, the innocent may be guilty, and the black activists may be part of the establishment. The Urban Revolutionaries occupy a dubious position, one that is enticing even to the hardened and cynical hero, Easy Rawlins. The character's first encounter with the group recalls both the style and political aspirations of the Panthers:

> The young black men and women wore dark clothes, talked and listened, posed and watched. Their voices might have seemed angry to someone who didn't know the gruff bark of the American Negro's soul. Those men and women were far beyond anger, though. They were expressing a desire for love and revenge and for something that didn't exist—had never existed. That's why they were there. They were going to create freedom out of the sow's ear called America. They believed in the spirit of the Constitution and not the direction of the cash register. Maybe if I stayed there long enough, I might have believed it, too.

Walter Mosley conjures these Black Panther look-alikes as neither heroes nor anti-heroes; they are part of the culture of dissent that characterized urban black America during this period. They comprise deeply committed youth and opportunists, sinister figures and the gullible, all readily recognizable human figures. As a member of the baby-boom generation, Walter Moseley writes both from imagination and his own recollections of the black power moment.[19]

Hip-hop generation novelist Paul Beatty serves up a very different version of critical memory of the Panthers in his novel *Tuff*. This text is situated in what scholars have termed the "new black aesthetic" or NBA. Popularized by writer Trey Ellis in the 1990s, these twenty-something authors sought to bring authentic black street sensibilities to popular literature. Ellis defined this literary movement as "a mongrel mix of classes and types, and their political music sounds out this hybrid." NBA authors are influenced by the models of black arts and politics from the sixties and seventies, but they also shamelessly parody black nationalism, a symbol of their parents' era. One writer has dubbed Paul Beatty a "ghetto-fab ethnographer and cultural critic" because of his ability to transcribe the language and texture of black and Latino urban cultures while keeping the media industries that capitalize on them under suspicion.[20]

The protagonist of *Tuff* is Winston "Tuffy" Foshay, a ne'er-do-well homeboy who typifies the contradictions of the contemporary urban underclass. He spends his time involved with petty drug dealing and hustling, has a child out of wedlock, and has only limited formal education. But Tuffy is an erudite cultural consumer, has a committed relationship with his child's mother, and has aspirations of social change that go beyond his individual gain. The book follows his transformation from street hood to local politician with a cast of supportive characters right out of the sixties. Perhaps the most troubling is Tuffy's father, who enjoys the trappings of fatherhood without any of the responsibility. The father, Clifford, is a would-be poet and former Black Panther—this latter association defines his life and his son's disdain. In one scene, Tuffy talks to his former high school teacher, who has arranged a poetry reading by Clifford. Tuffy is deeply annoyed: "my father's poems is worser than the shit you used to make us read. You all be falling for that Black Panther Up-with-People bullshit too," he bemoaned. Several of Clifford's Black Panther buddies also show up for the reading, and afterward Tuffy asks them to leave. Clifford leans toward his son with mock sincerity, saying, "Winston, these are four brothers who've been around the block. Proud black men who've sacrificed their youth so young people like yourself wouldn't have to go through what they did. Do you remember?" Silently, Tuffy does conjure up recollections of a childhood in which he felt strangely protected by these black men; back then, "though he was too young to know the war had been over for more than a decade, he longed to be old enough to fight on the Revolution's frontline."[21]

Beatty's meditation captures the essence of critical nostalgia about the Black Panther Party. They are always in the collective consciousness of black Americans, and they elicit a desire to experience the radical ferment of an earlier age. Former Black Panthers are often engaged in an active campaign to construct their legacy for the next generation. But the characters in *Tuff* differentiate between memory and substance, between the romance of heroic black masculinity and the realities of a failed revolution. Tuffy rails against the false nostalgia that elevates the Panthers in the narratives of the sixties without considering their deeds and individual lives. Like Roger Guenveur Smith, Beatty wants the Black Panthers to be remembered not as vestiges of some lost gallant struggle but as the flesh-and-blood visionaries who, for better or worse, left a lasting image of black power.

Documentary filmmakers who have taken on the Panthers as subjects find themselves in the continuum between novelists, historians, and journalists as they juxtapose creative and scholarly techniques that can both interrogate and reinforce collective memories. Perhaps the most influential documentary film project about the civil rights and black power era, *Eyes on the Prize*, is emblematic of these texts. The films in this series, released in 1986 and 1989, skillfully employ interviews, primary sources, and archival footage to present a comprehensive overview of the subject, hence accruing credibility as serious empirical projects. At the same time the films rely on cinematic conventions such as action visuals, dramatic storytelling, and narration by a voice that conjures memories of the era—that of civil rights icon Julian Bond. The Black Panthers appear as one of several crucial actors during the period 1967–68 as one volume of the documentary explains the rise of the black power movement. They represent the decline of the civil rights dream and the backlash that resulted from the nation's failures in race relations; while telling the story of the Panthers' evolution, the filmmakers assume they are already familiar fixtures in American culture. *Eyes on the Prize* offers critical memory in a conventional package; the films elevate black American protest and resistance to serious history, and situate these phenomena as predictable

responses to poverty, racial violence, discrimination, and disenfranchisement. The Black Panthers are part of a larger milieu of race relations in crisis, rather than objects of tribute or criticism.[22]

Numerous documentaries about the Black Panthers, their allies, and
their politics have been produced since the late 1980s, many intent on
using the conventions of *Eyes on the Prize* to right the historical record
or to introduce an alternative perspective to the ongoing memories.
Some are made in the tradition of the original Newsreel collective,
low-budget films designed to be provocative and to oppose mainstream
journalism. Many have been tributes to the Black Panther leadership
or its unsung heroes, particularly women in the party. Most are invested in a form of countermemory as they attempt to challenge prevailing myths and assumptions about the Panthers. One such film, *All
Power to the People*, takes an investigative approach to argue that the
U.S. government used assassinations, harassment, and imprisonment to
silence dissent during the 1960s and 1970s. The Panthers are the central metaphor in this film by Lee Lew-Lee, a former Panther and news
videographer. It traces the history of subjugation of racial minorities
in the United States, using the Panthers' popular rhetorical slogan to
once again resurrect their memory. Lee's intense, jarring film, released
in 1996, seeks to shake up public complacency about the state. He uses
interviews with former Panther Mumia Abu-Jamal and Native American activist Leonard Peltier, both on death row, to suggest that the government continues to hold political prisoners as a concerted strategy
of political repression. Despite Lew-Lee's personal ties to the party, *All
Power to the People* is less a tribute to the Panthers than an indictment of
the government. There is no love lost for the celebrated Panther leadership in this film. Lew-Lee laments the Panthers' decline and suggests
that megalomania and corruption undermined the group. Like other
cultural products, he wants individual personalities to stand apart from
the Panthers' larger vision.

One of the most recent films to add to the panoply of critical memories is *A Panther in Africa*, released in 2004 and broadcast on public
television and at festivals around the country. It tells the story of Pete
and Charlotte O'Neal, two relatively unknown former Panthers who
have lived in exile for more than thirty years. In 1970, Pete O'Neal was
barely out of his teens and a leader of the Panthers' Kansas City chapter. After being convicted on charges of transporting a gun across state

lines, he and his wife fled his hometown and joined the Cleavers in ex-ile in Algiers. Eventually they settled in Tanzania to launch a new life that remained committed to social justice and community service. The film examines the life and mind of a Black Panther while de-romanticizing the experience of exile. The filmmaker shows them as a couple negotiating a difficult life, unable to see family and friends, cut off from familiar culture and language, and cobbling together an in-come. But their experiences embody the longings of many African Americans—to be surrounded and embraced by a nation of black peo-ple, to become part of an ancestral community, and to leave behind the hostile gaze of the West. The O'Neals remain part of the extended Black Panther family, hosting a regular stream of visitors and support-ers over the years. When ex-Panther Geronimo Pratt is released from prison and exonerated after twenty-seven years, he builds a home near the O'Neals in the hope that Tanzania can provide him with a new start. Filmmaker Aaron Matthews does not dwell on the often-told story of the Black Panthers but rather tries to explain what drives a black revolutionary from this period—the dream of self-sufficiency, authority, and a world without racism underscores the O'Neals' diffi-cult quest.

Boondocks, the cartoon series by Aaron McGruder, may be the most ir-reverent and most popular project that sustains the Panthers' memory. The syndicated cartoon strip, which recently moved to television, tells the story of two black youths who live with their grandfather in a largely white suburb. The elder of the two, Huey, is named after Huey Newton, and his character retains many of the characteristics of the Panther mythology, down to the Afro, scowl, and doctrinaire language. Although Huey Freeman is too young to have personal recollections of the Black Panthers, he ardently defends their memory. In an early strip, the young Huey defiantly tells an upper-middle-class black neighbor that he is named after Newton, an "icon of the black power movement of the late sixties and early seventies." The neighbor is crestfallen that Huey was not named after pop star Huey Lewis. When Huey starts a new school and his academic file is presented, it is filled with surveillance photos and data similar to an FBI record. Huey is in despair when he finds out that his school is named after J. Edgar Hoover. The character spends his time try-ing to teach black people the correct politics of blackness that reaches back to the black power era—particularly his younger brother, Riley, who is drawn to the styling of gangster rap. Huey takes on white clue-lessness and black hypocrisy in equal measure; he even uses the term *bootlicker*, made popular in the *Black Panther* newspaper, to lambaste con-temporary Uncle Toms. Like Paul Beatty, Aaron McGruder is part of the generation of black cultural workers committed to putting their own slant on historical memory. McGruder has been criticized for his liberal use of the word *nigger* in the cartoon, and for airing black America's dirty laundry in front of mainstream audiences. He has chosen to "keep it real" through a critical—and satirical—invocation of the past.

Keepers of the Flame

In the last fifteen years, surviving members of the Black Panther Party have been in the forefront of the developing counternarratives about the sixties, the black power movement, and the Party. This small but vi-brant network has worked mightily to ensure that they have some say in the way the Panthers are remembered. Reunions, conferences, film festivals, and a host of more commercial activities attempt to shape public perceptions and build an enduring interpretive community. Many are committed to the task of freeing the Black Panther Party from its customary association with its celebrated leaders and focusing instead on the rank-and-file members who labored in obscurity to feed schoolchildren, publish the newspaper, run community clinics, and hold political education classes. Another motivation is to educate today's as-piring activists about the victories and failures of the Panthers, and to inspire another generation. And some are concerned that the legacy of the Black Panther Party for Self-Defense not be confused with recent groups that bear the organization's name but not their principles.

Former Black Panthers began to reappear in popular culture through the publication of several memoirs by mainstream presses, most notably Elaine Brown's *A Taste of Power: A Black Woman's Story* in 1992 and David Hilliard's *This Side of Glory* in 1993. An earlier auto-biography of Assata Shakur, first published in 1987, has become some-thing of a cult classic among scholars and readers interested in the Panthers and black women's experiences in the black power move-ment. But *Assata*, published by a relatively small press, never achieved mass market visibility. This was not the case for Brown's and Hilliard's projects. As both titles suggest, these Panther insiders focused on the heady days of the Panthers' celebrity tempered with the sober realities of the group's demise. In each instance, the individual's involvement in the Black Panther Party remains a core part of his or her identity and a vehicle for newfound celebrity. Like Newton and Seale in the sixties and seventies, these former Panthers had a story to sell and found a ready marketplace. Both texts offer personal perspectives; they are as much about the individual lives of the authors and what propelled them into the Panthers as they are about the actual organization. Brown's book gained immediate attention for her revelations of sexual impropriety and violence within the party ranks. Among the book's reviewers was novelist Alice Walker, who wrote in the *New York Times* that Brown unveiled and demystified the sexism and misogynist legacy of the black power movement. Because of this Elaine Brown became a black feminist icon of sorts, and the book won praise from reviewers and launched her successful career on the lecture circuit. David Hilliard's recollections sought to ensure his place alongside Newton and Seale in the history of the Panther leadership, and he offered an honest appraisal of his own struggles with alcohol and substance abuse as well as those of Newton and other high-ranking officials. David Hilliard presented the downfall of the Panthers as a struggle between two competing visions—those of Newton and those of Cleaver. He also outlined the failure of Newton's leadership during the 1970s and the Panthers' political missteps. In both memoirs, the authors walk a fine line between presenting a candid and original version of the Panther story while protecting the group's desired legacy as a positive force for social change. These books were followed by multiple memoirs of lesser-known Panthers, including William Lee Brent, Johnny Spain, and Evans Hopkins, as well as those fighting imprisonment such as Geronimo Pratt, Mumia Abu-Jamal, and Dhoruba Bin Wahad. Throughout the 1990s there seemed to be a revived appetite for anything written by ex-Panthers, regardless of how often they covered the same terrain.[23]

But not all of the memorializing projects were for public consumption. Following Newton's death in 1989, former Panthers from the Bay Area who had maintained contact with each other began to meet. Eventually the focus was on organizing a thirty-year anniversary celebration for 1996. A group calling itself the Committee to Celebrate the Founding of the Black Panther Party was organized. One of the

participants was Kathleen Cleaver. "We decided to put divisions behind us and have a reunion," she explained. "There was a book under
way by Charles Jones, the first serious book on the Panthers, and we realized it was time to deal with the party history." The first reunion was
a picnic held in Oakland that included speeches, a photo exhibit, and a
lot of reminiscing. The *San Francisco Examiner* recorded the event, noting that there were only a few glimpses of the fiery, explosive personalities of the past. "When they gathered at Oakland's Bushrod Park
Sunday, survivors of that militant movement were too busy greeting
long-lost friends and showing off their children and grandkids to be
moved to anger," said the reporter. Huey Newton was dead and Eldridge Cleaver far away, but Bobby Seale, David Hilliard, and Kathleen
Cleaver showed up to represent the early Central Committee. The
gathering was less about recognizing celebrities than about acknowl-
edging their past and celebrating their survival. In 2002, Oakland-
based novelist and playwright Ishmael Reed attended another Panther
reunion, now an annual event. He described a "humble gathering" at
DeFremery Park where a few former Panthers and their friends ate
barbecue and showed off their kids, surrounded by oversized photos of
Huey Newton, Bobby Hutton, and other celebrated figures. Reed recalled the Panthers' earlier glory and contrasted his memories with the
contemporary setting: "Back in the 1960s the Panthers used to pack
this park with thousands of people. Media from around the world covered their every utterance. Today there's one lone interviewer from
KALX, the University of California's student-operated radio station."
Reed, who moved to Oakland in 1979, credits the Black Panthers for
making the city a showcase for African American political clout. They
"helped to transform the city from a feudal backwater run by a few
families to a modern city with worldwide recognition," he declared.
Ishmael Reed's engagement with the Panthers is bound up in his
memories of Oakland, which he chronicles in *Blues City: A Walk in
Oakland*. For him, it is impossible to experience one without the
other.[24]

Kathleen Cleaver, who earned a law degree and launched a career as
a teacher, legal advocate, and scholar, found that one of the most meaningful aspects of the reunion was the opportunity for women to connect and share their histories. A group of women associated with the
Panthers held a retreat later that year to begin the healing process.

"There were Black Panther women who were underground, imprisoned, traumatized, and expelled—it was important for this group to come together. Once you were in it [the Panthers], the impact didn't end. Many still bear the scars from that time," said Cleaver. Two years later, her ex-husband Eldridge dropped dead, drawing Kathleen back to thinking about the Panthers' history. After organizing his funeral and meeting up with old friends and associates, Cleaver wanted to organize a different kind of gathering. "I realized this was on the West Coast; we wanted to do something on the East Coast. The way the Black Panther Party had been divided was so traumatic, I thought maybe this could be the time to bring people together," she recalled. Cleaver and friends organized a memorial concert featuring Max Roach and Nile Rodgers. Although nine hundred people attended, it was a financial disaster. Then Cleaver came up with the idea of organizing a film festival: "We could sell tickets, raise money, and have a meaningful cultural event," she explained. The first International Black Panther Film Festival was held in New York in 2000, featuring several days of film screenings, panel discussions, and more opportunities for former members to reconnect. By the next year, the Film Festival had become a significant occasion, and Kathleen Cleaver reissued some of the same iconography and rhetoric used in the 1960s to advertise the event. There was one key difference, however—instead of images of Huey Newton and Eldridge Cleaver, the iconic figure was a female Panther, herself. Cleaver asserts that the film festivals, which attracted a sizeable audience of twenty-something participants, were intended to reach out to a younger generation. Among the panelists at the 2001 festival were the hip-hop group Dead Prez and student organizers for the activist group Black August. "Another generation has come of age and they're discovering that thirty years ago, high school and college students were actually doing something—they were revolutionaries—and they say, 'I want to do that; I want to be in the Black Panthers or the Young Lords.' They have to have a vision of the possible, and we give them that: to expand consciousness, to expand the imagination for people to create their own avenues of resistance," said Cleaver. Not surprisingly, Kathleen Cleaver is at work on her memoirs. She has also taken up the role of reviving her ex-husband's prodigious literary output. In 2006 she published a volume of his writings, titled *Target Zero: A Life in Writing*, that includes excerpts from Eldridge Cleaver's unpublished autobiography.[25]

Back in California, the Committee to Celebrate the Founding of the Black Panther Party was so pleased with the first reunion that they organized a thirty-fifth-anniversary reunion in Washington, D.C., that included panel sessions, photo displays, a film-and-video festival, and social events. The event was held in Washington, D.C., to acknowledge the vitality of Panther chapters on the East Coast. Participants included Father Earl Neil, an early Oakland supporter; the mother of Fred Hampton; Illinois congressman Bobby Rush; the grandson of Marcus Garvey; and members representing chapters across the country. Elbert "Big Man" Howard, who was a significant party leader, wrote that "it was a healing process for many former members of the BP. . . . For me and many others, it was very satisfying to be recognized for the work that we did so many years ago to make the world and our communities a better place to live." A driving force behind the committee is Bill Jennings, who joined the Panthers as a teenager and watched the ebb and flow of the organization during his formative years. Now he is one of many devoted to preserving the historical memory. Jennings has made it his avocation to travel around the country talking about his experiences in the Panthers and showing videos and photographs from his enormous personal archive. Indeed, for some former Panthers such as Jennings, keeping the memory of the Panthers alive is a calling. He publishes a quarterly newspaper called *It's About Time* that carries articles by aging former members and new disciples. The paper's masthead bears the enduring snarling black cat on both ends. He has been struck by how many unsung former Panthers hunger to participate in the process of reclamation. "We're able to put people together who've lost contact; we've hooked up family members and friends," he explained. "Now we have a network. Everywhere I go I hear stories that need to be part of the Panthers' history. People send me photographs and videos that they find in their homes. The impact of the party is everywhere." Jennings now maintains a comprehensive Web site on the Black Panthers that includes scanned copies of archived publications and ephemera, background on former chapters across the United States, listings of upcoming events and reunions, and an online version of *It's About Time*. An especially poignant component of this Web site is its attention to memorializing departed members. One link offers memorials to historical figures such as Bobby Hutton, as well as more recently deceased former Panthers—an effort all the more relevant as this baby-boom-generation community passes into late middle age. Virtually all of the better-known ex-Panthers maintain Web sites, as do assorted spin-off organizations. The Internet has become the de facto networking and memorializing medium for maintaining the visibility of the personalities and politics of the organization.[26]

Resurrecting the Panthers' venerable publication, the *Black Panther*, has been another strategy for invigorating the group's memory. The Commemoration Committee for the Black Panther Party launched *The Commemorator*, a monthly newspaper, in 1990 following Newton's death. The publication, under the subheading "Serving All Oppressed Communities," employed the Panthers' standard iconography, including the snarling black cat. Much of its content has been articles and statements reprinted from the original *Black Panther* newspaper as well as commentary on current events. The publication was designed to pay tribute to the Panthers' leaders and philosophy; volunteers from Oakland and Berkeley could be found selling copies of the paper and Black Panther buttons at venues that harked back to the sixties. The *Commemorator* has established a small subscriber base and has used its reach to initiate a literacy campaign. In April 2006 the paper expanded its Berkeley headquarters, indicating confidence in their longevity. "We are not the Black Panther Party," editor Melvin Dickson told a local reporter; rather, the newspaper and its supporters see themselves carrying on the principles of intercommualism with a particular emphasis on the philosophies of Huey Newton. In 1991 another publication calling itself the *Black Panther: Black Community News Service* appeared as well. This paper's focus seemed to foster a commitment to the memory of the party rather than Newton as icon. This newspaper was a facsimile of the original, mimicking its layout, style, and language; it appeared on a quarterly basis for at least five years. The competing versions of the Panthers' history spilled over into these two projects, both published in the Bay Area. By 1997, a group of former Panthers on the East Coast started publishing the *Black Panther Collective Community News*, which combined nostalgic references to the founding group with a focus on the problem of race relations in New York City. The Black Panther Collective was organized following the New York police's assault on Abner Louima, a Haitian immigrant, and they revived the early Panther practice of monitoring police activities as part of their Brutality Prevention Project. The formation of the New York

group was evidence that some community activists were not only ven-
erating the legacy of the Black Panther Party but also using the group's
tactics and symbols to once again rally collective outrage and a spirit of
protest. The group hosted a reunion in 2003 and launched a Web site
and speakers bureau, adding to the proliferation of efforts to reinsert
the Panthers into public discourse.[27]

The Huey P. Newton Foundation, established in 1996 by David
Hilliard, Elaine Brown, and Newton's widow, Frederika Newton, was
yet another group designed to cultivate and preserve a version of the
Panthers' history. The foundation maintains its own Web site, manages
a speakers bureau, and sponsors special events. It also compiled Newton's extensive collection of documents, taped interviews, photographs, and films, which was sold to Stanford University. The move to
sell the Huey P. Newton Collection was both a historical enterprise
and a financial one—Stanford would organize the collection and make
it available to the public for an undisclosed price. Hilliard told a reporter that he had approached several universities, but "they were not
willing to pay us a fair market price for our collection." Stanford paid
more than $1 million for the archives of poet Allen Ginsberg that same
year, noted the *Examiner*. One cannot escape the irony that Newton's
archive rests side by side with Stanford's Hoover Institute, founded by
Herbert Hoover in 1919 and considered one of the nation's preemi-
nent conservative think tanks.[28]

David Hilliard has fashioned himself as the overseer of several Bay
Area projects, taking a decidedly entrepreneurial approach. In addition
to running the Huey P. Newton Foundation, he has published two new
books since his autobiography: a collection of Newton's writing and a
biography of the Panther co-founder. Frederika Newton referred to the
book as "the first authoritative biography of Huey P. Newton," and it
appears to replace Bobby Seale's original accounting and to stand in opposition to Hugh Pearson's. This objective is evident even in the title,
Huey: Spirit of the Panther, which contrasts with Pearson's *In the Shadow of
the Panther*. This metaphor is carried throughout the text: Newton was a
political visionary, and the spirit and energy of the Panthers must be pre-
served. This latest biography, published in 2006, followed the same narrative path as earlier accounts of Newton's life. Hilliard immediately
disrupted the idea that he and other former Panthers ignore the underside of their endeavors: the book's opening anecdote recounted how he

and Newton sold drugs to raise money for Bobby Seale's bail in 1967. He also recalled the events of the infamous night when Bobby Hutton was killed in April 1968. Hilliard gave an eyewitness account confirming that Cleaver was the catalyst for the conflagration when he went out looking for an armed confrontation with police despite Hilliard's protests. Hilliard maintained that he watched helplessly as the police shot Hutton in the back, and he blamed Cleaver for his reckless behavior. Like Lee Lew-Lee and other Panther chroniclers, Hilliard also focused on assorted details of the FBI campaign to bring down Newton and the organization; his primary sources were several interviews with former Panthers and Newton intimates, as well as Newton's unpublished manuscripts. He also devoted space to Newton's pursuit of a Ph.D. at the University of California, Santa Cruz, enshrining him as a revolutionary genius. Perhaps the most revealing moment of this narrative appears in the final chapter, by Frederika Newton and titled "Surviving Huey." Newton's widow told harrowing tales of his drug abuse history and violent character; she postulated that he may have suffered from a personality disorder as well. This project to reclaim Newton's legacy ends on a sad, dispirited note; bipolar, addicted to crack and prescription drugs, alcoholic, Huey Newton embodied the phrase he coined— "revolutionary suicide."[29]

Hilliard is involved in other memorializing projects as well. He leads a Black Panther tour in Oakland that starts at the office where Seale and Newton wrote the ten-point program and ends at DeFremery Park, where numerous Panther rallies were held. In so doing, the entire city of Oakland has become a Black Panther shrine. According to Ishmael Reed, the tour's highlights include the alley where Cleaver and Hutton were trapped by the police; Hilliard makes sure to point out the bullet holes that remain as a testimony to that historical event. Hilliard has also launched a number of financial ventures, including a clothing line and promoting a rap group. In 2001, a Los Angeles streetwear company got permission from Hilliard and Frederika Newton to use Panther images on a line of T-shirts, and Fresh Jive clothing, featuring Panther images, was launched. Hilliard told one reporter that this was a strategy to counter the prevailing media representations of the Panthers. "People are beginning to go beyond the media portrayal of us as militant, gun-toting young people who were just full of rhetoric, and beginning to look at us as a piece of the civil rights movement," he said. Some former

Panthers, including Bill Jennings, were incensed that Hillliard sought to capitalize on the Panthers' image. "None of that stuff belongs to any of those people," said Jennings, bemoaning the continued obsession with Panther celebrities. Undaunted, Hilliard more recently started Black Panther Records, with his son as co-founder. Their first music video was for a group called the Fugitives, which featured famous scenes of the Black Panthers from the 1960s. Currently, Black Panther Records and Productions is seeking sponsors for the Legacy Tour, which includes hip-hop and rap performances, video, and photography. The Fugitives are featured artists on the tour, and Hilliard, Frederika Newton, and Ericka Huggins are available for lectures. The group has also co-sponsored performances by Thomas Mapfumo, a Zimbabwean musician, in a venture designed to bring "revolutionary voices in the African and African American Struggle together."[30]

Bobby Seale, Panther founder and visionary, has waged his own campaign to maintain his own as well as the group's visibility. In the 1980s he was best known for his cookbook *Barbeque'n with Bobby*, but more recently he has been concerned with reclaiming his identity as the Party's leader. In 2002 he moved back to the Bay Area after living on the East Coast for many years. He manages his own Web site, which tells his version of the Panthers' history and sells his products, and he has railed against others using the Black Panther name. When the New Black Panther Party emerged in the early 1990s, members from the original group looked on with consternation. "They're a bunch of idiot extremists in the same way that a racist Ku Klux Klan and a racist Nazi is," said Seale. The new Panthers allied themselves with Khalid Abdul Muhammad, the controversial former spokesman for the Nation of Islam, known for his extreme anti-Semitic harangues. These "copycats," as they were labeled, reaped the benefits of the Panthers' celebrity but seemed far removed from their ideology. The Black Panther Party of Dallas, with roots in the original party, sued the new Panthers, saying the imitators damaged their image. Although the name "Black Panther" was not legally owned by any entity, the message was clear—the older Panthers did not want to be confused with this modern band of separatist blacks. "These guys are antithetical to what we represent," David Hilliard told the press. In 1997 a Texas court ordered the New Black Panthers to dissociate from the original group. But the issue resurfaced in 2002 when the original Panthers once again threatened legal action, claiming copyright and trademark infringement. Among other transgressions, the new group had a Web site featuring an image of Huey Newton, and it was increasingly apparent that they were attracting media attention because many assumed they were connected to the Oakland group. The attorney fighting the case on behalf of the original Panthers said, "The real concern is that 100 years from now, when the history of the 1960s is written, that the Black Panther Party be seen as a significant chapter in the civil rights struggle." The New Black Panthers were a threat to that legacy. Not surprisingly, the name, the image, and the memory of the Black Panther Party remain something worth fighting for.[31]

Notes

Introduction

1. *U.S. v. Zacarias Moussaoui*, U.S. District Court, Eastern District, 2001; *Time*, 2 February 2002.

2. Fox Network News, 18 July 2002; National Public Radio archive, *Weekend Edition*, 28 July 2002; a survey of the Vanderbilt Television News Archive and the *New York Times* yielded no mention of the Black Panthers' presence on that day; Nikhil Pal Singh, "The Black Panthers and the 'Undeveloped Country' of the Left," in Charles E. Jones, ed., *The Black Panther Party Reconsidered* (Baltimore: Black Classic Press, 1998), 61–62.

3. *New York Times*, 27 November 2004.

4. *Los Angeles Times*, 2 May 1998; *Los Angeles Times* 21 July, 25 July 2000; *San Francisco Examiner*, 19 July 2000.

5. *New York Times*, 20 July 1997; a kicker is a short, smaller-font headline just above the main headline, used to help classify articles. *New Republic*, 11 August 1997; *Los Angeles Times*, 20 February 2002.

6. H. Rap Brown, *Die Nigger Die!* (New York: Dial Press, 1969), 120; Stokely Carmmichael, speech at Wisconsin State University in Whitewater, 6 February 1967, reprinted in Robert L. Scott and Wayne Brockriede, *The Rhetoric of Black Power* (New York: Harper and Row, 1969), 99; Todd Gitlin, *The Whole World Is Watching: Mass Media in the Making and Unmaking of the New Left* (Berkeley: University of California Press, 1980), 3.

7. The essential source on the theory of framing is Erving Goffman, *Frame Analysis: An Essay on the Organization of Experience* (1974; reprint, Boston: Northeastern University Press, 1986). Other useful discussions include James K. Hertog and Douglas M. McLeod, "A Multiperspectival Approach to Framing Analysis: A Field Guide," in Stephen D. Reese, Oscar H. Gandy Jr., and August E. Grant, eds., *Framing Public Life: Perspectives on Media and Our Understanding of the Social World* (Mahwah, NJ: Lawrence Erlbaum Associates, 2001), 141–42; Stuart Hall, "The Whites of Their Eyes: Racist Ideologies and the Media," in George Bridges and Roseland Brunt, eds., *Silver Linings: Some Strategies for the Eighties* (London: Lawrence and Wishart, 1981), 28–52.

8. Bobby Seale, *Seize the Time: The Story of the Black Panther Party and Huey P. Newton* (New York: Vintage Books, 1968), 59–64. The Nation of Islam's platform, titled "What the Muslims Want, What the Muslims Believe," was published in each issue of *Muhammad Speaks* during the 1960s.

9. Huey Newton describes this ideological transition in *War Against the Panthers: A Study of Repression in America* (New York: Harlem River Press, 1996), 29; Wahneema Lubiano, "Black Nationalism and Black Common Sense: Policing Ourselves and Others," in *The House That Race Built: Black Americans, U.S. Terrain* (New York: Pantheon, 1997), 234.

10. *San Francisco Chronicle*, 11 June 2003; *Los Angeles Times*, 22 June 2003; History News Network, 14 July 2003.

Chapter 1: Thirty Years in Hindsight: The Black Panthers in Popular Memory

1. *Panther*, dir. Mario Van Peebles (Polygram Film Productions, 1995).

2. Noel Elyce Holton, " 'Panther' Is a Compelling Story on the Screen," *New York Beacon*, 17 May 1995; Kristal Brent Zook, " 'So Full Were They,' of Their Own Glory . . . ," *L. A. Weekly*, 5–11 May 1995, 21; Michael Robinson, "The Van Peebleses Prowl Through the Panthers' History," *American Visions*, April/May 1995, 16–18.

3. David Thelen, "Memory and American History," *Journal of American History* 75 (1989): 1117–29.

4. Marita Sturken, *Tangled Memories: The Vietnam War, the AIDS Epidemic, and the Politics of Remembering* (Berkeley: University of California Press, 1997), 9–10.

5. Charles E. Jones and Judson L. Jeffries, " 'Don't Believe the Hype': Debunking Panther Mythology," in Charles E. Jones, ed., *The Black Panther Party Reconsidered* (Baltimore: Black Classic Press, 1998), 37–44; George Lipsitz, *Time Passages: Collective Memory and American Popular Culture* (Minneapolis: University of Minnesota Press, 1990), 213–15. Lipsitz contends that such countermemories have particular power and efficacy in an era in which global capital, transnational mass media, and mass bureaucracy have contributed to a mounting sense of alienation and displacement among average citizens.

6. On Pierre Nora's theory, see Genevieve Fabre and Robert O'Meally, "Introduction," in Fahre and O'Meally, eds., *History and Memory in African-American Culture* (New York: Oxford University Press, 1994), 7.

7. Douglass quoted in David W. Blight, *Frederick Douglass' Civil War: Keeping Faith in Jubilee* (Baton Rouge: Louisiana State University Press, 1989), 223.

8. Patricia A. Turner notes that the FBI and CIA are regular subjects in African American legends and rumors of anti-black conspiracies; see her *I Heard It Through the Grapevine: Rumor in African-American Culture* (Berkeley: University of California Press, 1993), 112–13, 201.

9. Ed Guerrero, *Framing Blackness: The African American Image in Film* (Philadelphia: Temple University Press, 1993), 159, 160–61.

10. Misty Brown, "Panther: Close Up with Mario Van Peebles," *Washington Afro-American*, 6 May 1995; Gregg Kilday, "Power to the Peebles," *Entertainment Weekly*, 12 May 1995.

11. For an extensive discussion of the mass media's production of cultural authority, see Barbie Zelizer, *Covering the Body: The Kennedy Assassination, the Media, and the Shaping of Collective Memory* (Chicago: University of Chicago Press, 1992), 196–200, 201–9.

12. Esther Armah, "Taking a Leap Back into History," *Weekly Journal* (UK), 9 November 1995; Cheo Tyehimba, "Panthermania," *Essence*, February 1995, 108–12.

13. Melvin Van Peebles, *Panther* (New York: Thunder's Mouth Press, 1995), author's note; also see Guerrero, *Framing Blackness*, 86; "Parting Shots," *Life*, 13 August 1971, 61.

14. Jon Harmann, "The Trope of Blaxploitation in Critical Responses to Sweetback," *Film History* 6 (1994): 382–404; James Surowiecki, "Making It: An Interview with Melvin Van Peebles," *Transition* 0, 79 (1999): 182.

15. *San Francisco Chronicle*, 29 August 1994; program for Roger Guenveur Smith, *A Huey P. Newton Story*, Actors' Gang, Los Angeles, 19 January–12 February 1995. The board of directors of the Actors' Gang includes Harry Belafonte, Robert Altman, Robin Williams, and other show business luminaries; on Smith, also see *New York Times*, 9 February 1997.

16. See Melvin L. Oliver, James H. Johnson Jr., and Walter C. Farrell Jr., "Anatomy of a Rebellion: A Political-Economic Analysis," in Robert Gooding-Williams, ed., *Reading Rodney King—Reading Urban Uprising* (New York: Routledge, 1993), 117–34; Manning Marable, *Beyond Black and White: Transforming African-American Politics* (London: Verso, 1995), 203–15; Manning Marable, *Black Leadership* (New York: Columbia University Press, 1998), 151, 186–89.

17. Michael C. Dawson, *Black Visions: The Roots of Contemporary African-American Political Ideologies* (Chicago: University of Chicago Press, 2001). On the relationship between hip-hop and Malcolm X, see Michael Eric Dyson, *Making Malcolm: The Myth and Meaning of Malcolm X* (New York: Oxford University Press, 1995), 82. Also see Manning Marable, "Malcolm vs. Messiah: Cultural Myth Versus Historical Reality," in his *Beyond Black and White*, 137–41; Robin D.G. Kelley, *Yo' Mama's Dysfunctional: Fighting the Culture Wars in America* (Boston: Beacon Press, 1997); Maurice E. Stevens, "Subject of Countermemory: Disavowal and Black Manhood in Spike Lee's Malcolm X," *Signs: Journal of Women in Culture and Society* 28, 1 (2002): 281, 284.

18. "Generation Rap," *New York Times*, 3 April 1994.

19. Dawson, *Black Visions*, 129.

20. For an extensive discussion of masculinity, black nationalism, and rap music, see Charise L. Cheney, *Brothers Gonna Work It Out: Sexual Politics in The Golden Age of Rap Nationalism* (New York: New York University Press, 2005); Public Enemy, *Fear of a Black Planet* (Def Jam Records, 1990); Public Enemy, *It Takes a Nation of Millions to Hold Us Back* (Def Jam Records, 1988); Public Enemy, *Apocalypse 91 . . . The Enemy Strikes Back* (Def Jam Records, 1991); "It Was Rap Party Time at Nassau Coliseum," *Newsday*, 16 August 1988.

21. Common and Cee-lo, "A Song for Assata," on Common, *Like Water for Chocolate* (MCA Records, 2000); *Los Angeles Times*, 22 November 1992; Kara Keeling, "'A Homegrown Revolutionary'?: Tupac Shakur and the Legacy of the Black Panther Party," *The Black Scholar* 1999, 29, 2–3, 61; Cheney, *Brothers Gonna Work It Out: Sexual Politics in the Golden Age of Rap Nationalism*, 85.

22. Paris, *The Devil Made Me Do It* (Tommy Boy Music, 1989–90); Paris, *Guerrilla Funk* (Priority Records, 1994); *Los Angeles Times*, 4 February 1990; Tonya Pendleton, "The Black Panthers: Party of the People, Pt. 1," *Rap Pages*, November 1993; Errol A. Henderson, "Black Nationalism and Rap Music," *Journal of Black Studies* 26, 3 (1996): 308–39.

23. *Toronto Star*, 31 May 2000.

24. Gregg Kilday, "Power to the Peebles," *Entertainment Weekly*, 12 May 1995; *Daily Variety*, 2 May 1995, 5 May 1995, 12 May 1995.

25. Desson Howe, "Panther," *Washington Post*, 5 May 1995; Richard Corliss, "Power to the Peephole," *Time*, 15 May 1995; Caryn James, "They're Movies, Not Schoolbooks," *New York Times*, May 21, 1995.

26. Michael Eric Dyson, "The Panthers, Still Untamed, Roar Back," *New York Times*, 30 April 1995; Michael Robinson, "The Van Peebleses Prowl Through the Panthers' History," *American Visions*, April/May 1995, 16–18; Clarence Lusane, "To Fight for the People: The Black Panther Party and Black Politics in the 1990s," in Charles E. Jones, ed., *The Black Panther Party Reconsidered* (Baltimore: Black Classic Press, 1998), 445.

27. Tracye Matthews, " 'No One Ever Asks, What a Man's Place in the Revolution Is': Gender and the Politics of the Black Panther Party 1966–1971," in Charles E. Jones, ed., *The Black Panther Party Reconsidered* (Baltimore: Black Classic Press, 1998), 294–95; Robinson, "The Van Peebleses Prowl," 18; Kristal Brent Zook, " 'So Full Were They,' " 21.

28. Ellen Knickmeyer, "Is New Movie History Lesson or 'Poetic Lies?' " *Los Angeles Sentinel*, 21 June 1995.

29. Mario Van Peebles, Ula Y. Taylor, and J. Tarika Lewis, *Panther: The Pictorial History of the Black Panther Party and the Story Behind the Film* (New York: Newmarket Press, 1995); Ula Y. Taylor, *The Veiled Garvey: The Life and Times of Amy Jacques Garvey* (Chapel Hill: University of North Carolina Press, 1992). Thanks to Robin D.G. Kelley for pointing out the irony of Taylor and Lewis' participation. Spike Lee published books on the making of *School Daze*, *Do the Right Thing*, *She's Gotta Have It*, and *Malcolm X*, among others.

30. Robyn Wiegman, "Whiteness Studies and the Paradox of Particularity," *Boundary 2* 26, 3 (1999): 127.

Chapter 2: Black America in the Public Sphere

1. W.E.B. Du Bois, *The Souls of Black Folk*, in *Three Negro Classics* (New York: Avon Books, 1973), 215.

2. Eric Lott, *Love and Theft: Blackface Minstrelsy and the American Working Class* (New York: Oxford University Press, 1995), 25.

3. Ira Berlin, *Slaves Without Masters: The Free Negro in the Antebellum South* (New York: Pantheon Books, 1974), 95; George Fredrickson, *The Black Image in the White Mind: The Debate on Afro-American Character and Destiny, 1817–1914* (New York: Harper and Row, 1971), 53.

4. Thomas Jefferson, *Notes on the State of Virginia, Written in the Year 1781, Somewhat Cor-rected and Enlarged in the Winter of 1782, for the Use of a Foreigner of Distinction, in Answer to Certain Queries Proposed by Him*, excerpted in Wilson Jeremiah Moses, ed., *Classical Black Nationalism: From the American Revolution to Marcus Garvey* (New York: New York University Press, 1996), 46; on Jefferson's racial ideologies, also see Winthrop Jordan, *The White Man's Burden: Historical Origins of Racism in the United States* (New York: Oxford University Press, 1974); Fredrickson, *The Black Image*, 9.

5. Fredrickson, *The Black Image*, 17.

6. Ibid., 101.

7. Kenneth W. Goings, *Mammy and Uncle Mose: Black Collectibles and American Stereotyping* (Bloomington: Indiana University Press, 1994), 14.

8. Fredrickson, *The Black Image*, 255; also see Jordan, *The White Man's Burden*; and Thomas F. Gossett, *Race: The History of an Idea* (New York: Oxford University Press, 1997).

9. Fredrickson, *The Black Image*, 275–76; Donald Bogle, "Black Beginnings: From *Uncle Tom's Cabin* to *The Birth of a Nation*," in *Toms, Coons, Mulattoes, Mammies and Bucks* (New York: Continuum, 1989), 21; also see Clyde Taylor, "The Re-Birth of the Aes-thetic in Cinema," in Daniel Bernardi, ed., *The Birth of Whiteness: Race and the Emer-gence of U.S. Cinema* (New Brunswick, NJ: Rutgers University Press, 1996), 15–37.

10. Rayford W. Logan, *The Betrayal of the Negro from Rutherford B. Hayes to Woodrow Wilson* (New York: Collier Books, 1965), 219.

11. Ibid., 222–24.

12. Ibid., 230–38, 243, 252, 267.

13. Ibid., 390, 392.

14. George Eaton Simpson, *The Negro in the Philadelphia Press* (Philadelphia: University of Pennsylvania Press, 1936), 72, 102, 118–19.

15. Maurine Beasley, "The Muckrakers and Lynching: A Case Study in Racism," *Journal-ism History* 9, 3–4 (1982): 86–90.

16. T. Thomas Fortune, "We Know Our Rights . . . and Have the Courage to Defend Them," reprinted in John H. Bracey Jr., August Meier, and Elliot Rudwick, eds., *Black Nationalism in America* (New York: Bobbs-Merrill, 1970), 212–15.

17. Booker T. Washington, "The Atlanta Exposition Address, September 1895," in Wash-ington, *Up from Slavery*, reprinted in *Three Negro Classics* (New York: Avon Books, 1973), 145–57.

18. Du Bois, *Souls of Black Folk,* 240–52.

19. On Du Bois' turn to pan-Africanism, see W.E.B. Du Bois, *The Negro* (New York: 1915).

20. My survey of scholarship in the field found nothing on news content from this pe-riod. The *New York Times* was selected for analysis as it is one of very few newspapers that provides an index for those years.

21. *New York Times*, 13 October 1918.

22. *New York Times*, 29 July 1918.

23. *New York Times*, 12 January 1918.

24. *New York Times*, 18 February 1919; also see description in David Levering Lewis, *When Harlem Was in Vogue* (New York: Oxford University Press, 1979), 3–5.

25. *New York Times*, 11 May 1919.

26. *New York Times*, 20 July 1919.

27. *New York Times*, 31 July 1919.

28. Ibid.

29. *New York Times*, 28 July 1919.

30. *New York Times*, 26 August 1919.

31. *New York Times*, 3 June 1920, 3 August 1920.

32. *New York Times*, 4 August 1920.

33. Toni Morrison, *Playing in the Dark: Whiteness and the Literary Imagination* (Cambridge: Harvard University Press, 1992), 38.

34. Stuart Hall, "The Whites of Their Eyes: Racist Ideologies and the Media," in George Bridges and Rosalind Brunt, eds., *Silver Linings* (London: Lawrence and Wishart, 1981), 37.

35. Robert D. Leigh, ed., Commission on Freedom of the Press, *A Free and Responsible Press, A General Report on Mass Communication: Newspapers, Radio, Motion Pictures, Magazines, and Books* (Chicago: University of Chicago Press, 1947), 20–27.

36. Carolyn Martindale, *The White Press and Black America* (Westport, CT.: Greenwood Press 1986), 83.

37. Simeon Booker, "A New Frontier for Daily Newspapers," *Nieman Reports*, 1956, 25.

38. The Southern Regional Council report is discussed in Armistead S. Pride, "The News That Was," in Henry LaBrie, ed., *Perspectives of the Black Press: 1974* (Kennebunkport, ME: Mercer House Press, 1974); Ira Harkey, *The Smell of Burning Crosses: An Autobiography of a Mississippi Newspaperman* (Jacksonville, IL: Harris-Wolfe, 1967).

39. Taylor Branch, *Parting the Waters* (New York: Simon and Schuster, 1988), 21.

40. Susan M. Weill, "Mississippi's Daily Press in Three Crises," in David R. Davies, ed., *The Press and Race: Mississippi Journalists Confront the Movement* (Jackson: University Press of Mississippi, 2001), 24.

41. The *Readers' Guide to Periodical Literature*, the *New York Times* index, and other newspaper indexes were surveyed for the years 1955–1960 to determine the extent of attention to the Till case.

42. *New York Times*, 7 September 1955.

43. *New York Times*, 18 September 1955.

44. *Life*, 24 September 1956.

45. Wendy Kozol, *Life's America: Family and Nation in Postwar Photojournalism* (Philadelphia: Temple University Press, 1994), 154.

46. For an excellent example of television news coverage of the Till case, see the documentary *Eyes on the Prize*, part I, "Awakenings" (Henry Hampton: Blackside, Inc, 1986).

47. "The Media and the Movement: An Interview with Richard Valeriani," in Juan Williams, ed., *Eyes on the Prize: America's Civil Rights Year, 1954–1965* (New York: Viking, 1987), 270.

48. Ruby Hurley interview in Howell Raines, *My Soul Is Rested: The Story of the Civil Rights Movement in the Deep South* (New York: Viking Penguin, 1983), 136.

49. Julian Bond, "The Media and the Movement: Looking Back from the Southern Front," in Brian Ward, ed., *Media, Culture and the Modern African American Freedom Struggle* (Gainesville, FL: University Press of Florida, 2001). 19–26.

50. Branch, *Parting the Waters*, 175–78, 203.

51. Grover C. Hall, "Race Problem Coverage," *Bulletin of the American Society of Newspaper Editors* (1958).

52. A.H. Sulzberger, "The Word Negro Is Not to Appear Unless . . . ," *Nieman Reports*, 1958: 3, 4.

53. Journalist Dick Sanders, quoted in Allison Graham, *Framing the South: Hollywood, Television, and Race during the Civil Rights Struggle* (Baltimore: Johns Hopkins University Press, 2001), 10–11.

54. Gene Roberts and Hank Klibanoff, *The Race Beat: The Press, The Civil Rights Struggle, and the Awakening of a Nation* (New York: Alfred A. Knopf, 2006), 196.

55. Branch, *Parting the Waters*, 203; Richard Lentz, *Symbols, the News Magazines, and Martin Luther King* (Baton Rouge: Louisiana State University Press, 1990), 38.

56. Bond, "The Media and the Movement," 22; Branch, *Parting the Waters*, 225–28.

57. Jenny Walker, "A Media Made Movement?: Black Violence and Nonviolence in the Historiography of the Civil Rights Movement," in Brian Ward, ed., *Media, Culture, and the Modern African American Freedom Struggle*, 48.

58. Ibid., 52. On Robert Williams' encounters with the press, see Timothy B. Tyson, *Radio Free Dixie: Robert F. Williams and the Roots of Black Power* (Chapel Hill: University of North Carolina Press, 1999), 148–52; Simon Wendt, *The Spirit and the Shotgun: Armed Resistance and the Struggle for Civil Rights* (Gainesville, FL: University Press of Florida, 2007), 28–39.

59. Paul B. Johnson, David D. Sears, and John B. McConahay, "Black Invisibility, the Press and the Los Angeles Riot," *American Journal of Sociology* 76 no 4 (Jan. 1971): 698–721.

60. Taylor Branch, *Parting The Waters*, 633–34, 647–53; *New York Times*, 2 October 1962.

61. Branch quote is from *Parting The Waters*, 876; see also chapter 22, "The March on Washington."

62. *New York Times*, 1 September 1963; Lentz, *Symbols*, 104–5.

63. Taylor Branch, *Parting The Waters*, 888–92; Eugene Patterson essay quoted in Gene Roberts and Hank Klibanoff, *The Race Beat*, 352.

64. Charles M. Payne, *I've Got the Light of Freedom: The Organizing Tradition and the Mississippi Freedom Struggle* (Berkeley: University of California Press, 1995), 398; see Payne's discussion in chapter 14.

Chapter 3: Becoming Media Subjects

1. Quintard Taylor, *In Search of the Racial Frontier: African Americans in the American West, 1528–1990* (New York: W.W. Norton, 1998), 304; Robert Self, " 'To Plan Our Liberation': Black Power and the Politics of Place in Oakland, California, 1965–1977," *Journal of Urban History* 26, 6 2000, 766.

2. Taylor, *In Search of the Racial Frontier*, 289–92; Daniel Crowe, *Prophets of Rage: The Black Freedom Struggle in San Francisco, 1945–1969* (New York: Garland, 2000), 152–53, 208–9.

3. Gayle B. Montgomery and James W. Johnson, *One Step from the White House: The Rise and Fall of Senator William F. Knowland* (Berkeley: University of California Press, 1998), 274–79; Crowe, *Prophets of Rage*, 153.

4. Self, " 'To Plan Our Liberation,' " 773–75; Bobby Seale, *Seize the Time: The Story of the Black Panther Party and Huey P. Newton* (New York: Random House, 1970), 13–20, 35–36.

5. Robert F. Williams, *Negroes With Guns*, excerpted in Floyd B. Barbour, ed., *The Black Power Revolt* (Boston: Porter Sargent Publishers, 1968), 177–78; also see Timothy B. Tyson, *Radio Free Dixie: Robert F. Williams and the Roots of Black Power* (Chapel Hill: University of North Carolina Press, 1999); Lance Hill, *The Deacons for Defense: Armed Resistance and the Civil Rights Movement* (Chapel Hill: University of North Carolina Press, 2004), 56–8. See discussion in Michael Dawson, *Black Visions: The Roots of Contemporary African-American Political Ideologies* (Chicago: University of Chicago Press, 2001), 35–42.

6. Michael Omi and Howard Winant, *Racial Formation in the United States*; Clayborne Carson, *In Struggle: SNCC and the Black Awakening of the 1960s* (Cambridge: Harvard University Press, 1981), 191; Seale quoted in *Black Panther*, 2 June 1967; Stokely Carmichael and Charles V. Hamilton, *Black Power: The Politics of Liberation in America* (New York: Vintage Books, 1967), 44.

7. For background on the Lowndes County Black Panthers, see Carson, *In Struggle: SNCC and the Black Awakening of the 1960s* (Cambridge, MA: Harvard University Press, 1981), 164–66, 200; see also William Van Deburg, *New Day in Babylon: The Black Power Movement and American Culture, 1965–1975* (Chicago: University of Chicago Press, 1992), 12, 32–34.

8. *New York Times*, 5 May 1966.

9. *New York Times*, 17 May, 22 May 1966; also see discussion in Carson, *In Struggle*, 203–4.

10. *CBS Evening News*, 10 March 1966; *ABC Evening News*, 3 May 1966.

11. James L. Baughman, *The Republic of Mass Culture: Journalism, Filmmaking, and Broadcasting in America Since 1941* (Baltimore: Johns Hopkins University Press, 1994), 118–20; *Report of the National Advisory Commission on Civil Disorders* (New York: E.P. Dutton, 1968), 366.

12. Baughman, *The Republic of Mass Culture*, 91–115; Daniel C. Hallin, *We Keep America on Top of the World: Television Journalism and the Public Sphere* (New York: Routledge, 1994), 136–37.

13. Edward Jay Epstein, *Between Fact and Fiction: The Problem of Journalism* (New York: Vintage Books, 1975), 182–209.

14. Stuart Hall, "The Whites of Their Eyes: Racist Ideologies and the Media," in George Bridges and Rosalind Brunt, eds., *Silver Linings: Some Strategies for the Eighties* (London: Lawrence and Wishart, 1980), 28–52; also see David Theo Goldberg, "The Social Formation of Racist Discourse," in *The Anatomy of Racism* (Minneapolis: University of Minnesota Press, 1990), 298–301.

15. Julian Bond, "The Media and the Movement: Looking Back from the Southern Front," in Brian Ward, ed. *Media, Culture and the Modern African American Freedom Struggle* (Gainesville, FL: University Press of Florida, 2001), 34; Herman Gray, *Watching Race: Television and the Struggle for "Blackness"* (Minneapolis: University of Minnesota Press, 1995), 17.

16. Carson, *In Struggle*, 209–19; Van Deburg, *New Day in Babylon*, 32; James Forman, *The Making of Black Revolutionaries* (Seattle: University of Washington Press, 1977), 456–58.

17. John K. Jessup, "Negro Leaders' Growing Alarm," *Life*, 3 June 1966; Russell Sackett, "Plotting A War on 'Whitey'," *Life*, 10 June 1966; on Robert Williams and RAM, see Timothy B. Tyson, *Radio Free Dixie*, 297–98.

18. *Oakland Tribune*, 27 June, 5 July, 6 July, 7 July, 8 July, 28 July 1966.

19. *Oakland Tribune*, 8 November 1966.

20. *New York Times Magazine*, 25 September 1966.

21. *CBS Evening News,* 12 January 1967; *CBS Evening News* transcripts; Forman, *The Making of Black Revolutionaries,* 458.

22. Douglas interview from *Eyes on the Prize*, Part II (Blackside Productions, 1988).

23. David Hilliard and Lewis Cole, *This Side of Glory: The Autobiography of David Hilliard and the Story of the Black Panther Party* (Boston: Little, Brown, 1993), 116.

24. Seale, *Seize the Time*, 125–30.

25. *San Francisco Sunday Examiner and Chronicle*, 30 April 1967; John Fiske, *Media Matters: Everyday Culture and Political Change* (Minneapolis: University of Minnesota Press, 1994), xviii.

26. Hilliard and Cole, *This Side of Glory*, 122–23; Seale, *Seize the Time*, 162.

27. *Black Panther*, 2 June 1967.

28. Seale's comments from Philip S. Foner, *The Black Panthers Speak* (New York: Da Capo Press, 1995), xxxi; Seale's reprinted as "Executive Mandate Number One," *Black Panther*, 2 June 1967; Seale, *Seize the Time*, 153–66; network footage of the protest appears in *Eyes on the Prize*, Part II.

29. *Oakland Tribune*, 2 May 1967.

30. *Oakland Tribune*, 3 May 1967.

31. Ibid.

32. *Oakland Tribune*, 4 May 1967.

33. *Oakland Tribune*, 4 May 1967.

34. *San Francisco Examiner*, 2 May 1967; Seale, *Seize the Time*, 157.

35. *New York Times*, 3 May 1967; Foner, *The Black Panthers Speak*, xxx–xxxi.

36. *New York Times*, 3 May 1967.

37. Todd Gitlin, *The Whole World Is Watching: Mass Media in the Making and Unmaking of the New Left* (Berkeley: University of California Press, 1980).

38. Seale, *Seize the Time*, 162–63.

39. *New York Times*, 4 May 1967, 11 August 1967.

40. *New York Times*, 7 May 1967.

41. *New York Times*, 7 May 1967.

42. *U.S. News and World Report*, 15 May 1967; on the newsweeklies, see Richard Lentz, *Symbols, the News Magazines, and Martin Luther King* (Baton Rouge: Louisiana State University Press, 1990), 8, 14, 15–20.

43. *New York Times*, 17 May 1967; Kenneth O'Reilly, *Racial Matters: The FBI's Secret File on Black America, 1960–1972* (New York: Free Press, 1989), 294.

44. *U.S. News and World Report*, 29 May 1967.

45. *U.S. News and World Report*, 14 August, 4 September 1967; 15 January 1968.

46. *Oakland Tribune*, 18 May, 24 May, 7 June, 10 August 1967.

47. *San Francisco Examiner*, 24 May 1967.

48. *New York Times*, 21 May 1967.

49. For a comprehensive overview of the 1967 urban rebellions, see *Report of the National Advisory Commission on Civil Disorders* (New York: E.P. Dutton, 1968).

50. *New York Times*, 6 August 1967; David Horowitz, *Radical Son: A Generational Odyssey* (New York: Free Press, 1997), 102.

51. *New York Times*, 11 August 1967.

52. *New York Times*, 29 October 1967; *Oakland Tribune*, 28 October, 29 October, 30 October, 4 November 1967. A skyline head is a large headline placed above the paper's nameplate or flag for maximum emphasis; KPIX News, 28 October, 1967, San Francisco Bay Area Television Archives, San Francisco State University.

53. *Time*, 20 November 1967.

54. For background on the black press, see Jane Rhodes, *Mary Ann Shadd Cary: The Black Press and Protest in the Nineteenth Century* (Bloomington: Indiana University Press, 1998), and Frankie Hutton, *The Early Black Press in America, 1827–1860* (Westport, CT: Greenwood Press, 1993); on the black press and the public sphere, see Ronald N. Jacobs, *Race, Media and the Crisis of Civil Society* (Cambridge: Cambridge University Press, 2000), 24.

55. *Sun-Reporter*, 26 November 1966, 6 May, 13 May 1967.

56. *Sun-Reporter*, 4 November 1967.

57. *Sun-Reporter*, 4 November, 11 November, 18 November, 25 November 1967.

58. Among those who have claimed the Panthers were immediately embraced by the press are Hugh Pearson, *The Shadow of the Panther: Huey Newton and the Price of Black Power in America* (Reading, MA: Addison-Wesley Publishers, 1994); and Horowitz, *Radical Son*.

59. Robert Entman, "Framing: Toward Clarification of a Fractured Paradigm" *Journal of Communication* 43 (Autumn 1993) 4: 51–58; Omi and Winant, *Racial Formation*, 106.

60. Seale, *Seize the Time*, 149; Earl Anthony, *Picking Up the Gun: A Report on the Black Panthers* (New York: Dial Press, 1970), 19.

61. Hall, "The Whites of Their Eyes," 35.

62. Gitlin, *The Whole World Is Watching*, 3; on the context of television, see Daniel Hallin, *We Keep America on Top of the World: Television Journalism and the Public Sphere* (New York: Routledge, 1994), 136–37.

Chapter 4: Revolutionary Culture and the Politics of Self-Representation

1. This definition of culture is influenced by, among others, Pierre Bourdieu and Claude Lévi-Strauss; for a discussion of a ritual view of communication, see James Carey, *Communication as Culture: Essays on Media and Society* (Boston: Unwin Hyman, 1989), 23, 18.

2. Stokely Carmichael and Charles V. Hamilton, *Black Power: The Politics of Liberation in America* (New York: Vintage Books, 1967), 34–35; William Van Deburg, *New Day in Babylon: The Black Power Movement and American Culture, 1965–1975* (Chicago: University of Chicago Press, 1992), 28.

3. Haki R. Madhubuti, "Book of Life," in Haki R. Madhubuti (Don L. Lee), *Book of Life* (Detroit: Broadside Press, 1973), 63.

4. Frantz Fanon, *Black Skin, White Masks* (New York: Grove Press, 1967), 226.

5. Linda Harrison, "On Cultural Nationalism," *Black Panther,* 2 February 1969, reprinted in Philip S. Foner, ed., *The Black Panthers Speak* (New York: Da Capo Press, 1995), 152; Bobby Seale, *Seize the Time: The Story of the Black Panther Party and Huey P. Newton* (New York: Random House, 1970), 64.

6. David Hilliard and Lewis Cole, *This Side of Glory: The Autobiography of David Hilliard and the Story of the Black Panther Party* (Boston: Back Bay Books, 1993), 118.

7. Gilbert Moore, *Rage* (1971; reprint, Carroll and Graf, 1993), 64–65.

8. Hilliard and Cole, *This Side of Glory*, 121; William Lee Brent, *Long Time Gone: A Black Panther's True-Life Story of His Hijacking and Twenty-five Years in Cuba* (New York: Times Books, 1996), 96.

9. Assata Shakur, *Assata: An Autobiography* (London: Zed Books, 1987), 221.

10. Huey Newton, *War Against the Panthers: A Study of Repression in America* (New York: Harlem River Press, 1996), 34.

11. Robert J. Glessing, *The Underground Press in America* (Bloomington: Indiana University Press, 1970), 3. On Malcolm X, see Komozi Woodard, *A Nation with a Nation: Amiri Baraka (Leroi Jones) and Black Power Politics* (Chapel Hill: University of North Carolina Press, 1999), 59–60.

12. *Black Panther*, 20 July 1967; Benedict Anderson, *Imagined Communities: Reflections on the Origin and Spread of Nationalism* (London: Verso, 1987), 47.

13. On early black nationalism, see Floyd Miller, *The Search for a Black Nationality: Black Emigration and Colonization, 1787–1863* (Urbana: University of Illinois Press). Quote

is from David Morley, *Home Territories: Media, Mobility, and Identity* (New York: Routledge, 2000), 118.

14. Seale, *Seize the Time*, 134–46; *Black Panther Black Community News Service*, 25 April 1967.

15. *Black Panther Black Community News Service*, 25 April 1967; Seale, *Seize the Time*, 147–48; Hilliard and Cole, *This Side of Glory*, 122. Seale has revised some of this history on his personal Web site, www.bobbyseale.com.

16. Seale, *Seize the Time*, 148; *Black Panther*, 15 May 1967.

17. *Black Panther*, 15 May 1967; Seale, *Seize the Time*, 182.

18. Jane Rhodes interview with Emory Douglas, 28 February, 1995, San Francisco, CA; description of Black House in Robert Scheer, ed., *Eldridge Cleaver: Post-Prison Writings and Speeches by the Author of "Soul on Ice"* (New York: Random House, 1969), 25.

19. Seale, *Seize the Time*, 132; Hilliard and Cole, *This Side of Glory*, 128; Eldridge Cleaver, *Introduction to the Genius of Huey P. Newton*, Bancroft Library, University of California-Berkeley, n.p.

20. *Black Panther*, 20 July 1967, 19 October 1968; Jane Rhodes interview with Emory Douglas, 28 February 1995, San Francisco, CA; for an insider account of this history, see JoNina M. Abron, "'Raising the Consciousness of the People': The Black Panther Intercommunal News Service, 1967–1980," in Ken Wachsberger, ed., *Voices from the Underground: Vol. 1* (Tempe, AR: Mica Press, 1993), 348–51.

21. Jane Rhodes telephone interview with Earl Caldwell, 23 June 2002; *Black Power/House of Umoja Newsletter*, March 1967 and February-March 1968, Social Protest Collection, Bancroft Library, University of California at Berkeley.

22. Seale, *Seize the Time*, 182, 188.

23. *Black Panther*, 23 November 1967; Henry E. Weinstein, "Conversation with Cleaver," *The Nation*, 20 January 1969.

24. Julia Hervé, "Black Scholar Interviews Kathleen Cleaver," *Black Scholar* 2 (1971): 55; Jane Rhodes interview with Kathleen Cleaver, 18 November 2002, San Diego, CA.

25. Jane Rhodes interview with Kathleen Cleaver, 18 November 2002, San Diego, CA.

26. Seale, *Seize the Time*, 179; House of Representatives Report by the Committee on Internal Security, *Gun-Barrel Politics: The Black Panther Party, 1966–1971* (Washington, DC: U.S. Government Printing Office, 1971); for additional analysis of the paper, see Christian A. Davenport, "Reading the 'Voice of the Vanguard': A Content Analysis of the Black Panther Intercommunal News Service, 1969–1973," in Charles Jones, ed., *The Black Panther Party Reconsidered* (Baltimore: Black Classic Press, 1998), 193–207; and Jane Rhodes, "The *Black Panther* Newspaper: Standard-bearer for Modern Black Nationalism," *Media History* 7, 2 (2001): 151–58.

27. Jane Rhodes interview with Kathleen Cleaver, 18 November 2002, San Diego, CA; Jane Rhodes interview with Elaine Brown, 3 June 1998, San Diego, CA; Abron, "'Raising the Consciousness of the People,'" 349; John Dowling, *Radical Media: The Political Experience of Alternative Communication* (Boston: South End Press, 1984), 35.

28. *Black Panther*, 21 December 1968; Earl Anthony, *Picking Up the Gun: A Report on the Black Panthers* (New York: Dial Press, 1970), 25.

29. *Black Panther*, 14 September, 28 September 1968.

30. Carmichael and Hamilton, *Black Power: The Politics of Liberation in America*, 160; on what has become known as the Moynihan Report, see U.S. Department of Labor, *The Negro Family, the Case for National Action* (Washington, DC: U.S. Government Printing Office, 1965); Fanon, *Black Skin, White Masks*, 41.

31. *Black Panther*, 15 May 1967; Eldridge Cleaver, *Soul on Ice* (New York: McGraw Hill, 1968), 96–107, 68.

32. For a critique of the complimentarity theory, see Patricia Hill Collins, *Fighting Words: Black Women and the Search for Justice* (Minneapolis: University of Minnesota Press, 1998), chap. 5.

33. *Black Panther*, 20 July 1967, 28 September 1968; see Elaine Brown, *Taste of Power: A Black Woman's Story* (New York: Pantheon Books, 1992), and Shakur, *Assata*.

34. Jane Rhodes interview with Elaine Brown, 3 June 1998, San Diego, CA; Brown, *A Taste of Power*, 137; Ericka Huggins and Lynn French appear in the documentary film *Comrade Sister: Voices of Women in the Black Panther Party* (producers: Christine L. Minor and Phyllis J. Jackson, 1997); *Black Panther*, 23 November 1967; for a thorough discussion, see Tracye Matthews, "No One Ever Asks What a Man's Place in the Revolution Is," in Charles E. Jones, ed., *The Black Panther Party Reconsidered* (Baltimore: Black Classic Press, 1998), 277.

35. Erika Doss, "Imagining the Panthers: Representing Black Power and Masculinity, 1960s–1990s," *Prospects: An Annual of American Studies* 23 (1998): 470–93. Sam Greenlee's novel *The Spook Who Sat by the Door* (New York: Bantam Books, 1970) was a spoof on how blacks were used as tokens in corporate America.

36. *Black Panther*, 28 September 1968.

37. See Lauren Berlant, *Anatomy of a National Fantasy* (Chicago: University of Chicago Press, 1991); Weinstein, "Conversation with Cleaver."

38. *Black Panther Community Newsletter,* 26 November 1970. Examples of the *Black Panther Ministry of Information Bulletin* are located in the Bancroft Library of the University of California at Berkeley; examples of the *Black Panther Community Newsletter* are located at the Southern California Library for Social Science and Research, Los Angeles.

39. Copies of *FOCUS: The Black Panther Caucus* and *Auto Workers Newsletter* are in Bancroft Library, University of California, Berkeley; Report of Union Meeting, 21 August 1969, California Associations/Black Panther Party File, San Francisco Public Library.

40. On the black jeremiad, see David Howard-Pitney, "The Enduring Black Jeremiad: The American Jeremiad and Black Protest Rhetoric, From Frederick Douglass to W.E.B. Du Bois, 1841–1919," *American Quarterly* 38 (1986): 481–92; Hilliard and Cole, *This Side of Glory*, 128; John A. Courtright, "Rhetoric of the Gun: An Analysis of the Rhetorical Modifications of the Black Panther Party," *Journal of Black Studies* 4, 3 (1974): 259–60.

41. *Black Community Bulletin*, August 1970; for a discussion of black power rhetoric before the Black Panthers, see Robert L. Scott and Wayne Brockriede, *The Rhetoric of Black Power* (New York: Harper and Row, 1969); David Hilliard interview with CBS News, 28 December 1969, reprinted in Philip S. Foner, ed., *The Black Panthers Speak*, 133.

42. In addition to *Gun-Barrel Politics*, see, for example, House of Representatives Committee on Internal Security, *The Black Panther Party: Its Origin and Development as Reflected in its Official Weekly Newspaper The Black Panther Black Community News Service* (Washington: 1970); Seale, *Seize the Time*, 180; also see Kenneth O'Reilly, *Racial Matters: The FBI's Secret File on Black America, 1960–1972* (New York: Free Press, 1989); see, for example, *Black Panther* Distribution Report for 11/17/72–11/23-72, and complaints filed with airlines, Huey P. Newton Papers, Special Collections, Stanford University Library.

43. Jane Rhodes interview with Kathleen Cleaver, 18 November 2002, San Diego, CA.

Chapter 5: Free Huey: 1968

1. *Oakland Tribune*, 5 January 1969.

2. Interview with Kathleen Cleaver, 18 November 2002, San Diego, CA.

3. As previously noted, a kicker is a title placed above the headline for added emphasis.

4. *Oakland Tribune*, 11 January 1968.

5. *Black Panther Ministry of Information Bulletin*, no. 2, n.d., Black Panther Collection, San Francisco Afro-American Historical Society.

6. *Oakland Tribune*, 3 February 1968.

7. Bobby Seale, *Seize the Time* (New York: Random House, 1970), 207–8; David Hilliard and Lewis Cole, *This Side of Glory* (Boston: Back Bay Books, 1993), 141; *Berkeley Barb*, 22 December 1967. The definitive study on this relationship is Joel R. Wilson, " 'Free Huey': The Black Panther Party, the Peace and Freedom Party, and the Politics of Race in 1968," Ph.D. dissertation, University of California, Santa Cruz, 2002, 24.

8. *New York Times*, 4 February 1968.

9. *San Francisco Examiner*, 28 February 1968; see Eric Lott, *Love and Theft: Blackface Minstrelsy and the American Working Class* (New York: Oxford University Press, 1993).

10. Pacifica Radio Archives, 15 February 1968; *Oakland Tribune*, 18 February 1968; *San Francisco Examiner*, 19 March 1968.

11. *Black Panther*, 16 March 1968; Eldridge Cleaver, Ministry of Information Black Paper, 16 March 1968, Black Panther Collection, San Francisco Afro-American Historical Society.

12. Paul Jacobs' Peace and Freedom Party Senatorial Race Campaign Book, Bancroft Library, University of California at Berkeley; *Why Free Huey?,* n.d., Black Panther Collection, San Francisco Afro-American Historical Society; *Black Panther Candidates*, n.d., Black Panther Collection, San Francisco Afro-American Historical Society.

13. *U.S. News and World Report*, 15 January 1968; Newton discusses SNCC in Executive Mandate No. 2, *Black Panther*, 29 July 1967; Stokely Carmichael with Ekwueme Michael Thelwell, *Ready for Revolution: The Life and Struggles of Stokely Carmichael* (New York: Scribner, 2003), 659–61.

14. Seale, *Seize the Time*, 214–22, quote 221; see discussion in Clayborne Carson, *In Struggle: SNCC and the Black Awakening of the 1960s* (Cambridge, MA: Harvard University Press, 1981), 278–86; *Oakland Tribune*, 17 February 1968.

15. *Oakland Tribune*, 17 February 1968; Hilliard and Cole, *This Side of Glory*, 172–73.

16. James Forman, *The Making of Black Revolutionaries* (1972; reprint, Seattle: University of Washington Press, 1985), 530–31.

17. Text of speeches and descriptions of the rally are based on the film *Black Panther: Huey Newton*, distributed by International Historic Films, 1985; also see UC Berkeley Library, Social Activism Project, which has links to transcripts of the speeches.

18. *Oakland Tribune*, 17 February, 19 February 1968.

19. *Oakland Tribune*, 19 February 1968; Seale, *Seize the Time*, 222; Elaine Brown, *A Taste of Power: A Black Woman's Story* (New York: Pantheon Books, 1992), 126–27; flyer for Free Huey! Mass Rally, 18 February 1968, Southern California Library for Social Studies and Research, Los Angeles.

20. On KPFA see John D.H. Downing, *Radical Media: Rebellious Communication and Social Movements* (Thousand Oaks, CA: Sage, 2001), 325–53, and Matthew Lasar, *Pacifica Radio: The Rise of an Alternative Network* (Philadelphia: Temple University Press, 1999). The Pacifica Radio Archive is available online. Abe Peck, *Uncovering the Sixties: The Life and Times of the Underground Press* (New York: Pantheon, 1985), 87–88, 130; *San Francisco Express Times*, 22 February 1968; *Berkeley Barb*, 23–29 February 1968; *Movement*, April 1968.

21. Peck, *Uncovering the Sixties*, 148; quote from Roz Payne's Web site, www.newsreel.us; Cynthia Ann Young, "Soul Power: Cultural Radicalism and the Formation of a US Third World Left," Ph.D. diss., Yale University, May 1999, 135, 140, 145.

22. *Black Panthers: Huey Newton, Black Panther Newsreel* was packaged and distributed by International Historical Films in the 1980s, *Off the Pigs* is distributed by Roz Payne's Newsreel archives, and *Black Panthers* is distributed by California Newsreel. See also David James, *Allegories of Cinema: American Film in the Sixties* (Princeton, NJ: Princeton University Press, 1989), 177–78, 181; Jerry Stoll to David Hilliard, 16 December 1969, Huey P. Newton Archives, Special Collections, Stanford University Libraries; Cynthia Young, "Soul Power," 141.

23. *Oakland Tribune*, 26 February, 27 February, 28 February 1968; *San Francisco Examiner*, 28 February 1968; press release, Huey P. Newton Defense Fund, 26 February 1968, Social Protest Collection, Bancroft Library, UC Berkeley.

24. *Black Panther*, 16 March 1968.

25. Joan Didion, "Black Panther: May 1968," *Saturday Evening Post*, 4 May 1968; Tom Wolfe "Introduction," Tom Wolfe and E. W. Johnson, eds., *The New Journalism* (New York: Harper and Row, 1973).

26. *Black Panther*, 16 March 1968; KPFA archives; Didion, "Black Panther."

27. Didion, "Black Panther."

28. *Sun-Reporter*, 20 January 1968.

29. *Sun-Reporter*, 10 February, 17 February, 2 March 1968.

30. *Sun-Reporter*, 6 April 1968.

31. Kathleen Cleaver, "Three Ways that Martin Luther King Changed My Life," *Black Renaissance/Renaissance Noire* 2, 1 (1998): 59.

32. There are numerous accounts of the incident, including Seale, *Seize the Time,* 232–36, and Kathleen Cleaver, "Three Ways," 61. David Hilliard's narrative accuses Eldridge Cleaver of planning and executing an armed assault on the police in his quest to gain revolutionary credentials; see Hilliard and Cole, *This Side of Glory,* 182–92. See also Henry Louis Gates' interview with Eldridge Cleaver on *Frontline,* "The Two Nations of Black America," WGBH, 1998.

33. *San Francisco Examiner,* 7 April 1968.

34. Quotes from press conference broadcast on KPFA, Pacifica Radio Archive BB5543.

35. *San Francisco Examiner,* 8 April 1968. For example, the House Committee on Internal Security published a report titled *Gun-Barrel Politics: The Black Panther Party, 1966–1971* (Washington, DC: U.S. Government Printing Office, 1971) that was based largely on the content of the *Black Panther.*

36. *Oakland Tribune,* 8 April 1968. Eldridge Cleaver presented several alternative versions of the events that night, including a detailed account in the *Black Panther,* 10 June 1968.

37. *Oakland Tribune,* 9 April 1968.

38. *San Francisco Examiner,* 8 April 1968.

39. *New York Times,* 8 April 1968.

40. Ibid.

41. *Oakland Tribune,* 13 April, 16 April 1968; *San Francisco Examiner,* 13 April 1968.

42. *Sun-Reporter,* 20 April 1968.

43. *New York Times,* 13 April 1968; Paul Jacobs' Peace and Freedom Party Senatorial Race Campaign Book, Bancroft Library, University of California at Berkeley.

44. *Time,* 19 April 1968.

45. *New York Review of Books,* 23 May 1968.

46. *Ramparts,* May 1968, 49–50; *Commonweal,* 10 May 1968, 223–24.

47. *National Guardian,* 13 April 1968; Robert L. Allen, *Dialectics of Black Power* (New York: Weekly Guardian Associates, 1968), 7, 18. Since that time, Allen has become a recognized scholar, award-winning author, and editor of the *Black Scholar.*

48. James H. Pickerell to Charles Garry, 10 May 1968, Huey P. Newton Papers, Special Collections, Stanford University Libraries; Gitlin, *The Whole World Is Watching; Mass Media in the Making and Unmaking of the New Left* (Berkeley: University of California Press, 1988), 52; London *Sunday Telegraph,* 18 August 1968.

Chapter 6: A Trial of the Black Liberation Movement

1. Black Panther Party Speaker's Kit, Huey P. Newton Papers, Special Collections, Stanford University Libraries.

2. *Oakland Tribune,* 24 April, 1968; *San Francisco Examiner,* 25 April, 26 April 1968.

3. *San Francisco Chronicle,* 20 May, 21 May 1968.

4. San Francisco *Sun-Reporter,* 20 April 1968.

5. San Francisco *Sun-Reporter,* 27 April, 1 June 1968.

6. AP report in *Oakland Tribune,* 21 May 1968; Seale, *Seize the Time: The Story of the Black Panther Party and Huey Newton* (New York, Random House, 1970), 237–38.

7. *San Francisco Examiner,* 2 May 1968; *Oakland Tribune,* 3 May 1968.

8. *Ramparts,* May 1968, 48–50, 15 June 1968, 17–20.

9. *Ramparts,* 29 June 1968, 37–46.

10. *Oakland Tribune,* 12 June, 13 June 1968; *Berkeley Barb,* 14–20 June 1968.

11. *Oakland Tribune,* 14 July, 15 July, 16 July, 17 July 1968.

12. *Sun-Reporter,* 20 July, 3 August, 17 August 1968.

13. *Oakland Tribunal,* June 1968, Black Panther Collection, San Francisco Afro-American Historical Society; *Oakland Observer,* 13 July 1968; *Oakland Montclarion,* 10 July 1968.

14. *New York Times,* 16 July 1968.

15. *New York Times,* 20 July 1968.

16. *Washington Post,* 28 July 1968.

17. On the context of television news, see Daniel Hallin, *We Keep America on Top of the World: Television Journalism and the Public Sphere* (New York: Routledge, 1994), 136–37.

18. KPIX Film Library, San Francisco Bay Area Television Archives, San Francisco State University Library; *ABC Evening News,* 18 July 1968.

19. Kathleen Cleaver, "How TV Wrecked the Black Panthers," *Channels of Communications* (November/December 1982): 98–99.

20. David Hilliard and Lewis Cole, *This Side of Glory,* 159–70.

21. *ABC Evening News,* 18 July, 24 July 1968; James Forman, *The Making of Black Revolutionaries* (Seattle: University of Washington Press, 1997), 535–38; *Black Panther,* 14 September 1968.

22. KNXT news transcripts, 7 August, 8 August 1968.

23. Gerald Horne, *The Fire This Time: The Watts Uprising and the 1960s* (Charlottesville: University Press of Virginia, 1995), 197, 202–3; Elaine Brown, *A Taste of Power: A Black Woman's Story* (New York: Pantheon, 1992), 119–20. NBC, *Huntley-Brinkley Report,* 6 August 1968.

24. James Baughman, *The Republic of Mass Culture: Journalism, Filmmaking and Broadcasting in America since 1941* (Baltimore: Johns Hopkins University, Press, 1992), 112–16; *Report of the National Advisory Commission on Civil Disorders* (New York: E.P. Dutton, 1968), 366. I am arguing against Todd Gitlin's assertion that "the more closely the concerns and values of social movements coincide with the concerns and values of elites in politics and in media, the more likely they are to become incorporated in the prevailing news frames," in his *The Whole World is Watching: Mass Media in the Making and Unmaking of the New Left* (Berkeley: University of California Press, 1980), 284. This was not necessarily the case for black radical activists.

25. *Report of the National Advisory Commission on Civil Disorders,* 385.

26. David James, *Allegories of Cinema: American Film in the Sixties* (Princeton, NJ: Princeton University Press, 1989).

27. Ibid., 183. I screened an original print of *Black Panthers* at the British Film Institute in London; videotape copies are available through International Historic Films.

28. Celia Rosebury, *Black Liberation on Trial: The Case of Huey Newton* (Berkeley: Bay Area Committee to Defend Political Rights, 1968), Bancroft Library, University of California; Hilliard and Cole, *This Side of Glory*, 144–45.

29. *Huey Newton Talks to the Movement* (San Francisco: Students for a Democratic Society, August 1968), copy at the Schomburg Center for Research in Black Culture, New York Public Library; *Huey Newton Talks to the Movement* (San Diego: San Diego Commune, August 1968), copy at the San Francisco Afro American Historical Society; Eldridge Cleaver, *Soul on Ice* (1968; reprint, New York: Dell Books, 1991), 153.

30. For an extensive discussion of the Chicago 1968 Democratic National Convention, see Todd Gitlin, *The Sixties: Years of Hope, Days of Rage* (New York: Bantam Books, 1987), 319–40; on the media framing of the convention, see Gitlin, *The Whole World Is Watching*, 187; *CBS Evening News*, 19 August 1968.

31. *Oakland Tribune*, 5 August, 8 August, 16 August, 25 August 1968.

32. *San Francisco Examiner*, 28 July, 30 July 1968.

33. *San Francisco Examiner*, 6 August, 11 August, 25 August 1968; on Greenlee, see his obituary in *The Black Scholar* 30 (Summer 2000) 2:50.

34. *San Francisco Examiner*, 28 July, 27 August 1968.

35. *New York Times*, 6 August, 16 August 1968; *CBS Evening News*, 5 September 1968; *ABC Evening News*, 5 September 1968; *San Francisco Examiner*, 4 September 1968.

36. *Newsweek*, 16 September 1968.

37. *New York Times*, 9 September 1968; *Oakland Tribune*, 9 September 1968.

38. NBC, *Huntley-Brinkley Report*, 10 September, 16 September 1968; *ABC Evening News*, 10 September 1968.

39. NBC, *Huntley-Brinkley Report*, 16 September 1968; *CBS Evening News*, 13 September 1968.

40. NBC, *Huntley-Brinkley Report*, 17 September 1968.

41. *Time*, 20 September 1968; *Newsweek*, 23 September 1968.

42. E. Franklin Frazier, *Black Bourgeoisie: The Rise of a New Middle Class in the United States* (New York: Collier Books, 1962), 190; *Ebony*, January 1968.

43. *Jet,* 26 September 1968, 14–23.

44. *Los Angeles Sentinel*, 18 July, 25 July 1968; New York *Amsterdam News*, 14 September 1968.

45. Gitlin, *The Whole World Is Watching*, 80–82; Jane Rhodes telephone interview with Earl Caldwell, 23 June 2002.

46. *The Caldwell Journals*, chapter 14, available at www.maynardije.org; on 1960s journalists and critical culture, see Michael Schudson, *Discovering the News: A Social History of American Newspapers* (New York: Basic Books, 1978), 176–83.

47. Caldwell interview.

48. *New York Times*, 10 September 1968. Editors, not reporters, write headlines; thus Caldwell was probably not the author of this headline.

49. *New York Times*, 15 September 1968; Gitlin, *The Whole World Is Watching*, 210.

50. *New York Times*, 15 September 1968.

51. *New York Times*, 28 September 1968.

52. *San Francisco Examiner*, 27 September 1968; *Oakland Tribune*, 27 September 1968.

Chapter 7: From Campus Celebrity to Radical Chic

1. The organizational figures were reported in the *Black Panther*, 14 September 1968; on the Chicago chapter, see Jon Rice, "The World of the Illinois Panthers," in Jeanne F. Theoharris and Komozi Woodard, eds., *Freedom North: Black Freedom Struggles Outside the South, 1940–1980* (New York: Palgrave MacMillan, 2003), 41–64; *ABC Evening News*, 5 September 1968; NBC, *Huntley-Brinkley Report*, 5 September 1968; *CBS Evening News*, 5 September 1968.

2. *Seattle*, October 1968, 36–47, 57–61.

3. David Hilliard and Lewis Cole, *This Side of Glory* (Boston: Little, Brown, 1993), 212; "Eldridge Cleaver Discusses Revolution: An Interview From Exile," in Phillip Foner, ed., *The Black Panthers Speak* (New York: Da Capo Press, 1995), 115; Kathleen Cleaver, "How TV Wrecked the Black Panthers" *Channels of Communications* (November/December 1982): 99.

4. Stokely Carmichael with Ekwueme Michael Thelwell, *Ready for Revolution: The Life and Struggles of Stokely Carmichael (Kwame Ture)* (New York: Scribner, 2003), 664.

5. See Ward Churchill, " 'To Disrupt, Discredit and Destroy': The FBI's Secret War Against the Black Panther Party," in Kathleen Cleaver and George Katsiaficas, eds., *Liberation, Imagination and the Black Panther Party* (New York: Routledge, 2001), 81; Senator Frank Church, chairman, *The Intelligence Community: History, Organization, and Issues* (New York: R.R. Bowker, 1977), 401, 413; Kenneth O'Reilly, *Racial Matters: The FBI's Secret File on Black America, 1960–1972* (New York: Free Press, 1991), 261; Clayborne Carson, *In Struggle* (Cambridge, MA: Harvard University Press, 1981), 261–64.

6. The language of the 29 February 1968 memo is reproduced in several studies, including Carson, *In Struggle*, and O'Reilly, *Racial Matters*; 25 November 1968 FBI memo quoted in Churchill, " 'To Disrupt, Discredit and Destroy,' " 83; O'Reilly, *Racial Matters*, 294.

7. See O'Reilly, *Racial Matters*, 300, citing numerous FBI letters and memoranda.

8. Clayborne Carson, *In Struggle*, 284–85; Carmichael with Thelwell, *Ready for Revolution*, 671–72; Church, *The Intelligence Community*, 401; *New York Times*, 23 August 1968.

9. *New York Times*, 23 August 1968.

10. *New York Times*, 7 October 1968; James Forman, *The Making of Black Revolutionaries* (Seattle: University of Washington Press, 1997), 522–23; Cleveland Sellers with Robert Terrell, *The River of No Return: The Autobiography of a Black Militant and the Life and Death of SNCC* (New York: William Morrow, 1973), 249; Earl Anthony, *Spitting in*

the Wind (Santa Monica, CA: Rountable Publishers, 1990), 199. Winston Grady-Willis believes Forman's denial was intended to prevent further damage to the movement. I am less inclined to find credible the memoirs of a former FBI operative, Earl Anthony, whose book is filled with factual errors and paranoid ravings. See Grady-Willis, "The Black Panther Party: State Repression and Political Prisoners," in Charles Jones, ed., *The Black Panther Party Reconsidered* (Baltimore: Black Classic Press, 1998), 386 n. 33.

11. Documents from Mayor Joseph Alioto Collection, San Francisco Public Library.

12. *New York Times*, 7 October 1968.

13. Peniel E. Joseph, "Dashikis and Democracy: Black Studies, Student Activism, and the Black Power Movement," *Journal of African American History* 88, 2 (2003): 182–203; also see Robert Cohen and Reginald E. Zelnik, eds., *The Free Speech Movement: Reflections on Berkeley in the 1960s* (Berkeley: University of California Press, 2002) and Terry Anderson, *The Movement and the Sixties* (New York: Oxford University Press, 1995), 101–10.

14. William Van Deburg, *New Day in Babylon* (Chicago: University of Chicago Press, 1992), 66.

15. *San Francisco Chronicle*, 9 March 1968.

16. Harry Edwards, *The Revolt of the Black Athlete* (New York: Free Press, 1969), 40–47; *San Jose Mercury News*, 23 September 2000.

17. *San Francisco Chronicle*, 12 April 1968.

18. *Oakland Tribune*, 12 September 1968; *San Francisco Examiner*, 12 September 1968.

19. *San Francisco Examiner*, 17 September 1968; *Oakland Tribune*, 18 September 1968.

20. *San Francisco Examiner*, 18 September, 19 September 1968.

21. *Oakland Tribune*, 19 September, 20 September 1968.

22. *Oakland Tribune*, 21 September 1968; *San Francisco Examiner*, 21 September 1968.

23. *Sun-Reporter*, 21 September 1968.

24. *Oakland Tribune*, 22 September, 23 September, 24 September, 25 September, 26 September 1968; *San Francisco Examiner*, 25 September, 26 September 1968.

25. *Oakland Tribune*, 26 September 1968; San Francisco *Sun-Reporter*, 28 September, 5 October 1968.

26. *Oakland Tribune*, 27 September 1968

27. *Oakland Tribune*, 28 September 1968; *San Francisco Examiner*, 27 September 1968.

28. *Oakland Tribune*, 1 October, 2 October, 3 October 1968; *New York Times*, 3 October 1968.

29. Cleaver's speech was broadcast on KPFA radio in December 1968 (Pacifica Radio Archives); *Oakland Tribune*, 3 October 1968; *San Francisco Examiner*, 5 October 1968.

30. *Jet*, 24 October 1968.

31. *Oakland Tribune*, 3 October 1968; Hilliard and Cole, *This Side of Glory*, 210.

32. *San Francisco Examiner*, 4 October, 6 October, 7 October, 8 October, 9 October 1968; *Oakland Tribune*, 7 October, 8 October 1968.

33. *New York Times*, 27 October 1968.

34. *CBS Evening News*, 31 October 1968; *ABC Evening News*, 28 October 1968.

35. Don A. Schanche, "Law and Order: Burn the Mother Down," *Saturday Evening Post*, 16 November 1968.

36. *San Francisco Examiner*, 12 September, 15 September 1968.

37. *The Movement*, January 1968, 6–7, 11; *Golden Gater*, 8–9 February, 15 February 1968.

38. *San Francisco Examiner*, 27 September, 1 October 1968; for a thorough review of the issues, see William Orrick Jr., *Shut It Down! A College in Crisis: San Francisco State College, October 1968–April 1969, a Report to the National Commission on the Causes and Prevention of Violence* (Washington, DC: Government Printing Office, 1969), 30–33.

39. *Oakland Tribune*, 24 October, 25 October 1968.

40. *Oakland Tribune*, 31 October, 1 November, 2 November 1968; *San Francisco Examiner*, 1 November 1968; for background see Orrick, *Shut It Down*, 34–35. The editor of the student newspaper, the *Gater*, did hear Murray's speech and wrote his account in Dikran Karagueuzian, *Blow It Up! The Black Student Revolt at San Francisco State College and the Emergence of Dr. Hayakawa* (Boston: Gambit Press, 1971), 38–39.

41. *Oakland Tribune*, 31 October, 1 November, 2 November 1968; *San Francisco Examiner*, 1 November, 2 November 1968; for background see Orrick, *Shut It Down*, 34–35.

42. Kay Boyle, *The Long Walk at San Francisco State* (New York: Grove Press, 1970), 6–13, quote 12; Orrick, *Shut It Down*, 20–29.

43. *San Francisco Examiner*, 4 November 1968.

44. Orrick, *Shut It Down*, 37–40; Boyle, *The Long Walk*, 21. Carmichael's speech was recorded by *Gater* editor Dikran Karagueuzian and reproduced in *Blow It Up*, 96–102.

45. *San Francisco Examiner*, 9 November 1968.

46. Karagueuzian, 96–102.

47. Karagueuzian, *Blow It Up*, 139–40; Boyle, *The Long Walk*, 16–17, 25; *San Francisco Examiner*, 13 November 1968; *Golden Gater*, 14 November 1968.

48. *Oakland Tribune*, 14 November 1968.

49. *Oakland Tribune*, 16 November 1968; *San Francisco Examiner*, 16 November 1968; Orrick, *Shut It Down*, 45–47.

50. *Oakland Tribune*, 16 November 1968; *San Francisco Examiner*, 17 November 1968.

51. *San Francisco Examiner*, 19 November 1968.

52. *Oakland Tribune*, 20 November 1968.

53. William Lee Brent, *Long Time Gone* (New York: Times Books, 1996), 119–20.

54. *San Francisco Examiner*, 20 November 1968

55. NBC, *Huntley-Brinkley Report*, 19 November 1968; *ABC Evening News*, 19 November 1968.

56. *San Francisco Examiner*, 20 November 1968; press release, San Francisco Recreation and Park Department, 20 November 1968; press release, Council for Civic Unity, 22 November 1968; Rules and Regulations, Garden Center of San Francisco and Hall of Flowers; Reservation Application for Garden Center of San Francisco and Hall of Flowers by Weekly Guardian Associates, Joseph Alioto Jr. Papers, San Francisco History Center, San Francisco Public Library.

57. Flyer for the International Committee to Defend Eldridge Cleaver, 1968, Huey P. Newton Collection, Stanford University Library; Pacifica Radio Archives, KPFA, 21 November 1968. The text of Cleaver's speech is included in *Eldridge Cleaver: Post-Prison Writings and Speeches* (New York: Random House, 1968), 147–60.

58. Letter from Milton Zaslow to Friends of Newton-Cleaver Defense Committee, n.d. Huey P. Newton Collection, Stanford University Library.

59. *Oakland Tribune*, 20 November 1968.

60. *San Francisco Examiner*, 21 November 1968.

61. *San Francisco Examiner*, 21 November 1968; *Oakland Tribune*, 21 November 1968.

62. *San Francisco Examiner*, 26 November 1968.

63. *Oakland Tribune*, 22 November 1968; *San Francisco Examiner*, 22 November 1968.

64. *San Francisco Examiner*, 25 November 1968.

65. *New York Times*, 26 November 1968.

66. *San Francisco Examiner*, 26 November 1968; *Oakland Tribune*, 26 November 1968.

67. *New York Times*, 27 November 1968.

68. *New York Times*, 24 November 1968; *San Francisco Examiner*, 27 November 1968.

69. *Oakland Tribune*, 27 November 1968.

70. NBC, *Huntley-Brinkley Report*, 27 November 1968.

71. *San Francisco Examiner*, 28 November 1968; *Oakland Tribune*, 28 November 1968; *New York Times*, 28 November 1968.

72. *Oakland Tribune*, 29 November, 30 November, 2 December 1968; *San Francisco Examiner*, 29 November, 30 November 1968; *International Herald Tribune*, 30 November–1 December 1968; for a recounting of Cleaver's exile, see Kathleen Neal Cleaver, "Back to Africa: The Evolution of the International Section of the Black Panther Party (1969–1972)," in Charles Jones Jr., ed, *The Black Panther Party Reconsidered*, 217.

73. *San Francisco Examiner*, 1 December 1968; *New York Times*, 1 December 1968.

74. *Oakland Tribune*, 27 November 1968; *New York Times*, 27 November 1968.

75. *Oakland Tribune*, 27 November 1968; *San Francisco Examiner*, 26 November, 27 November 1968; Orrick, *Shut It Down*, 59; Karagueuzian, *Blow It Up*, 152.

76. Karagueuzian, *Blow It Up*, 164–65; San Francisco *Sun-Reporter*, 7 December 1968; *Oakland Tribune*, 10 December 1968.

77. *Oakland Tribune*, 6 December, 11 December, 17 December, 21 December 1968; *San Francisco Examiner*, 2 December, 3 December, 5 December, 9 December, 10 December, 11 December 1968.

78. *Black Panther*, 7 December 1968.

79. *San Francisco Examiner*, 10 December, 12 December, 20 December 1968; *Oakland Tribune*, 28 December 1968; *New York Times*, 21 December 1968.

80. Nat Hentoff, "Playboy Interview: Eldridge Cleaver," *Playboy*, December 1968, 89–108, 238.

81. Ibid.

82. *Jet*, 16 December 1968.

83. *Wall Street Journal*, 6 December 1968.

Chapter 8: Servants of the People: The Black Panthers
as Natural and Global Icons

1. *Ramparts*, 26 October, 17 November 1968; Eldridge Cleaver, *Post-Prison Writings and Speeches* (New York: Random House, 1969), 156.
2. *New York Times*, 17 June 1970.
3. Eldridge Cleaver, *The Genius of Huey P. Newton* (Black Panther Party Ministry of Information, n.d.), Bancroft Library, University of California at Berkeley.
4. *I Was a Black Panther, as Told to Chuck Moore* (New York: Doubleday, 1970).
5. Ibid., 92.
6. Earl Anthony, *Picking Up the Gun: A Report on the Black Panthers* (New York: Dial Press, 1970); Elaine Brown, *A Taste of Power: A Black Woman's Story* (New York: Anchor Books, 1994), 113–15.
7. *New York Times*, 1 May 1970; Earl Anthony, *Spitting in the Wind: The True Story Behind the Violent Legacy of the Black Panther Party* (Santa Monica, CA: Roundtable Publishing, 1990), 7–9, 39.
8. Cleaver, *Post-Prison Writings*, introduction.
9. Ibid., xxxii.
10. Gene Marine, *The Black Panthers* (New York: New American Library, 1969).
11. Ibid., 212, 213.
12. Mona Bazaar, ed., *The Trial of Huey Newton* (Oakland: M. Bazaar, 1968), n.p.
13. Eldridge Cleaver, *Soul on Ice* (New York: McGraw-Hill, 1968), dedication page; Edward M. Keating, *Free Huey!* (Berkeley: Ramparts Press, 1970), 280; Keating obituary, *Palo Alto Daily News*, 4 April 2003. Laurence Moore to Huey P. Newton, 22 June 1971, Huey P. Newton Papers, Special Collections, Stanford University Library.
14. Ruth-Marion Baruch, "Preface," *The Vanguard: A Photographic Essay on the Black Panthers* (Boston: Beacon Press, 1969), 11; interview with Pirkle Jones, *Los Angeles Times*, 16 May 2004.
15. Baruch, "Preface," 12, 14; Jones interview.
16. *New York Times*, 16 December 1968.
17. *The Black Panthers in Action*, (Wheaton, IL: Church League of America, 1969), 5, 31.
18. Norman Hill, ed., *The Black Panther Menace: America's Neo-Nazis* (New York: Popular Library, 1971), 9–15.
19. *Black Panther*, 4 January 1969; on the publishing success of *Soul on Ice*, see *Wall Street Journal*, 13 March 1969.
20. *Look*, 7 January 1969.
21. *The Nation*, 20 January 1969.
22. *New York Times*, 26 February 1969.
23. *New York Times Book Review*, 27 April 1969.
24. *Wall Street Journal*, 13 March 1969.
25. Central Committee press release, 2 January 1969, Huey P. Newton Collection, Stanford University Libraries (the announcement was reprinted in *Ministry of Information*

Bulletin no. 9, 6 January 1969); "Set Bill Brent Free," flyer, December 1968, Bancroft Library, University of California, Berkeley; *San Francisco Examiner*, 13 January 1969.

26. *Oakland Tribune*, 3 January 1969; *The Movement*, January 1969; *New York Times*, 21 June 1969; *Oakland Tribune*, 17 June, 18 June, 21 June 1969.

27. Bobby Seale, *Seize the Time* (New York: Vintage Books, 1970), 413; Robyn C. Spencer, "Repression Breeds Resistance: The Rise and the Fall of the Black Panther Party in Oakland, CA., 1966–1982," Ph.D. diss., Columbia University, 2001, 125–26; an ad in the *Ministry of Information Bulletin*, 6 January 1969, sought donations for the breakfast program.

28. *San Francisco Examiner*, 31 January 1969; *Black Panther*, 26 March 1969.

29. NBC, *Huntley-Brinkley Report*, 5 May 1969.

30. *Newsweek*, 5 May 1969.

31. *ABC Evening News*, 27 August 1969.

32. *New York Times*, 18 August 1969.

33. *Wall Street Journal*, 29 August 1969.

34. Ibid.; *Wall Street Journal*, 13 January 1970.

35. David Hilliard and Lewis Cole, *This Side of Glory* (Boston: Little, Brown, 1993), 164; Brown, *A Taste of Power*, 153; Scot D. Brown, "The US Organization: African-American Cultural Nationalism in the Era of Black Power, 1965 to the 1970s," Ph.D. diss., Cornell University, 1999, 302–4; Jack Olson, *Last Man Standing: The Tragedy and Triumph of Geronimo Pratt* (New York: Anchor Books, 2001), 45.

36. See discussion in Brown, "The US Organization"; also Olson, *Last Man Standing*, 46; *UCLA Daily Bruin*, 20 January 1969, Black Panther Party Papers, Southern California Library for Social Studies and Research, Los Angeles; *ABC Evening News*, 20 January 1969.

37. *Oakland Tribune* 18 January, 19 January 1969.

38. *San Francisco Examiner,* 18 January, 21 January 1969.

39. *Los Angeles Sentinel*, 23 January 1969.

40. *Los Angeles Sentinel*, 23 January, 30 January 1969; on Booker Griffin and Los Angeles black politics, see Gerald C. Horne, *Fire This Time: The Watts Uprising and the 1960s* (Charlottesville: University of Virginia Press, 1995), 185–202.

41. *Black Panther*, 2 February 1969; *Ministry of Information Bulletin*, No. 2, southern California edition, 22 January 1969, Black Panther Party Papers, Southern California Library for Social Studies and Research, Los Angeles.

42. *Oakland Tribune*, 20 January, 22 February, 2 April, 24 April, 1 May 1969; *San Francisco Examiner*, 25 March, 1 May, 2 May 1969; *New York Times*, 21 January 1969; *ABC Evening News,* 2 April 1969.

43. *New York Times*, 25 May 1969; Lee Lockwood, *Conversation with Eldridge Cleaver: Algiers* (New York: McGraw-Hill, 1970), 22; Henry Louis Gates Jr., "Eldridge Cleaver on Ice," reprinted in *Transition* 75/76 (1997): 301.

44. Lockwood, *Conversation with Eldridge Cleaver,* Gates, "Eldridge Cleaver on Ice"; *New York Times*, 1 June, 3 July 1969; *San Francisco Examiner*, 25 June 1969; *Oakland Tribune*, 1 June, 2 July 1969.

45. *San Francisco Examiner*, 13 July 1969; *New York Times*, 13 July 1969; Gates, "Eldridge Cleaver on Ice," 302–3.

46. Lockwood, *Conversation with Eldridge Cleaver*, 27, 57; Kathleen Neal Cleaver, "Back to Africa: The Evolution of the International Section of the Black Panthers Party (1969–1972)," in Charles Jones, ed., *The Black Panther Party Reconsidered* (Baltimore: Black Classic Press, 1998), 216–25.

47. Don A. Schanche, *The Panther Paradox: A Liberal's Dilemma* (New York: David McKay Co., 1970), ix, xiv, 4, 137, 153.

48. *New York Times Magazine*, 7 September 1969.

49. *Black Panther*, 5 July, 12 July, 9 August 1969; *San Francisco Examiner*, 13 July 1969; *New York Times*, 13 July, 16 July, 18 July, 25 July 1969; for background, see Cleaver, "Back to Africa."

50. *San Francisco Examiner*, 17 July, 1 August, 16 December 1969.

51. Cleaver, "Back to Africa," 228–99, 231.

52. Obi Egbuna, *Destroy This Temple: The Voice of Black Power in Britain* (London: MacGibbon and Kee, 1971), 18; BBC News, 18 July 1967, BBC Archives, Middlesex, England; *Times* (London), 17 July 1967; Derek Humphry and David Tindall, *False Messiah: The Story of Michael X* (London: Hart-Davis, MacGibbon, 1977), 63–65; the Congress on the Dialectics of Liberation was organized by renowned psychoanalyst R.D. Laing.

53. Nicholas Deakin, *Colour, Citizenship and British Society: Based on the Institute of Race Relations Report* (London: Panther Books, 1970), 121; *Times* (London), 11 September 1967; Egbuna, *Destroy This Temple*.

54. *Times* (London), 11 September, 9 November, 16 November 1967.

55. Peter Fryer, *Staying Power: The History of Black People in Britain* (London: Pluto Press, 1984), 381–82; *Time,* 28 April 1967, 3 May 1968; BBC News, 23 February 1968, BBC Archives, Middlesex, England; also see Harry Goulbourne, *Race Relations in Britain Since 1945* (New York: St. Martin's Press, 1998).

56. *Times* (London), 29 April 1968; BBC News, 28 April 1968, BBC Archives, Middlesex, England; *Daily Mirror*, 19 April 1968; Stephen Small, *Racialized Barriers: The Black Experiences in the U.S. and England in the 1980s* (London: Routledge, 1994), 3; Humphrey and Tindall, *False Messiah*, 62.

57. BBC News, 14 April 1968, BBC Archives, Middlesex, England; *This Week*, 16 May 1968, British Film Institute Archives, London.

58. *Black Power Speaks*, June 1968, Institute of Race Relations Archives, London; *Black People's News Service* (London: n.d.); also see Egbuna, *Destroy This Temple*, 21–22.

59. *Black Panther News Service* (London), March 1970, Institute of Race Relations Archives, London; see Harry Goulbourne, "The Contributions of West Indian Groups to British Politics," in H. Goulbourne, ed., *Black Politics in Britain* (Aldershot: Avebury, 1990), 109; Michael L. Clemons and Charles E. Jones, "Global Solidarity: The Black Panther Party in the International Arena," in Kathleen Cleaver and George Katsiaficas, eds., *Liberation, Imagination and the Black Panther Party* (New York: Routledge, 2001), 25.

60. *Times* (London), 26 July, 13 August 1968; Egbuna, *Destroy This Temple*, 10–12, 21; Flyer, Black Power Movement, 3 October 1968, Institute of Race Relations Archives, London.

61. *Times* (London), 4 March 1968.

62. *Times* (London), 13 March 1968; *Manchester Guardian*, 27 September 1968.

63. Mike Phillips and Trevor Phillips, *Windrush* (London: Harper Collins, 1998), 232; Obi Egbuna, *The ABC of Black Power Thought*, n.d., British Library, 16; *Times* (London), 12 December 1969.

64. Vijay Prashad, "Bruce Lee and the Anti-imperialism of Kung Fu: A Polycultural Adventure," *Positions* 11(2003): 61, 64; *Wall Street Journal*, 30 April 1969; Carlos Munoz Jr., *Youth, Identity, Power: The Chicano Movement* (London: Verso, 1989), 87–88; Daryl J. Maeda, "Black Panthers, Red Guards, and Chinamen: Constructing Asian American Identity Through Performing Blackness, 1969–1972," *American Quarterly* 57, 4 (2005): 1079–104; also see Michael L. Clemons and Charles E. Jones, "Global Solidarity: The Black Panther in the Global Arena," in Kathleen Cleaver and George Katsiaficas, 23–26. *Liberation, Imagination and the Black Panther Party* (New York: Routledge, 2001): 20–39.

65. *Black Panther*, 20 July 1967.

66. *New York Times*, 15 June 1969; *Oakland Tribune*, 15 June, 18 June, 19 June 1969.

67. *New York Times*, 28 October, 30 October, 2 November, 6 November 1969; *San Francisco Examiner*, 11 November 1969; *Life*, 14 November 1969.

68. *Los Angeles Times*, 4 July 1969.

69. *New York Times*, 27 July 1969.

70. *New York Times*, 5 December 1969; *Oakland Tribune*, 4 December 1969.

71. *New York Times*, 5 December, 10 December, 13 December 1969.

72. *Oakland Tribune*, 8 December 1969; *New York Times*, 10 December 1969; BBC News, 21 December 1969, BBC Archives, Middlesex, England.

73. *New York Times*, 29 December 1969; *San Francisco Examiner*, 29 December 1969.

74. *San Francisco Examiner*, 22 December, 28 December 1969.

75. *Wall Street Journal*, 29 December 1969.

76. The *New Yorker* article is reprinted in Edward J. Espstein, *Between Fact and Fiction: The Problem of Journalism* (New York: Vintage Books, 1975), 75–77.

77. *Jet*, 16 December 1969.

Chapter 9: The Rise and Fall of a Media Frenzy: The 1970s

1. G. Louis Heath, ed., *Off the Pigs: The History and Literature of the Black Panther Party* (Metuchen, NJ: Scarecrow Press, 1976), 133; Gerald Emanuel Stearn, "Rapping with the Panthers in White Suburbia," *New York Times Magazine*, 8 March 1970, 28.

2. *New York Times*, 3 April 1969; *Look for Me in the Whirlwind: The Collective Autobiography of the New York 21* (New York: Random House, 1971); *New York Times*, 5 April, 22 April, 2 May 1970.

3. Radio Free People flyer, n.d., Social Protest Collection, Bancroft Library, University of California, Berkeley; see Roz Payne's Web site (www.newsreel.us) for a collection of photographs from the trial.

4. *New York Times*, 2 May 1970.

5. Jean Genet to Bobby Seale and Huey Newton, n.d., Huey P. Newton Papers, Special Collections, Stanford University Libraries; Kathleen Neal Cleaver, "Back to Africa: The Evolution of the International Section of the Black Panther Party," in Charles E. Jones, *The Black Panther Party Reconsidered* (Baltimore: Black Classic Press, 1998), 250; *New York Times*, 1 May 1970; for a thorough overview of Genet's activities on the Panther's behalf, see Robert Sandarg, "Jean Genet and the Black Panther Party," *Journal of Black Studies* 16, 3 (March 1986): 269–82; Jean Genet, *May Day Speech, Description by Allen Ginsberg* (San Francisco: City Lights, 1970); Jean Genet, *Here and Now for Bobby Seale: Essays* (New York: Committee to Defend the Panthers, 1970).

6. Gail Sheehy, "Black Against Black: The Agony of Panthermania," *New York*, 16 November 1970; Gail Sheehy, "The Consequences of Panthermania," *New York*, 23 November 1970; also see Michael Staub, "Black Panthers, New Journalism, and the Rewriting of the Sixties," *Representations* 57 (1997): 56, 63.

7. Charles R. Garry to Legal Dept., Random House, 11 January 1971; Joseph M. Kraft to Charles R. Garry, 29 January 1971, Huey P. Newton Collection, Special Collections, Stanford University Libraries; Gail Sheehy, *Panthermania: The Clash of Black Against Black in One American City* (New York: Random House, 1971), 69, 113.

8. The *Yale Daily News* strips by Garry Trudeau are available at www.doonesbury.com.

9. Ovid P. Adams, *The Adventures of Black Eldridge: The Panther* (San Francisco: Marcus Books, 1970), Bancroft Library, University of California at Berkeley.

10. *Black Panther* #1 (Marvel Comics, 1976), author's collection; see discussion by Omar Bilal at www.blacksuperhero.com.

11. *New York Times*, 16 May, 14 July, 4 September 1970.

12. Commission of Inquiry into the Black Panthers and Law Enforcement, "Preliminary Investigation of the Relations Between the Black Panther Party and Local Law Enforcement Agencies," 1970, 17–18, Bancroft Library, University of California at Berkeley; Roy Wilkins and Ramsey Clark, Chairmen, *Search and Destroy: A Report* (New York: Metropolitan Applied Research Center, 1973).

13. U.S. Senate, Supplementary Detailed Staff Reports on Intelligence Activities and the Rights of Americans, Book III, *Final Report of the Select Committee to Study Governmental Operations with respect to Intelligence Activities*, S. Rep. No. 755, 94th Congress, 2d Session. See also Senator Frank Church, chairman, *The Intelligence Community: History, Organization and Issues* (New York: R.R. Bowker, 1977).

14. *San Francisco Examiner*, 5 August, 6 August 1970; Panther Communications inventory, 3 June, 11 June 1971, Huey P. Newton Papers, Stanford University Library. An entire volume of *National Lawyer Guild Practitioner*, 29, 3/4 (1972), focused on prison law with special attention to Newton's case, Huey P. Newton Papers, Stanford University Library.

15. *Black Panther Party Part 1: Investigation of Kansas City Chapter; National Organization Data*, Hearings before the Committee on Internal Security, House of Representatives, 91st Congress (Washington, DC: U.S. Government Printing Office, 1970), 2613–15.

16. *Black Panther Party Part 1: Investigation of Kansas City Chapter* and *Black Panther Party Part 3: Investigation of Activities in Detroit, Mich.; Philadelphia, Pa. and Indianapolis, Indiana*, Richardson Pryor, Chairman, Sub-Committee of the Committee on Internal Security to National Offices of Black Panther Party, 24 September 1970, Huey P. Newton Papers, Stanford University Library; Reynaldo Anderson, "Practical Internationalists: The Story of the Des Moines, Iowa, Black Panther Party," in Jeanne Theoharis and Komozi Woodard, eds., *Groundwork: Local Black Freedom Movements in America* (New York: New York University Press, 2005), 290–95.

17. Newspaper Distribution Reports, 1971–72, Huey P. Newton Papers, Stanford University Library; Books in Progress, Stronghold Consolidated Productions, Inc., 20 July 1971, Huey P. Newton Papers, Stanford University Library; letter from Martin Kenner, Stronghold Consolidated Productions, 7 July 1971, Huey P. Newton Papers, Stanford University Library; Agreement, Black Panther Party and Stronghold Consolidated Productions, 15 December 1970, Huey P. Newton Papers, Stanford University Library.

18. "Call for Revolutionary People's Constitutional Convention, June 23–July 3, 1970," reprinted in Philip S. Foner, ed., *The Black Panthers Speak* (New York: Da Capo Press, 1995), 267–71; *Black Panther*, 20 June 1970.

19. *Black Panther*, 5 September 1970.

20. *Black Panther*, 21 August 1970.

21. Nora Sayre, "The Revolutionary People's Constitutional Convention," *Esquire*, January 1971.

22. Elaine Woo, "Nora Sayre; Essayist on Cold War Era," *Los Angeles Times*, 11 August 2001; Joan Didion, *The White Album* (New York: Pocket Books, 1979), 31; Robert E. Smith, "They Still Write It White," *Columbia Journalism Review* (1969), reprinted in Alfred Balk and James Boylan, eds., *Our Troubled Press: Tens Years of the* Columbia Journalism Review (Boston: Little, Brown, 1971), 67–71.

23. *Wall Street Journal*, 13 March 1969.

24. James Baldwin, *No Name in the Street* (New York: Dell, 1972), 165.

25. Application of Caldwell, 311 F.Supp. 358 (N. D. Cal., 1970); *Caldwell v. U.S.*, 434 F. 2d 1081 (9th Cir. 1970); *Branzburg v. Hayes*, 408 U.S. 665, 92 S.Ct. 2646 (1972). Caldwell's claim that the FBI tried to turn him into an informant is made in his collection of essays, *Black American Witness: Reports from the Front* (Washington, DC: Lion House Publishing, 1994), introduction.

26. Ekwueme Michael Thelwell, afterword to Gilbert Moore, *Rage* (New York: Carroll & Graf, 1993), 275–77.

27. Angela LeBlanc-Ernest, " 'The Most Qualified Person to Handle the Job': Black Panther Party Women, 1966–1982," in Charles Jones, ed., *The Black Panther Party Reconsidered* (Baltimore: Black Classic Press, 1998), 316–17; *New York Times*, 1 March, 10 March 1971; *Black Panther*, 17 April 1971; Kathleen Cleaver, "Back to Africa," in

Charles Jones, ed., *The Black Panther Party Reconsidered* (Baltimore: Black Classic Press, 1998), 238–39; *Black Panther*, 13 February 1971.

28. Black Panther Party Central Committee meeting minutes, 24 May 1972, Huey P. Newton Papers, Stanford University Library; Elaine Brown, *A Taste of Power* (New York: Anchor Books, 1994), 323–24, 333.

29. For an overview on the final days of the Black Panther Party, see Ollie A. Johnson III, "Explaining the Demise of the Black Panther Party: The Role of Internal Factors," in Charles Jones, ed., *The Black Panther Party Reconsidered* (Baltimore: Black Classic Press, 1998), 406–9; Brown, *A Taste of Power*, 437–50.

30. Peter Goldman and Gerald Lubenow, "The Party's Over," *Newsweek*, 5 September 1977.

31. Kate Coleman, "The Party's Over," *New Times*, 10 July 1978; see discussion in Hugh Pearson, *The Shadow of the Panther* (Reading, MA: Addison-Wesley Pub. Co., 1994), 288–89; Jane Rhodes interview with Kate Coleman, 9 July 2003, Berkeley, CA.

Conclusion

1. G. Louis Heath, ed., *Off the Pigs: The History and Literature of the Black Panther Party* (Metuchen, NJ: Scarecrow Press, 1976), 214; Gail Sheehy, *Panthermania: The Clash of Black Against Black in One American City* (New York: Harper and Row, 1971), 8; House of Representatives Committee on Internal Security, *Gun-Barrel Politics: The Black Panther Party, 1966–1971* (Washington, DC: U.S. Government Printing Office, 1971), 16.

2. *Look for Me in the Whirlwind: The Collective Autobiography of the New York 21* (New York: Random House, 1971), 303, 299, 285.

3. Nikhil Pal Singh, *Black Is a Country* (Cambridge: Harvard University Press, 2004), 202.

4. Jack Lule, "News Strategies in the Death of Huey Newton," *Journalism Quarterly* 70 (1993): 287–99; Todd Fraley and Ellie Lester-Roushanzamir, "Revolutionary Leader or Violent Thug? A Comparative Analysis of the Chicago *Tribune* and *Chicago Daily Defender*'s Reporting on the Death of Fred Hampton," *Howard Journal of Communications* 15 (2004): 147–67; Gail Sheehy, *Panthermania: The Clash of Black Against Black in One American City* (New York: Harper and Row, 1971), 8–9.

5. Michael Staub, "Black Panthers, New Journalism, and the Rewriting of the Sixties," *Representations* 57 (1997): 57; Hugh Pearson, *The Shadow of the Panther* (Reading, MA: Addison-Wesley Pub. Co., 1994), 339.

6. Harris Poll, 1970; *Wall Street Journal*, 13 January 1970; House of Representatives Committee on Internal Security, *Gun-Barrel Politics: The Black Panther Party, 1966–1971* (Washington, DC: U.S. Government Printing Office, 1971), 16.

7. For a useful discussion of the narrowness of sixties scholarship, see Andrew Hunt, "'When Did the Sixties Happen?' Searching for New Directions," *Journal of Social History* 33, 1 (1999): 147–61.

8. James Miller, *Democracy Is in the Streets: From Port Huron to the Siege of Chicago* (New York: Simon and Schuster, 1987), 320, 301; see also Terry H. Anderson, *The Movement*

and the Sixties: Protest in America from Greensboro to Wounded Knee (New York: Oxford University Press, 1995).

9. Todd Gitlin, *The Sixties: Years of Hope, Days of Rage* (New York: Bantam Books, 1987), 348–51.

10. Meta Mendel-Reyes, *Reclaiming Democracy: The Sixties in Politics and Memory* (New York: Routledge, 1995), 72–73, 146.

11. Manning Marable, *Race, Reform and Rebellion: The Second Reconstruction in Black America, 1945–1990,* 2nd ed. (Jackson: University Press of Mississippi, 1991), 108; William L. Van Deburg, *New Day in Babylon: The Black Power Movement and American Culture, 1965–1975* (Chicago: University of Chicago Press, 1992), 155–56, 300; Rod Bush, *We Are Not What We Seem: Black Nationalism and Class Struggle in the American Century* (New York: New York University Press, 1999), 196, 205.

12. See Jeffrey O.G. Ogbar, *Black Power: Radical Politics and African American Identity* (Baltimore: Johns Hopkins University Press, 2004), 191; Singh, *Black Is a Country*, 195–97.

13. See Kathleen Neal Cleaver and George Katsiaficas, eds., *Liberation, Imagination and the Black Panther Party* (New York: Routledge, 2001); Charles Jones, ed., *The Black Panther Party Reconsidered* (Baltimore: Black Classic Press, 1998), 12.

14. Hugh Pearson, *The Shadow of the Panther: Huey Newton and the Price of Black Power in America* (Reading, MA: Addison-Wesley, 1994), 338–39, 341–42; see Avery F. Gordon, *Ghostly Matters: Haunting and the Sociological Imagination* (Minneapolis: University of Minnesota Press, 1997), 7–8.

15. Pearson, *The Shadow of the Panther*, 340; for a thorough critical analysis of Pearson's book, see Errol A. Henderson, "The Lumpenproletariat as Vanguard? The Black Panther Party, Social Transformation, and Pearson's Analysis of Huey Newton," *Journal of Black Studies* 28, 2 (1997): 171–99, quote on 190.

16. Marita Sturken, *Tangled Memories* (Berkeley: University of California Press, 1997), 75–76.

17. Houston A. Baker Jr., "Critical Memory and the Black Public Sphere," in the Black Public Sphere Collective, eds., *The Black Public Sphere* (Chicago: University of Chicago Press, 1995), 7–37.

18. Victor Leo Walker II, "Review of *A Huey P. Newton Story*," *African American Review* 31, 4 (1997): 727–28.

19. Walter Mosley, *Bad Boy Brawly Brown* (New York: Warner Books, 2002), 47–48.

20. Trey Ellis, "The New Black Aesthetic," *Callaloo* 12 (1989): 119–40; Mark Anthony Neal, *Soul Babies: Black Popular Culture and the Post-Soul Aesthetic* (New York: Routledge, 2002), 134.

21. Paul Beatty, *Tuff* (New York: Random House, 2000), 105, 109–10.

22. Henry Hampton, producer and creator, *Eyes on the Prize: America at the Racial Crossroads, 1965–1985,* episode 3 (Boston: WGBH Films, 1989).

23. Alice Walker, "Black Panthers or Black Punks?" *New York Times*, 5 May 1991.

24. *San Francisco Examiner*, 22 February, 19 May 1996; Ishmael Reed, *Blues City: A Walk in Oakland* (New York: Crown Publishers, 2003), 19, 71.

25. Jane Rhodes interview with Kathleen Cleaver, 16 November 2002, San Diego, CA; Eldridge Cleaver, *Target Zero: A Life in Writing*, ed. Kathleen Cleaver (New York: Palgrave Macmillan, 2006).

26. Jane Rhodes interview with Bill Jennings, 10 July 2003, Sacramento, CA; www .itsabouttimebpp.com.

27. East Bay News Service, 29 April 2006. The author picked up a copy of the *Commemorator* in 1996 in front of Cody's Bookstore on Telegraph Avenue in Berkeley, a counterculture landmark. Both the *Commemorator* and the new *Black Panther* are located in several libraries in the University of California system. A copy of the *Black Panther Collective Community News* is posted at www.itsabouttimebpp.com; also see CNN News online, 3 October 1997.

28. *San Francisco Examiner*, 14 October 1996.

29. David Hilliard with Keith and Kent Zimmerman, *Huey: Spirit of the Panther* (New York: Thunder's Mouth Press, 2006).

30. Press kit, Anonym Records and Black Panther Records; Ishmael Reed, *Blues City*, 71; www.blackpanthertours.com; *San Francisco Chronicle*, 25 October 1977; *Alameda Times-Star*, 4 July 2003; *New Times* (Los Angeles), 9 August 2001; Associated Press, 27 January 2003.

31. *San Francisco Chronicle*, 28 August 1996, 26 September 2002; "Copycats," *Utne Reader*, February 1997, 25–27; Salim Muwakkil, "The New Black Panthers," *In These Times*, 23 November 1997, 13–15; *Los Angeles Times*, 12 November 2002.

Bibliography

Manuscript and Archival Collections

African American Museum and Library at Oakland
Black Panther Files, Oakland History Room, Oakland Public Library

Black Panther Files, Bancroft Library, U.C. Berkeley
Paul Jacobs' Peace and Freedom Party Senatorial Race Campaign Book, Bancroft Library,
   U.C. Berkeley
Social Activism Project, U.C. Berkeley Libraries
Social Protest Collection, Bancroft Library, U.C. Berkeley

Black Panther Collection, San Francisco African American Historical and Cultural Society

Black Panther Files, San Francisco History Center, San Francisco Public Library
Joseph Alioto Jr. Papers, San Francisco History Center, San Francisco Public Library

Black Panther Files, Schomburg Center for Research in Black Culture, New York Public
   Library

Black Power Files, Institute for Race Relations Archives, London
The British Library, London
The British Library Newspaper Collection, Collindale

Huey P. Newton Archives, Special Collections, Green Library, Stanford University

Southern California Library for Social Studies and Research, Los Angeles

Audio/Video Archives

BBC Archive, Middlesex, U.K.
British Film Institute Archive, London
CBS News Archive, New York
Pacifica Radio Archive, Los Angeles

San Francisco Bay Area Television Archive, San Francisco State University Library
Vanderbilt University Television News Archive, Nashville

Newspapers and Periodicals

African American Review
Alameda Times-Star
American Visions
Amsterdam News (New York)
Berkeley Barb
Black Panther
Black Scholar
Columbia Journalism Review
Commonweal
Daily Variety
Ebony
Entertainment Weekly
Esquire
Essence
Golden Gater
In These Times
International Herald Tribune
Jet
L.A. Weekly
Life
London Sunday Telegraph
Look
Los Angeles Sentinel
Los Angeles Times
Manchester Guardian (UK)
The Movement
Muhammad Speaks
The Nation
National Guardian
Neiman Reports
The New Republic
Newsday (New York)
Newsweek
New York Beacon
The New York Review of Books
The New York Times
Oakland Montclarion

The Oakland Observer
The Oakland Tribune
Playboy
Ramparts
Rap Pages
San Diego Union
San Francisco Chronicle
San Francisco Examiner
San Francisco Express Times
San Jose Mercury News
The Saturday Evening Post
The Sun-Reporter (San Francisco)
Time
The Times (London)
Toronto Star
UCLA Daily Bruin
U.S. News and World Report
Utne Reader
The Wall Street Journal
Washington Afro-American
The Washington Post
The Weekly Journal (UK)

Film and Video

All Power to the People! (Lee Lew-Lee, 1996)
Black Panther: Huey Newton (Newsreel, 1968)
The Black Panthers—Les Panthers Noires (Agnes Varda, 1968)
Comrade Sister: Voices of Women in the Black Panther Party (Christine L. Minor and Phyllis J. Jackson, 1997)
Eyes on the Prize: America at the Racial Crossroads, 1965–1985 (Henry Hampton, 1990)
Frontline: The Two Nations of Black America (PBS and WGBH, 1998)
Off the Pigs (Newsreel, 1968)
Panther (Mario Van Peebles, 1995)
A Panther in Africa (Aaron Matthews, 2004)

Interview Sources

Brown, Elaine. June 3, 1998. San Diego, CA.
Caldwell, Earl. June 23, 2002. Telephone interview.
Cleaver, Kathleen. November 18, 2002. San Diego, CA.
Coleman, Kate. July 9, 2003, Berkeley, CA.

Douglas, Emory. February 28, 1995, San Francisco, CA.

Jennings, Bill. July 10, 2003. Sacramento, CA.

Books

Anderson, Benedict. *Imagined Communities: Reflections on the Origin and Spread of Nationalism.* London: Verso, 1987.

Anderson, Terry. *The Movement and the Sixties.* New York: Oxford University Press, 1995.

Anthony, Earl. *Picking Up the Gun: A Report on the Black Panthers.* New York: Dial Press, 1970.

————. *Spitting in the Wind: The True Story Behind the Violent Legacy of the Black Panther Party.* Santa Monica, CA: Roundtable Publishing, Inc., 1990.

Baldwin, James. *The Fire Next Time.* New York: Dial Press, 1963.

————. *No Name in the Street.* New York: Dell Publishers, 1972.

Barbour, Floyd B., ed. *The Black Power Revolt.* Boston: Porter Sargent Publishers, 1968.

Baruch, Ruth-Marion and Pirkle Jones. *The Vanguard: A Photographic Essay on the Black Panthers.* Boston: Beacon Press, 1969.

Baughman, James L. *The Republic of Mass Culture: Journalism, Filmmaking, and Broadcasting in America since 1941.* Baltimore: Johns Hopkins University Press, 1994.

Beatty, Paul. *Tuff.* New York: Random House, 2000.

Berlant, Lauren. *Anatomy of a National Fantasy.* Chicago: University of Chicago Press, 1991.

Berlin, Ira. *Slaves Without Masters: The Free Negro in the Antebellum South.* New York: Pantheon Books, 1974.

Blanchard, Margaret A. *Revolutionary Sparks: Freedom of Expression in Modern America.* New York: Oxford University Press, 1992.

Blight, David W. *Frederick Douglass' Civil War: Keeping Faith in Jubilee.* Baton Rouge: Louisiana State University Press, 1989.

Bogle, Donald. *Toms, Coons, Mulattoes, Mammies and Bucks: An Interpretive History of Blacks in American Films.* New York: Continuum Publishing, 1989.

Bourdieu, Pierre. *The Field of Cultural Production: Essays on Art and Literature.* New York: Columbia University Press, 1993.

————. *On Television.* New York: New Press, 1998.

Boyle, Kay. *The Long Walk at San Francisco State.* New York: Grove Press, 1970.

Bracey, John H. Jr., August Meier, and Elliot Rudwick, eds. *Black Nationalism in America.* New York: Bobbs-Merrill, 1970.

Branch, Taylor. *Parting the Waters: America in the King Years 1954–63.* New York: Simon and Schuster, 1988.

Brent, William Lee. *Long Time Gone: A Black Panther's True-Life Story of His Hijacking and Twenty-five Years in Cuba.* New York: Times Books, 1996.

Brown, Elaine. *A Taste of Power: A Black Woman's Story.* New York: Pantheon Books, 1992.

Brown, H. Rap. *Die Nigger Die!* New York: The Dial Press, 1969.

Brown, Scot. *Fighting for US: Maulana Karenga, The US Organization, and Black Cultural Nationalism.* New York: New York University Press, 2003.

Broussard, Albert S. *Black San Francisco: The Struggle for Racial Equality in the West, 1900–1954.* Lawrence, KS: University of Kansas Press, 1993.

Bush, Rod. *We Are Not What We Seem: Black Nationalism and Class Struggle in the American Century.* New York: New York University Press, 1999.

Caldwell, Earl. *Black American Witness: Reports from the Front.* Washington, D.C.: Lion House Publishing, 1994.

Carmichael, Stokely and Charles V. Hamilton. *Black Power: the Politics of Liberation in America.* New York: Vintage Books, 1967.

———— with Ekwueme Michael Thelwell. *Ready for Revolution: The Life and Struggles of Stokely Carmichael.* New York: Scribner, 2003.

Carson, Clayborne. *In Struggle: SNCC and the Black Awakening of the 1960s.* Cambridge: Harvard University Press, 1981.

Carey, James. *Communication as Culture: Essays on Media and Society.* Boston: Unwin Hyman, 1989.

Cheney, Charise L. *Brothers Gonna Work It Out: Sexual Politics in the Golden Age of Rap Nationalism.* New York: New York University Press, 2005.

Church, Senator Frank, Chairman. *The Intelligence Community: History, Organization, and Issues.* New York: R.R. Bowker, Co., 1977.

Cleaver, Eldridge. *Soul on Ice.* New York: McGraw-Hill, 1968.

————. *Post-prison Writings and Speeches.* New York: Random House, 1969.

————. *Target Zero: A Life in Writing.* New York: Palgrave Macmillan, 2006.

Cleaver, Kathleen and George Katsiaficas, eds., *Liberation, Imagination and the Black Panther Party.* New York and London: Routledge, 2001.

Cohen, Robert and Reginald E. Zelnik, eds. *The Free Speech Movement: Reflections on Berkeley in the 1960s.* Berkeley: University of California Press, 2002.

Collins, Patricia Hill. *Fighting Words: Black Women and the Search for Justice.* Minneapolis: University of Minnesota Press, 1998.

Commission on Freedom of the Press. *A Free and Responsible Press, A General Report on Mass Communication: Newspapers, Radio, Motion Pictures, Magazines, and Books.* Chicago: University of Chicago Press, 1947.

Crowe, Daniel. *Prophets of Rage: The Black Freedom Struggle in San Francisco, 1945–1969.* New York: Garland Publishing Co., 2000.

Davis, Angela. *If They Come in the Morning: Voices of Resistance.* New York: Third Press, 1971.

Dawson, Michael. *Black Visions: The Roots of Contemporary African-American Political Ideologies.* Chicago: University of Chicago Press, 2001.

Deakin, Nicholas. *Colour, Citizenship and British Society: Based on the Institute of Race Relations Report.* London: Panther Books, 1970.

Didion, Joan. *The White Album.* New York: Pocket Books, 1979.

Dowling, John. *Radical Media: The Political Experience of Alternative Communication*. Boston: South End Press, 1984.

Du Bois, W.E.B. *The Souls of Black Folk* in *Three Negro Classics*. New York: Avon Books, 1973.

Dyson, Michael Eric. *Making Malcolm: The Myth and Meaning of Malcolm X*. New York: Oxford University Press, 1995.

Edwards, Harry. *The Revolt of the Black Athlete*. New York: Free Press, 1969.

Egbuna, Obi. *Destroy This Temple: The Voice of Black Power in Britain*. London: MacGibbon and Kee, 1971.

Epstein, Edward Jay. *Between Fact and Fiction: The Problem of Journalism*. New York: Vintage Books, 1975.

Fabre, Genevieve and Robert O'Meally, eds. *History and Memory in African-American Culture*. New York: Oxford, 1994.

Fanon, Frantz. *Black Skin, White Masks*. New York: Grove Press, 1967.

————. *The Wretched of the Earth*. New York: Grove Press, 1968.

Fiske, John. *Media Matters: Everyday Culture and Political Change*. Minneapolis: University of Minnesota Press, 1994.

Foner, Philip S. *The Black Panthers Speak*. New York: Da Capo Press, 1995.

Forman, James. *The Making of Black Revolutionaries* (1972). Reprint—Seattle: University of Washington Press, 1985.

Frazier, E. Franklin. *Black Bourgeoisie: The Rise of a New Middle Class in the United States*. New York: Collier Books, 1962.

Fredrickson, George. *The Black Image in the White Mind: The Debate on Afro-American Character and Destiny, 1817–1914*. New York: Harper and Row, 1971.

Fryer, Peter. *Staying Power: The History of Black People in Britain*. London: Pluto Press, 1984.

Gans, Herbert. *Deciding What's News: A Study of CBS Evening News, NBC Nightly News, Newsweek and Time*. New York: Pantheon, 1979.

Garry, Charles and Art Goldberg. *Streetfighter in the Courtroom: The People's Advocate*. New York: Dutton, 1977.

Gilroy, Paul. *The Black Atlantic: Modernity and Double Consciousness*. Cambridge: Harvard University Press, 1993.

Gitlin, Todd. *The Whole World is Watching: Mass Media in the Making and Unmaking of the New Left*. Berkeley: University of California Press, 1980.

————. *The Sixties: Years of Hope, Days of Rage*. New York: Bantam Books, 1987.

Glessing, Robert J. *The Underground Press in America*. Bloomington: Indiana University Press, 1970.

Goffman, Erving. *Frame Analysis: An Essay on the Organization of Experience* (1974). Reprint—Boston: Northeastern University Press, 1986.

Goings, Kenneth W. *Mammy and Uncle Mose: Black Collectibles and American Stereotyping*. Bloomington: Indiana University Press, 1994.

Goldberg, David Theo. *The Anatomy of Racism*. Minneapolis: University of Minnesota Press, 1990.

Gordon, Avery F. *Ghostly Matters: Haunting and the Sociological Imagination*. Minneapolis: University of Minnesota Press, 1997.

Gossett, Thomas F. *Race: The History of an Idea*. Reprint—New York: Oxford University Press, 1997.

Graham, Allison. *Framing the South: Hollywood, Television and Race During the Civil Rights Struggle*. Baltimore: Johns Hopkins University Press, 2001.

Gray, Herman. *Watching Race: Television and the Struggle for "Blackness."* Minneapolis: University of Minnesota Press, 1995.

Greenlee, Sam. *The Spook Who Sat By the Door*. New York: Bantam Books, 1970.

Guerrero, Ed. *Framing Blackness: The African American Image in Film*. Philadelphia: Temple University Press, 1993.

Hall, Stuart, et al. *Policing the Crisis: Mugging, the State, and Law and Order*. London: MacMillan, 1978.

Hallin, Daniel C. *We Keep America on Top of the World: Television Journalism and the Public Sphere*. New York: Routledge, 1994.

Harkey, Ira. *The Smell of Burning Crosses: An Autobiography of a Mississippi Newspaperman*. Jacksonville, Illinois: Harris-Wolfe, 1967.

Heath, G. Louis, ed. *Off the Pigs: The History and Literature of the Black Panther Party*. Metuchen, NJ: Scarecrow Press, 1976.

Hill, Lance. *The Deacons for Defense: Armed Resistance and the Civil Rights Movement*. Chapel Hill: University of North Carolina Press, 2004.

Hill, Norman, ed. *The Black Panther Menace: America's Neo-Nazis*. New York: Popular Library, 1971.

Hilliard, David and Lewis Cole. *This Side of Glory: The Autobiography of David Hilliard and the Story of the Black Panther Party*. Boston: Little, Brown and Co., 1993.

_____ and Donald Weise, eds. *The Huey Newton Reader*. New York: Seven Stories Press, 2002.

_____ with Keith and Kent Zimmerman. *Huey: Spirit of the Panther*. New York: Thunders Mouth Press, 2006.

Horne, Gerald C. *Fire This Time: The Watts Uprising and the 1960s*. Charlottesville: University of Virginia Press, 1995.

Horowitz, David. *Radical Son: A Generational Odyssey*. New York: Free Press, 1997.

Humphry, Derek and David Tindall. *False Messiah: The Story of Michael X*. London: Hart-Davis, MacGibbon, 1977.

Hutton, Frankie. *The Early Black Press in America, 1827–1860*. Westport, CT: Greenwood Press, 1993.

Jacobs, Ronald N. *Race, Media and the Crisis of Civil Society*. Cambridge: Cambridge University Press, 2000.

James, David. *Allegories of Cinema: American Film in the Sixties*. Princeton, NJ: Princeton University Press, 1989.

Jeffries, Judson. *Huey P. Newton: The Radical Theorist*. Jackson, MS.: University of Mississippi Press, 2002.

Jones, Charles E. ed. *The Black Panther Party Reconsidered*. Baltimore: Black Classic Press, 1998.

Jordan, Winthrop. *The White Man's Burden: Historical Origins of Racism in the United States*. New York: Oxford University Press, 1974.

Joseph, Peniel E. *Waiting 'Til the Midnight Hour: A Narrative History of Black Power in America*. New York: Henry Holt and Company, 2006.

Kargueuzian, Dikran. *Blow it Up! The Black Student Revolt at San Francisco State College and the Emergence of Dr. Hayakawa*. Boston: Gambit Press, 1971.

Keating, Edward M. *Free Huey!* Berkeley: The Ramparts Press, 1970.

Kelley, Robin D.G. *Yo' Mama's Dysfunctional: Fighting the Culture Wars in America*. Boston: Beacon Press, 1997.

―――. *Freedom Dreams: The Black Radical Imagination*. Boston: Beacon Press, 2002.

―――. *Race Rebels: Culture, Politics and the Black Working Class*. New York: Free Press, 1994.

Kozol, Wendy. *Life's America: Family and Nation in Postwar Photojournalism*. Philadelphia: Temple University Press, 1994.

Lasar, Matthew. *Pacifica Radio: The Rise of an Alternative Network*. Philadelphia: Temple University Press, 1999.

Lentz, Richard. *Symbols, the News Magazines, and Martin Luther King*. Baton Rouge: Louisiana State University Press, 1990.

Lewis, David Levering. *When Harlem Was In Vogue*. New York: Oxford University Press, 1979.

Lipsitz, George. *Time Passages: Collective Memory and American Popular Culture*. Minneapolis: University of Minnesota Press, 1990.

Lockwood, Lee. *Conversation with Eldridge Cleaver: Algiers*. New York: McGraw-Hill, 1970.

Logan, Rayford W. *The Betrayal of the Negro from Rutherford B. Hayes to Woodrow Wilson*. New York: Collier Books, 1965.

Look For Me in the Whirlwind: The Collective Autobiography of the New York 21. New York: Random House, 1971.

Lott, Eric. *Love and Theft: Blackface Minstrelsy and the American Working Class*. New York: Oxford University Press, 1995.

Lubiano, Wahneema, ed. *The House That Race Built: Black Americans, U.S. Terrain*. New York: Pantheon, 1997.

Madhubuti, Haki R. (Don L. Lee). *Book of Life*. Detroit: Broadside Press, 1973.

Major, Reginald. *A Panther is a Black Cat: A Study in Depth of the Black Panther Party—Its Origins, Its Goals, Its Struggle for Survival*. New York: William Morrow, 1971.

Marable, Manning. *Beyond Black and White: Transforming African-American Politics*. London: Verso, 1995.

―――. *Black Leadership*. New York: Columbia University Press, 1998.

―――. *Race, Reform and Rebellion: The Second Reconstruction in Black America, 1945–1990*. Jackson, MS: University Press of Mississippi, 1991.

Marine, Gene. *The Black Panthers*. New York: New American Library, 1969.

Martindale, Carolyn. *The White Press and Black America*. Westport, CN: Greenwood Press, 1986.

McCartney, John T. *Black Power Ideologies: An Essay in African-American Political Thought*. Philadelphia: Temple University Press, 1993.

Mendel-Reyes, Meta. *Reclaiming Democracy: The Sixties in Politics and Memory*. New York: Routledge, 1995.

Miller, Floyd. *The Search for a Black Nationality: Black Emigration and Colonization, 1787–1863*. Urbana, IL: University of Illinois Press, 1975.

Miller, James. *Democracy Is In the Streets: From Port Huron to the Siege of Chicago*. New York: Simon and Schuster, 1987.

Montgomery, Gayle B. and James W. Johnson. *One Step from the White House: The Rise and Fall of Senator William F. Knowland*. Berkeley: University of California Press, 1998.

Moore, Gilbert. *Rage* (1971). Reprint—Carroll and Graf, 1993.

Morley, David. *Home Territories: Media, Mobility, and Identity*. New York: Routledge, 2000.

Morrison, Toni. *Playing in the Dark: Whiteness and the Literary Imagination*. Cambridge: Harvard University Press, 1992.

Mosley, Walter. *Bad Boy Brawly Brown*. New York: Warner Books, 2002.

Moses, Wilson Jeremiah, ed. *Classical Black Nationalism: From the American Revolution to Marcus Garvey*. New York: NYU Press, 1996.

Munoz, Carlos Jr. *Youth, Identity, Power: The Chicano Movement*. London: Verso, 1989.

Neal, Mark Anthony. *Soul Babies: Black Popular Culture and the Post-Soul Aesthetic*. New York: Routledge, 2002.

Newton, Huey P. *War Against the Panthers: A Study of Repression in America*. New York: Harlem River Press, 1996

_____. *Revolutionary Suicide*. New York: Harcourt Brace Jovanovich, 1973.

_____. *To Die for the People: The Writings of Huey P. Newton*. New York: Random House, 1972.

Newton, Michael. *Bitter Grain: Huey Newton and the Black Panther Party*. Los Angeles: Holloway House Publishing Company, 1980.

Ogbar, Jeffrey O.G. *Black Power: Radical Politics and African American Identity*. Baltimore: Johns Hopkins University Press, 2004.

Olson, Jack. *Last Man Standing: The Tragedy and Triumph of Geronimo Pratt*. New York: Doubleday, 2000.

Omi, Michael and Howard Winant. *Racial Formation in the United States*. New York: Routledge, 1994.

O'Reilly, Kenneth. *Racial Matters: The FBI's Secret File on Black America, 1960–1972*. New York: Free Press, 1989.

Payne, Charles M. *I've Got the Light of Freedom: The Organizing Tradition and the Mississippi Freedom Struggle*. Berkeley: University of California Press, 1995.

Pearson, Hugh. *The Shadow of the Panther: Huey Newton and the Price of Black Power in America*. Reading, MA: Addison-Wesley, 1994.

Peck, Abe. *Uncovering The Sixties: The Life and Times of the Underground Press*. New York: Pantheon, 1985.

Phillips, Mike and Trevor Phillips. *Windrush*. London: HarperCollins, 1998.

Prashad, Vijay. *Everybody Was Kung Fu Fighting: Afro-Asian Connections and the Myth of Racial Purity*. Boston: Beacon Press, 2001.

Raines, Howell. *My Soul Is Rested: The Story of the Civil Rights Movement in the Deep South*. New York: Viking Penguin, 1983.

Reed, Ishmael. *Blues City: A Walk in Oakland*. New York: Crown Publishers, 2003.

Report of the National Advisory Commission on Civil Disorders. New York: E.P. Dutton, 1968.

Rhodes, Jane. *Mary Ann Shadd Cary: The Black Press and Protest in the Nineteenth Century*. Bloomington: Indiana University Press, 1998.

Roberts, Gene and Hank Klibanoff. *The Race Beat: The Press, The Civil Rights Struggle, and the Awakening of a Nation*. New York: Alfred A. Knopf, 2006.

Robinson, Cedric. *Black Marxism: The Making of the Black Radical Tradition* (1983). Reprint—Chapel Hill: University of North Carolina Press, 2000.

Schanche, Don A. *The Panther Paradox: A Liberal's Dilemma*. New York: David McKay Co., 1970.

Schudson, Michael. *Discovering the News: A Social History of American Newspapers*. New York: Basic Books, 1978.

———. *Watergate in American Memory: How We Remember, Forget, and Reconstruct the Past*. New York: Basic Books, 1992.

Scott, Robert L. and Wayne Brockriede. *The Rhetoric of Black Power*. New York: Harper and Row, 1969.

Seale, Bobby. *Seize the Time: The Story of the Black Panther Party and Huey P. Newton*. New York: Random House, 1970.

Self, Robert O. *American Babylon: Race and the Struggle for Postwar Oakland*. Princeton: Princeton University Press, 2003.

Sellers, Cleveland with Robert Terrell. *The River of No Return: The Autobiography of a Black Militant and the Life and Death of SNCC*. New York: William Morrow, 1973.

Shakur, Assata. *Assata: An Autobiography*. London: Zed Books, 1987.

Sheehy, Gail. *Panthermania: The Clash of Black Against Black in One American City*. New York: Random House, 1971.

Simpson, George Eaton. *The Negro in the Philadelphia Press*. Philadelphia: University of Pennsylvania Press, 1936.

Singh, Nikhil Pal. *Black Is a Country: Race and the Unfinished Struggle for Democracy*. Cambridge: Harvard University Press, 2004.

Small, Melvin. *Covering Dissent: The Media and the Anti-Vietnam War Movement*. New Brunswick: Rutgers University Press, 1994.

Small, Stephen. *Racialized Barriers: The Black Experience in the U.S. and England in the 1980s*. London: Routledge, 1994.

Smith, Jennifer B. *An International History of the Black Panther Party*. New York: Garland, 1999.

Stone, Willie. *I Was a Black Panther, As Told to Chuck Moore*. New York: Doubleday, 1970.

Sturken, Marita. *Tangled Memories: The Vietnam War, the AIDS Epidemic, and the Politics of Remembering*. Berkeley: University of California Press, 1997.

Taylor, Quintard. *In Search of the Racial Frontier: African Americans in the American West, 1528–1990*. New York: W.W. Norton, 1998.

Taylor, Ula Y. *The Veiled Garvey: The Life and Times of Amy Jacques Garvey*. Chapel Hill: University of North Carolina Press, 1992.

Theoharis, Jeanne and Komozi Woodard, eds. *Groundwork: Local Black Freedom Movements in America*. New York: NYU Press, 2005.

_____. *Freedom North: Black Freedom Struggles Outside the South, 1940–1980*. New York: Palgrave McMillan, 2003.

Turner, Patricia A. *I Heard It Through the Grapevine: Rumor in African-American Culture*. Berkeley: University of California Press, 1993.

Tyson, Timothy B. *Radio Free Dixie: Robert F. Williams and the Roots of Black Power*. Chapel Hill: University of North Carolina Press, 1999.

Van Deburg, William. *New Day in Babylon: The Black Power Movement and American Culture, 1965–1975*. Chicago: University of Chicago Press, 1992.

Van Peebles, Mario, Ula Y. Taylor, and J. Tarika Lewis, *Panther: The Pictorial History of the Black Panther Party and the Story Behind the Film*. New York: Newmarket Press, 1995.

Van Peebles, Melvin. *Panther*. New York: Thunder's Mouth Press, 1995.

Wachsberger, Ken, ed. *Voices from the Underground: Vol. 1*. Tempe, AZ: Mica Press, 1993.

Ward, Brian, ed. *Media, Culture, and the Modern African American Freedom Struggle*. Gainesville, FL: University Press of Florida, 2001.

Washington, Booker T. *Up From Slavery* in *Three Negro Classics*. New York: Avon Books, 1965.

Wendt, Simon. *The Spirit and the Shotgun: Armed Resistance and the Struggle for Civil Rights*. Gainesville, FL: University Press of Florida, 2007.

Wiegman, Robyn. *American Anatomies: Theorizing Race and Gender*. Durham: Duke University Press, 1995.

Williams, Juan, ed. *Eyes on the Prize: America's Civil Rights Years, 1954–1965*. New York: Viking.

Williams, Robert F. *Negroes With Guns*. New York: Marzani and Munsell, 1962.

Williams, Yohuru. *Black Politics/White Power: Civil Rights, Black Power, and the Black Panthers in New Haven*. St. James, NY: Brandywine Press, 2000.

Wolfe, Tom. *Radical Chic & Mau-Mauing the Flak Catchers*. New York: Farrar, Straus and Giroux, 1970.

_____. and E. W. Johnson, eds. *The New Journalism*. New York: Harper and Row, 1973.

Woodard, Komozi. *A Nation Within a Nation: Amiri Baraka (Leroi Jones) and Black Power Politics*. Chapel Hill: University of North Carolina Press, 1999.

Young, Cynthia A. *Soul Power: Culture, Radicalism, and the Making of a U.S. Third World Left*. Durham, NC: Duke University Press, 2006.

Zelizer, Barbie. *Covering the Body: The Kennedy Assassination, the Media, and the Shaping of Collective Memory*. Chicago: University of Chicago Press, 1992.

Pamphlets

Adams, Ovid P. *The Adventures of Black Eldridge: The Panther*. San Francisco: Marcus Books, 1970. Bancroft Library, University of California at Berkeley.

Bazaar, Mona, ed. *Free Huey: Or, the Sky's the Limit*. Oakland: M. Bazaar, 1968. Bancroft Library, University of California at Berkeley.

The Black Panthers in Action. Wheaton, IL.: Church League of America, 1969. Bancroft Library, University of California at Berkeley.

Cleaver, Eldridge. *The Genius of Huey P. Newton*. 1970. Bancroft Library, University of California at Berkeley.

———. *Revolution in the Congo*. 1971. Bancroft Library, University of California at Berkeley.

———. *Revolution and Education*. n.d. Bancroft Library, University of California at Berkeley.

Commission of Inquiry into the Black Panthers and the Police. Roy Wilkins and Ramsey Clark, Chairmen. *Search and Destroy: A Report*. New York: Metropolitan Applied Research Center, 1973. Bancroft Library, University of California at Berkeley.

Egbuna, Obi. *The ABC of Black Power Thought*, n.d. British Library, London.

Genet, Jean. *May Day Speech, Description by Allen Ginsberg*. San Francisco: City Lights, 1970. Bancroft Library, University of California at Berkeley.

Huey Newton Talks to the Movement. San Francisco: Students for a Democratic Society, August 1968. Schomburg Center for Research in Black Culture, New York.

Newton, Huey. *The Original Vision of the Black Panther Party*. 1973. Bancroft Library, University of California at Berkeley.

Report from Lowndes County. *The Black Panther Party*. 1966. Bancroft Library, University of California at Berkeley.

Rosebury, Celia. *Black Liberation on Trial: The Case of Huey Newton*. Berkeley: Bay Area Committee to Defend Political Rights, 1968. Bancroft Library, University of California at Berkeley.

Articles and Book Chapters

Abron, JoNina M. " 'Raising the Consciousness of the People': The Black Panther Intercommunal News Service, 1967–1980." In Ken Wachsberger, ed., *Voices from the Underground: Vol. 1*. Tempe AZ: Mica Press, 1993.

———. "The Legacy of the Black Panther Party." *The Black Scholar* 17 (1986): 33–36.

Anderson, Reynaldo. "Practical Internationalists: The Story of the Des Moines, Iowa, Black Panther Party." In Jeanne Theoharis and Komozi Woodard, eds., *Groundwork: Local Black Freedom Movements in America*. New York: NYU Press, 2005, 282–99.

Baker, Houston A. Jr. "Critical Memory and the Black Public Sphere." In The Black Public Sphere Collective, eds., *The Black Public Sphere*. Chicago: University of Chicago Press, 1995, 7–37.

Barker-Plummer, Bernadette. "News as Political Resource: Media Strategies and Political Identity in the U.S. Women's Movemnet, 1966–1975." *Critical Studies in Mass Communication* 12 (1995): 306–24.

Beasley, Maurine. "The Muckrakers and Lynching: A Case Study in Racism." *Journalism History* 9 (1982): 86–90.

Bond, Julian. "The Media and the Movement: Looking Back from the Southern Front." In Brian Ward, ed., *Media, Culture and the Modern African American Freedom Struggle*, Gainesville, FL: University Press of Florida, 2001, 16–40.

Booker, Simeon. "A New Frontier for Daily Newspapers." *Nieman Reports* 1956: 25.

Calloway, Carolyn R. "Group Cohesiveness in the Black Panther Party." *Journal of Black Studies.* 8 (1977): 55–74.

Churchill, Ward. " 'To Disrupt, Discredit and Destroy': The FBI's Secret War against the Black Panther Party." In Kathleen Cleaver and George Katsiaficas, eds. *Liberation, Imagination and the Black Panther Party: A New Look at the Panthers and their Legacy.* New York: Routledge, 2001, 78–117.

Cleaver, Kathleen Neal. "How TV Wrecked the Black Panthers." *Channels of Communications* (November/December 1982): 98–99.

———. "Three Ways That Martin Luther King Changed My Life," *Black Renaissance/Renaissance Noire* 2,1 (1998): 51–62.

———. "Back to Africa: The Evolution of the International Section of the Black Panther Party (1969–1972)." In Charles E. Jones, ed., *The Black Panther Party Reconsidered.* Baltimore: Black Classic Press, 1998, 211–54.

Clemons, Michael L. and Charles E. Jones, "Global Solidarity: The Black Panther Party in the International Arena." In Kathleen Cleaver and George Katsiaficas, eds., *Liberation, Imagination, and the Black Panther Party: A New Look at the Panthers and their Legacy.* New York: Routledge, 2001, 20–39.

Courtright, John A. "Rhetoric of the Gun: An Analysis of the Rhetorical Modifications of the Black Panther Party." *Journal of Black Studies* 4, 3 (1974): 249–67.

Davenport, Christian A. "Reading the 'Voice of the Vanguard': A Content Analysis of the Black Panther Intercommunal News Service, 1969–1973." In Charles E. Jones, ed., *The Black Panther Party Reconsidered.* Baltimore: Black Classic Press, 1998, 193–209.

Domke, David. "Journalists, Framing, and Discourse about Race Relations." *Journalism and Mass Communication Monographs.* 164 (1997).

Doss, Erika. "Imagining the Panthers: Representing Black Power and Masculinity, 1960s–1990s." *Prospects: An Annual of American Studies* 23 (1998): 470–93.

Ellis, Trey. "The New Black Aesthetic." *Callaloo* 12 (Winter 1989): 119–40.

Entman, Robert. "Framing: Toward Clarification of a Fractured Paradigm." *Journal of Communication* 43, no. 4 (1993): 51–58.

Fraley, Todd and Ellie Lester-Roushanzamir. "Revolutionary Leader or Violent Thug? A Comparative Analysis of the *Chicago Tribune* and *Chicago Daily Defender*'s Reporting on the Death of Fred Hampton." *Howard Journal of Communication* 15 (2004): 147–67.

Gates, Henry Louis Jr. "Eldridge Cleaver on Ice." *Transition.* 0 (1997): 294–311.

Grady-Willis, Winston A. "The Black Panther Party: State Repression and Political Prisoners." In Charles E. Jones, ed., *The Black Panther Party Reconsidered*. Baltimore: Black
Classic Press, 1998, 363–89.

Hall, Grover C. "Race Problem Coverage." *Bulletin of the American Society of Newspaper Editors*. 5 (1958).

Hall, Stuart. "The Whites of Their Eyes: Racist Ideologies and the Media." In George
Bridges and Rosalind Brunt, eds., *Silver Linings: Some Strategies for the Eighties*. London:
Lawrence and Wishart, 1981, 28–52.

———. "Gramsci's Relevance for the Study of Race and Ethnicity." *Journal of Communication Inquiry*. 10 (1986): 5–27.

———. "Culture, the Media and the 'Ideological Effect'." In James Curran, Michael
Gurevitch, and Janet Woollacott, eds., *Mass Communication and Society*. London: Edward
Arnold in association with the Open University Press, 1977.

Harmann, Jon. "The Trope of Blaxploitation in Critical Responses to *Sweetback*." *Film
History* 6 (1994): 382–404.

Henderson, Errol A. "Black Nationalism and Rap Music." *Journal of Black Studies* 26
(1996): 308–39.

———. "The Lumpenproletariat As Vanguard? The Black Panther Party, Social Transformation, and Pearson's Analysis of Huey Newton." *Journal of Black Studies* 28 (1997):
171–99.

Hertog, James K. and Douglas M. McLeod. "A Multiperspectival Approach to Framing
Analysis: A Field Guide." In Stephen D. Reese, Oscar H. Gandy Jr., and August E.
Grant, eds., *Framing Public Life: Perspectives on Media and Our Understanding of the Social
World*. Mahwah, NJ: Lawrence Erlbaum Associates, 2001, 139–62.

Herve, Julia. "Black Scholar Interviews Kathleen Cleaver." *Black Scholar* 2 (December
1971): 54–59.

Howard-Pitney, David. "The Enduring Black Jeremiad: The American Jeremiad and Black
Protest Rhetoric, From Frederick Douglass to W.E.B. Du Bois, 1841–1919." *American
Quarterly* 38 (1986): 481–92.

Hunt, Andrew. " 'When Did the Sixties Happen?' Searching for New Directions." *Journal
of Social History* 33 (1999): 147–61.

Jameson, Fredric. "Periodizing the Sixties." In Sohnya Sayers, et. al., eds., *The Sixties Without Apology*. Minneapolis: University of Minnesota Press, 1984, 178–208.

Johnson, Ollie A. III. "Explaining the Demise of the Black Panther Party: The Role of Internal Factors." In Charles E. Jones, ed., *The Black Panther Party Reconsidered*. Baltimore:
Black Classic Press, 1998, 391–409.

Johnson, Paula B., David O. Sears, and John B. McConahay. "Black Invisibility, the
Press and the Los Angeles Riot." *American Journal of Sociology* 76, no. 4 (1971):
698–721.

Jones, Charles E. and Judson L. Jeffries. " 'Don't Believe the Hype': Debunking Panther
Mythology." In Charles E. Jones, ed., *The Black Panther Party Reconsidered*, Baltimore:
Black Classic Press, 1998, 25–55.

Joseph, Peniel E. "Dashikis and Democracy: Black Studies, Student Activism, and the Black Power Movement." *Journal of African American History* 88 (2003): 182–203.

Keeling, Kara. "'A Homegrown Revolutionary'?: Tupac Shakur and the Legacy of the Black Panther Party." *The Black Scholar* 29:2–3, 1999: 178–82.

LeBlanc-Ernest, Angela. "'The Most Qualified Person to Handle the Job': Black Panther Party Women, 1966–1982." In Charles E. Jones, ed., *The Black Panther Party Reconsidered*. Baltimore: Black Classic Press, 1998, 305–34.

Lule, Jack. "News Strategies in the Death of Huey Newton." *Journalism Quarterly* 70 (1993): 287–99.

Lusane, Clarence. "To Fight for the People: The Black Panther Party and Black Politics in the 1990s." In Charles E. Jones, ed., *The Black Panther Party Reconsidered*. Baltimore: Black Classic Press, 1998, 443–67.

Maeda, Daryl J. "Black Panthers, Red Guards, and Chinamen: Constructing Asian American Identity through Performing Blackness, 1969–1972." *American Quarterly* 57 (December 2005): 1079–1104.

Matthews, Tracye. "'No One Ever Asks, What a Man's Place in the Revolution Is': Gender and the Politics of The Black Panther Party 1966–1971." In Charles E. Jones, ed., *The Black Panther Party Reconsidered*. Baltimore: Black Classic Press, 1998, 267–304.

Morgan, Edward P. "From Virtual Community to Virtual History: Mass Media and the American Antiwar Movement of the 1960s." *Radical History Review* 78 (2000): 85–122.

Murphree, Vanessa D. "The Selling of Civil Rights: The Communication Section of the Student Nonviolent Coordinating Committee." *Journalism History* 29, 1 (2003): 21–31.

Oliver, Melvin L., James H. Johnson Jr., and Walter C. Farrell Jr. "Anatomy of a Rebellion: A Political-Economic Analysis." In Robert Gooding-Williams, ed., *Reading Rodney King/Reading Urban Uprising*. New York: Routledge, 1993, 117–41.

Prashad, Vijay. "Bruce Lee and the Anti-imperialism of Kung Fu: A Polycultural Adventure." *Positions*. 11 (2003): 51–90.

Pride, Armistead S. "The News That Was." In Henry LaBrie, ed., *Perspectives of the Black Press: 1974*. Kennebunkport, ME: Mercer House Press, 1974.

Rhodes, Jane. "Black Radicalism in 1960s California: Women in the Black Panther Party." In Quintard Taylor and Shirley Ann Moore, eds., *African American Women Confront the West, 1600–2000*. Norman, OK: University of Oklahoma Press, 2003, 346–62.

———. "The *Black Panther* Newspaper: Standard-bearer for Modern Black Nationalism." *Media History* 7(2), 2001: 151–58.

———. "Fanning the Flames of Racial Discord: The National Press and the Black Panther Party." *Harvard International Journal of Press/Politics* 4 (1999): 95–118.

Rice, Jon. "The World of the Illinois Panthers." In Jeanne F. Theoharris and Komozi Woodard, eds., *Freedom North: Black Freedom Struggles Outside the South, 1940–1980*. New York.: Palgrave MacMillan, 2003, 41–64.

Sandarg, Robert. "Jean Genet and the Black Panther Party." *Journal of Black Studies* 16 (1986): 269–82.

Self, Robert. " 'To Plan Our Liberation: Black Power and the Politics of Place in Oakland, California, 1965–1977." *Journal of Urban History* 26 (2000): 759–92.

Singh, Nikhil Pal. "The Black Panthers and the 'Undeveloped Country' of the Left." In Charles E. Jones, ed., *The Black Panther Party Reconsidered*. Baltimore: Black Classic Press, 1998, 57–105.

Staub, Michael. "Black Panthers, New Journalism, and the Rewriting of the Sixties." *Representations* 57 (1997): 57–72.

Stevens, Maurice E. "Subject to Countermemory: Disavowal and Black Manhood in Spike Lee's *Malcolm X*." *Signs: Journal of Women in Culture and Society* 28 (2002): 277–301.

Sulzberger, A.H. "The Word Negro is Not to Appear Unless . . ." *Nieman Reports* (1958): 3, 4.

Surowiecki, James. "Making It: An Interview with Melvin Van Peebles." *Transition* 79 (1999): 176–92.

Thelen, David. "Memory and American History." *Journal of American History* 75 (1989): 1117–29.

Walker, Jenny. "A Media Made Movement?: Black Violence and Nonviolence in the Historiography of the Civil Rights Movement." In Brian Ward, ed., *Media, Culture, and the Modern African American Freedom Struggle*. Gainesville, FL: University Press of Florida, 2001, 41–66.

Wiegman, Robyn. "Whiteness Studies and the Paradox of Particularity." *Boundary 2* 26 (1999): 115–50.

Weill, Susan M. "Mississippi's Daily Press in Three Crises." In David R. Davies, ed., *The Press and Race: Mississippi Journalists Confront the Movement*. Jackson: University Press of Mississippi, 2001, 17–55.

Unpublished Manuscripts

Austin, Neffetiti. "A Look at the Intersectional Experience of Black Women in the Black Panther Party." M.A. Thesis. University of California, Los Angeles, 1996.

Brown, Scot D. "The US Organization: African-American Cultural Nationalism in the Era of Black Power, 1965 to the 1970s." Ph.D. Dissertation. Cornell University, 1999.

Cheney, Charise. "Phallic/ies and Hi(S)stories: Masculinity and the Black Nationalist Tradition, From Slave Spirituals to Rap Music." Ph.D. Dissertation. University of Illinois at Urbana-Champaign, 1999.

Holder, Kit Kim. "The History of the Black Panther Party, 1966–1972: A Curriculum Tool for Afrikan American Studies." Ph.D. Dissertation. University of Massachusetts at Amherst, 1990.

Spencer, Robyn C. "Repression Breeds Resistance: The Rise and the Fall of the Black Panther Party in Oakland, CA., 1966–1982." Ph.D. Dissertation. Columbia University, 2001.

Wilson, Joel R. " 'Free Huey': The Black Panther Party, The Peace and Freedom Party, and the Politics of Race in 1968." Ph.D. Dissertation. University of California, Santa Cruz, 2002.

Young, Cynthia Ann. "Soul Power: Cultural Radicalism and the Formation of a U.S. Third World Left." Ph.D. Dissertation. Yale University, 1999.

Government Reports

Orrick, William Jr. *Shut It Down! A College in Crisis: San Francisco State College, October 1968-April 1969. A Report to the National Commission on the Causes and Prevention of Violence.* Washington, D.C.: Government Printing Office, 1969.

U.S. Department of Labor, *The Negro Family, the Case for National Action.* Washington, D.C.: U.S. Government Printing Office, 1965.

U.S. House of Representatives Committee on Internal Security. *The Black Panther Party: Its Origin and Development as Reflected in its Official Weekly Newspaper* The Black Panther Black Community News Service. Washington: 1970.

U.S. House of Representatives Report by the Committee on Internal Security. *Gun-Barrel Politics: The Black Panther Party, 1966–1971.* Washington, D.C.: U.S. Government Printing Office, 1971.

U.S. House of Representatives, Hearings before the Committee on Internal Security, 91st Congress. *Black Panther Party Part 1: Investigation of Kansas City Chapter; National Organization Data.* U.S. Government Printing Office: Washington, 1970.

U.S. House of Representatives, Hearings before the Committee on Internal Security, 91st Congress. *Black Panther Party Part 3: Investigation of Activities in Detroit, Mich.; Philadelphia, Pa. and Indianapolis, Indiana;* U.S. Government Printing Office: Washington, 1970.

U.S. Senate, Supplementary Detailed Staff Reports on Intelligence Activities and the Rights of Americans, Book III, *Final Report of the Select Committee to Study Governmental Operations with Respect to Intelligence Activities,* S. Rep. No. 755, 94th Congress, 2d Session.

Index